Intellectual Property Protection of Fact-based Works

Intellectual Property Protection of Fact-based Works

Copyright and Its Alternatives

Edited by

Robert F. Brauneis
The George Washington University Law School, USA

Edward Elgar
Cheltenham, UK • Northampton, MA, USA

Published by
Edward Elgar Publishing Limited
The Lypiatts
15 Lansdown Road
Cheltenham
Glos GL50 2JA
UK

Edward Elgar Publishing, Inc.
William Pratt House
9 Dewey Court
Northampton
Massachusetts 01060
USA

A catalogue record for this book
is available from the British Library

Library of Congress Control Number: 2009936226

Mixed Sources
Product group from well-managed forests and other controlled sources
www.fsc.org Cert no. SA-COC-1565
© 1996 Forest Stewardship Council
FSC

ISBN 978 1 84844 183 5

Typeset by Cambrian Typesetters, Camberley, Surrey
Printed and bound by MPG Books Group, UK

Contents

Contributors

Miriam Bitton is an Assistant Professor at Bar-Ilan University Faculty of Law, Israel.

Robert F. Brauneis is an Associate Professor of Law at The George Washington University Law School, USA.

Alan L. Durham is a Professor of Law at the University of Alabama School of Law, USA.

Daniel J. Gervais is a Professor of Law at the Vanderbilt University Law School, USA.

Michael Steven Green is a Professor of Law at the College of William and Mary, Marshall-Wythe School of Law, USA.

Justin Hughes is a Professor of Law at the Cardozo School of Law, USA.

Elizabeth F. Judge is an Associate Professor of Law at the University of Ottawa Faculty of Law, Canada.

David McGowan is a Professor of Law at the University of San Diego School of Law, USA.

Kristen Osenga is an Associate Professor of Law at the University of Richmond School of Law, USA.

Elizabeth A. Rowe is an Associate Professor of Law at the University of Florida, Levin College of Law, USA.

Sharon K. Sandeen is a Professor of Law at the Hamline University School of Law, USA.

Preface

The chapters in this book are based on papers presented at a symposium entitled 'Feist, Facts, and Functions: IP Protection for Works Beyond Entertainment', which was held in Washington, DC on 28 September 2007. The symposium was co-sponsored by The George Washington University Law School and the Software and Information Industry Association. For their support of the project, I would like to thank Frederick M. Lawrence, the Dean of the Law School; Michael Ryan, Director of the Law School's Creative and Innovative Economy Center; Ken Wasch, President of the Software and Information Industry Association; and Keith Kupferschmid, Senior Vice President of the Association. For their aid in organizing and staffing the event, I would like to thank Sarah Huisentruit Orye, Shauna Eisenberg, and Thomas Lee of the Creative and Innovative Economy Center. For his superlative assistance in compiling the indices, I would like to thank David Yung Ho Kim, whose work was generously supported by the Cardozo Law School during my visit there in the Spring of 2009; for his timely support in finalizing the indices, I would like to thank Thomas Mittenzwei. Finally, and most importantly, I would like to thank the participants in the Symposium for their presentations and for their subsequent contributions to this volume, from which I have learned a great deal.

Robert F. Brauneis
The George Washington University Law School
December 2008

Acknowledgements

An earlier version of Miriam Bitton's contribution to this volume was published as Miriam Bitton, 'Trends in Protection for Informational Works Under Copyright Law During the 19th and 20th Centuries', 13 *Mich. Telecomm. Tech. L. Rev*. 115 (2006).

An earlier version of Alan Durham's contribution to this volume was published as Alan Durham, 'Speaking of the World: Fact, Opinion and the Originality Standard of Copyright', 33 *Ariz. St. L. J*. 791 (2001).

A version of Justin Hughes's contribution to this volume was published as Justin Hughes, 'Created Facts and the Flawed Ontology of Copyright Law', 83 *Notre Dame L. Rev*. 43 (2007).

A version of Kristen Osenga's contribution to this volume was published as Kristen Osenga, 'Information May Want to Be Free, But Information Products Do Not: Protecting and Facilitating Transactions in Information Products', 30 *Cardozo L. Rev.* 2099 (2009).

The publisher and editor of this volume wish to thank the publishers of these journals and all of the authors for their permission to publish the contributions to this volume.

Cases and legislation

CASES

National Cases

Canada

England & Wales

Germany

India

United States

LEGISLATION

EU Directives

National Legislation

Canada

United Kingdom

United States

TREATIES, CONVENTIONS, AND OTHER INTERNATIONAL INSTRUMENTS

PART I

Copyright and facts: historical and comparative perspectives

1. *Feist*, facts and functions: historical perspective

Miriam Bitton[1]

INTRODUCTION

The 1990s brought significant developments in the field of information technology. These in turn stimulated the creation of a new global market for electronic information services and products, a market that is occupied substantially by electronic databases. The emergence of these new technological developments challenged many branches of the law, including intellectual property law. A particularly prominent part of this debate is how the law should address the protection of electronic databases.

The debate over database protection in the United States can be traced back to the Supreme Court's seminal decision in *Feist Publications, Inc. v Rural Telephone Service Co.*[2] In *Feist*, the Court found white pages telephone directories to be non-copyrightable. The Court held that the touchstone for copyright protection is creative originality, and that this requirement is constitutionally mandated. The Court's decision also clarified that its holding 'inevitably means that the copyright in a factual compilation is thin. Notwithstanding a valid copyright, a subsequent compiler remains free to use the facts contained in another's publication to aid in preparing a competing work, so long as the competing work does not feature the same selection and arrangement.'[3] *Feist* thus ended the tradition in some courts of providing copyright protection based on the labor invested in creating the work and declared the death of the 'sweat of the brow' and 'industrious collection' doctrines.

---

1 Assistant Professor, Bar-Ilan University Faculty of Law, Israel; LL.B., M.A., Bar-Ilan University Faculty of Law, Israel; LL.M, S.J.D., University of Michigan Law School; Visiting Fellow, George Washington University Law School; Microsoft Research Fellow, The Berkeley Center for Law & Technology, Boalt Law, University of California. This chapter is based on an earlier version that was published as Miriam Bitton, 'Trends in Protection for Informational Works Under Copyright Law During the 19th and 20th Centuries', 13 *Mich. Telecomm. Tech. L. Rev.* 115 (2006).

2 499 U.S. 340 (1991).

3 *Id.* at 349.

The debate gained additional prominence due to a number of worldwide initiatives that extended protection to databases and considered the provision of a much more extensive legal protection for databases. Notably, the *Agreement on Trade Related Aspects of Intellectual Property Rights* ('TRIPs Agreement')[4] introduced minimum standards regarding copyright protection for databases, and the ongoing discussion in the World Intellectual Property Organization ('WIPO') considered the provision of broader intellectual property rights in databases than does the United States under *Feist*.[5] Furthermore, the European Union's Directive on the Legal Protection for Databases ('Database Directive'), adopted in 1996, constituted the most comprehensive attempt to provide protection to databases. It granted a 15-year, renewable, *sui generis* right to prevent the extraction and utilization of raw data in a database.

The adoption of the Database Directive, especially the reciprocity provision that conditions protection of non-EU databases upon reciprocal provision of comparable protection in non-EU jurisdictions, has sparked an ongoing debate over bills drafted in the US Congress to address the legal protection of databases.

In particular, a number of legal scholars have voiced their opinions on the question of how Congress should react to the Supreme Court's holding in *Feist* and the EU's subsequent enactment of the Database Directive. Most of this scholarship, however, has simply accepted the argument, advanced by some segments of the database industry and others, that *Feist* creates a problem, that this problem is exacerbated by the EU's Database Directive, and that this problem needs to be solved.[6] Much of the scholarly discussion has also been dedicated to criticizing the United State's proposed bills because of the risks they supposedly pose to the database industry in general and to specific groups such as the scientific and educational communities in particular.[7] The academic debate has, therefore, also focused on suggesting new and improved forms of protection that Congress could enact.[8]

---

4 Agreement on Trade-Related Aspects of Intellectual Property Rights, Apr. 15, 1994, 33 I.L.M. 81 (1994) [hereinafter TRIPs Agreement].

5 *Basic Proposal for the Substantive Provisions of the Treaty on Intellectual Property in Respect of Databases,* WIPO Doc. CRNR/DC/6 (30 August 1996).

6 See, for example, *Database and Collections of Information Misappropriation Act of 2003: Joint Hearing on H.R. 3261 Before the Subcomm. On Courts, the Internet, and Intellectual Prop. of the House Comm. on the Judiciary and the Subcomm. on Commerce, Trade, and Consumer Prot. of the House Comm. on Energy and Commerce,* 108th Cong. 27 (2003) [hereinafter H.R. 3261 Hearing] (statement of David Carson, General Counsel, Copyright Office of the U.S., Library of Cong.).

7 See, for example, Esanu Julie M. and Paul F. Uhlir (eds) (2003), *The Role of Scientific and Technical Data and Information in the Public Domain: Proceedings Of a Symposium.*

8 See Ginsburg, Jane C. (1992), 'No "Sweat"? Copyright and Other Protection

Despite the extensive discussion on the subject of legal protection for databases, the questionable bases for the assumptions underlying the debate are routinely overlooked. One major issue that has been ignored is the historical dimension of the debate. This chapter provides a historical analysis of the protection of databases under modern intellectual property law. Specifically, it addresses the popular claim, often raised by proponents of legislation advocating broader database ownership rights, that the United States Supreme Court's decision in *Feist* brought about a dramatic change in the legal landscape. According to this argument, *Feist* disturbed the status quo and overturned legal protections based on the industrious collection doctrine, which governed copyright law for 200 years. Under this long-standing doctrine, database producers had reasonably believed that their databases were entitled to copyright protection. Advocates of legislative action providing broader database ownership rights contend that the legal system flourished under the sweat-of-brow regime, and that Congress should therefore 'restore' what the *Feist* decision changed.[9]

Opponents of such restrictive legislation, by contrast, argue that the industrious collection doctrine was never the prevailing approach for the protection of databases. They argue that the legal landscape prior to *Feist* reflected an information policy that consistently supported unfettered access to factual information[10] and that it would be a mistake to overturn 200 years of legal

---

of Works of Information after *Feist v Rural Telephone*', 92 *Colum. L. Rev.* 338 (suggesting a federal anticopying statute with collective licensing); Reichman, J.H. and Pamela Samuelson, 'Intellectual Property Rights in Data?', 50 *Vand. L. Rev.* 51 (1997) (suggesting a modified liability approach).

[9] See *H.R. 3261 Hearing*, *supra* note 6, at 27 (statement of David Carson, General Counsel, Copyright Office of the U.S. Library of Congress) (urging 'restoration of the general level of protection provided in the past under copyright "sweat of the brow" theories'); *Collections of Information Antipiracy Act: Hearing on H.R. 354 Before the Subcomm. on Courts and Intellectual Prop. of the House Comm. on the Judiciary*, 106th Cong. 157 (1999) [hereinafter H.R. 354 Hearing] (statement of Marilyn Winokur, Executive Vice President, Micromedex, Inc. on behalf of the Coalition Against Database Piracy) (asking to maintain 'the traditional balance between the respective interests of the owners and users of informational products'); *Collections of Information Antipiracy Act; Trade Dress Protection Act; and Continued Oversight of Internet Domain Name Protection: Hearing on H.R. 2652 and H.R 3163 Before the Subcomm. on Courts and Intellectual Prop. of the House Comm. on the Judiciary*, 105th Cong. 128 (1998) [hereinafter H.R. 2652 and H.R. 3163 Hearing] (statement of Jane C. Ginsburg, Columbia University School of Law) (seeking to 'restore the *status quo ante-Feist*').

[10] See *H.R. 354 Hearing*, *supra* note 9, at 127 (statement of James G. Neal, Dean, University Libraries, John Hopkins University) ('H.R. 354 would overturn our 200 years of information policy in this country which has consistently supported unfettered access to factual information.'); *H.R. 2652 and H.R. 3163 Hearing*, *supra* note 9,

tradition by passing legislation that suddenly restricts access to fact-based works.

A historical analysis of database protection from the inception of US copyright law until *Feist* reveals that at various times, however, what was perceived to be the copyrightable element of a work ranged along a continuum between creativity and originality at one end and industriousness and labor at the other. In other words, judicial thought in the United States has swung back and forth like a pendulum, alternating between a focus on investment of labor and a focus on creativity as the proper basis for copyright. The following historical analysis clearly indicates that the arguments on both sides of the debate over potential legislative action are inaccurate, and that prior to *Feist* the legal landscape was very complex in its treatment of information-based works.

In order to assess these arguments, it is important to thoroughly examine the treatment of works of facts in general and compilations in particular over time. Relying primarily on the seminal work of Professor Jane C. Ginsburg,[11] this chapter begins with an overview of the emergence of the industrious collection doctrine and concludes with an examination of the legal landscape of the industrious collection doctrine under the 1976 Copyright Act. This analysis clearly illustrates the complex and rich legal landscape in the years preceding *Feist* and points to a general uneasiness and confusion about the doctrine. Moreover, it shows that most courts in their decisions were preparing the ground for an eventual repudiation of the doctrine. This analysis also supports the argument that US policy on fact-based intellectual property has consistently fostered unrestricted access to the factual content contained in these works. Such access is based on an appreciation that unrestricted access is necessary to stimulate innovation, support the educational process, and 'promote the Progress of Science and useful Arts'.[12]

The historical evidence thus demonstrates that neither those who advocate strong legislative protection of databases nor those who oppose it are entirely correct in their characterization of the last 200 years of copyright jurisprudence in the United States. Contrary to what the proponents of protective legislation would claim, the industrious collection doctrine has not consistently been the governing legal regime in the United States for the past 200 years, particularly after passage of the 1976 Copyright Act. By the same token, the claims of the opponents of such legislation are also incorrect since the industrious collection doctrine was, at least for a certain period of time, a

---

at 151 (testimony of Jonathan Band, Partner, Morrison & Foerster LLP, General Counsel of the Online Banking Association) ('In fact, sweat of the brow was never the prevailing approach for the protection of databases').

11 Ginsburg, Jane C. (1990), 'Creation and Commercial Value: Copyright Protection of Works of Information', 90 *Colum. L. Rev.* 1865.

12 US Const. art. I, § 8, cl. 8.

significant, if not the prevailing, doctrine governing copyright protection. Accordingly, the Supreme Court's decision in *Feist* could not have worked a sea change in copyright jurisprudence in either direction, but rather is more accurately described as merely ending the movement of that jurisprudence along the continuum between authorship based purely on labor and authorship based purely on creativity, finding the latter approach as the only possible basis for copyrightability.

I. THE EMERGENCE OF THE INDUSTRIOUS COLLECTION DOCTRINE

In 1789, the Framers of the Constitution empowered Congress to 'promote the Progress of Science . . . by securing for limited Times to Authors . . . the exclusive Right to their respective Writings. . . .'[13] The Framers appear primarily to have intended to promote learning, with secondary concerns of protecting authors and providing them with incentives and expanding the range of ideas and information within the public domain.[14] However, because no extensive history of the Copyright and Patent Clause exists, difficulties abound in determining exactly what types of works the Framers intended copyright to cover. On its face, the Copyright Clause says nothing about originality as a prerequisite for legal protection; however the text of the Clause implies such a requirement. By granting exclusive rights only to 'authors', the clause implies that originality is the essence of the right to protection. Moreover, the Clause's reference to 'progress' suggests that a work entitled to copyright protection must contain more than merely trivial originality. Nevertheless, the terms of the Clause are so general that it offers little help in determining the minimum original contribution necessary to create a copyrightable work from facts and data.

After the Constitution was ratified, Congress quickly enacted the Copyright Act of 1790 to provide limited periods of protection for original works of authorship such as books, maps, and charts. Under this statute, compilations were considered to be 'books',[15] and, indeed, compilations constitute one of the oldest forms of authorship protected under US law.[16] As Professor

13 *Id.*

14 Patterson, L. Ray and Craig Joyce (1989), 'Monopolizing the Law: The Scope of Copyright Protection for Law Reports and Statutory Compilations', 36 *UCLA L. Rev.* 719, 783.

15 Copyright Act of May 31, 1790, ch. 15, 1 Stat. 124, reprinted in Solberg, T. (1906), *Copyright Enactments of the United States 1783–1906* at 32 [hereinafter Act of May 31, 1790].

16 See, for example, *Kilty v Green*, 4 H. & McH. 345 (Md. 1799).

Ginsburg writes, the works at issue in early copyright disputes were most often highly useful, informational works such as calendars, maps, law books, and arithmetic and grammar primers.[17] The overwhelming presence of informational works reflects, in Professor Ginsburg's opinion, an important legislative policy of encouraging fact-based works underlying English and American law.[18]

Professor Ginsburg has also identified the development of two discrete bases on which the concept of authorship has been founded: investment of labor and investment of individuality.[19] She argues that '[p]erhaps because of the predominance of informational subject matter, the concept of authorship and the basis for copyright protection underlying judicial decisions until the mid-nineteenth century seemed to focus on the labor, rather than the inspiration, invested in the work.'[20] Professor Ginsburg also examined the idea that later in the nineteenth century 'courts and commentators began to offer . . . a different rationale for copyright coverage', stating that these authorities viewed authorship as not purely the product of labor, but rather as the 'emanation of an author's personality'.[21] The author's subjective judgment in arranging data, rather than her diligence in collecting it, was held to be the protectable essence of the work. Thus, a work was protectable because it incorporated something of its creator's unique individuality.[22]

Nonetheless, this conclusion does not suggest that courts required that the work possess high levels of the requisite 'subjectivity'.[23] 'Sufficient original authorship' could be found 'because each author is a distinct individual and inevitably stamps some part of herself upon the work'.[24] Moreover, as Professor Ginsburg remarked, 'this shift in copyright philosophy toward a more subjective view of authorship' did not in fact suddenly 'spur abandonment of the prior labor-oriented approach. Instead, the two views continued to

---

17 See Ginsburg, *supra* note 11, at 1873. See also Ginsburg, Jane C. (1990), 'A Tale of Two Copyrights: Literary Property in Revolutionary France and America', 64 *Tul. L. Rev.* 991, 998–1005.

18 Ginsburg, *supra* note 11, at 1873.

19 *Id.* at 1873–93.

20 *Id.* at 1873–74.

21 *Id.* at 1874.

22 *Id.* See, for example, *Bleistein v Donaldson Lithographing Co.*, 188 U.S. 239, 250 (1903) (Holmes, J.); *Jeffreys v Boosey*, (1854) 4 H.L.C. 815, 866–81, 10 Eng. Rep. 681, 702–07 (Erle LJ); Ginsburg, *supra* note 11, at 1874.

23 *Id.*

24 *Id.* See also *Jeffreys,* 4 H.L.C. 815 at 869; *Jewelers' Circular Publ'g Co. v Keystone Publ'g Co.*, 274 F. 932, 934 (S.D.N.Y. 1921) (Hand J.), aff'd, 281 F. 83 (2d Cir. 1922).

coexist'.[25] Consequently, throughout the nineteenth and into the twentieth century, the concept of original authorship embraced investment of *both* labor and originality.

A. Labor as a Basis for Authorship

As Professor Ginsburg has explained, many English and American copyright decisions in the eighteenth and early to mid-nineteenth centuries characterized copyrightable authorship in terms of the labor invested in the work.[26] This analysis was adopted in the 1806 decision *Matthewson v Stockdale*,[27] in which the court held that the plaintiff's East India calendar was a protectable work because of the 'considerable expence and labour' involved in creating the work.[28]

In the United States, many courts followed the English precedent.[29]As Professor Ginsburg shows, when '[c]ombined with the United States constitutional and legislative goals to 'promote the Progress of Science' and learning, the labor concept of copyrightability appears to furnish ample rationale for protecting all kinds of informational works, from narratives to catalogues'.[30] Inquiry into the personal or subjective character of the author's investment in his work seemed to have been irrelevant.[31]

A regime of exclusive ownership rights in information itself seems to have been consistent with the early principles of copyright protection in the United States. Professor Ginsburg argues, however, that such a conclusion is somewhat misleading. Even during that period of jurisprudence, a copyright did not

---

25 Ginsburg, *supra* note 11, at 1873–74. See, for example, *Alfred Bell & Co. v Catalda Fine Arts, Inc.*, 191 F.2d 99, 102–03 (2d Cir. 1951). *Cf. L. Batlin & Son v Snyder*, 536 F.2d 486, 489 (2d Cir. 1976) (en banc).

26 See Ginsburg, *supra* note 11, at 1873–74.

27 (1806) 12 Ves. Jun. 270, 33 Eng. Rep. 103 (Ch.).

28 *Id.* at 105–06. *Accord Lewis v Fullarton*, (1839) 2 Beav. 6, 8, 48 Eng. Rep. 1080 (Rolls Ct.). See also *Kelly v Morris* (1866) LR 1 Eq 697, 701. *Accord Morris v Ashbee* (1868) LR 7 Eq 34, 40. Subsequent English decisions adopted the rule laid down in *Kelly v Morris*. See, for example, *Hogg v Scott* (1874) LR 18 Eq 444, 458 (1874); *Morris v Wright* (1870) LR 5 Ch App 279 ; *Scott v Stanford* (1867) LR 3 Eq 718.

29 See, for example, *Emerson v Davies*, 8 F. Cas. 615, 619 (C.C.D. Mass. 1845) (No. 4,436); *List Public Co. v Keller*, 30 F. 772, 772-73 (C.C.S.D.N.Y. 1887). See also Ginsburg, *supra* note 11, at 1875.

30 Ginsburg, *supra* note 11, at 1876.

31 See Act of May 31, 1790, at 32 (reflecting this principle by providing protection for any 'map, chart, book or books', the first two categories of which are rather information-laden and labor-intensive works).

necessarily grant such expansive rights.[32] Indeed, the scope of early copyright protection in informational works was narrow; it extended to the precise contribution of the first author,[33] but it generally did not prevent competitors from duplicating the actual information in the copyrighted work as long as they themselves acquired that same information directly from the primary sources.[34] In this way, copyright protection under early court decisions operated in much the same manner as the unfair competition tort of misappropriation currently operates.[35]

B. Individuality as a Basis for Authorship

While the late eighteenth and early nineteenth century Anglo-American courts tended to view original authorship as a function of labor, authors tended to characterize their work as an expression of their personality.[36] Only later did the courts also finally begin to recognize individual author personality as a basis for copyright protection.[37] In an 1854 House of Lords decision, one Lord proclaimed:

> The order of each man's words is as singular as his countenance, and although if two authors composed originally with the same order of words, each would have a property therein, still the probability of such an occurrence is less than that there should be two countenances that could not be discriminated.[38]

While neither the United States Constitution nor the copyright laws prior to 1976 expressly required originality, American courts in the latter half of the nineteenth century began to infer such a requirement from the Constitution's textual reference to granting protection to 'authors'. Because the term 'author' means 'beginner', 'first mover', 'creator' or 'originator',[39] the Constitution's

---

32 Ginsburg, *supra* note 11, at 1876–77.

33 *Id.* at 1877–81. See, for example, English Cases: *Cary v Kearsley* (1802) 4 Esp. 168, 170–71, 170 Eng. Rep. 679, 680 (KB) (Lord Ellenborough); U.S. cases: *Webb v Powers*, 29 F. Cas. 511, 517 (C.C.D. Mass. 1847) (No. 17,323).

34 See Ginsburg, *supra* note 11, at 1876–81. See, for example, *Hogg v Kirby*, 8 Ves. Jun. 215, 222, 32 Eng. Rep. 336, 339 (Ch. 1803).

35 Ginsburg, *supra* note 11, at 1876–81. The classic misappropriation decision is *International News Service v Associated Press,* 248 U.S. 215 (1918) [hereinafter *INS*], in which the Supreme Court announced a federal common law 'quasi-property' right against misappropriation of commercial value. *Id.* at 239–40.

36 Ginsburg, *supra* note 11, at 1881. See, for example, Colman, George (1787), 'The Gentleman' No. 6 (1775), in 1 *Prose On Several Occasions.*

37 See Ginsburg, *supra* note 11, at 1882–84.

38 *Jeffreys v Boosey*, 4 H.L.C. 815, 869, 10 Eng. Rep. 681, 703 (1854) (Erle LJ).

39 See *Burrow-Giles Lithographic Co. v Sarony*, 111 U.S. 53, 58 (1884); see also 1 Melville B. Nimmer and David Nimmer, *Nimmer On Copyright* § 1.06[A] (2004).

grant of protection to 'authors' necessarily requires originality; if a work lacks originality, it is not the creation of an 'author'.[40]

Eventually, the US Supreme Court also inferred from the Copyright Clause a requirement that a work be original in order to be copyrighted, noting that the Framers of the Constitution understood 'the nature of copyright and the objects to which it was commonly applied, for copyright, as the exclusive right of a man to the production of his own genius or intellect, existed in England at that time'.[41] Ultimately, the case law eliminated any doubt that the prevailing prerequisite for copyright protection, regardless of the type of work at issue, is originality.[42] As the following discussion shows, however, the case law also applied a more specific threshold standard below which originality will not be found.

In the seminal case *Burrow-Giles Lithographic Co. v Sarony*[43] the Court justified a more expansive construction of the term 'writings' by noting that the first federal copyright statute protected maps, charts and books, none of which are literally 'writings'.[44] Because those who drafted this first copyright statute were the same authors who drafted the Constitution, the Court concluded that the Framers of the Constitution must have intended a broader and less literal definition of the term 'writings'.[45] The Court therefore interpreted the term 'authors' in the Copyright Clause to include anyone 'to whom anything owed its origin', such that the term 'writings . . . meant the literary productions of those authors, and Congress very properly has declared these to include all forms of writing, printing, engraving, etching, etc., by which the ideas in the mind of the author are given visible expression'.[46] Accordingly, the original photographer who was the plaintiff in this case qualified as an 'author' who could be protected under the Copyright Clause.

Burrow-Giles imparts two important lessons. First, in order to be copyrightable, a given subject matter must owe its origin to a particular identifiable author.[47] Secondly, the Court held that despite the general rule that pre-existing objects do not satisfy the 'origination by the author' requirement, a particular selection and arrangement of such pre-existing items *can* qualify as

---

40 See 1 Nimmer and Nimmer, *supra* note 39, § 2.01; *Reiss v Nat'l Quotation Bureau, Inc.*, 276 F. 717, 719 (S.D.N.Y. 1921).

41 *Burrow-Giles*, 111 U.S. at 58.

42 *L. Batlin & Son, Inc. v Snyder*, 536 F.2d 486, 489–90 (2d Cir. 1976); 1 Nimmer and Nimmer, *supra* note 39, § 2.01.

43 111 U.S. at 53.

44 *Id.* at 56–57.

45 *Id.* at 57.

46 *Id.* at 58.

47 *Id.* at 58.

copyrightable subject matter if that selection or arrangement is the author's original conception.[48]

Once the *Burrow-Giles* Court established 'originality' as a prerequisite for copyright protection, lower courts were required to distinguish original from unoriginal works, which they did by defining original works as works that display some artistic merit.[49] Such decisions were perfectly consistent with the *Burrow-Giles'* Court's language. As the *Burrow-Giles* Court noted, the 'ordinary production of a photograph' by itself would not have been copyrightable, suggesting that genuinely creative works are distinct from merely 'ordinary' works.[50]

Nineteen years after *Burrow-Giles*, the Court substantially, but not completely, withdrew its requirement of artistic merit as a prerequisite for copyright. In *Bleistein v Donaldson Lithographic Co.*, Justice Oliver Wendell Holmes wrote an opinion rejecting artistic merit as a prerequisite for copyright, and also adopted a 'copyright-as-personality' approach.[51] Justice Holmes explained that the source of an author's protection under copyright law lies in the author's investment of unique individuality into his work. Copyrightable originality thus requires only some minimal level of unique expression by the author, some irreducible quantum that most people cannot define, but which they can nevertheless recognize when they see it.[52]

Holmes' interpretation also built upon another early Supreme Court interpretation of originality. In *United States v Steffens*[53] the Court concluded that the Trade-Mark Act was unconstitutional because trademarks come into being only through extended periods of use, not from spontaneous creativity or design.[54] Because the establishment of a trademark relies only on the 'priority of appropriation' and displays 'no fancy or imagination, no genius, no laborious thought', trademarks do not meet the originality requirement of the Copyright Clause.[55] Thus, in *Steffens*, as in *Bleistein*, a key criterion for copyright protection is the individual author's personality or creative thoughts as embodied in his work.

---

48 *Id.* at 59.

49 See, for example, *J.L. Mott Iron Works v Clow*, 82 F. 316, 318 (7th Cir. 1897).

50 *Burrow-Giles*, 111 U.S. at 59.

51 188 U.S. 239 (1903). See also *Courier Lithographing Co. v Donaldson Lithographing Co.*, 104 F. 993 (6th Cir. 1900).

52 188 U.S. at 250. See also *Alfred Bell & Co. v Catalda Fine Arts, Inc.*, 191 F.2d 99 (2d Cir. 1951); Yen, Alfred C. (1990), 'Restoring the Natural Law: Copyright as Labor and Possession', 51 *Ohio St. L.J.* 517, 522, 537.

53 100 U.S. 82 (1879).

54 *Id.* at 94.

55 *Id.*

The Supreme Court offered yet further insight into what constitutes originality in *Baker v Selden*.[56] Denying copyright protection to a book providing an arrangement and explanation of a bookkeeping system, the Court noted that copyright is supposed to be 'for the encouragement of learning', not merely for the 'encouragement of industry or labor unconnected to the advancement of learning and the sciences'.[57] The Court also emphasized that originality does not require novelty, but rather only independent creation.[58] Moreover, material drawn from the public domain will support a copyright if put together as a 'distinguishable' or 'substantial' variation of pre-existing material.[59] Thus, the Court did not require that the author create something never done before. Instead, creativity required some expression or product that was the result of more than mere labor.[60] 'All that is needed to satisfy both the Constitution and the statute is that the "author" contributed something more than a "merely trivial" variation, something recognizably "his own".'[61]

As for the scope of protection under the 'copyright as personality' approach, former Justice Kaplan has suggested that the introduction of the personality rationale led both to a greater disapproval of compositions heavily dependent on predecessors' works and to an increasing intolerance of copying in the nineteenth century.[62] This development led to an expansion in the scope of copyright protection over an increasing range of activities.[63] Examination of the first 100 years of United States copyright laws from 1790 to 1891 reveals movement from 'rights simply in "printing, reprinting, publishing and vending" to the additional rights of "completing, copying, executing, finishing, and vending . . . and in the case of a dramatic composition, of publicly performing . . . [a]nd authors may reserve the right to dramatize or to translate their own works".'[64]

---

56 101 U.S. 99 (1879). See also Kaplan, Benjamin (1967), *An Unhurried View of Copyright* 64.

57 *Baker*, 101 U.S. at 105.

58 *Id.* at 102. See also *Roth Greeting Cards v United Card Co.*, 429 F.2d 1106, 1110 (9th Cir. 1970); *Wihtol v Wells*, 231 F.2d 550, 553 (7th Cir. 1956); *Alfred Bell & Co. v Catalda Fine Arts, Inc.*, 191 F.2d 99, 102 (2d Cir. 1951); *Merritt Forbes Co. v Newman Inv. Sec. Inc.*, 604 F. Supp. 943, 951 (S.D.N.Y. 1985).

59 *Gerlach-Barklow Co. v Morris & Bendien, Inc.*, 23 F.2d 159, 161 (2d Cir. 1927).

60 *Baker*, 101 U.S. at 105.

61 *Alfred Bell*, 191 F.2d at 102–03 (citing *Chamberlin v Uris Sales Corp.*, 150 F.2d 512, 513 (2d Cir. 1945)).

62 Kaplan, *supra* note 56, at 22–25.

63 Ginsburg, *supra* note 11, at 1885.

64 *Id.*

II. THE INDUSTRIOUS COLLECTION DOCTRINE

A. The Emergence of the Industrious Collection Doctrine Under the Copyright Act of 1909

It was only after the Copyright Act of 1909 ('1909 Act') was enacted that the industrious collection doctrine truly made its first appearance in American copyright jurisprudence. The 1909 Act allowed putative authors to register their works for copyright protection. Under s. 5 of the Act, the applicants for such protection had to identify their work from among certain specific categories. One of those categories was 'directories'.[65] Although the 1909 Act did not say that all categories of works listed in s. 5 were automatically copyrightable, some courts nevertheless inferred that directories must be copyrightable and that no further showing was required in order to benefit from protection.[66] Thus was born the 'industrious collection' doctrine, otherwise known as the 'sweat of the brow' doctrine in American law.[67]

The first expression of the industrious collection doctrine in American jurisprudence can be traced back to the 1921 Second Circuit decision in *Jeweler's Circular Publishing Co. v Keystone Publishing Co.*, in which the court upheld the copyright of a trade directory containing various jewelers' addresses and trademark illustrations, which were themselves unoriginal and non-copyrightable.[68] Stating that the 'law is now well established' regarding copyright protection of directories,[69] the court concluded that the right to copyright a book depends on 'nothing more than industrious collection'.[70] Thus, although the directory lacked original thought and creativity, took no particular insight to produce, and evidenced no original form, according to the court:

---

65 1909 Copyright Act, Pub. L. No. 349, 35 Stat. 1075 (1909) (previously codified at 17 U.S.C. §§ 1–216) (repealed 1976) [hereinafter the 1909 Act].

66 However, the legislative history of the 1909 Act might be interpreted as requiring creativity:

> As thus interpreted, the word 'writings' would to-day in popular parlance be more nearly represented by the word 'works'; and this the bill adopts; referring back, however, to the word 'writings' by way of safe anchorage, but regarding this as including 'all forms of record in which the thought of an author may be recorded and from which it may be read or reproduced.

S. Rep. No. 59-6187, at 4 (1907).

67 See *supra* Part I.A.

68 281 F. 83 (2d Cir 1922). See also *Donald v Zack Meyer's TV Sales & Serv.*, 426 F.2d 1027 (5th Cir. 1970); *Markham v A.E. Borden Co.*, 206 F.2d 199 (1st Cir. 1953).

69 *Jeweler's Circular Pub. Co.*, 281 F. at 85.

70 *Id.* at 88.

> [T]he man who goes through the streets of a town and puts down the names of each of the inhabitants, with their occupations and street numbers, acquires material of which he is the author. He produces by his labor a meritorious composition, in which he may obtain a copyright. . . .[71]

Accordingly, with this decision the court moved the concept of originality, with its focus on individuality and the creative process, to the background and placed renewed emphasis on labor as a basis for copyrighting compilations.

Furthermore, like its eighteenth and nineteenth century predecessors, the industrious collection doctrine also extended copyright protection to the original author's investment in collecting the facts contained in the compilation, thereby providing protection that goes beyond simply the original selection and arrangement the compiler contributed. In addition, under the industrious collection doctrine, the only defense to infringement was independent creation. A subsequent compiler was 'not entitled to take one word of information previously published', but had to 'independently [work] out the matter for himself. . . .'[72]

Although the doctrine therefore lacked justification under copyright theory, it was serviceable when most compilation-related copyright litigation at that time dealt with old-fashioned databases such as telephone directories. Later courts seized upon the doctrine to deal with situations in which a compiler would make a substantial contribution of labor in collecting factual data only to have someone else freely reap the benefit.[73] In applying copyright protection in this manner, courts were probably trying to decrease the risk of a market failure in situations in which people spent large amounts of time and money compiling data. The abundance of cases that dealt with *Jeweler's*-type factual scenarios suggests that old-fashioned database piracy was probably a significant problem in the pre-digital era.[74] As shown elsewhere, unlike electronic database producers, old-fashioned database producers did not have the same non-legal tools and features at their disposal to overcome such a risk.[75]

---

71 *Id.*

72 *Id.* at 89.

73 Denicola, Robert C. (1981), 'Copyright in Collections of Facts: A Theory for the Protection of Nonfiction Literary Works', 81 *Colum. L. Rev.* 516, 530. See also *Patry, supra* note 39; *Harper & Row, Publishers, Inc. v Nation Enters.*, 471 U.S. 539, 589 (1985) (Brennan J., dissenting).

74 See Symposium (2002), 'Bioinformatics and Intellectual Property Law, April 27, 2001 – Boston, Massachusetts, Data Protection Statutes and Bioinformatics Databases', 8 *B.U.J. Sci. & Tech. L.* 171, 172. See also Lum, Sarah (1988) Note, 'Copyright Protection for Factual Compilations – Reviving the Misappropriation Doctrine', 56 *Fordham L. Rev.* 933, 952.

75 Bitton, Miriam (2006), 'A New Outlook on the Economic Dimension of the Database Protection Debate', 47 *IDEA* 93.

All they could do was offer data and organize it in a manner that best served users and hope that the courts would step in to protect them when necessary.

1. The prohibition on exclusive ownership in facts and fact-based materials under the Copyright Act of 1909 and the emergence of a new emphasis on the public domain

Despite the swing of copyright jurisprudence back toward the investment of labor end of the copyright continuum after the 1909 Act, an important, albeit often overlooked, piece in the historical puzzle is the treatment of factual works under the 1909 Act and the emergence of a new emphasis on the public domain. The prevailing approach under the 1909 Act, even in those courts adhering strictly to the industrious collection doctrine, was that facts and other indispensable materials are non-copyrightable. Evidence of the prevalence of these values can be found in copyright doctrines developed by the courts, most notably the idea/expression dichotomy, the fact/expression dichotomy, and the merger doctrine.

Furthermore, there was a growing awareness of and a new emphasis on the importance of maintaining a broad public domain of fact-based works. This analysis thus gives a broader perspective on the historical argument that the industrious collection doctrine has always been the ruling principle of copyright law and shows this assumption is not entirely valid.

a. The fact/expression dichotomy The fact/expression dichotomy and its twin, the idea/expression dichotomy, are classic doctrines of copyright law.[76] They reflect the balance that copyright law seeks to achieve between encouraging authors to create new works by protecting their original creations from unauthorized copying, while, at the same time, preserving the basic building blocks of facts and ideas for the public domain so that others may use them to create new works.[77] The 1879 Supreme Court decision in *Baker v Selden*[78] represents the beginning of the modern fact/expression doctrine.[79] In *Baker*, the Court emphasized that, while a copyright in a bookkeeping treatise

---

[76] See *Feist Publ'ns, Inc. v Rural Tel. Serv. Co.*, 499 U.S. 340, 344–45 (1991) ('The most fundamental axiom of copyright law is that "[n]o author may copyright his ideas or the facts he narrates".' (quoting *Harper & Row Publishers, Inc. v Nation Enters.*, 471 U.S. 539, 556 (1985))). See also Ginsburg, *supra* note 11, 1868.

[77] See Gorman, Robert A. (1982), 'Fact or Fancy? The Implications for Copyright', 29 *J. Copyright Soc'y* U.S.A. 560, 560. See also *Nash v CBS*, 899 F.2d 1537, 1540 (7th Cir. 1990). See generally 4 Nimmer and Nimmer, *supra* note 39, § 13.03[B][2], at 13–69 to 13–70.

[78] 101 U.S. 99 (1879). See Gorman, *supra* note 77, at 560.

[79] See, for example, *Triangle Publ'ns, Inc. v Sports Eye, Inc.*, 415 F. Supp. 682 (E.D. Penn. 1976).

protects the author's explanation of his bookkeeping system, it does not protect the bookkeeping system itself.[80]

Later decisions, most notably *Nichols v Universal Pictures Corp.*,[81] elaborated upon the doctrine and explored its difficulties as well. Judge Learned Hand, the author of the *Nichols* opinion, recognized that the major problem with the idea/expression dichotomy and, by implication, the fact/expression dichotomy, is uncertainty over where to draw the line between the idea or fact and the expression.[82]

A seminal expression of the prohibition on copyrighting facts themselves came in the 1918 Supreme Court decision, *International News Service v Associated Press*,[83] in which the Supreme Court announced a federal common-law 'quasi-property' right in the dissemination of information. At issue in that case were the news reports the Associated Press ('AP') published on the East Coast. Rival International News Service ('INS') had been copying those reports and relaying them to its Midwest and West Coast papers simultaneously or even ahead of their receipt by the AP's local counterparts. In rejecting the AP's complaint, the Court made a clear, *constitutionally*-based statement regarding the non-copyrightability of factual information.[84]

This generally accepted aversion to copyrighting facts has broadly carried through to the federal circuits and district courts as well.[85]

Taking this rationale further, the *Rosemont Enterprises, Inc. v Random House, Inc.* court, using language that would be repeated 25 years later in *Feist*,[86] vehemently rejected the view that a second-comer is absolutely precluded from saving time and effort by referring to and relying upon prior published material. It clearly rejected the industrious collection doctrine approach, stating that '[i]t is just such wasted effort that the proscription against the copyright of ideas and facts, and to a lesser extent the privilege of fair use, are designed to prevent'.[87]

---

80 *Baker v Selden*, 101 U.S. 99 (1980). See also 17 U.S.C. § 102(b) (2005) (incorporating *Baker*).

81 45 F.2d 119 (2d Cir. 1930).

82 See *id.* at 121. See also *Nash v CBS*, 899 F.2d 1537, 1540 (7th Cir. 1990); *CCC Info. Servs. Inc. v Maclean Hunter Mkt. Reports, Inc.*, 44 F.3d 61, 69 n.16 (2d Cir. 1994).

83 248 U.S. 215 (1918).

84 *Id.* at 234.

85 *Greenbie v Noble*, 151 F. Supp. 45 (S.D.N.Y. 1957). See also *Lake v Columbia Broad. Sys. Inc.*, 140 F. Supp. 707, 708–09 (S.D. Cal. 1956); *Rosemont Enter. Inc. v Random House, Inc.*, 366 F.2d 303, 307 (2d Cir. 1966).

86 *Feist Publ'n, Inc. v Rural Tel. Serv. Co., Inc.*, 499 U.S. 340, 354 (1991).

87 *Rosemont*, 366 F.2d at 310.

b. The merger doctrine The merger doctrine is a collateral branch of the idea/expression dichotomy, although it somewhat blurs the line between idea and expression. Under the merger doctrine, first announced in *Morrissey v Procter & Gamble Co.*,[88] a court may exclude from copyright protection expressions of ideas that can be expressed only in one way or in a very limited number of ways based on the logic that copyrighting such an expression would effectively copyright the idea as well. Although it ostensibly prohibits copyrights in what would otherwise be protectable expression, the merger doctrine, like the idea/expression dichotomy, also reflects the law's general aversion to exclusive ownership in facts.

c. The emergence of new emphasis on the public domain As a number of other scholars have demonstrated,[89] since 1960 the United States Supreme Court has repeatedly emphasized the constitutional dimensions of the public domain, including the principle that it is the public that 'owns' public domain materials and that these 'ownership' rights are irrevocable. For example, in the famous *Sears/Compco*[90] decisions, the Court held that the states could not prohibit copying of unpatentable public domain materials which represent too slight an advance to be patented:

> An unpatentable article, like an article on which the patent has expired, is in the public domain and may be made and sold by whoever chooses to do so . . . .[91]

B. The Industrious Collection Doctrine Under the 1976 Copyright Act

After the introduction of the industrious collection doctrine more than 80 years ago and the concomitant swing back toward investment of labor as a justification for copyright protection, the lower courts began to struggle with the very underpinnings of the industrious collection doctrine, particularly after the

---

88 379 F.2d 675 (1st Cir. 1967). See also *Concrete Mach. Co. v Classic Lawn Ornaments, Inc.*, 843 F.2d 600, 606 (1st Cir. 1988).

89 See, for example, Ochoa,Tyler T. (2002), 'Origins and Meanings of the Public Domain', 28 *U. Dayton. L. Rev*. 215.

90 See *Sears, Roebuck & Co. v Stiffel Co.*, 376 U.S. 225 (1964); *Compco Corp. v Day-Brite Lighting, Inc.*, 376 U.S. 234.

91 *Sears*, 376 U.S. at 231–32. See also *Graham v John Deere Co.*, 383 U.S. 1, 5–6 (1966); *Kewanee Oil Co. v Bicron Corp.*, 416 U.S. 470, 484 (1974). But see *Goldstein v California*, 412 U.S. 546 (1973); Pollack, Malla (1995), 'Unconstitutional Incontestability? The Intersection of the Intellectual Property and Commerce Clauses of the Constitution: Beyond A Critique of *Shakespeare Co. v Silstar Corp.*', 18 *Seattle U.L. Rev*. 259, 305–20 (describing *Goldstein* as inconsistent with public domain principles).

enactment of the 1976 Copyright Act. Under the 1976 Act, courts were divided regarding the doctrine's continued viability. Although the majority of federal courts had never embraced the industrious collection doctrine,[92] the doctrine had considerable staying power in some circuits.[93] Some courts continued to apply the doctrine, viewing it as the only viable method by which to provide meaningful protection for factual compilations. Other courts tried to avoid any direct discussion of whether factual works are indeed copyrightable, preferring instead to assume that they are, and relying instead on the fair use defense as an indirect way of allowing defendants to freely use the underlying factual material.

Some courts, however, began showing overt uneasiness with the industrious collection doctrine and its questionable underpinnings, leading to confusion and internal inconsistency in the reasoning of their decisions. Other courts went even further and explicitly repudiated the doctrine, turning their focus instead back to the creative elements of a compilation as the touchstone of copyrightability. These unsuccessful attempts to reconcile the industrious collection doctrine with modern copyright jurisprudence, laid the groundwork for an outright repudiation of the industrious collection doctrine in *Feist*.

Despite these simultaneous but divergent trends in the copyrightability of compilations, lower courts continued to hold that actual facts and other information-based materials themselves are not copyrightable. Courts interpreting the 1976 Act also continued to emphasize the importance of the public domain, pointing to its constitutional underpinnings. After promulgation of the 1976 Act, however, the case law on copyrightable subject matter began to give detailed, policy-based analyses as well. Unlike the industrious collection decisions that followed in the wake of the 1909 Act, post-1976 decisions were careful to adhere to the basic goals that copyright law aims to promote.

---

92 See *infra* Part II.B. 3–5. See also Wood, Ethan L. (1994), Note, 'Copyrighting the Yellow Pages: Finding Originality in Factual Compilations', 78 *Minn. L. Rev.* 1319, 1322–23.

93 See, for example, *Rural Tel. Serv. Co. v Feist Publ'ns, Inc.*, 916 F. 2d 718 (10th Cir. 1990), *cert. granted,* 498 U.S. 808 (1990); *S. Bell Tel. & Tel. Co. v Associated Tel. Directory Publishers*, 756 F.2d 801 (11th Cir. 1985); *Ill. Bell Tel. Co. v Haines & Co.*, 683 F. Supp. 1204 (N.D. Ill. 1988), *aff'd*, 905 F.2d 1081 (7th Cir. 1990), *vacated,* 499 U.S. 944 (1991); *Hutchinson Tel. Co. v Fronteer Directory Co. of Minn.*, 586 F. Supp. 911 (D. Minn. 1984), *rev'd* 770 F.2d 128 (8th Cir. 1985); *Fin. Info. Inc. v Moody's Investors Serv. Inc.*, 599 F. Supp. 994, 997–98 (S.D.N.Y. 1983), *rev'd*, 751 F.2d 501 (2d Cir. 1984).

1. Copyrights in facts and other information-based materials, preservation of the public domain, and the policy underlying copyright law

Unlike the 1909 Act, the 1976 Copyright Act included an express definition of the term 'compilation', which, for the first time, drew an express statutory connection between compilations and 'original works of authorship':

> A 'compilation' is a work formed by the collection and assembling of preexisting materials or of data that are selected, coordinated, or arranged in such a way that the resulting work as a whole constitutes an original work of authorship. . . .[94]

A separate section of the 1976 Act also clarified the scope of protection for compilations, specifying that:

> The copyright in a compilation or derivative work extends only to the material contributed by the author of such work, as distinguished from the preexisting material employed in the work. . . .[95]

This definition expressly applies the originality requirement to compilations. It also compels a court to examine the nature of a compilation's 'selection, coordination, or arrangement' in order to determine whether the compilation is 'an original work of authorship' protectable under 35 U.S.C. § 102(a).

Likewise, s. 102(b) of the 1976 Act also expressly codified the common-law concepts of the idea/expression and fact/expression dichotomies.[96] Under s. 102(b), 'in no case does copyright protection for an original work of authorship extend to any idea, procedure, process, system, method of operation, concept, principle or discovery'.[97] Sections 102(a) and 103 also implicitly codify the fact/expression dichotomy by according copyright protection only to 'original works of authorship'[98] and granting protection of compilations and derivative works 'only to the material contributed by the author of such work, as distinguished from the preexisting material employed in the work'.[99] The 1976 Act does not, however, resolve the ambiguities in the idea/expression doctrine that Judge Hand identified in the *Nichols* decision. Nowhere among the definitions in s. 101 is there a definition of 'fact' or 'expression'.

Furthermore, the 1976 Act's use of the phrase 'original work of authorship', which replaced the phrase 'all the writings of an author' in the 1909 Act, was

---

94 17 U.S.C. § 101 (2005).
95 17 U.S.C. § 103(b) (2005).
96 See *supra* text accompanying notes 56–60.
97 17 U.S.C. § 102(b) (2005).
98 17 U.S.C. § 102(a).
99 17 U.S.C. § 103(b).

left purposefully undefined. Much like the Copyright Clause of the Constitution, the 1976 Act provides guidance in defining originality only in very general terms. Courts were thus left to develop an understanding of 'originality' in their own terms. Nevertheless, the legislative history of the 1976 Act shows that Congress intended for courts to incorporate their own standards for the necessary level of originality, as established in their interpretations of the 1909 Act.[100]

After the enactment of the 1976 Act, courts dealing with historical and other fact-based works began to take a much more policy-oriented approach to these cases, growing increasingly aware of the risks of granting exclusive rights in facts and knowledge. They show a heightened understanding of the possible chilling effects that such exclusivity could have on other authors who were trying to tackle other issues or pursue other endeavors. A few courts also began to emphasize the constitutional origins of the ideal of the public domain.

For example, in *Alexander v Haley*, the court dealt with, *inter alia*, the defendant's alleged infringement of the plaintiff's copyright in a novel and pamphlet that were amalgams of fact and fiction derived from the somber history of slavery in the United States.[101] In determining whether there had been a taking of copyrightable elements of the work, the court agreed with the defendant that 'each of the similarities asserted by the plaintiff is in one or more of several categories of attributes of written work which are not subject to the protection of the copyright laws',[102] pointing to three such categories in particular. First, the court rejected the plaintiff's claim of infringement based on 'matters of historical or contemporary fact', for '[n]o claim of copyright protection can arise from the fact that the plaintiff has written about such historical and factual items. . . .'[103] Secondly, the court rejected the plaintiff's claim based on material traceable to common sources or to the public domain.[104] Thirdly, the court rejected the claim based on borrowed scenes a faire,[105] which are incidents, characters, or settings that, as a practical matter, are indispensable to the treatment of a given topic.

---

100 H.R. Rep. No. 94-1476, at 51, 54 (1976). See also *Harper & Row, Publ'g, Inc. v Nation Enters.*, 471 U.S. 539, 581 (1985) (Brennan J., dissenting).

101 460 F. Supp. 40 (S.D.N.Y. 1978).

102 *Id.* at 44.

103 *Id.* at 44–45. See also *Sid & Marty Krofft Television Prod. Inc. v McDonald's Corp.*, 562 F.2d 1157, 1163 (9th Cir. 1977); *Signo Trading Int'l Ltd. v Gordon*, 535 F. Supp. 362 (N.D. Cal. 1981).

104 *Alexander*, 460 F. Supp. at 45.

105 *Id.* See also *Landsberg v Scrabble Crossword Game Players, Inc.*, 736 F.2d 485, 489 (9th Cir. 1984); *Hoehling v Universal City Studios, Inc.*, 618 F.2d 972, 979 (2d Cir. 1980).

Similarly, the courts perceived as the leading authorities in the formulation of United States' copyright laws, such as the Second and Ninth Circuits, have permitted extensive reliance on prior works of history and emphasized that factual information must remain in the public domain.[106] For instance, in *Hoehling v Universal City Studios, Inc.*,[107] the Second Circuit held that second comers must be allowed to rely extensively on prior works of history, thus rejecting case law in other circuits that held the results of original research are copyrightable.[108]

The Second Circuit's holding touched upon a fundamental policy underlying copyright law:

> The rationale for this doctrine is that the cause of knowledge is best served when history is the common property of all, and each generation remains free to draw upon the discoveries and insights of the past.[109]

In its 1984 decision, *Landsberg v Scrabble Crossword Game Players, Inc.*, the Ninth Circuit followed the path set by the Second Circuit.[110] Because of the limited number of ways in which certain facts and factual information can be presented, the court held that protecting the public's interest in such limited modes of expression requires that the 'similarity of expression may have to amount to verbatim reproduction or very close paraphrasing before a factual work will be deemed infringed'.[111] Any other approach might allow the first few writers to tackle a factual topic to exhaust the limited modes of expression available to convey it.

Likewise, in the wake of the 1976 Act, the Supreme Court touched upon the essence of modern copyright law in *Harper & Row, Publishers Inc. v Nation Enterprises*.[112] Although the Court's decision in *Harper & Row* was at face value concerned with the 'fair use' defense as applied to *The Nation*'s publication of numerous extracts from President Ford's biography, the Court also

---

[106] See discussion *supra* Part II.A.1, which deals, *inter alia*, with trends in the Second Circuit before the enactment of the 1976 Act. See also *Oxford Book Co. v Coll. Entrance Book Co.*, 98 F.2d 688, 691 (2d Cir. 1938).

[107] 618 F.2d 972. See also *Miller v Universal City Studios, Inc.*, 650 F.2d 1365, 1369–71 (5th Cir. 1981).

[108] The Second Circuit clearly repudiated such an approach in *Rosemont Enterprises Inc. v Random House Inc.*, 366 F.2d 303, 310 (2d Cir. 1966).

[109] *Hoehling*, 618 F.2d at 974.

[110] 736 F.2d 485 (9th Cir. 1984). See also *Ekern v Sew/Fit Co.*, 622 F. Supp. 367, 370 (N.D. Ill. 1985); *Evans v Wallace Berrie & Co.*, 681 F. Supp. 813, 817 (S.D. Fla. 1988).

[111] *Landsberg*, 736 F.2d at 488. See also *Worth v Selchow & Righter Co.*, 827 F.2d 569, 572 (9th Cir. 1987).

[112] 471 U.S. 539 (1985).

took this opportunity to discuss more generally exactly what protective scope fact-based works enjoyed under copyright law. Quoting from the Court's earlier opinion in *Sony Corp. of America v Universal City Studios, Inc.*,[113] Justice O'Connor's opinion for the Court in *Harper & Row* touched upon the underlying principle of the Copyright Clause and its application to works of fiction and non-fiction alike:

> [Copyright] is intended to motivate the creative activity of authors and inventors by the provision of a special reward, and to allow the public access to the products of their genius after the limited period of exclusive control has expired.[114]

O'Connor wrote that 'no author may copyright facts or ideas',[115] since 'copyright is limited to those aspects of the work – termed "expression" – that display the stamp of the author's originality'.[116] Subsequent users are therefore free to 'copy from a prior author's work those constituent elements that are not original', such as 'facts, or materials in the public domain – as long as such use does not unfairly appropriate the author's original contributions'.[117] By refusing to recognize a copyright in facts alone, the law is able to serve the public's interest in the free flow of information.[118] Consequently, although the Supreme Court did not deal directly with the viability of the industrious collection doctrine, it did plant the seeds for its later decision in *Feist.*[119]

The *Harper & Row* Court also placed the idea/expression dichotomy within its broader constitutional context, pointing out that the doctrine 'strike[s] a definitional balance between the First Amendment and the Copyright Act by permitting free communication of facts while still protecting an author's expression'.[120] Even Justice Brennan, in dissent, commented on why facts cannot be copyrighted. First noting the economic rationale for this rule, Justice Brennan explained that, 'were an author able to prevent subsequent authors from using concepts, ideas, or facts contained in his or her work, the creative process would wither, and scholars would be forced into unproductive replication of the research of their predecessors.'[121] He then looked at the broader

---

113 464 U.S. 417 (1984).

114 *Harper & Row*, 471 U.S. at 546 (quoting *Sony*, 464 U.S. at 429).

115 *Id.* at 547.

116 *Id.*

117 *Id.* at 548.

118 *Id.*

119 But see *Black's Guide, Inc. v Mediamerica, Inc.*, No. C-90-0819, 1990 U.S. Dist. LEXIS 16272, at *9 (N.D. Cal. Aug. 15, 1990).

120 *Harper & Row*, 471 U.S. at 556 (quoting *Harper & Row Publishers, Inc. v Nation Enters.*, 723 F.2d 195, 203 (2d Cir. 1983)).

121 *Id.* at 582.

constitutional rationale for this rule, explaining that such a limitation on copyright protections also ensures consonance with important First Amendment values.[122]

Using works of history as an example, Justice Brennan emphasized that, at its core, copyright law does not protect the most valuable aspect of factual works:

> The value this labor produces lies primarily in the information and ideas revealed, and not in the particular collocation of words through which the information and ideas are expressed.[123]

Accordingly, the impulse to compensate authors for subsequent use of the information and ideas produced by their labors is entirely understandable, for there is an 'inequity [that] seems to lurk in the idea that much of the fruit of the historian's labor may be used without compensation'.[124] And yet, Justice Brennan continued, in a passage that would be adopted seven years later by the majority in *Feist*:

> This, however, is not some unforeseen byproduct of a statutory scheme intended primarily to ensure a return for works of the imagination. Congress made the affirmative choice that the copyright laws should apply in this way.[125]

2. The decline of the industrious collection doctrine

Although the industrious collection doctrine both originated in and was subsequently rejected by both the Second and Ninth Circuits,[126] the Seventh, Eighth and Tenth Circuits continued strongly to support the doctrine until the Supreme Court's decision in *Feist*.

A recent example of the doctrine at work is the Seventh Circuit decision in *Schroeder v William Morrow & Co.*,[127] in which the court addressed the

---

122 *Id.*

123 *Id.* at 589.

124 *Id.*

125 *Id.* (quoting H.R. Rep. No. 94-1476, at 56–57 (1976)). But see *San Francisco Arts & Athletics, Inc. v U.S. Olympic Comm'n*, 483 U.S. 522 (1987); *Harper & Row Publishers, Inc. v Nation Enters.*, 471 U.S. 539 (1985); *Zacchini v Scripps-Howard Broad. Co.*, 433 U.S. 562 (1977).

126 The Ninth Circuit originally embraced the industrious collection doctrine as a basis for copyright protection in *Leon v Pacific Telephone & Telegraph Co.,* 91 F.2d 484 (9th Cir. 1937) (citing *Jeweler's Circular Publishing Co. v Keystone Publishing,* 281 F. 83 (2d Cir. 1922)).

127 566 F.2d 3 (7th Cir. 1977). Prior to *Schroeder* the Seventh Circuit had already adopted the industrious collection doctrine in a few cases. See, for example, *G.R. Leonard & Co. v Stack*, 386 F.2d 38 (7th Cir. 1967); *Adventures in Good Eating, Inc. v Best Places to Eat, Inc.*, 131 F.2d 809, 812–13 (7th Cir. 1942).

alleged copying of a gardening directory. The names and addresses in the garden directory were arranged alphabetically, requiring no original insights on the part of the compiler.[128] The court, citing the Second Circuit's now rejected application of the industrious collection doctrine in *Jeweler's Circular Publishing Co.*, found the directory warranted copyright protection. It asserted that 'only industrious collection' is required since 'copyright protects not the individual names and addresses but the compilation, the product of the compiler's industry',[129] thus protecting the fruits of any substantial and independent effort, regardless of the originality or creativity involved.

Another relatively recent example of the industrious collection doctrine is the Eighth Circuit's decision in *United Telephone Co. of Missouri v Johnson Publishing Co.*[130] The defendant had updated its own independent directory by verifying new listings obtained from the local telephone company's directory. The court found that by comparing its directory to and obtaining new subscriber listings from the telephone company's directory, the defendant had created a second work of substantial similarity to the telephone company's directory, thereby infringing the telephone company's legitimately asserted copyright in its directory.[131]

In addition to this line of cases overtly applying the industrious collection doctrine, there is a second line of cases that purported to require originality as a prerequisite for copyright protection, but, in practice, simply measured originality as a function of industry. For example, the Eighth Circuit's 1986 decision in *West Publishing Co. v Mead Data Central, Inc.* revolved around Mead Data's proposal to cite page numbers from West Publishing's legal reporters in Mead Data's computerized LEXIS reports of the same opinions.[132]

The Eighth Circuit affirmed the lower court's grant of a preliminary injunction against Mead Data.[133] At first, the court correctly pointed out that an arrangement of pre-existing materials may receive copyright protection and that 'in each case the arrangement must be evaluated in light of the originality and intellectual-creation standards' of prior case law.[134] The court seemed to lose this standard, however, for although West Publishing had arranged the

128 *Schroeder*, 566 F.2d at 6.

129 *Id.* at 5. *Accord Feist Publ'ns, Inc. v Rural Tel. Serv. Co.*, 916 F.2d 718 (10th Cir. 1990), *rev'd*, 499 U.S. 340 (1991); *Illinois Bell Tel. Co. v Haines & Co.*, 905 F.2d 1081 (7th Cir. 1990), *vacated*, 111 S. Ct. 1408 (1991); *Hutchinson Tel. Co. v Fronteer Directory Co. of Minn., Inc.*, 770 F.2d 128 (8th Cir. 1985).

130 855 F.2d 604 (8th Cir. 1988).

131 *Id.* at 608–09.

132 799 F.2d 1219, 1222 (8th Cir. 1986) ('*Mead*'). See also *Oasis Publishing Co. v West Publishing Co.*, 924 F. Supp. 918 (D. Minn. 1996).

133 *Mead*, 799 F.2d at 1222.

134 *Id.* at 1225.

cases in a purely mechanical fashion with no original insight or creativity, the court stated that 'a work need only be the product of a modicum of intellectual labor' to be protectable, a test that West's reporters easily met.[135] In response to the argument that this essentially granted copyright protection to page numbers, the court rejoined that 'protection for the numbers is not sought for their own sake. It is sought, rather, because access to these particular numbers . . . would give users of LEXIS a large part of what West has spent so much labor and industry in compiling',[136] thus overlooking the lack of originality in the arrangement of page numbers.[137]

As discussed below, however, many other courts decisions, and ultimately *Feist* itself, not only rejected the premise of the 'industrious collection' doctrine but also required an affirmative showing that the allegedly infringed material demonstrates originality of authorship.[138]

3. The fair use defense as a shield against exclusive ownership of facts

A few courts have tried to avoid the question of database protection in general and the industrious collection doctrine in particular. Instead, they simply assumed that the work at issue was entitled to copyright protection and tried to resolve the disputes indirectly via the fair use defense as a means of 'freeing' factual information. These courts, however, went to such extraordinary lengths as to stretch the defense beyond its limits.

The fair use defense is a limitation on the copyright owner's exclusive rights. Section 107 of the 1976 Act[139] provides that 'the fair use of a copyrighted work . . . for purposes such as criticism, comment, news reporting, teaching . . . , scholarship, or research is not an infringement of copyright'. It also provides that '[i]n determining whether the use made in any particular case is a fair use the factors to be considered shall include – (1) the purpose and character of the use, including whether such use is for a commercial nature or is for nonprofit educational purposes; (2) the nature of the copyrighted work; (3) the amount and substantiality of the portion used in relation to the copyrighted work as a whole; and (4) the effect of the use upon the potential market for or value of the copyrighted work.'

---

135 *Id.* at 1227.

136 *Id.*

137 But see *id.* at 1248 (Oliver J., concurring in part and dissenting in part); see also *Toro Co. v R & R Prods. Co.*, 787 F.2d 1208, 1213 (8th Cir. 1986); *Eggers v Sun Sales Corp.*, 263 F. 373 (2d Cir. 1920); *Banks Law Publ'g Co. v Lawyers' Co-op. Publ'g Co.*, 169 F. 386 (2d Cir. 1909), *appeal dismissed*, 223 U.S. 738 (1911).

138 *See infra* Part II.B.5.

139 17 U.S.C. § 107 (2005).

The case of *New York Times Co. v Roxbury Data Interface*[140] serves as a good example of this trend. The court dealt with whether a copyrighted work may be indexed by an outsider without the permission of the copyright holder. The plaintiff's newspaper, *The New York Times*, published its own annual indices of citations to names and other data in newspaper issues from that year.[141] Finding the plaintiff's indices inadequate, the defendants published their own index to those indices but collated the citations over several years.[142] The court refused to grant a preliminary injunction, despite the defendants' confession to copying names directly from the plaintiff's directory.[143]

Because the defendants did not appropriate the corresponding citations to pages and columns, the court held that the defendants' index likely either was not an infringement or was excused under the doctrine of fair use.[144]

Although the court thus focused upon the expression inherent in the author's final product, it recognized that copyrightable expression goes beyond the mere superficial arrangement or ordering of the data.[145] Although correlations drawn between facts may still be criticized as lacking the required creativity, the scope of protection afforded by this broadened view of what is copyrightable in a compilation of facts is still significantly more than that afforded under an unadulterated application of the originality requirement. Even under a pure application of the industrious collection doctrine, the court's attempt to distinguish between different forms of data is, at best, baseless. In terms of solely the labor invested or saved, copying only the names gathered by the plaintiff is not in any meaningful way very different from copying the entire work. In both situations the defendants were simply free-riding on the labor already invested by the plaintiff. Something else must therefore have motivated the court's analysis – most likely the court's disinterest in dealing with the uneasy question of copyrightability of compilations.

The court's application of the four 'fair use' factors in this case is particularly revealing. In a typical fair-use analysis, a court will look first at whether the alleged fair use is commercial or non-commercial. In *Roxbury*, however, the court looked first at the purpose and character of the use, identifying at least two main motives that the defendants had in copying from the plaintiff's indices: (1) to make money, and (2) to facilitate public access to useful information in the

140 *N.Y. Times Co. v Roxbury Data Interface, Inc.*, 434 F. Supp. 217 (D.N.J. 1977) ('*Roxbury*').

141 *Id.* at 218.

142 *Id.* at 219.

143 *Id.* at 222.

144 *Id.* at 226–27.

145 *Fin. Info., Inc. v Moody's Investors Serv., Inc.*, 808 F.2d 204, 208 n.3 (2d Cir. 1986).

plaintiff's newspapers.[146] Although the court was undoubtedly correct in finding that the defendants' index would serve the public interest, this hardly seems significant since an alleged infringing work usually serves the public interest in at least some manner. Perhaps for this very reason, the typical 'fair use' analysis does not begin by looking at the public interest. Instead, public interest is typically a factor reserved for the threshold question of whether the plaintiff's work is in fact protected by copyright, and not whether the defendants' work infringes that protection. Such a public interest analysis could have led the court to conclude that the plaintiff's work was factual and useful rather than creative in nature and thus was non-copyrightable material. Nevertheless, in struggling to protect the free flow of facts, the court in *Roxbury* went to extraordinary lengths to emphasize the defendants' contribution to the public interest: 'save researchers a considerable amount of time and, thus, facilitate the public interest in the dissemination of information'.[147]

Only as the second step in its fair use analysis did the court finally consider the nature of the plaintiff's copyrighted work. The court found that the Times indices were basically a collection of facts, and '[s]ince the Times Index is a work more of diligence than of originality or inventiveness, defendants have greater license to use portions of the Times Index under the fair use doctrine'.[148] Such explorations of a work's factual or creative nature should be conducted during the threshold copyrightability analysis. Classifying the work as one 'more of diligence than of originality' suggests that, in the court's eyes, it does not deserve copyright protection.

As the third step in its fair use analysis, the court considered whether the amount and substance of the copied parts in relation to the copyrighted work as a whole were reasonable in light of the defendants' purpose in copying the plaintiff's work. Here the court emphasized again that the protected element in the plaintiff's work is the correlation of names to page citations, an element that the defendants had not copied.[149] The court thereby distinguished other directory cases that had employed the industrious collection doctrine, stressing that these other cases involved defendants who had copied the essence of the plaintiff's work in its entirety as a new and virtually identical directory in direct competition with the plaintiff's directory.[150]

The court also noted the extent to which producing the defendants' index required copying the names directly from the Times Index, and that for all practical purposes, the defendants could not have published their index with-

146 *Roxbury*, 434 F. Supp. at 221.
147 *Id.*
148 *Id.*
149 *Id.* at 222.
150 *Id.* at 222–23.

out such direct copying.[151] The plaintiff, however, correctly pointed out that the defendants could have obtained the same information directly from the newspaper issues, as had the compilers of the Times Index.[152] Had the court been loyal to the industrious collection doctrine, it would not have allowed the defendants such leeway because the Times Index required a significant expenditure of time and effort. The court, however, did not take this path, holding that such an argument could be successful only upon copying of both the personal names and their correlated citations.[153]

It is unclear, however, why the defendants would have had to appropriate both the names and their correlative citations under the industrious collection doctrine. Even the court itself acknowledged that its distinction between taking the names alone and taking both names and citations was 'not determinative' to its 'fair use' analysis, but simply 'must be noted'.[154]

Interestingly, the court seems to suggest in a footnote that, regardless of the amount or substance of the material copied, what the defendants copied was not the true, copyrightable essence of the plaintiff's work. The court essentially divided compilations into two categories, factual compilations and subjective compilations, hinting that the latter category merited greater protection than the former.[155] The former is mechanical compilation of facts while the latter is the product of the compiler's judgment and discretion in choosing which entries to include. Content selected on inevitably objective criteria for automatic inclusion in a compilation should remain in the public domain, for there are very few ways to create such compilations.

Fourth and last, the court considered the effect of the defendants' name index on the potential market for the Times Index, which the court found to be slight.[156] The defendants' index was useless without the corresponding Times Index volume because only the Times indices themselves cited the actual articles.[157] The defendants' index therefore did not compete directly with the plaintiff's indices.[158]

Even more revealing is the court's response to the argument that the defendants' index deprived the plaintiffs of their right to exploit their copyrights.[159] The court viewed this argument as stating that a copyrighted work cannot be

151 *Id.* at 223.
152 *Id.*
153 *Id.*
154 *Id.*
155 *Id.* at 222 n.2.
156 *Id.* at 223.
157 *Id.*
158 *Id.* at 224.
159 *Id.*

indexed without permission from the copyright holder in much the same way that filmmakers cannot make a movie from a copyrighted play or novel. The court rejected this analogy, first because the defendants had not copied the essence of the plaintiff's work, the correlation of names and other data with page cites.[160] As discussed above, however, this explanation would fail under the industrious collection doctrine. Secondly, the court rejected the analogy because the defendants' index had a different function and format.[161] However, this fact is irrelevant under the industrious collection doctrine if the defendants drew significantly and extensively from the plaintiff's copyrighted materials. Thirdly, the court cited the fact that the Times Indices themselves contained nothing comparable to the defendants' index,[162] yet another factor that would have been irrelevant under a pure industrious collection analysis.[163]

4. Questioning the underpinnings of the industrious collection doctrine

Some courts at both the appellate court and district court level started to explicitly doubt the foundation of the industrious collection doctrine. These courts included some that had previously applied the doctrine, such as the Seventh Circuit. The discussion that follows provides an illustration of such uneasiness at its peak, showing how courts voiced their concerns regarding the consistency of the industrious collection doctrine with copyright doctrine while at the same time 'excusing' in economic terms their continued adherence to the doctrine as the only meaningful means of supporting compilation creators. These courts' decisions thus reflect confusion and internal inconsistency in their reasoning and final resolutions. In their own way, however, these cases prepared the ground for *Feist*'s later repudiation of the doctrine.

A good example is found in a 1982 district court decision, *National Business Lists, Inc. v Dun & Bradstreet, Inc.*[164] The court started by describing the copyright protection of compilations as 'a doctrine in search of conceptual underpinnings',[165] and a 'troublesome legal issue because it involves consideration of competing interests within the confines of a statutory scheme better suited to other literary works'.[166] Describing the compiler's contribu-

160 *Id.* at 224–25.
161 *Id.* at 225.
162 *Id.* at 225.
163 See, for example, *Dow Jones & Co. v Bd. of Trade*, 546 F. Supp. 113, 120 (S.D.N.Y. 1982); *Nat'l Bus. Lists, Inc. v Dun & Bradstreet, Inc.*, 552 F. Supp. 89 (N.D. Ill. 1982).
164 552 F. Supp. 89.
165 *Id.* at 93.
166 *Id.* at 91.

tion to knowledge as the collection of information, the court expressed concerns about the compilation industry and the possible undermining of the economic incentives to create such works.[167] The court admitted, however, that such economic concerns nevertheless do not explain why courts fall back on copyright law when other legal doctrines, such as the misappropriation doctrine, can accomplish the same ends.[168]

The court went even further, pointing to the questionable constitutionality of protecting factual compilations.[169] Its grave doubts notwithstanding, however, the court followed the industrious collection doctrine, providing a two-fold explanation for its decision. First, it noted that 'there appears to remain a lingering recognition that "[t]he second historian or second directory publisher cannot bodily appropriate the research of his predecessor".'[170] Secondly, it adverted to the fact that 'the directory cases, rather than being a breed apart, are the most striking illustrations in copyright law that the misappropriation doctrine . . . . has there long found a house if not a home'.[171]

In another case, *Rand McNally & Co. v Fleet Management Systems, Inc.*,[172] the court found a roadway mileage guide non-copyrightable as a compilation, and expressed its uneasiness with the industrious collection doctrine. This decision is unusual in a few respects. On the one hand, the court accepted the long-established idea that '[c]ompilations of facts, however, have "long rested securely within the scope of copyright".'[173] Nevertheless, relying on *National Business List*,[174] the court also acknowledged that 'the rationale behind protecting such compilations, however, is unclear'.[175] On the other hand, despite its recognition that 'another justification for protecting compilations of facts relies on the compiler's "subjective judgment and selectivity in choosing items to a list",'[176] the court asserted that factual compilations may still be protected by copyright by simple virtue of being the 'result of some level of compiler effort and industry'.[177]

---

167 *Id.* at 92. See also *Black's Guide, Inc. v Mediamerica, Inc.*, No. C-90-0819, 1990 U.S. Dist. LEXIS 16272, at *8 (N.D. Cal. Aug. 15, 1990).

168 *Nat'l Bus. Lists*, 552 F. Supp. at 95. See also *id.* at 92; *Fin. Info. Inc. v Moody's Investors Serv. Inc.*, 599 F. Supp. 994, 999 (S.D.N.Y. 1983), *rev'd*, 751 F.2d 501 (2d Cir. 1984). But see Denicola, *supra* note 73, at 530.

169 *Nat'l Bus. Lists*, 552 F. Supp. at 93.

170 *Id.* at 95 (quoting *Huie v Nat'l Broad. Co.*, 184 F. Supp. 198 (S.D.N.Y. 1960)).

171 *Id.* (citation omitted).

172 591 F. Supp. 726 (N.D. Ill. 1983).

173 *Id.* at 731.

174 See *supra* text accompanying notes 164–171.

175 *Rand McNally & Co. v Fleet Mgmt. Sys., Inc.*, 591 F. Supp. 726, 731 (D.C. Ill. 1983).

176 *Id.* at 732 n.4.

177 *Id.* at 733.

Soon thereafter, the Seventh Circuit's 1985 decision in *Rockford Map Publishers, Inc. v Directory Service Co. of Colorado*[178] declared that 'copyright laws protect the work, not the amount of effort expended',[179] thus de-emphasizing labor and finding originality only in creative arrangements. The defendant, relying on the industrious collection doctrine affirmed in *Schroeder*, argued that because the plaintiff had spent little time preparing its maps, its efforts were 'not very "industrious" ' and its product was thus not copyrightable.[180] Rejecting this argument, the court emphasized that the amount of time invested is irrelevant.[181] Though the court appeared to reject the industrious collection doctrine as a basis for protection, the court actually made no explicit judgment as to whether labor, in and of itself, is protectable. Rather, the court simply re-interpreted *Jeweler's* and *Schroeder*, two classic industrious collection cases, as hinging on whether the compiler produced a 'new' or original arrangement, not on whether the compiler had invested a significant amount of time and effort.[182]

Rockford Map created confusion within the Seventh Circuit probably because it studiously avoided adopting the industrious collection doctrine while at the same time borrowing heavily from classical industrious collection cases such as *Jeweler's*.[183]

In light of the court's ruling in *Rockford Map,* the defendant in *Rand McNally I* brought a motion for reconsideration.[184] The court conceded that after *Rockford Map*, its previous reliance on the level of effort involved in compiling data was erroneous.[185] Instead, the proper analysis is whether the compilation as a whole evinced originality in its arrangement of facts.[186]

The *Rand McNally III* court expressed its uneasiness with the industrious collection doctrine, calling the law on factual compilation copyrights a 'tangled web'[187] and admitting that it presents 'intellectual difficulties in determining where protectable copying of facts ends and unlawful copying of

---

178 768 F.2d 145 (7th Cir. 1985).

179 *Id.* at 148.

180 *Id.*

181 *Id.*

182 *Id.* But see *Black's Guide, Inc. v Mediamerica, Inc.*, No. C-90-0819, 1990 U.S. Dist. LEXIS 16272, at *8 (N.D. Cal. Aug. 15, 1990); *Nat'l Bus. Lists, Inc. v Dun & Bradstreet, Inc.*, 552 F. Supp. 89, 97 (N.D. Ill. 1982).

183 See *Rockford Map Publishers,* 768 F.2d at 148–49.

184 *Rand McNally & Co. v Fleet Mgmt. Sys., Inc.*, 634 F. Supp. 604–05 (N.D. Ill. 1986) ('Rand McNally III').

185 *Id.* at 606.

186 *Id.* at 606–07.

187 *Id.* at 608.

the compilation begins'.[188] As to the continued viability of the industrious collection doctrine, however, it concluded that *Schroeder*[189] remained solid law in the Seventh Circuit,[190] and rejected the proposition that *Rockford Map* moved away from concentrating on labor expended to concentrating on originality.[191] Trying to reconcile *Rockford Map*'s confusing pronouncements,[192] the *Rand McNally III* court tried to draw formalistic distinctions between infringing map-makers and infringing compilers.[193] Ignoring the conflicting case law and the 1976 Act's express requirement that compilations constitute *original* works of authorship, the *Rand McNally III* court instead relied exclusively on the industrious collection doctrine as the basis for protection.

The Eleventh Circuit showed its own discomfort with the industrious collection doctrine in *Southern Bell Telephone & Telegraph Co. v Associated Telephone Directory Publishers*.[194] There, the court found the Atlanta Yellow Pages to be a copyrightable work of original authorship because of its subjective selection, organization, and arrangement of pre-existing materials. Although the court discounted the substantial line of cases relying on the industrious collection doctrine, it misinterpreted the originality requirement since the arrangement and selection of data in a typical Yellow Pages directory is mechanical and conventional, not original, and although laborious, does not reflect the compiler's personality. Moreover, notwithstanding its apparent rejection of the industrious collection doctrine, the court expressly refused to reject the notion that 'the principle characterized as the "sweat of the brow" theory is to apply in a determination of originality under the act'.[195] The court opined that originality should 'be tested by the nature of the selection and arrangement of the preexisting material in the compilation'[196] and that 'protection of original research of information in the public domain is better afforded under an unfair competition theory'.[197]

---

188 *Id.*

189 *Schroeder v William Morrow & Co.*, 566 F.2d 3 (7th Cir. 1977).

190 *Rand McNally III*, 634 F. Supp. at 608.

191 *Id.*

192 See *supra* text accompanying notes 182–183.

193 *Rand McNally III*, 634 F. Supp. at 608. See also *Clark Equip. Co. v Lift Parts Mfg. Co.*, 32 Copyright L. Rep. (CCH) P 20, 528, 530 (N.D. Ill. 1986); *Ill. Bell Tel. Co. v Haines & Co.*, 683 F. Supp. 1204, 1207–10 (N.D. Ill. 1988) (adopting *Rand McNally III*'s holding), *aff'd*, 905 F.2d 1081 (7th Cir. 1990).

194 756 F. 2d 801 (11th Cir. 1985).

195 *Id.* at 809 n.9.

196 *Id.*

197 *Id.* See also *Bellsouth Adver. & Publ'g Corp. v Donnelley Info. Publ'g Inc.*, 719 F. Supp. 1551, 1557 (S.D. Fla. 1988).

5. Repudiation of the industrious collection doctrine and the minimum level of originality necessary for copyright protection of compilations

After the 1976 Act was implemented, most courts rejected the industrious collection doctrine,[198] requiring instead that compilations contain sufficient creativity in their 'select[ion], coordinate[ion] or arrange[ment]' as to render them 'original works of authorship' entitled to copyright protection.[199] The line, however, between mere labor producing little or no originality and 'intellectual labor' producing original and newly created material can be very fine.

The basic problem with the industrious collection doctrine was that it failed to incorporate the concept of originality.[200] Courts that rejected the industrious collection doctrine, however, began to draw the line between 'intellectual labor' and mere unoriginal labor according to the fundamental principles underlying copyright law. These courts understood that facts do not owe their origin to the author who simply describes them. They also recognized that originality is not only a constitutionally mandated requirement but also a requirement that serves the important function of balancing the public's interest in stimulating creative activity against the public's need for unrestricted access to information by allowing subsequent authors to build upon and add to prior knowledge without unnecessary duplication of effort. These courts therefore established a minimum threshold of originality to deny copyright protection to fact compilations that failed to exhibit some level of subjective arrangement, thoughtful selection, or creativity.

The 1978 Ninth Circuit decision in *United States v Hamilton*[201] provided the first explicit rejection of the industrious collection doctrine. A Third Circuit decision from the 1950s had held that only those portions of a map that were recorded by direct observation of the geography described could be copyrighted.[202] The *Hamilton* court, however, found this rule theoretically unsound and instead made clear that only originality is the basis for a copyright.[203]

---

[198] See, for example, *Worth v Selchow & Righter Co.*, 827 F. 2d 569, 572–73 (9th Cir. 1987); *Fin. Info. Inc. v Moody's Investors Serv. Inc.*, 808 F. 2d 204, 207 (2d Cir. 1986); *Eckes v Card Prices Update*, 736 F.2d 859, 862 (2d Cir. 1984).

[199] 17 U.S.C. § 101 (2005).

[200] See, for example, 1 Nimmer and Nimmer, *supra* note 39, § 3.04.

[201] 583 F.2d 448 (9th Cir. 1978).

[202] *Amsterdam v Triangle Publ'ns*, 93 F. Supp. 79, 82 (E.D. Pa. 1950), *aff'd*, 189 F.2d 104 (3d Cir. 1951).

[203] *Hamilton*, 583 F.2d 448, 451. See also *Signo Trading Int'l Ltd. v Gordon*, 535 F. Supp. 362, 364 (N.D. Cal. 1981); *Roy Export Co. v Columbia Broad. Sys. Inc.*, 672 F.2d 1095, 1103 (2d Cir. 1982).

The *Hamilton* court further cited early cases recognizing that '(t)he elements of the copyright (in a map) consist in the selection, arrangement, and presentation of the component parts'.[204]

Explicit and direct rejection of the industrious collection doctrine also appeared in the Fifth Circuit's *Miller v Universal City Studios, Inc.*[205] decision, in which the court held that research itself is merely an alternative form of fact compilation and therefore also non-copyrightable. In doing so, the court provided for the first time a full-blown legislative, constitutional, economic, and policy-based analysis repudiating the industrious collection doctrine. Comparing the collection of facts to the compilation of names and addresses in a directory, the circuit court concluded that copyrightability for such a work rests 'on the originality of the selection and arrangement of factual material, rather than on the industriousness of the efforts to develop the information'.[206]

The court started its analysis with the idea/expression dichotomy, explaining that it 'derives from the concept of originality which is the premise of copyright law'.[207] Originality, the court continued, is a constitutional requirement, as illustrated by the Copyright Clause's use of the word 'Author'.[208] Facts, however, do not meet the threshold of originality because a 'fact does not originate with the author of a book describing the fact. . .'.[209]

Although the court was aware of the possibility of diminished incentives to create databases, it understood that the only question at bar was whether the copyright laws were intended to provide such protection.[210] Under the law, the only element of a compilation of facts that can be protected is the original selection and arrangement.[211] Otherwise, directories are a problematic breed that cannot be reconciled with the principle that facts are non-copyrightable; the 'mere use of the information contained in a directory without a substantial copying of the format does not constitute infringement'.[212] Accordingly, the *Miller* court found the Second Circuit's approach in *Hoehling* and *Rosemont*

---

204 583 F.2d at 452 (quoting *Gen. Drafting Co. v Andrews*, 37 F.2d 54, 55 (2d Cir. 1930)). See also *Emerson v Davies*, 8 F. Cas., 615, 619 (C.C.D. Mass. 1845) (No. 4436).

205 650 F.2d 1365 (5th Cir. 1981). See also *Southern Bell Tel. & Tel. Co. v Associated Tel. Dir. Publishers*, 756 F.2d 801, 809 (11th Cir. 1985).

206 *Miller*, 650 F.2d at 1369.

207 *Id.* at 1368.

208 *Id.* (citing U.S. Const. art. I, § 8, cl. 8). See also *Burrow-Giles Lithographic Co. v Sarony*, 111 U.S. 53, 58 (1884)).

209 *Miller*, 650 F.2d at 1368–69.

210 *Id.* at 1369.

211 *Id.* at 1368.

212 *Id.* at 1369–70.

more in line with the purpose and intended scope of copyright law because it 'allows a subsequent author to build upon and add to prior accomplishments without unnecessary duplication of effort'.[213]

Another Second Circuit case, *Eckes v Card Prices Update*,[214] also rejected the industrious collection doctrine. The court rested its holding squarely on the 'selection, creativity, and judgment' it found in the baseball card guidebook at issue in the case.[215] Although the Second Circuit found a tension between the proposition that facts alone are not copyrightable while a collection of them is, it resolved this tension by applying the rule that only original selection or creative arrangement may be protected.[216] This solution was ultimately adopted seven years later in *Feist*.[217]

The Ninth Circuit followed the steps of the Second Circuit in *Eckes* in its 1987 decision *Worth v Selchow & Righter Co.*[218] *Worth* is notable for the minimal scope of protection it affords compilations of facts. It is also instructive because of its endorsement of the original selection or arrangement requirement[219] and its reliance on cases disavowing the industrious collection doctrine.[220] The Ninth Circuit held that the discovery of a fact, regardless of the quantum of labor and expense invested in that discovery, is simply not a copyrightable work of an 'author'.[221]

In addition to these court decisions, the Copyright Office's registration practices during the years that preceded *Feist* are also informative. In its report on legal protection of databases, the Copyright Office outlined its registration practices during these pre-*Feist* years.[222] One of the primary roles of the Copyright Office is to register copyright claims in works of authorship.[223] Generally, the Copyright Office has always applied an originality standard. Until the late 1980s, however, based on the industrious collection doctrine it

---

213 *Id.* at 1371–72.

214 736 F.2d 859 (2d Cir. 1984).

215 *Id.* at 863.

216 *Id.* at 862. See also *Fin. Info., Inc. v Moody's Investors Serv., Inc.*, 751 F.2d 501, 510 (2d Cir. 1984) (Newman, J., concurring); *Fin. Info., Inc. v Moody's Investors Serv., Inc.*, 808 F.2d 204, 207 (2d Cir. 1986).

217 499 U.S. 340 (1991).

218 827 F.2d 569 (9th Cir. 1987).

219 *Id.* at 573.

220 *Id.* at 572–3.

221 *Id.* at 573–4 (citing *Rosemont Enters., Inc. v Random House, Inc.*, 366 F.2d 303, 310 (2d Cir. 1966)). See also *Black's Guide, Inc. v Mediamerica, Inc.*, No. C-90-0819, 1990 U.S. Dist. LEXIS 16272, at *10 (N.D. Cal. Aug. 15, 1990); *Cooling Sys. & Flexibles v Stuart Radiator*, 777 F.2d 485, 491 (9th Cir. 1985).

222 U.S. Copyright Office, Report on Legal Protection for Databases 29–38 (1997).

223 17 U.S.C. §§ 410, 701(a) (2005).

also registered compilations including, but not limited to, telephone directories and other factual databases.[224] Such works, however, were registered under a 'rule of doubt'.[225] This practice obviously stemmed from the fact that the case law at the time simultaneously upheld both the industrious collection doctrine and the 1976 Act's explicit originality standard.[226]

Beginning in 1987, however, the Copyright Office began to question the copyrightability of works where the industrious collection doctrine was the only basis for registration.[227] By 1989, it had abandoned this standard for most compilations, continuing to apply it only to works like commercial telephone, street, and business directories and parts catalogues and inventory lists that were not 'clearly *de minimis*'.[228] Thus, database producers had fair warning that copyright protection might not extend to the facts contained in their databases.

In light of this long, complex, and vacillating history of copyright protection of databases in the US, one must wonder whether the Supreme Court really did 'drop a bomb'[229] when it issued its decision in *Feist*. As the discussion above shows, the legal landscape prior to *Feist* was much more complex than what has been argued on either side of the *Feist* debate. The pre-*Feist* courts' constant struggle over the industrious collection doctrine set the stage for the Supreme Court's consideration of the issue and not surprisingly the Supreme Court ultimately granted certiorari in a Tenth Circuit case that applied the industrious collection doctrine to protect a white pages telephone directory against wholesale copying.[230]

CONCLUSIONS

The current debate over the legal protection of databases has lasted for almost ten years. As this chapter has shown, however, the debate has failed to identify and discuss some of the most basic and preliminary historical aspects of the issue. This chapter has therefore sought to challenge these underlying assumptions by providing a fresh look at the historical dimension of the debate.

---

224 U.S. Copyright Office, supra note 222, at 32.

225 *Id.* at 30, 32–33.

226 *Id.* at 32.

227 *Id.* at 32–34.

228 *Id.* at 32, 34.

229 Polivy, Denise R. (1998), '*Feist* Applied: Imagination Protects, But Perspiration Persists – the Bases of Copyright Protection for Factual Compilations', 8 *Fordham Intell. Prop. Media & Ent. L.J.* 773, 782.

230 *Feist Publ'ns, Inc. v Rural Tel. Serv. Co.*, 916 F.2d 718 (10th Cir. 1990), cert. granted, 498 U.S. 808 (1990), rev'd 499 U.S. 340 (1991).

Indeed, as can be seen from the more comprehensive review provided above on the history of informational works before the Court's decision in *Feist*, the law's prevailing approach has long been to support unfettered access to facts and other materials considered indispensable for academic, economic progress. In particular, the discussion showed that the 'sweat of the brow' doctrine had been in constant decline under the 1976 Copyright Act even before the Court finally repudiated it in *Feist*, clearly rebutting the commonly accepted argument that the Court dropped a bomb when issuing its decision in *Feist*.

Based on this historical analysis it becomes evident that the actual decision in *Feist* did not really establish any new law that would have come as a surprise to the database industry. Instead, *Feist* simply reflected the prevailing approach of the time. Most importantly, however, *Feist* reaffirmed the originality requirement and thus guaranteed the continued unfettered access to facts and information in a new and constantly evolving information environment.

2. The debate over copyright in news and its effect on originality doctrine

Robert F. Brauneis*

For the first three-quarters of the nineteenth century, the notion that copyright incorporated an originality requirement which excluded factual matter from protection was unknown to Anglo-American law. Courts routinely found infringement of fact-based works, such as maps, charts, road-books, directories, and calendars, on the basis of the copying of their factual content, and concluded that the industry of plaintiffs in gathering and presenting facts should be protected under copyright law. By the first decade of the twentieth century, however, the creativity-based view of originality, which denies protection to factual matter on the ground that it is not the subjective creation of an author, had found prominent expression in judicial opinions and treatises. Although a number of commentators have noted the relationship between the creativity-based view of originality and the ideology of the 'romantic author',[1] this relationship does not explain the late nineteenth-century

* Associate Professor of Law and Co-Director of the Intellectual Property Law Program, The George Washington University Law School; Member, Managing Board, Munich Intellectual Property Law Center. I would like to thank the participants in the 28 September 2007 Symposium on 'Feist, Facts, and Functions: IP Protection for Works Beyond Entertainment,' co-sponsored by the Intellectual Property Law Program of The George Washington University Law School and the Software and Information Industry Association. For assistance in retrieving petitions and other original documents relating to the news copyright bills of 1884, I would like to thank Rod Ross and William Davis of the Center for Legislative Archives, National Records and Archives Administration. For assistance in locating the briefs of the parties in *National Tel. News Co. v Western Union Co.*, 119 F. 294 (7th Cir. 1902), I would like to thank the staff of the Chicago office of the National Archives and Records Administration, Great Lakes Region. For comments on drafts of this piece, I would like to thank Ellen Goodman, Michael Carroll, Dawn Nunziato, Bob Tuttle, Lionel Bently, Robert Burrell, Justin Hughes, Frederick Lawrence, the students in my Fall 2008 IP History seminar, and the participants in the October 2008 WIP IP Conference at Tulane University Law School and in the faculty workshops at The George Washington University Law School and the Cardozo Law School.

1 See, for example, Rose, Mark (1993), *Authors and Owners: The Invention of Copyright* 113–129; Woodmansee, Martha (1984), 'The Genius and the Copyright: Economic and Legal Conditions of the Emergence of the "Author"', 17 *Eighteenth-*

rise of creativity-based originality in American law, since romantic author narrative was well known a century before.

This chapter argues that the rise of creativity-based originality in copyright law has strong ties to the debate over legal protection for news in the last decades of the nineteenth century. Until the 1880s, the American news industry remained in a pre-copyright era, and played no part in copyright discourse. Most newspapers were partisan organs that sought financial support at least as much from political sponsors as from sales or advertising. Newspaper editors followed a widespread custom of freely copying text from other newspapers. That custom was acknowledged and encouraged by a massive government subsidy in the form of free postage for newspaper copies that editors were exchanging. Newspaper owners never registered their papers before publication, and thus forsook copyright protection for them.

In the middle decades of 1800s, however, social and technological changes radically changed the structure of the news industry. Political subsidies for newspapers shrank, and newspapers became more heavily dependent on sales and advertising. The introduction of the telegraph provided newspapers with an opportunity to invest in more timely news; yet together with improvements in typesetting, printing, and transportation technology, the telegraph also created an appropriability problem. It shrank the lead-time advantage that newspapers traditionally had relied upon to realize the value of their investment in news, and also exposed them to competition from which they had previously been geographically isolated. At the same time, the new communications technologies led to the emergence of companies and large associations that dominated markets, often with the aid of anti-competitive practices. Prominent among these were the news industry organizations of the Associated Press and the Western Union.

Within this context, the Associated Press, Western Union and others began in the 1880s to press for legal protection of news reports, in both legislative and judicial arenas. On the legislative front, the Associated Press backed an 1884 effort to amend the Copyright Act to provide protection for news items. Opposition to that effort led to the first prominent articulations of the notion that facts are not created by authors, and are therefore not copyrightable subject matter. After that effort failed, the Associated Press and others turned to the courts. Paradoxically, their efforts to seek judicial protection for news ended up reinforcing the creativity-based view of originality, because they decided for strategic reasons to seek protection outside of federal copyright law, in common law misappropriation, and decided to argue that news was not copyrightable in order to avoid copyright pre-emption of their common law claims.

Century Std. 425; Jaszi, Peter (1991), 'Toward a Theory of Copyright: The Metamorphoses of "Authorship",' *Duke L. J.* 455.

Part I of this chapter reviews the intellectual-labor-based model of originality that dominated Anglo-American copyright law in the nineteenth century. Part II describes the structure of the American news industry up through the mid-nineteenth century, and explains why that industry operated entirely independently of copyright. Part III describes the changes in news industry structure caused by the telegraph and other new technologies, and explains how those changes led the industry to push for legal protection for news. Part IV follows the legislative and judicial campaign for legal protection for news, and traces the development of creativity-based originality rhetoric on both sides of that campaign. Part V draws some conclusions about the broader history of copyright doctrine from this episode.

I. ORIGINALITY IN NINETEENTH-CENTURY COPYRIGHT: INTELLECTUAL LABOR AND 'ORIGINAL SOURCES OF INFORMATION OPEN TO ALL'

For most of the nineteenth century, American publishing, and hence copyright litigation, was dominated by various types of practical, nonfiction works.[2] Following English precedent, American courts crafted a doctrine of originality that included the factual content gathered in these works as copyrightable subject matter. The 1828 case that first discussed the originality requirement in American copyright law, *Blunt v Patten*,[3] presented an analysis that would be used in dozens of cases throughout the rest of the nineteenth century. In *Blunt*, Supreme Court Justice Smith Thompson, writing as a circuit judge, considered mapmaker Edmund Blunt's claim that Richard Patten had infringed his copyright in a nautical chart of the coast of northeastern North America. Thompson writes:

> The natural objects from which the charts are made are open to the examination of all, and any one has a right to survey and make a chart. And if such surveys and charts are all correct, all will be alike, but no one would complain of his rights having been infringed, and each one may be considered an original chart. A right,

2 See Ginsburg, Jane (1990), 'Creation and Commercial Value: Copyright Protection of Works of Information', 90 *Colum. L. Rev.* 1865; Bitton, Miriam (2006), 'Trends in Protection for Informational Works under Copyright Law in the Nineteenth and Twentieth Centuries', 13 *Mich. Telecomm. Tech. L. Rev.* 115.

3 3 F. Cas. 763 (No. 1580) (1828). This is the report of Blunt's action in equity seeking an injunction; a companion report of Blunt's qui tam action seeking a monetary penalty is found at 3 F. Cas. 762 (No. 1579)(1828).

> in such a subject, is violated only when another copies from the chart of him who has secured the copyright, and thereby availing himself of his labor and skill.[4]

This passage approaches originality as a matter of independent creation. If many people survey the same coastal region and make charts, states Justice Thompson, each of those charts will be original. Conversely, however, if one person copies a copyrighted chart made by another, he will infringe that copyright. That the copyrighted chart merely accurately represents the position of shores and the depth of the water in a particular area is not a defense to infringement. Those representations are part of the protected subject-matter of the map. The representations should be protected because they were the product of the 'labor and skill' of the chart maker. Thus, although *Blunt v Patten* does not use the phrase 'sweat of the brow',[5] the theory that factual representations should be protected as the intellectual labor of an author enters American copyright law in the very first case to discuss originality.

Dozens of similar examples from English and American cases and treatises could be cited. The most important example in an American treatise is probably a passage in Joseph Story's influential and widely distributed *Commentaries on Equity Jurisprudence*,[6] first published in 1836:

> The difficulty [in cases of maps, charts, translations, and road books] is to distinguish, what belongs to the exclusive labors of a single mind, from what is the common source of the materials of the knowledge used by all. . . . [A second man]

---

4 *Blunt*, 3 F. Cas. 763, 764-65. Justice Thompson cites no sources, but he almost certainly drew his analysis from existing English cases and treatises. See, for example, *Longman v Winchester*, 16 Ves. Jun. 269, 270, 33 Eng. Rep. 987, 987 (1809); Eden, Robert Henley, *A Treatise on the Law of Injunctions* 282–83; Jeremy, George (1828), *A Treatise on the Equity Jurisdiction of the High Court of Chancery* 322.

5 The phrase 'sweat of his own brow' first appeared in conjunction with copyright in *Amsterdam v Triangle Publications*, 93 F. Supp. 79 (D. Pa. 1950). It was used to express the somewhat unusual and now-discredited view that the mere combination of features from other maps cannot result in copyright in the compiled map so generated, as copyright in maps could only arise when the mapmaker had himself made observations of the world. In a discussion of this case in 1963, Robert Gorman used the phrase 'sweat of the brow.' See Gorman, Robert A. (1963), 'Copyright Protection for the Collection and Representation of Facts', 76 *Harv. L. Rev.* 1569, 1572. It may surprise some to learn that it was not until 1984 that a court used the phrase in its now well-recognized sense as referring to a theory of originality that does not require creativity. See *Financial Information, Inc. v Moody's Investors Service, Inc.* 751 F.2d 501, 506 (2d Cir. 1984).

6 Story, Joseph (1836), *Commentaries on Equity Jurisprudence as Administered in England and America.*

may work on the same original materials; but he cannot exclusively and evasively use those already collected and embodied by another.'[7]

Courts and commentators continued to use this analysis and logic right into the 1880s. American cases like *Lawrence v Dana* (1869),[8] *Farmer v Calvert Lithographic, Engraving & Map Publishing Co.* (1872),[9] *Banks v McDivitt* (1875),[10] and *List Publishing Co. v Keller* (1887),[11] and English cases like *Kelly v Morris* (1866),[12] *Morris v Ashbee* (1868),[13] and *Hogg v Scott* (1874)[14] all followed the pattern, as did American treatises like James Appleton Morgan's *The Law of Literature* (1875)[15] and Eaton Drone's *Treatise on the Law of Property in Intellectual Productions* (1879),[16] and English treatises like Walter Arthur Copinger's *Law of Copyright* (1881).[17] The Supreme Court did not have occasion to decide whether copyright protection extended to representations of facts; before 1879, it had only decided seven cases that touched on copyright issues.[18] As already mentioned above, however,

---

7 *Id.* at 216. Three years later, in *Gray v Russell*, 10 F. Cas. 1035 (C.C.D. Mass. 1839) (No. 5728), Justice Story had the opportunity to present the same analysis in a judicial opinion; see also Curtis, George Ticknor (1847), *A Treatise on the Law of Copyright* 174.

8 15 F.Cas. 26 (C.C.D. Mass. 1869) (No. 8136) ('[W]here there are certain common objects of information which must, if described correctly, be described in the same words, a subsequent compiler is bound to do for himself that which was done by the first compiler.').

9 8 F. Cas. 1022 (E.D. Mich. 1872) (No. 4651) ('The defendant, no doubt, had the right to go to the common source of information, and having ascertained those boundaries, to have drawn them upon his map, notwithstanding that in this respect it would have been precisely like plaintiff's map (which of course it would have been if they were both correct). But he had no right to avail himself of this very labor on the part of complainant in order to avoid it himself.').

10 2 F. Cas. 759 (1875) (No. 961).

11 30 F. 772 (C.C.S.D.N.Y. 1887) ('No compiler of a book such as directories, guide-books, road-books, statistical tables, can acquire, by copyright, a monopoly of the matter published, but the subsequent compiler must investigate for himself from the original sources of information which are open to all.').

12 L.R. 1 Eq. 697 (1866).

13 L.R. 7 Eq. 34 (1868).

14 L.R. 18 Eq. 444 (1874).

15 Morgan, James Appleton (1875), *The Law of Literature* 328–331.

16 Drone, Eaton S. (1879), *A Treatise on the Law of Property in Intellectual Productions* 201–202 ('Collections of Well-Known Facts').

17 Copinger, Walter Arthur (1881), *The Law of Copyright in Works of Literature and Art*.

18 See *Wheaton v Peters*, 33 U.S. 591 (1834); *Backus v Gould*, 48 U.S. 798 (1849); *Stephens v Cady*, 55 U.S. 528 (1852); *Stevens v Gladding*, 58 U.S. 447 (1854); *Little v Hall*, 59 U.S. 165 (1855); *Paige v Banks*, 80 U.S. 608 (1871); *Parris v Hexamer*, 99 U.S. 674 (1878).

Supreme Court Justices Joseph Story and Smith Thompson did have occasion to do so while riding circuit, and both held that copying of factual content could amount to copyright infringement.[19]

One other case deserves extended discussion. In 1829, a year after *Blunt v Patten*, Justice Thompson, again riding circuit, decided in a case called *Clayton v Stone*[20] that a 'price-current' – a daily newspaper that reported commodity prices – was not a 'book' within the meaning of the Copyright Act, which at the time extended copyright protection only to 'maps, charts and books'. First, reasoned Justice Thompson, the Copyright Act should be read in light of the purpose of copyright as stated in the constitution, namely, to promote the progress of Science. To contribute to science, works had to be of a 'permanent and durable character'; [21] the plaintiff's newspaper was of too 'fluctuating and fugitive a form'.[22] Secondly, the copyright act prescribed formalities that seemed so lengthy and cumbersome – most pointedly, a requirement that a copy of the work's registration be published for four weeks in at least one newspaper – that it seemed unlikely that Congress intended them to apply to 'a work of so ephemeral a character as that of a newspaper'.[23]

It is tempting to read current categories back on to the *Clayton* case and conclude that the newspaper was denied copyright because its contents – commodity price quotations – were purely factual and thus unoriginal. But the analysis in the case does not proceed along those lines, and, indeed, one would not expect Justice Thompson, the author of *Blunt v Patten*, to use such an analysis. Rather, the relevant distinctions were between lasting contributions and ephemeral ones, and between learning and mere industry. An 1848 case which uses the same analysis makes it clear that the *Clayton* distinctions did

---

[19] The acceptance of factual representations as copyrightable subject matter does not mean that copying such representations would always amount to copyright infringement. Courts used two doctrines to avoid such a result: the 'new toil' or improvement doctrine, under which a charge of infringement might be avoided by demonstrating that the defendant substantially improved an older work, and the 'market substitute' approach to infringement, under which a new work would not infringe an older work if it served a different market. See, for example. *Webb v Powers*, 29 F. Cas. 511 (C.C. 1st Cir. 1847) (No. 17,323) ('new toil' doctrine); *Gray v Russell*, 10 F. Cas. 1035 (C.C.D. Mass. 1839) (per Story, J.) (employing a 'market substitute' analysis). Importantly, neither of these doctrines was thought to be limited to factual works. Thus, they provided a kind of 'safety valve,' allowing the copying of significant factual matter that, if prohibited, might call the institution of copyright into question, without singling out factual accounts as needing a special exemption from copyright protection.

[20] 5 F. Cas. 999 (C.C.S.D.N.Y. 1829) (No. 2872).

[21] *Id.*

[22] *Id.*

[23] *Id.*

not exclude factual matter from copyright protection. In *Scoville v Toland*,[24] Justice John McLean held that labels, which served the purely commercial purpose of identifying goods for sale, were not copyrightable. At the same time, he commented that 'lunar tables' – tables showing the dates on which the moon is in its various phases – were copyrightable books even if only printed on single sheets. That the lunar tables were purely factual was not a matter of which Justice McLean took any note. Rather, he was satisfied that they made a lasting contribution to learning or science, instead of being ephemeral or commercial in character.

The holding of *Clayton v Stone* is of uncertain scope – was it supposed to disqualify from copyright only commodity price reports, or did it extend more broadly to cover the contents of all daily newspapers?[25] There was never any chance to find out, because, in spite of the dominance of nonfiction works in American copyright litigation over the next 50 years, no reported case concerned a newspaper. Why was that? One answer is that newspapers might have been deterred from seeking copyright by the burdensome requirements of registration. That answer is not satisfactory, however, because if copyright protection were important to newspapers, they would have sought reform of the registration requirement, and they did not do so until the 1880s. Thus the question remains, and because the answer is crucial to understanding originality doctrine for most of the nineteenth century, this chapter now turns to the task of providing one.

II. PRE-TELEGRAPH NEWS GATHERING AND DISSEMINATION: THE DOMINANCE OF THE EXCHANGE SYSTEM AND THE PARTISAN PRESS

Throughout the first half of the nineteenth century, newspapers gathered out-of-town news primarily by means of exchanging copies of their papers with

---

24 21 F. Cas. 893 (1848) (No. 12,553).

25 There was a distinctly separate business press in the United States in the early 1800s, and Justice Thompson may have taken for granted that he was focusing on business papers, and that that would continue to be a stable, distinct category. Interestingly, time has proven that Justice Thompson was right about the ephemeral nature of such papers. As historian John McCusker has noted, '[i]t seems the peculiar fate of business newspapers that, despite being published in reasonable press runs, they appear to have been less likely to have been preserved than the more general purpose papers'. McCusker, John J. (2005), 'The Demise of Distance: The Business Press and the Origins of the Information Revolution in the Early Modern Atlantic World', 110 *The American Historical Review* 295, n. 60.

newspapers from other cities. Well-established newspapers in large cities would have exchange relationships with dozens and even hundreds of other newspapers. Thus, for example, the Washington, DC-based *Daily National Intelligencer* boasted in 1820: 'We receive at our office about three hundred papers, printed in all parts of the United States, from Mobile and New Orleans south, to Detroit north; and from Eastport in the east, to Arkansaw in the west . . . From Upper and Lower Canada, we receive several newspapers . . .'[26]

This exchange system was promoted and heavily subsidized by the colonial post office, and after independence by the federal post office, which until 1873 carried newspaper exchanges without charge. The practice started by custom in the early 1700s, and was officially sanctioned in a 1758 policy statement by Benjamin Franklin and William Hunter, joint deputy postmasters general for the American colonies.[27] In 1792, Congress enacted the exchange privilege into federal law, declaring 'That every printer of newspapers may send one paper to each and every other printer of newspapers within the United States, free of postage . . .'[28]

The scale of the resulting exchange system was vast. In 1843, just before the advent of the telegraph, an estimated seven million exchanges were carried by the post office free of charge.[29] As Richard Kielbowicz has calculated, that meant that, on average, each of the 1600 newspapers in the country was receiving about 4400 exchanges per year, or about a dozen every day.[30]

Why was news gathered and spread through this informal system of exchanges, rather than through propertization and sale of news items? If the legal structure for propertization was not in place, why didn't newspapers more actively lobby for it? Likely economic explanations include the difficulty of enforcing any such rights, the purely local nature of newspaper publishing (which avoided direct competition with all out-of-town papers), and the lead-time advantage within local markets due to existing typesetting

---

26 *Daily National Intelligencer*, Wednesday, 2 August 1820, p. 3.

27 Kielbowicz, Richard B. (1987), 'News Gathering by Mail in the Age of the Telegraph: Adapting to a New Technology', 28 *Technology and Culture* 26, 29.

28 Post Office Act of 1792, 1 U.S. Statutes at Large 238.

29 Kielbowicz, Richard B., *supra* note 27, at 30 n. 16. In total, about 39 million newspapers were carried by the U.S. postal system in 1840. See John, Richard R. (2000), 'Recasting the Information Infrastructure for the Industrial Age', in Chandler, Alfred Dupont, *Nation Transformed by Information: How Information Has Shaped the United States from Colonial Times to the Present* 55, 61. The 32 million that were not exchanges were not carried free of charge, but they were carried at very low rates, as compared to those charged for letters: 'newspapers made up as much as 95 percent of the weight of the mail, while accounting for no more than about 15 percent of the revenue.' *Id.*

30 *Id.*

and printing technology. In addition, many newspapers looked as much to partisan subsidies and patronage as to markets for support.

As for the difficulty of enforcement, intercity transportation and hence communication in the pre-telegraph era was slow. Historical geographer Allan Pred has measured the mean lag-time of information between American cities from the 1790s to the 1840s. In 1794, it took about seven days on average for news to travel between New York and Washington, DC, and 45 days for news to travel from New York to Cincinnati.[31] Twenty-one years later, in 1817, the time-lag from New York to Washington was three days; New York to Cincinnati was 19 days; and New York to Chicago was 43 days.[32] By 1841, with the coming of the railroad, news could travel from New York to Washington in as fast as ten hours,[33] but the average time lag was still longer; the lag between New York and Cincinnati was about eight days, and from New York to Chicago about 10 days.

The slow speed of communication also made it difficult to manage businesses that had locations in many different cities. Almost all newspapers, just as most other businesses at the time, served purely local markets, and therefore did not care if newspapers in other cities copied their stories.

The pre-electronic delivery of news through the transportation system, by means of the physical delivery of newspapers, could also lead to evidentiary difficulties in demonstrating that one newspaper had copied from another. The same carriage, ship, or railroad that brought one newspaper brought others, and also usually brought people who themselves knew the news from the departure city. Under the exchange system, it was the custom for newspapers to credit the source of news items, both as a courtesy and to enhance credibility; but if newspapers had wanted to conceal the source of their news, it is likely that they often could have.

Many larger cities had more than one newspaper, and there certainly was competition between them. But newspapers could often effectively compete against other local papers without propertizing news, given the time and cost of copying. Although typesetting and printing technology improved dramatically over the nineteenth century, for most of the century it still took several hours to print and assemble an edition of a newspaper in any volume. In addition, most

---

31 See Pred, Allan R. (1971), 'Urban Systems Development and the Long-Distance Flow of Information Through Preelectronic U.S. Newspapers', 47 *Economic Geography* 498, 511. Other important time-lag studies include Shaw, Donald Lewis (Summer 1981), 'At the Crossroads: Change and Continuity in American Press News', 1820–1860', *Journalism History*, VIII, 38; Brooker-Gross, Susan R. (Winter 1981), 'Timeliness: Interpretations from a Sample of 19th Century Newspapers', *Journalism Quarterly* 58, 594–98.

32 *Id.* at 513–515.

33 *Id.* at 517.

newspapers worked on a daily schedule; it cost them more to print an 'extra' that was released outside the normal schedule. As a result, a newspaper that obtained a 'scoop' on a news story usually got a lead-time advantage of at least several hours, and often an entire day. That was probably enough to sell a large number of newspapers, and over time to gain a reputation as a better newspaper. In 1851, Horace Greeley, editor of the *New York Tribune*, went to London to testify before a parliamentary committee, and gave an account of the lead-time advantage he thought his paper enjoyed:

> The fact that certain journals have the earliest news soon becomes notorious, and almost every one wants his newspaper with his breakfast, delivered between the hours of five and half past seven. They take the morning papers to read with their breakfast; and those who take the news after we issue it can not have it in time to deliver it to a very large number in a suitable morning season, and we regard it as of no consequence.[34]

Another important factor in the first half of the nineteenth century was the dominance of the partisan press. Most newspapers were identified with a political party, and were heavily subsidized to serve as the party organ. At every level and from every branch of government, newspaper owners received lucrative printing contracts and patronage appointments from the party in power.[35] Newspapers of the era thus tended to be focused on politics and political news,[36] and sought their rewards more from governments and political parties

---

[34] Hudson, Frederic (1873), *Journalism in the United States from 1690 to 1872*, 542 (Hudson reprints generous excerpts of the transcript of Greeley's testimony). Greeley also acknowledges that, in the case of important news, the *Tribune* would take precautions to ensure that no copy of the story left the hands of its confidential agents until the moment that the printed copies of the newspapers were distributed at 5:00 a.m. See *id.*

For similar comments, see 'Copyright in News', *New York Times*, 2 February 1884, p. 4; ('Priority of publication is so enormous an advantage in the business of printing news, that when that advantage is secured the newspaper that has secured it can afford to look with complacent indifference upon copyists.'); *The Milwaukee Sentinel* (Milwaukee, WI), 22 February 1884, p. 3.

[35] See Baldasty, Gerald J. (1992), *The Commercialization of News in the Nineteenth Century* 20 & 20 n. 68 (from 1819 to 1846, Congress awarded lucrative contracts to favored newspaper publishers to publish its proceedings; President Andrew Jackson also awarded printing contracts to favored newspapers across the country, and appointed 50 to 60 newspaper editors to patronage jobs such as postmaster; state and local support of partisan newspapers was also common).

[36] Gerald Baldasty shows the enormous shift in the content of newspapers from the 1830s to the 1890s. In 1831–32, his survey of five metropolitan newspapers reveals that 50.5 per cent of their column space was devoted to politics, and only 11.6 per cent to crime and courts, accidents, society and women, and leisure activities; by 1897, his

than from subscribers, single-copy purchasers, or advertisers. In this respect, newspaper editors were like composers of just a few generations before – they looked to patrons rather than markets as their primary source of support.[37]

The end result of these technological and social conditions was that newspapers had little or no need for copyright, and embraced a culture of copying. It would thus be a mistake to conclude that the placement of the newspapers outside of the copyright system was the result of a single judicial decision like *Clayton v Stone,* or of a single statutory requirement like that of registration. Undoubtedly, registering each daily issue of a paper could amount to a significant expense, and several authors mention the inconvenience of registration as a reason why newspapers were not copyrighted.[38] Yet in weighing the impracticability of registration, one has to consider the potential benefits of registration, as well as the burden. The fact is that the potential benefits were slight, so that taking on even a modest burden did not seem worthwhile.

The fact that newspapers, for economic reasons, remained outside of the copyright system had a significant if completely unnoticed impact on the prevailing intellectual-labor view of the originality requirement for copyright. That view purported to be quite broad in scope: any factual representation was the result of mental labor and was therefore copyrightable, and no one could copy wholesale that representation as a substitute for going out into the world and doing the hard work of gathering the factual details himself. By its own terms, that logic should apply to narrative accounts of current events, as well as non-narrative representations of persistent states of affairs like maps and city directories. In practice, however, so long as newspapers remained outside of copyright, originality doctrine did not have to come to grips with copyright issues concerning such news accounts.[39]

---

survey of eight metropolitan newspapers found that only 19.3 per cent was devoted to politics, and 39.1 per cent to the latter categories. See *id.* at 123.

37 On the transition of composers from support by churches and courts to orientation towards markets, see Scherer, F.M. (2004), *Quarter Notes and Bank Notes: The Economics of Music Composition in the Eighteenth and Nineteenth Centuries*.

38 See, for example, Morgan, James Appleton (1875), *The Law of Literature*, vol. II, p. 381; Drone, Eaton S. (1879), *A Treatise on the Law of Property in Intellectual Productions* 170.

39 The effect of newspapers remaining outside of copyright undoubtedly spread beyond the papers themselves to any historical or biographical account that was not based on first-hand observation, since the great bulk of second-hand accounts could be traced through uncopyrighted newspapers. In *Folsom v Marsh,* 9 F. Cas. 342 (C.C. Mass. 1841) (No. 4901), for example, Justice Story noted that certain historical narrative introducing George Washington's letters 'is either original, or derived (at least as far as the matter has been brought before the court) from common sources of information, open to all authors', *Id.* at 347. The 'common sources of information' Justice Story was contemplating must have included public domain accounts of events, including those in uncopyrighted newspapers.

III. MID-CENTURY CHANGES IN NEWS GATHERING AND DISSEMINATION: THE TELEGRAPH AND THE DEMISE OF THE PARTY PRESS.

The invention and deployment of the electric telegraph dramatically changed many industries, and the news industry was prominent among them. Telegraph lines began commercial operation in the mid-1840s. Within two decades, they blanketed the country. By 1866, Western Union controlled 37,380 miles of telegraph lines and 2250 telegraph offices in almost every town and city of any size in the United States.[40] 1866 also marked the completion of the first successful transatlantic cable,[41] thus enabling telegraphic communication between the Old World and the New.[42] A transcontinental telegraph line from Chicago to San Francisco had been completed in 1861, eight years before the transcontinental railroad. Through a combination of effects, this revolutionary telecommunications technology enabled and spurred on calls for increased legal protection for news.

First, the speed of communication over long distances made possible the development of geographically dispersed, and hence larger, business organizations. Management in one city could receive reports from and send orders to employees in other cities within minutes, if necessary, and daily interaction could become routine.[43] Two prime examples of the development of larger organizations were those intimately associated with news gathering and dissemination: Western Union and the Associated Press. By 1866, Western Union became the first industrial monopoly, controlling over 90 per cent of the telegraph business in the United States.[44] The Associated Press, founded in 1848 just after the commercialization of the telegraph, underwent several reorganizations in the second half of the nineteenth century, but in one form or another dominated news gathering and dissemination in the United States after

---

40 See Thompson, Robert Luther (1947), *Wiring a Continent: The History of the Telegraph Industry in the United States 1832–1866*, 426. There were 75,686 miles of wire strung along those lines. *Id.*

41 See Lubrano, Annteresa (1997) *The Telegraph: How Technology Innovation Caused Social Change* 9, 155.

42 The telegraph was not the first telecommunications technology. Newspapers, governments, and others had been experimenting with carrier pigeons, semaphore systems, and the like. But the telegraph far outstripped these in speed and distance.

43 Richard Du Boff argues that telegraph use had scale effects, control effects, and intelligence effects that led to dominance of single firms in many markets. See DuBoff, Richard B. (1984), 'The Telegraph in Nineteenth-Century America: Technology and Monopoly', in 26 *Comparative Studies in Society and History* 571, 573–579.

44 See *id.* at 572.

the Civil War. Although most individual newspapers remained locally owned, they were members of associations that competed on a national scale. Exchanges of news between members were now centrally controlled, and exchanges of news with non-members were prohibited, on pain of revocation of membership.[45]

Telegraphic communication also made it easier to pursue enforcement actions in places remote from a business's head office – communications between attorney and client allowed for effective pursuit and control of litigation. By the 1890s, the Associated Press was involved in lawsuits against newspapers in New York, Washington, DC, Minneapolis, Milwaukee, Chicago, and St. Louis, a geographic reach of litigation that would have been unthinkable without communication by telegraph.[46] Moreover, telegraphic communication would often make it easier to prove that the plaintiff's news dispatch was the source of the defendant's story. The telegraph message carrying the news arrived long before any people who might be carrying it as word-of-mouth, and as long as Western Union and Associated Press were dominant, there were unlikely to be other telegraph lines or news services through which the defendant could have gotten the story.

Secondly, the telegraph could effectively destroy the lead-time advantage that had previously protected news organizations. Several competitive scenarios irked newspapers that had spent money to gather news. Large-city newspapers had begun to gain audiences in the surrounding countryside as improved railroad lines made far-flung distribution possible in less than a day. Small-town papers along those railroad lines, however, would arrange for agents to telegraph the news as soon as the big-city papers were available in the big cities, and the small-town papers could then go to press before the train from the big city arrived. Thus, Frederic Hudson reported in 1873, a 'journalist that was desirous of an influence beyond the limits of the city where his newspaper is published' did not always view the telegraph kindly, 'especially when he reads an announcement that "the *Elmira* (N.Y.) *Advertiser* publishes telegraph news fifteen hours in advance of the receipt of the New York dailies".'[47]

---

45 See Rosewater, Victor (1930), *History of Cooperative News-Gathering in the United States* 260–261.

46 See *The Law of the Associated Press*, Vol. I (1914) (republishing documents from Associated Press litigation against the publishers of the *Chicago Inter Ocean*, p. 3; the *St. Louis Star*, p. 89; the *New York Sun*, p. 286; the *Washington News*, p. 446; the *Minneapolis Tribune*, p. 472; and the *Milwaukee Daily News* and *Milwaukee Germania*, p. 506).

47 Hudson, Frederic (1873), *Journalism in the United States from 1690 to 1872*, p. 595. Another new source of competition for big-city newspapers were the producers of 'patent insides' for smaller-town papers – pre-set printing plates that would be

Lead-time advantage was also destroyed when telegraphic transmissions cut across time zones. The Associated Press and some of the New York newspapers complained about this scenario in the early 1880s:

> The complaint is made that the New York correspondents for newspapers in Chicago and other points west to San Francisco, by reason of the difference of time in their favor, can, without credit, telegraph all there is worth telegraphing from New York to their respective journals. They not only can, but do. One or two San Francisco newspapers, because of this, have given notice of a desire to withdraw from the Associated Press.[48]

The facts of *International News Service v Associated Press*,[49] the famous case that ended up in the Supreme Court in 1918 (and to which this chapter will return), involve such a scenario. The International News Service was allegedly copying Associated Press news stories as they were published in New York newspapers, and telegraphing them to the west coast, three time zones earlier. West Coast newspapers that were INS subscribers could then print the news in time for their morning or evening editions, and compete head-on against their AP-subscriber competitors.

Another scenario involving the loss of lead time arose with the development of 'tickers', machines that could print text from a telegraphic signal without the need of a human operator. Without the need for a human intermediary, telegraphed news began to be distributed directly and continuously to end-user subscribers, who had such machines installed in their offices, shops, hotels, or restaurants. A competing company could have an employee read a ticker tape in a public place or in the office of a conspiring subscriber, and then enter the news dispatches into its own distribution system, which would have its own subscribers. Instead of typesetting and printing, the only action required was telegraphic keying or typing, and there were no editions on a daily cycle,

---

shipped out to smaller towns for printing together with local content on the covers. See *Galveston Daily News*, 8 February 1884, p. 4 ('In Chicago and other cities the patent newspaper fiends take the early morning newspapers, clip them up before daylight, and in the course of a couple of hours have the pith of the news in type for patent insides for country dailies which appear in the afternoon in smaller cities along the lines of the railroad that distribute the larger city papers.')

48 *Oshkosh Daily Northwestern* (Oshkosh, WI), 29 February 1884, p. 3 (quoting the *Cincinnati Enquirer*, 20 February 1884); see *New York Times*, 18 February 1884, p. 2 ('The difference in time between points relatively east and west in our vast country enable a publisher who chooses to do so to make use of the enterprise of others. Should the thief at a distant point be enabled by the use of the telegraph to steal the property of those men who have gone to great care and cost to obtain it?') (quoting Henry Watterson, who had been engaged by the Associated Press to lobby for a bill to extend copyright to newspapers, see *infra* p. 88).

49 248 U.S. 215 (1918).

because the ticker tape ran continuously. In such circumstances, lead time could be cut from hours to a minute or less.[50]

Thirdly, communication by telegraph was of great value to many people, but it was also very expensive. The initial capital costs of setting up a telegraph line across hundreds or thousands of miles could be enormous, and operating and maintenance costs were also substantial. While the newspaper exchange system had been heavily subsidized by the federal government through free postal carriage, the telegraph system did not benefit from government largesse on such a scale.

Of course, some of the messages carried by telegraph were private and of value only to particular individuals or businesses; those individuals or businesses who wanted to send or receive them would pay for the privilege. Other messages, such as timely commodity or stock price reports, were particularly valuable to a relatively small group of investors and traders. Those individuals and firms would also pay for that information; channels of communication could be relatively well-protected against unauthorized tapping; authorized recipients could be bound by subscription contracts not to pass it on to others; and enforcement against third parties who were inducing breaches of those contracts could be sought under trade secret law.

That still left a lot of information about current events that was of interest to, and valued by, the general public. How could the cost of gathering and transmitting that information be borne by the public, to whom it was of value? Newspapers had not previously had to face this problem, in part because they were often supported as partisan organs by governments and political parties, and in part because they enjoyed lead-time advantages over copiers. If technological developments cut lead time, social developments cut political patronage. It is not within the scope of this chapter to trace those complicated social developments. It is clear, however, that during the middle decades of the nineteenth century, newspapers moved dramatically away from political parties, and began to rely much more on sales and advertising for revenue.[51] Thus, one might see the adoption by Congress in 1846 of a low-bid system for awarding printing contracts as signaling the end of an era.[52]

Arguably, therefore, the decline of patronage and lead time left news organizations to deal with an appropriability problem.[53] Of course, as we will see,

---

50 Such facts formed the basis of the dispute in *National Telegraph News Co. v Western Union Telegraph Co.*, 119 F. 294 (7th Cir. 1902).

51 These developments are traced in Baldasty, *supra* note 35, at 36–58.

52 See *id.* at 42.

53 The problem of appropriability has been defined and extensively discussed in the context of innovation: if information about an innovation spreads as a public good, then firms may lack an adequate incentive to invest in the research and development

opponents of protection for the news strongly disputed the existence of such a problem, and the issue whether any particular level of protection for news or newspapers would optimize the production of news is beyond the scope of this chapter. It is clear, however, that some news organizations sought to convince Congress and the courts of the existence of an appropriability problem; that they had a plausible story to tell; and that developments in communications technology made possible a new business model for journalism – the selling or licensing of news stories, rather than informal exchange and sharing – that was more difficult to put into practice without some legal protection for news.

IV. EFFORTS TO PROTECT NEWS IN CONGRESS AND THE COURTS AND THE RISE OF CREATIVITY-BASED ORIGINALITY RHETORIC

During the 1880s and 1890s, news organizations like the Associated Press and Western Union (which, although mainly a telegraph company, made occasional forays into the news dissemination business) attempted to gain legal protection for news in both the Congress and the courts. The one serious attempt in Congress took place in 1884. For purposes of this chapter, the most important attempt in the courts culminated in a federal court of appeals decision in 1902. In both cases, I will argue, those attempts led to the articulation of a creativity-based view of the originality requirement in copyright.

A. The News Copyright Bill of 1884

In late 1883, the Associated Press sent Henry Watterson to Washington, DC to seek passage of a bill that would grant short-term protection to articles published in newspapers.[54] Watterson was the founder and editor of the *Louisville Courier-Journal*; he had served a partial term in the US House of Representatives in 1876 and 1877, having been elected to serve out the remaining term of a Kentucky Congressman who had died in office.

On 4 March 1884, Senator John Sherman of Ohio introduced 'A Bill

---

that would produce innovation. See, for example, Kenneth Arrow (1962), 'Economic Welfare and the Allocation of Resources for Invention,' in *The Rate and Direction of Inventive Activity: Economic and Social Factors*. Conference No. 13, Universities – National Bureau of Economic Research (Princeton, Princeton University Press); Nelson, Richard (1959), 'The Simple Economics of Basic Research,' 67 *J. Pol. Econ.* 297.

[54] Watterson, Henry (1919), *Marse Henry: An Autobiography*, vol. II, p. 104 [available on Google Books, http://books.google.com/books?id=ZSKbwauEbnIC&].

Granting Copyright in Newspapers'.[55] Six days later, Representative John Randolph Tucker of Virginia introduced an identical bill in the House.[56] The bills sought to grant newspapers and newspaper associations 'the sole right to print, issue and sell for the term of eight hours, dating from the hour of going to press, the contents of [the] newspaper, or the collected news of said newspaper association, exceeding one hundred words'.[57] Thus, the rights were granted directly to the newspaper or the association, rather than to the author of the contents;[58] and they were good for eight hours from going to press.

Newspapers across the United States quickly learned of the bill, and devoted their own column space to engaging in vigorous debate about it. The opponents of the news copyright bill sent scores of petitions to Congress. Entries in the Congressional Record document the receipt of at least 60 separate petitions in opposition, received from citizens of at least 19 of the 38 states then in the Union, and of the Dakota Territory.[59] Many of those petitions have been preserved at the National Archives.[60] Most of the petitions opposing the bills were sent on identical printed forms with blank spaces to be filled in with the name, newspaper affiliation, and address of the petitioner, which

---

55 S. 1728, 48th Cong., see 15 Cong. Rec. 1578. The full text of the bill was:
A Bill Granting Copyright to Newspapers

Be it enacted by the Senate and House of Representatives of the United States of America in Congress assembled, That any daily or weekly newspaper or any association of daily or weekly newspapers, published in the United States, or any of the Territories thereof, shall have the sole right to print, issue and sell for the term of eight hours dating from the hour of going to press, the contents of said daily or weekly newspaper, or the collected news of said newspaper association exceeding one hundred words.

Section 2. That for any infringement of the copyright granted by the first section of this Act, the party injured may sue in any court of competent jurisdiction, and recover in any proper action the damages sustained by him from the person making the infringement, together with the costs of suit.

56 H.R. 5850, 48th Cong., see 15 Cong. Rec. 1758.

57 *Id.* Apparently, drafts of the bill before it was introduced had set the period of exclusivity at 48 hours, and then at 24 hours, before settling on the period of eight hours. See *The Saturday Evening Observer*, Dunkirk, NY, 15 March 1884, p.1.

58 In committee hearings on the bill, one of the questions raised was whether Congress had the power under the constitution to grant rights directly to newspapers, since the Copyright Clause refers only to a power to grant exclusive rights to Authors. See *Galveston Daily News*, 20 March 1884.

59 See 15 Cong. Rec. 111 (1884) (index listing all of the entries for petitions relating to the bills).

60 They are located in Record Group 233, in folders HR 48A–H 12.5 (Committee on the Judiciary) and HR 48A–H 21.3 (Committee on Patents); and in Record Group 46, in folders S 48A–H 14 (Committee on the Library) and S 48A–J6 (Tabled Petitions).

suggests that there was organized opposition to the bills. By contrast, Congress apparently received only one petition in favor of the bill, though that was from the Southern Press Association, which represented 22 newspaper members.[61]

The bill divided newspapers along four overlapping fault lines. First and most prominently, it divided the 'metropolitan' papers – big-city papers with large circulations that could afford to hire their own reporting staffs and to pay to belong to a news association and receive telegraph dispatches – from the 'country press', small-town papers that continued to rely heavily on borrowed material to fill their pages.[62] Secondly, the news copyright bills set the Associated Press and its members (many of whom were the 'metropolitan' papers) against the members of the United Press – at that time a two-year-old competitor of the AP[63] – and against independent papers that were not members of either association.[64] Thirdly, the bill set afternoon papers, which were often accused of lifting material from morning-paper competitors, against the morning papers that were the alleged victims of the borrowing.[65] Similarly and fourthly, it set East Coast papers, which were the first to go to

---

61 See *id.*

62 Compare *New York Times*, 2 February 1884, p. 4 ('the country newspapers [were] beneath the rule of men with whom the scissors are mightier than the pen') with *Newark Daily Advocate* (Newark, Ohio), 19 February 1884, p. 1 (arguing that the news copyright bill was 'a monopoly scheme to force the readers in the smaller towns to depend for their news upon the metropolitan press ring, to the exclusion of the home journals.').

63 See Schwarzlose, Richard A., *The Nation's Newsbrokers*, Vol. II, p. 133, p. 248 table 1 (UP had grown from 'barely one hundred subscribers' in 1882 to 166 subscribers in 1884; AP had 425 subscribers in 1883). Schwarzlose portrays the news copyright bill as an effort of the AP to 'tackl[e] the UP competition'. *Id.* at 135.

64 The United Press did not itself publicly oppose the bills, but some of its prominent members did. See, for example, *Boston Daily Globe*, 27 March 1884, p. 2 (criticizing the news copyright bill and predicting that it would fail: 'We are inclined to believe that the Associated Press will have to take its chances with the rest of the journalistic world in getting the news.'); Schwarzlose, *The Nation's Newsbrokers*, *supra* note 63, p. 133 (describing the *Boston Daily Globe* as a 'mainstay' of the United Press). Opposition to the bill was often tied to animosity towards the 'monopolies' of the Associated Press and the Western Union. See, for example, *Newark Daily Advocate* (Newark, OH), 3 March, 1884, p. 1.

65 See, for example, *Galveston Daily News*, 17 February 1884, p. 2. '[T]he smaller morning dailies . . . are just able to take the state report of Associated Press matter and a few specials, are naturally somewhat badly affected when an afternoon pirate springs up beside them and takes nearly all they are able to give by an expenditure serious enough to them in their circumstances, and puts his subscription price lower than it could be if he paid part of the price for the telegrams. The pirate can sometimes run the local morning paper hard enough to keep it poor, and thus keep readers from obtaining as good a paper as they would otherwise have in their town.'

press every day, against western papers located in time zones that lagged one to three hours behind the East Coast, putting them in a position to borrow material from published East Coast papers.

For purposes of this chapter, the most important thing about this debate is to note how opponents of the bill contested it, and how supporters defended it. One of the most prominent arguments used against the bill articulated and depended upon a creativity-based view of originality. For example, the printed petition against the bill, copies of which were sent by dozens of newspaper editors to Congress, asked 'What is news? The statement of facts, the history of current events. Can any one create or invent a fact or event? If he cannot create or invent a fact or event, how can he copyright it?'[66] Similarly, the *Newark Daily Advocate* of Newark, Ohio reported a speech by Representative John Anderson of Kansas, railing against the bills:

> While there may be a possible ground for copyrighting the editorial, as the product of the editor's brain, what ground is there for copyrighting, say, election returns, or the news of Garfield's murder! Does the editor create them in the sense that an author creates a book? In my mind the measure is a glaring wrong, glittering with impertinence . . .'[67]

Almost two decades after *Feist Publications, Inc. v Rural Telephone Service Co, Inc.*,[68] the contention that facts are not copyrightable because they aren't created by authors appears perfectly familiar to us. Yet in 1884, existing case law and treatises did not contain such reasoning. Courts and treatise writers uniformly supported the view that a work which presented facts that had been gathered by observation of the world should be protected under copyright law. On the other hand they had not been faced with the issue of protecting facts about current events – news. To opponents of the news copyright bill, news seemed different, and they hoped that they could convince Congress it was.

News seemed different in several respects. First, current events did not seem to be a suitable subject for methodical, sustained study. Map and chart makers went on surveying expeditions using special tools to measure distances that would eventually be represented in their maps or charts. Authors of directories systematically canvassed neighborhoods or institutions. By contrast,

---

66 Petition, The News Copyright Bill, *supra* n. 68. This language is echoed by *The Evening Observer*, Dunkirk, NY, the editor of which must have either read or wrote the petition: 'What is news? The statement of facts, the history or current events. Can anyone create or invent a fact? Unquestionably not. What therefore are the reasonable grounds for a copyright?' 3 April 1884, p. 2.

67 *Newark Daily Advocate* (Newark, OH), 3 March 1884, p. 1.

68 499 U.S. 340 (1991).

events that formed the basis of the news could often not be predicted in advance, and thus it seemed fortuitous that a particular person would learn of a newsworthy event. As an article in 21 February 1884 issue of *The Nation*, commenting on the newspaper copyright bill, put it:

> [I]t is absurd to talk of a man who picks up a piece of news or an 'item' as an 'author' at all. The reason why copyright laws are passed is to secure the fruits of original, intellectual labor. But the proposed copyright in 'news' does not do this. Any one may collect news without any original intellectual effort, and with very little effort of any kind. Some people do it by listening at keyholes, most people in the ordinary course of conversation with the persons whom they meet in the way of business or pleasure. If a collector of news in London telegraphs to New York that . . . Lord Cairns has offered Miss Fortescue £10,000 to release his son from his marriage engagement, who is the person whose 'property' in the news ought to be protected, or who is the 'author' of it?[69]

This view of how news was gathered – 'in the ordinary course of conversation with the persons whom they meet in the way of business or pleasure' – was outdated even in 1884. Newspapers and news associations had already begun to employ reporters to go out and find news, not just to report whatever they happened to hear in casual conversations. And, of course, much of the investment was not in finding news, but in transmitting it quickly over great distances. Yet this image that news was acquired largely by chance was quite powerful, and fit in well with the argument that copyright required intellectual labor that was missing in newsgathering.

Secondly, fact-based works that were already protected under copyright law – maps, directories, calendars, road-books, and the like – were rarely in narrative form. Rather, they presented information in the form of lists, charts, maps, and the like. Not all news in newspapers was presented in narrative form; stock prices and weather reports weren't, for example. Both sides in the news copyright debate, however, assumed that much of what the bill would protect would be news *stories* – literary works in narrative form. This presented a new issue – how should copyright law deal with factual material presented in narrative form? For narrative literary works, copyright law already had developed a distinction between form and content.[70] Thus, in

---

69 *The Nation*, Volume 38, n. 973 (21 February 1884), p. 159.

70 Another way to illuminate this difference draws on Jane Ginsburg's distinction between 'high authorship' and 'low authorship' works. See Ginsburg, *supra* note 2, at 1866–1870. 'High authorship' – the manifestation of a 'personal authorial presence' – is much more easily accomplished or perceived in works of literary narration. Lists, maps and the like are much more likely to be associated with 'low authorship', Of course, it is an illusion to think that lists of numbers and names are bereft of personal interpretation. As Justin Hughes has pointed out, there may be plenty of inter-

Stowe v Thomas,[71] Justice Grier wrote: 'A "copy" of a book must, therefore, be a transcript of the language in which the conceptions of the author are clothed; of something printed and embodied in a tangible shape. The same conceptions clothed in another language cannot constitute the same composition, nor can it be called a transcript or "copy" of the same "book".'[72] Both opponents and proponents of the newspaper copyright bill seemed to proceed from the assumption that copyright in newspapers would only protect the literal language of a news story, and that any newspaper editor would be able to rewrite the story so that it recounted the same facts but avoided infringement liability.[73]

Thirdly, news was important to the political and cultural life of the country, and to political and cultural speech, in a way that directories and maps weren't. As the *Milwaukee Sentinel* put it, '[news] becomes a matter of common information as soon as it is printed, and men may spread it by word of mouth or may write to one another about it . . . . To prevent other journals from commenting upon it is to stifle free discussion, and to permit them to comment is to permit them to republish the matter.'[74] The concern about freedom of the press was particularly pointed in light of the size and power of the Associated Press – many were sure that the practical result of the news copyright bill would be, not the decentralized sale and purchase of news stories by many newspapers, but further concentration of the news business. As *The Evening Observer* (Dunkirk, NY) put it, 'The Sherman copyright bill [is] designed to create a monopoly of newsgathering. It was instigated and was backed by the associated press and the metropolitan newspapers. The associated press is the worst kind of a monopoly, and yet additional protection is asked for! . . . We cannot understand how a monopoly of newsgathering can in any way advantage the people.'[75]

---

pretation in numbers – one person's notion of whether to divide a population count into Caucasians and Negroes, and how to count them, might be quite different from another's. See Hughes, Justin (2007), 'Created Facts and the Flawed Ontology of Copyright Law', 83 *Notre Dame L. R.* 43, 53–54.

71 23 F. Cas. 201 (1853) (No. 13, 514).

72 *Id.* at 207.

73 See, for example, *The Atlanta Constitution*, 20 March 1884, p. 4 (opposing the news copyright bill) ('Neither facts nor incidents can be copyrighted, but only the form in which they are presented. This is no remedy at all, for the papers that steal their news would not be balked by the copyright of form merely, and this is all that any copyright can cover.'); *Galveston Daily News*, 17 February 1884, p. 2 (supporting the news copyright bill) ("Copyright . . . would not prevent any writer from making in his own words a statement of the facts alleged in the telegram. The so-called newspapers that feed on other newspapers would . . . have to dismiss the scissors brigade and do some writing instead of clipping . . . .').

74 *Milwaukee Sentinel*, 22 February 1884, p. 4.

75 *The Evening Observer* (Dunkirk, NY), 1 April 1884, p. 2. The Associated

Fourthly, with works such as directories and maps, application of a 'market substitute' doctrine of infringement could accommodate the most pressing concerns about free speech while protecting the core economic interests of copyright owners.[76] Directories and maps documented large numbers of names, addresses, geographical relationships, and the like, and were bought as reference works. Purchasers would consult them many times over an extended period, and would likely consult different parts of the works at different times. That market for reference works was only endangered if a copier reproduced all or a substantial portion of a work. Thus, in the market for reference works a 'market substitute' doctrine would leave room for the kind of copying that authors who did not set out to duplicate the work in question were likely to want to do. An author would be free to use and incorporate a single directory entry or some information incorporated on a map without fear of infringement.

Newspapers were different, however. Each daily edition was modest in size, and its market value was short-lived. People often bought the daily paper to read the lead story about some sensational event, and then discarded it. Subsequent authors might well want to repeat the essential facts of that lead story. Under these circumstances, the 'market substitute' doctrine had much less maneuvering room to mediate between the economic interests of the copyright owner and the interests of the reader in speaking freely about what he or she had learned. The situation was even worse with news tickers, which dispensed content in a continuous stream, making it difficult to identify a 'work' of any size greater than a single news item.

In light of these conditions, the logic that lay behind the intellectual-labor view of originality, and the consequent protection of fact-based works, probably seemed quaint to the opponents of the news copyright bill, and the 'market substitute' infringement doctrine did not seem to offer any clear relief. Were the events that formed the basis of news reports 'common sources of information open to all'? Once one heard of the report of an event, it was too late to go witness it oneself – time had moved forward – and those who did witness it were already dispersing. Moreover, the means of transmitting the report from the distant site of the event to one's own location were not open on equal terms to all: the Western Union owned the telegraph lines, and it offered the

---

Press was supposed to be neutral, but Menahem Blondheim has argued that its selection of news items was actually biased in favor of the Republican Party and against the Democrats, and has noted that the Associated Press was also not above agreeing to refrain from any criticism of the Western Union Telegraph Company in its dispatches, in return for favorable access to telegraph lines and a promise that Western Union would not itself enter the news business. See Blondheim, Menahem (1994), *News Over the Wires: The Telegraph and the Flow of Public Information in America, 1844–1897*, pp. 151, 175–187.

[76] For a description of the market substitute doctrine, see n. 19, *supra*.

Associated Press special terms. Thus, maps, directories, and news reports might be equated at some abstract level, but they did not seem similar when placed in their concrete social context.

In the end, the news copyright bill died. The *New York Times* had predicted that the political influence of the country press, widespread throughout the Union, could decide the issue: 'If country members of Congress are instructed by their constituents that the news copyright bill is a defense for metropolitan journals, (as is very likely the case,) the country members will defeat the bill beyond peradventure.'[77] The 'country members' never got to vote on the bill; it was reported out of the Committee of the Library with a recommendation that it not pass, and was allowed to disappear quietly.[78]

B. Seeking Protection for News in the Courts

By the late spring of 1884, the Associated Press realized that its quest to obtain legislative protection for news was going to be futile. From the vantage point of 1919, Henry Watterson looked back on his trip to Washington to lobby for the bill as 'fool's errand'.[79] But the legislature wasn't the only forum in which the Associated Press could pursue protection for news. Watterson recounted that while he was in Washington, 'a learned but dissolute lawyer said to me, "You need no act of Congress to protect your news service. There are at least two, and I think four or five, English rulings that cover the case. Let me show them to you".'[80] Watterson then commented, 'To a recent date the Associated Press has relied on these decisions under the common law of England.'[81]

Watterson no doubt received this advice before he testified in front of the House Committee on the Judiciary on 24 March 1884, because his testimony on that occasion featured the argument that English courts had already decided in favor of copyright for news.[82] Watterson relied principally on the 1869

77 *New York Times*, 18 February, 1884, p. 4.

78 See 15 Cong. Rec. 3077 (18 April 1884).

79 Watterson, Henry (1919), *Marse Henry: An Autobiography*, vol. II, p. 104 [available on Google Books http://books.google.com/books?id=ZSKbwauEbnIC&].

80 *Id.* at 105.

81 *Id.*

82 See *The Evening Observer* (Dunkirk, NY), 29 March 1884, p. 1. Indeed, Watterson's visit with the 'learned but dissolute old lawyer' can probably be more precisely placed between 14 March and 24 March, because *The Evening Observer*'s account of Watterson's testimony on the 24 March notes that it was 'substantially identical with his testimony before the joint Library Committee on the 14th inst., except that he submitted the following comprehensive statement of principles adjudicated in cases on the subject.' *Id.*

English Court of Chancery case of *Cox v Land and Water Journal Company*.[83] In that case, the court held that a newspaper that had published a directory of hunts, which included 'the name of each hunt, with the nearest town convenient for strangers, the number of the hounds in the pack, the hunting days, the names of the masters, huntsmen, and whips, and the address of the kennel',[84] had an action for copyright infringement against another periodical that had copied the directory. Although the facts of *Cox* did not involve news, the *Cox* court considered a hypothetical news scenario that was particularly relevant to telegraph news services like Watterson's Associated Press:

> Now, suppose, for instance, the proprietor of a newspaper employs a correspondent abroad, and that correspondent, being employed and sent abroad at great expense, makes communications to a newspaper which are highly appreciated by the public, can it be said that another newspaper, published, perhaps, in the evening of the same day, may take and publish those communications in extenso, with or without acknowledgment?[85]

It was clear that the question was rhetorical, and the answer was supposed to be 'no'; that was exactly the answer the news agencies wanted.

In spite of *Cox* and other similarly supportive cases and commentary,[86] however, the news agencies still faced a problem under US copyright law. In England, there was a special registration provision for periodicals, which allowed the owner of copyright in the periodical to register just once for the entire series; that registration was good so long as the periodical maintained regular publication.[87] The US Copyright Act did not contain any special registration provision for works published in series. It continued to require registration for each separately published work covered under the Act. Daily newspapers continued not to register their individual issues as they were published; and if under certain circumstances telegraph dispatches themselves were going to count as publications, they would face even greater difficulties meeting the registration requirement. Thus, news agencies

---

83 [L R] 9 Eq 324 (1869).

84 *Id.*

85 *Id.*

86 See,for example, *Wilson v Luke*, 1 Vict. L. R. Eq. 127 (1875); Copinger, Walter Arthur (1881), *The Law of Copyright in Works of Literature and Art* 100–101 (2nd edn); Fisher, Joseph R. and James Andrew Strahan (1891), *The Law of the Press* 32–33.

87 Section 19 of the Copyright Act provided that the proprietor of copyright in 'any encyclopedia, review, magazine, periodical work, or other work published in a series of books or parts', could register the entire series prospectively, so long as it maintained regular publication. Act 5 & 6 Vict. c. 45, s. 19, quoted in *Cox v Land and Water Journal Co* (1869) LR 9 Eq 324.

needed a legal strategy for avoiding the registration requirement under US copyright law.

This issue came to a head in 1901, when Western Union sued a company called the National Telegraph News Company. Western Union had itself entered the news business, in a limited fashion. It had purchased the Gold & Stock Telegraph Company, which owned the rights to an early telegraph ticker machine, and had continued the Gold & Stock business of providing news service directly to ticker machines. Those tickers were installed in hotels, saloons, and private companies that wanted 'instant information of passing events of more or less importance throughout the world', and sometimes, in particular, news of sporting events, no doubt of especial interest to gamblers and bookmakers.[88] The National Telegraph News Company had a competing business of providing a news service through tickers. It admitted that it had been copying news items from the Western Union tickers, and sending them out on its own wires, 'so that within a very few minutes from the time th[e] news appears upon the tapes of the [Western Union] tickers it re-appears upon the tapes of the [National Telegraph News Company] tickers'.[89] Western Union argued that the National Telegraph News Company charged less for its subscriptions because it had no expenses for gathering news, and that Western Union had been forced to lower its prices to retain subscribers.[90]

Western Union obtained a preliminary injunction from the District Court prohibiting National Telegraph News from using any news items it had gathered from Western Union tickers for 60 minutes after they appeared on those tickers. National Telegraph News appealed. National's chief argument on appeal was that Western Union had published the ticker tapes without registration, notice, or deposit, and had therefore abandoned common-law copyright in them without acquiring copyright under federal law.[91] Western Union decided to argue that the reports that it transmitted to the tickers were not copyrightable subject matter under federal law, and hence that federal requirements of registration, notice and deposit upon publication did not apply:

> [W]e respectfully protest at the outset, and in the holy name of arts and letters, that the reports of passing events sent over [Western Union] tickers to saloons, hotels and brokers' offices, is not, properly speaking, literature; that it does not come

---

88 Brief for Appellee at 2, *National Telegraph News Co. v Western Union Telegraph Co.*, No. 789 (7th Cir. 1901).

89 *Id.* at 3.

90 *Id.* at 4.

91 See Brief for Appellant at 8-34, *National Telegraph News Co. v Western Union Telegraph Co.*, No. 789 (7th Cir. 1901). National also argued that Western Union was a common carrier and was thus obligated to offer it a ticker subscription on terms equal to those of other subscribers. See *id.* at 34-43.

> within the purview of the copyright statutes; that it would not be entitled to the protection of such statutes even if every condition precedent prescribed by them had been punctiliously complied with; and that it would not, therefore, be subject to diminution because of any failure to comply therewith.[92]

Why were the reports not copyrightable subject matter? Western Union cited the old 1829 case of *Clayton v Stone*,[93] and argued as Justice Thompson had in *Clayton* that the ticker reports provided only 'a history of inconsequential contemporaneous events which adds nothing to the learning of the world'.[94] However, perhaps aware that *Clayton* had not remained a strong precedent, it also argued that news was not copyrightable because it was not the product of any author: 'Could you call the writer of [a telegraph message giving the result of a baseball match or a horse-race, or the fluctuations of the stock market] an "author?" The very absurdity of the proposition is its own refutation.'[95] Thus, a prominent force in the news industry, Western Union, had itself decided to adopt a creativity-based view of originality to avoid a charge of abandonment under federal copyright law, and to try its luck arguing that common law still protected its reports.

The Seventh Circuit affirmed the preliminary injunction, and Judge Peter Grosscup wrote an opinion that provides a pioneering, astoundingly clear articulation of creativity-based originality, and of the associated notion of the romantic author. 'Authorship', he wrote, 'implies that there has been put into the production something meritorious from the author's own mind; that the product embodies the thought of the author, as well as the thought of others; and would not have found existence in the form presented, but for the distinctive individuality of mind from which it sprang.'[96] News reports, he concluded, did not usually bear the stamp of a particular mind, and therefore were not the products of an author that copyright law should protect.

> A mere annal . . . is the reduction to copy of an event that others, in a like situation, would have observed; and its statement in the substantial form that people generally would have adopted. . . . [I]f . . . writings are a mere notation of the figures at which stocks or cereals have been sold, or of the result of a horse race, or base-ball game, they cannot be said to bear the impress of individuality, and fail, therefore, to rise to the plane of authorship. In authorship, the product has some likeness to the mind underneath it; in a work of mere notation, the mind is guide only to the fingers that

---

[92] Brief for Appellee at 8, *National Telegraph News Co. v Western Union Telegraph Co.*, No. 789 (7th Cir. 1901).

[93] 5 F. Cas. 999 (C.C.S.D.N.Y. 1829) (No. 2872).

[94] *Id.* at 10.

[95] *Id.* at 9.

[96] *National Tel. News Co. v Western Union Tel. Co.*, 119 F. 294, 297-98 (7th Cir. 1902).

> make the notation. One is the product of originality; the other the product of opportunity.[97]

Nevertheless, Grosscup and his brethren held, the news service provided by Western Union has a commercial and social value that deserves legal protection – it is a 'modern enterprise – one of the distinctive achievements of our day – which, combining the genius and accumulations of men, with the forces of electricity, combs the earth's surface, each day, for what the day has brought forth, that whatever befalls the sons of men shall come, almost instantaneously, into the consciousness of mankind.'[98] Thus, the court upheld the injunction on common-law grounds. The release of *National Telegraph News* decision marks a significant moment in American copyright history. For the first time, a federal court concluded that a large category of products of intellectual labor – news accounts that were 'mere annals' – was not copyrightable subject matter, on the basis of a creativity-based interpretation of the originality requirement.

C. The Aftermath

Both the debate on the Newspaper Copyright Bill and the *National Telegraph News* decision influenced commentators and courts. In his 1912 book *Copyright: Its History and Its Law*, Richard Rogers Bowker contended that the failure to pass the Newspaper Copyright Bill meant that there was no copyright protection for news, but only for the literary form in which it was recounted:

> A bill to protect news for twenty-four hours was at one time before Congress, but was never passed. There is, therefore, no copyright protection for news as such, but the general copyright of the newspaper or a special copyright may protect the form of a dispatch, letter or article containing news.[99]

(Bowker then noted that the *National Telegraph News* case provided common-law protection for news on ticker tapes.[100]) The following year, a Southern District of New York opinion cited the Bowker account with approval in support of a broad statement that facts were not copyrightable: '[T]here can be no piracy of facts, because facts are public property',[101] stated Judge Hough; he then opined that 'a fair summary of the law on [the impossibility of copyrighting

---

97 *Id.* at 298.
98 *Id.* at 300.
99 Bowker, Richard Rogers (1912), *Copyright: Its History and Its Law* 89.
100 *Id.*
101 *Davies v Bowes*, 209 F. 53, 56 (S.D.N.Y. 1913).

news] is, I think, contained in Bowker on Copyright, pp. 88, 89.'[102] The case proceeded to hold that fiction presented as news should also be uncopyrightable, essentially adopting a theory of estoppel.

In his 1917 copyright law treatise,[103] Arthur William Weil quoted extensive passages from *National Telegraph News*, which he praised as 'an extremely able opinion'.[104] In particular, Weil quoted approvingly the passage from *National Telegraph News* denying copyright to 'mere annals' while criticizing Justice Holmes's apparent acceptance of the copyrightability of directories in *Bleistein v Donaldson Lithographing Co.*[105] In the same year, William B. Hale, whose copyright treatise was published as volume 13 of *Corpus Juris*,[106] cited *National Telegraph News* in support of two related propositions: that there is no copyright in news,[107] but that there is common law protection of news, which is not destroyed by publication because news is not literary property.[108]

1917 is also the year that Judge Augustus Hand issued the District Court decision in *Associated Press v International News Service.*[109] This litigation, of course, culminated in the Supreme Court's decision in *International News Service v Associated Press*[110] the following year. The Supreme Court's recognition of a property right in news in this litigation has been widely recognized and extensively analyzed. The role of the *INS* case in establishing that news is not copyrightable, however, has received somewhat less emphasis. Judge Hand's opinion directly addressed the policy question – should news be given some post-publication protection? – with little discussion of the legal issue of how to avoid dedication to the public under the federal copyright scheme, which by that time had dropped the registration requirement, but still required proper notice upon publication.[111] As for that policy issue, Hand announced that he was 'personally satisfied . . . that the right exists to prevent the sale by

102 *Id.*

103 Weil, Arthur William (1917), *American Copyright Law.*

104 *Id.* at 35; for the quoted passages, see *id.* at 36, 42–43.

105 See *id.* at 43.

106 Hale, William B. (1917), *A Treatise on the Law of Copyright and Literary Property*, published as volume 13 of William Mack and William B. Hale, *Corpus Juris.*

107 *Id.* at 1109, 1109 n. 93.

108 *Id.* at 956, 956 n. 34 (containing a 500-word quotation from the *National Telegraph News* decision).

109 240 F. 983 (S.D.N.Y. 1917).

110 248 U.S. 215 (1918).

111 The *National Telegraph News* case was litigated before 1909, when federal copyright law still required registration before publication. The 1909 Act removed the registration requirement, so that the principal requirement for obtaining federal copyright protection became publication with proper copyright notice.

a competing news agency of news which is taken from early publications of complainant's members before sufficient time has elapsed to afford opportunity for general publication'.[112] In support of such a proposition, Hand rested heavily on *National Telegraph News*, and his opinion contained a three-paragraph, 700-word quote from Judge Grosscup's opinion in that case.[113] Yet Judge Hand concluded that the legal issue was not sufficiently free from doubt to grant a preliminary injunction prohibiting copying altogether. Rather, he issued a preliminary injunction that only forbade INS from inducing agents of the Associated Press, or of its member newspapers, to furnish it with news in breach of AP policy. That meant that INS was still free to obtain published copies of East Coast newspapers and transmit that news to West Coast clients.

Both sides appealed the preliminary injunction. As appellate counsel, the Associated Press engaged none other than Peter Stenger Grosscup himself, author of the *National Telegraph News* opinion, who had resigned from his Seventh Circuit judgeship in 1911.[114] In a split decision, the Second Circuit, citing *National Telegraph News* with approval,[115] extended the preliminary injunction to cover copying of Associated Press news even when it was procured from publicly available newspapers. Judge Charles Merrill Hough's opinion directly addressed the issue of whether news content was copyrightable, and embraced a creativity-based view of originality: 'It may be granted that . . . publication at common law terminated an author's rights in his manuscript and the fruits of his brain; yet it still remains true that plaintiff's property in news is not literary at all, that it is not capable of copyright, and that "publication", as that word is used in the long line of decisions regarding literary rights, has no determinative bearing on this case.'[116]

When the case reached the Supreme Court, it split the Justices six to three, but not on the issue whether copyright law incorporated a creativity-based originality requirement. For the majority, Justice Pitney concluded that 'the news element – the information respecting current events contained in the literary production – is not the creation of the writer',[117] and therefore was not copyrightable. Justice Pitney echoed concerns expressed in both the Newspaper Copyright Bill debates and the *National Telegraph News* decision

---

112 *Associated Press v International News Service*, 240 F. at 996.

113 See *id.* at 993-94.

114 See *Associated Press v International News Service*, 245 F. 244, 247 (2d Cir. 1917) (listing Peter S. Grosscup as lead counsel for plaintiffs); Federal Judicial Center, Biographical Directory of Federal Judges, http://www.fjc.gov/public/home.nsf/hisj (entry for 'Grosscup, Peter Stenger' notes that he resigned on 23 October 1911).

115 See *Associated Press v International News Service*, 245 F. 244, 249 (2d Cir. 1917).

116 *Id.* at 250.

117 *International News Service v Associated Press*, 248 U.S. 215, 234 (1918).

about granting exclusive rights over 'the history of the day'.[118] The Framers of the Constitution, he argued, could not have 'intended to confer upon one who might happen to be the first to report a historic event the exclusive right for any period to spread the knowledge of it.'[119] In dissent, Justice Brandeis expressed similar support for a creativity-based originality standard that would exclude factual matter. '[I]ntellectual productions', he contended, 'are entitled to such protection only if there is underneath something evincing the mind of a creator or originator, however modest the requirement. The mere record of isolated happenings, whether in words or by photographs not involving artistic skill, are denied such protection'.[120] In support, he cited, among other cases, *National Telegraph News*.[121]

As an experiment in common-law protection of intellectual property, *International News Service v Associated Press* can probably be counted as a failure. It has not spawned a broad jurisprudence of common-law intellectual property, but has been given a narrow reading, limited to 'hot news' misappropriation;[122] and as a matter of federal court jurisdiction it has been thoroughly repudiated.[123] As the statement of a view of originality that excludes independently created factual accounts from copyright protection, however, it can be counted as a success. Although some post-*INS* courts continued to protect compilations of facts without a showing of creative selection or arrangement, the Supreme Court eventually vindicated *INS* in *Feist Publications, Inc. v Rural Telephone Service Co, Inc.*[124] Thus, the debate over copyright in news, beginning with the Newspaper Copyright Bill in 1884 and continuing through the *National Telegraph News* case, resulted in the rise of a

---

118 *Id.*

119 *Id.*

120 *Id.* at 254 (Brandeis, J., dissenting).

121 *Id.* at 254 n. 6. Justice Holmes's separate dissent did not touch directly on the issue, but he could be safely counted on the side of creativity-based originality as well. See *Bleistein v Donaldson Lithographing Co.*, 188 U.S. 239, 250 (1903) ('The copy is the personal reaction of an individual upon nature. . . a very modest grade of art has in it something irreducible, which is one man's alone. That something he may copyright . . .').

122 See, for example, *National Basketball Ass'n v Motorola*, 105 F.3d 841 (2d Cir. 1997).

123 See, example, *McKevitt v Pallasch*, 339 F.3d 530 (7th Cir. 1993) (*INS v AP* 'no longer is legally authoritative because it was based on the federal courts' subsequently abandoned authority to formulate common law principles in suits arising under state law though litigated in federal court.').

124 499 U.S. 340 (1991). But see Ginsburg, Jane C. (1992), 'No "Sweat"? Copyright and Other Protection of Works of Information After *Feist v Rural Telephone*', 92 *Colum. L. Rev.* 338, 352 ('Nonetheless, judicial inclination to reprimand sweat theft remains strong.').

creativity-based model of originality that received unanimous Supreme Court approval in 1918 and has only been strengthened and broadened by *Feist*.

V. LESSONS FROM THE NEWSPAPER COPYRIGHT DEBATE

What can we learn from the debate over copyright in news, and the transformation of originality doctrine in that debate?

First, it is a reminder that although copyright doctrine and rationale may be framed at high levels of abstraction, they are likely to enjoy success only under a much more particular set of conditions, and those conditions are likely to change over time. Nineteenth-century judges and commentators articulated a view of copyright originality under which factual matter was entitled to copyright protection; those who wanted to sell works that imparted information were exhorted to go out and gather it themselves, rather than free-ride on the intellectual labor of those who had already gathered it. Yet while that view is stated in general enough terms to make it applicable to news and news-gathering, the view became settled orthodoxy without ever being tested within the news industry, because at that time the news industry had no interest in protection for news. Once it gained such an interest, the intellectual labor theory was severely tested, because news, as it functioned within late-nineteenth-century American culture, did not fit the presuppositions of that theory very well. Witnessing a current event seemed to many to be as much a matter of chance as of labor and investment. News often came in narrative form, which allowed for a greater distinction between form and content than was possible with directories and maps. News seemed to be of more immediate political and cultural importance, and its free dissemination seemed particularly important when non-local news gathering was dominated by a very small number of large organizations. Moreover, 'market substitute' infringement doctrine had much less maneuvering space to mediate between the economic interests of copyright owners and the interest in free dissemination when individual news items could become the selling points for newspaper issues, and could become independent works in the continuous stream of the news ticker.

Secondly, the news copyright debate demonstrates the interdependence of the myriad doctrines that constitute copyright law. It was no particular surprise that the 'country press', which was opposed to any form of protection for news, advanced a creativity-based view of the originality requirement under which news matter was not copyrightable. Yet under copyright law as it existed at the turn of the twentieth century, the Western Union, which strongly desired protection for its news items, decided that it also wanted to advance a creativity-based view of originality, because its news ticker service could not satisfy the formalities of registration and notice; better to argue that news was outside of the reach of copyright altogether, and could therefore still qualify for common-law protection. The removal of news content from copyright – a contraction of copyright protection along the dimension of copyrightable subject matter – may also have made it easier for copyright to expand in other dimensions. If copyright was going to focus less on news, and more on fiction and entertainment, then the opposition to increases in scope of protection, such as protection of derivative works, and in length of copyright term, would decrease. This continues to be relevant to the current debate about whether patent and copyright law should have special rules for each industry that avails itself of patent or copyright protection.[125] It remains to be seen whether tailoring is a useful tool to ensure that each industry receives protection at a level that is optimal for society as a whole, or is an opportunity for each industry to ensure that as much market surplus as possible is captured by producers rather than consumers.

Several important developments remain outside the scope of this chapter. There is no doubt that issues raised by the addition of photographs as copyrightable subject matter also contributed to the rise of creativity-based originality. Before photography, the pathway from states of affairs in the world to fixed, copyrightable representations of them always went through the human mind: the minds of mapmakers, directory compilers, and engravers directed the hands that fixed factual representations. Photography took human minds out of that pathway: light, reflected off objects in the world and bent through a lens, fixed an image directly on a tangible, photosensitive medium. Infringement defendants took advantage of this novelty to argue that photographs did not have an author, and therefore could not constitutionally be protected under the Patent and Copyright Clause, which granted Congress the power to protect only authors and inventors. When the issue reached the Supreme Court in 1884 – at exactly the same time the Newspaper Copyright Bill was being brought before Congress[126] – the Court was forced to articulate

---

[125] See, for example, Carroll, Michael W. (2006), 'One for All: The Problem of Uniformity Cost in Intellectual Property Law', 55 *Am. Univ. L. Rev.* 845; Burk, Dan L. and Mark A. Lemley (2002), 'Is Patent Law Technology Specific?', 17 *Berkeley Tech. L. J.* 1155, 1159; Lunney, Jr., Glynn S. (2004), 'Patent Law, the Federal Circuit, and the Supreme Court: A Quiet Revolution', 11 *Sup. Ct. Econ. Rev.* 1.

[126] In his autobiography, Henry Watterson reports: 'through my uncle, Stanley Matthews [who at the time was an Associate Justice of the Supreme Court], I interested the members of the Supreme Court [in the issue of copyright for newspapers].' Watterson, Henry (1919), *Marse Henry: An Autobiography*, vol. II, p. 104. This suggests the tantalizing possibility that Supreme Court Justices were actually pondering originality issues involving photographs and news at the same time. Alas, I have found no evidence that they actually did so.

exactly what it was that made photographs works of authorship. The Court's answer – that photographs were copyrightable 'so far as they are representatives of original intellectual conceptions of the author'[127] – went far towards adopting a creativity-based view of originality, as it placed originality inside the mind of the author.

Yet photography was not the battleground that news was, in part because the form and content of photographs seems to be more tightly bound together than that of literary works. It is possible to rewrite a news story that has appeared in a competitor's newspaper and claim that one was only taking unprotected facts; it is not possible to 'rewrite' a photograph that a competitor has published. And while Justice Brandeis, in dissent in *International News Service v Associated Press*,[128] contended that 'photographs not involving artistic skill' were uncopyrightable,[129] the law was moving in the opposite direction. As Arthur Weil had phrased it in his copyright treatise, published the year before the *INS* decision: 'The elements of thought, arrangement and selection, which appealed to the Court in the Sarony case, are present . . . in the taking of all photographs. Their manifestation is a matter of degree, but their presence, to some extent, no matter how small, is always demonstrable.'[130] If creativity-based originality is found in all photographs, even those that document the world, and if any work that is not an exact copy of that photograph – say, a verbal description of the scene revealed by the photograph, or a computer graphic that simulates the scene portrayed from a different angle – does not have the audience appeal and therefore the commercial value of the original, then the debate between labor-based and creativity-based views of originality will not find much to work with in the field of photography.[131]

---

[127] *Burrow-Giles Lithographic Co. v Sarony*, 111 U.S. 53, 58 (1884). For a discussion of *Burrow-Giles* and the effect of photography on copyright law, see Farley, Christine Haight (2004), 'The Lingering Effects of Copyright's Response to the Invention of Photography', 65 *U. Pitt. L Rev*. 385.

[128] 248 U.S. 215 (1918).

[129] *Id.* at 254 (Brandeis, J., dissenting).

[130] Weil, Arthur William (1917), *American Copyright Law* 29–30; see *Pagano v Charles Beseler Co.,* 234 F. 963, 964 (S.D.N.Y. 1916) (finding originality in a photograph of the New York Public Library because 'It undoubtedly requires originality to determine just when to take the photograph, so as to bring out the proper setting for both animate and inanimate objects, with the adjunctive features of light, shade, position, etc.').

[131] There remains the special issue of derivative-work copyright in photographic reproductions of works of graphic art that are in the public domain, which raises the particular concern that the owner of the original is attempting, in effect, to extend copyright term on the original by limiting physical access to it and claiming that all authorized photographs of it are protected by new copyrights. See, for example, *The Bridgeman Art Library v Corel Corp.*, 36 F. Supp. 2d 191 (S.D.N.Y. 1999).

Finally, there is the issue of the distinction between news reports, on the one hand, and other fact-based works like directories and maps, on the other. If, indeed, news reports posed different issues than directories and maps, thus requiring a rethinking of prevailing originality doctrine, why doesn't copyright law continue to distinguish between them? Why did the *Feist* Court end up treating them all the same, with a broad, sweeping statement about the non-copyrightability of facts? There is certainly more work to be done on this issue, but perhaps the reader will indulge a few preliminary observations. First, the distinction between 'compilations', such as directories and calendars, and news accounts, persisted for decades, albeit somewhat inconsistently given the number of federal courts involved and the confusion in the law. Important lower courts, such as the Second Circuit, gave notice that in spite of *INS v AP* they were sticking to the view that the copyright in directories was not limited to creative selection and arrangement.[132] Secondly, the argument against copyright in news that had the most immediate and simplest intuitive appeal – that reporters did not create the facts that they documented – had implications beyond news, and those implications were difficult to ignore. Thirdly, the Copyright Act provided little or no textual grounds for making such a distinction. Interestingly, the Berne Convention, which began to be drafted in 1884 – the same year as the Newspaper Copyright Bill – contemplated that its signatories would treat news differently. It provided for a default rule of free copying of news stories, another sign that the custom of news copying was not confined to the United States.[133] Yet if the United States never adopted special statutory protection for news stories, it never adopted a special exclusion from protection for them either, and that made it difficult to maintain a distinction.

Thus, all that remains is to reiterate the main thesis of this chapter. An intellectual-labor-based view of originality, and of the scope of copyright protection, developed during an era when the news industry was uninterested in

---

132 See, for example, *Jeweler's Circular Pub. Co. v Keystone Pub. Co.*, 281 F. 83 (2d Cir. 1922).

133 Article 7 of the original Berne Convention of 9 September 1886 provided that newspaper and magazine articles published in any country that was a member of the Berne Union could be reproduced, in the original language or in translation, unless the authors or editors expressly prohibited it; furthermore, the prohibition would not apply to articles that discussed political matters or news of the day. It was not until the Stockholm Conference in 1967 that this default blanket license provision was deleted; the current text contains one vestige of the original provision, the statement in Article 2(8) that 'The Protection of the Convention shall not apply to news of the day or to miscellaneous facts having the character of mere items of press information.' See Ricketson, Sam (1987) *The Berne Convention for the Protection of Literary and Artistic Works: 1886–1986*, 302–06.

copyright. When major news industry players became interested in protection for news, due to technological and social changes that reshaped that industry, debate about the appropriateness and shape of that protection in Congress and the courts gave a substantial boost to a creativity-based view of originality that grew in dominance during the twentieth century and today is established orthodoxy.

3. Of silos and constellations: comparing notions of originality in copyright law

Elizabeth F. Judge* and Daniel J. Gervais**

Originality is simply a pair of fresh eyes.
Thomas Wentworth Higginson (1823–1911)

1. INTRODUCTION

Originality is a central theme in efforts to understand human evolution, thinking, innovation and creativity. Artists strive to be original, however the term is understood by each of them. It is also one of the major concepts in copyright law. In a previous discussion of the notion,[1] one of the authors noted that (a) the notion is defined neither in international treaties nor in the vast majority of national laws and (b) it is the most important notion of copyright law because it is the sieve that determines which 'productions[2] of the human spirit' are protected by copyright and acquire the status of 'work'. The other main condition, namely that the production should belong to the literary or artistic

* Associate Professor of Law, University of Ottawa Faculty of Law (Common Law Section).
** Professor of Law, Vanderbilt University Law School.
We gratefully acknowledge support from the Social Sciences and Humanities Research Council of Canada, the Law Foundation of Ontario, and the Faculty of Law at the University of Ottawa. We thank Leanne Fioravanti, Kiernan Murphy, Anna Wysocka, and Martin Zatowkaniuk for their excellent research assistance.

1 Gervais, Daniel (2002), '*Feist* Goes Global: A Comparative Analysis of the Notion of Originality in Copyright Law', 49:4 *J. Copyright Soc'y of the USA* 949 ['*Feist* Goes Global'].

2 We use this generic term as it is used in Article 2 of the *Berne Convention for the Protection of Literary and Artistic Works*, 9 September 1886, as last revised at Paris on 24 July 1971, 1161 U.N.T.S. 30, S.Treaty Doc. No. 99- 27 (1986) [Berne Convention].

domain,[3] has not precluded databases or computer programs from being protected by copyright.[4]

In '*Feist* Goes Global', it was suggested that the notions of originality developed by courts in civil law and major common law jurisdictions tended to converge around a notion based on what the United States Supreme Court referred to as a 'modicum of creativity'.[5] In some jurisdictions the threshold of creativity was somewhat higher. In others it was referred to in different terms. For example, in the Canadian Supreme Court case of *CCH Canadian Ltd. v Law Society of Upper Canada*,[6] the Court found that originality required non-mechanical, non-trivial skill and judgment (and that the work must originate from an author and not be copied from another work). In parsing the content of those notions, '*Feist* Goes Global' argued that originality stemmed from creative choices made by the author. 'Creative choices' were defined in that context as those made by a human author which are not dictated by the function of the work, the method or technique used, or by applicable standards or relevant 'good practice'.[7]

In this chapter we consider the evolution of the notion since 2002 (when '*Feist* Goes Global' was published) and continue the analysis. In Part 2, we consider the four traditional silo-like notions of originality used in national legal systems. In Part 3, we look at the major international treaties for guidance in defining the parameters of an international notion of originality. In Part 4, we analyze the silos and suggest that they take the form of constellations which cannot be defined or compared hierarchically or indeed as completely separate notions; rather, they overlap in myriad ways. In the last part, we conclude that while normatively *Feist* had a very significant impact, the notion of originality it strived to define was perhaps best explained and operationalized in the *CCH* case.

---

3 The Berne Convention protects 'literary and artistic works'. The role of the Convention, which is the most important copyright convention in both age and coverage (number of member countries), was further enhanced when most of its substantive provisions were incorporated into the Agreement on *Trade-Related Aspects of Intellectual Property Rights*, 15 April 1994, Marrakesh Agreement establishing the World Trade Organization, Annex 1C, *Results of the Uruguay Round of Multilateral Trade Negotiations: The Legal Texts*, 1869 U.N.T.S. 299, 33 I.L.M. 1125, 1197 [TRIPS Agreement].

4 There remains a third condition in a few legal systems, namely that the production should be fixed in a tangible medium of expression. See, for example, 17 U.S.C. §102(a).

5 *Feist Publications, Inc. v Rural Telephone Service Co., Inc.*, 499 U.S. 340, 346 (1991) [*Feist*].

6 [2004] SCC 13 (Can.) [*CCH*].

7 '*Feist* Goes Global', *supra* note 1, at 976–977.

2. SILOS OF ORIGINALITY STANDARDS

Under the orthodox interpretation of originality for purposes of copyright law, there are four different families of standards, speaking broadly, which, ranged from most restrictive to most generous, are the European Union's personal intellectual creation,[8] the United States's *Feist* minimal degree of creativity,[9] Canada's *CCH* standard of non-mechanical and non-trivial exercise of skill and judgment,[10] and the United Kingdom's skill and labour standard.[11] This section discusses the origin, development, complexities, and critiques of copyright originality standards in continental Europe, the United States, Canada, the United Kingdom and other commonwealth jurisdictions, and a discussion of originality under international treaties follows in Part 3.

2.1 Personal Intellectual Creation

2.1.1 Originality in continental European systems and national law

Interestingly, the notion of originality appeared rather late in French jurisprudence. It had emerged first in doctrine, as is often the case in civil law systems. Professor Henri Desbois is credited with using the notion as a filter or criterion to determine what deserves protection.[12]

The classic originality test in France is that the work must express or reflect the author's personality. In theory this is consistent with a Hegelian derived intellectual property philosophy, but in application it is a fairly subjective standard to be sure.[13] According to a French commentator, it was not surprising that such a subjective test would emerge during the nineteenth century because it fit 'the modes of expression then in vogue – sculpture, painting and writings –', that is to say, 'the expression of (inner) turmoil (*tourmente*) of the author, the emotional, subjective and non-rational aspect of human thought. In a way, what differentiates one work from another is its irrationality, a reflection of the author's own irrational mind.'[14] The personality test is still regularly invoked by courts.[15]

---

8 *Infra* Part 2.1.

9 *Infra* Part 2.2.

10 *Infra* Part 2.3.

11 *Infra* Part 2.4.

12 Lucas, Andre and H.J. Lucas (2006), *Traite de la Propriété Littéraire et Artistique* 72 (3rd edn).

13 *Ibid.*, 73–74: 'The classic thesis is simple: Originality must be understood as the mark of the author's personality.' [authors' translation].

14 Martin, Jean (1991), 'Le droit d'auteur applicable au logiciel', in Isabelle de Lamberterie, ed, *Le Droit d'Auteur Aujourd'hui* 111 [authors' translation].

15 See *Sawkins v Harmonia Mundi*, Nanterre Tribunal de Grande Instance, 19

This approach, while understandable for expressive works, such as sculpture, writings and painting, did not mesh well with more utilitarian works, such as compilations and databases. For these works, the French courts did not jettison the traditional notion of originality when deciding which of these works were protected, or to what extent. Instead, they searched for a more objective test than personality because it became unrealistic to find the personality of the author of a database or of a computer operating system. These problems, though *quantitatively* unprecedented in the evolution of copyright given the size of the computer industry, which saw itself suddenly as both a newcomer and the largest player among copyright holders, and which were certainly made more acute by information technologies,[16] were not altogether *qualitatively* new, for authors' rights did apply to utilitarian works, such as encyclopedias, maps and other works in which the search for a subjective mark of the author's personality was unlikely to be convincingly fruitful.

The test that courts developed in France and a number of other European countries is creative choices: which choices did the author make that were guided neither by applicable standards, the method used to create the works, nor considerations of optimal functionality and efficiency.[17] Professor André Lucas refers to this as 'l'arbitraire de l'auteur'.[18]

For example, in a case involving a bilingual dictionary, the Court of Appeal of Paris found that 'the choices and intellectual operations required to create the [dictionary] tend to give the resulting work a certain degree of originality,

---

January 2005. English translation at (2006) 37:1 *International Review of Intellectual Property and Competition Law* (IIC) 116, concluding that a performance edition restoring the music of a French Baroque era composer where the only surviving copy was posthumous was original as he was 'obliged to make personal and arbitrary artistic choices on the basis of his personal interpretation'. 'In order to be eligible for copyright protection, a work must bear the intellectual and personal stamp of the author's contribution, irrespective of its degree of originality… Given the state of the sources, the defendant have not proven a degree of strict faithfulness of the restored work to de Lalande's intention that would be capable of denying any personal character in the restoration and composition work such that it became a mere act of transcription.' *Ibid.* at 118–119. See *infra* note 109 for Sawkins's successful litigation involving a similar work before England's Court of Appeal applying the skill, labour and judgment originality standard.

16 When measured in dollar terms. Worldwide revenues in 2006 for companies in the *Software 500* list were $394 billion. This can be compared to the $891 billion that the core copyright industries generated in the US in 2006. See Siwek, Stephen E., *Copyright Industries in the U.S. Economy: The 2006 Report*, available at <http://www.iipa.com/pdf/2006_siwek_full.pdf> and *SoftwareMagazine – 2008 Software 500: Innovation Alive and Well*, available at <http://www.softwaremag.com/L.cfm?Doc=1175-10/2008>.

17 See *supra* note 7 and accompanying text.

18 Lucas, *supra* note 12, at 84–85.

even when dealing with a technical type of work'.[19] The Court made it clear that the fact of sorting data that was difficult to generate in alphabetical order was not original, thus refusing a sweat of the brow or labour-based (dessert) approach. Originality can only follow, it said, from intellectually creative (as opposed to mechanical or functional or format-driven choices.[20] A similar conclusion was reached by the same court a few years later concerning a catalog of Cajun words.[21] A test similar to creative choices is applied by the French courts when deciding who the author of a collective work is. In a case involving a 'multimedia work', the author was determined to be the person who selected the texts, music, and displays, not the person who took all the necessary technical steps to give the work its 'materiality'.[22]

Another interesting case which illustrates the standard applied to a compilation involved a compilation of short stories based on traditional folklore.[23] Because the stories themselves were in the public domain through the expiration of the term of protection, copyright could only subsist in the (original) selection and arrangement of stories. The Court found that 'by choosing the stories, by narrating them with his own style and by arranging them according to a sequence chosen by him and which was not necessary,[24] and by giving the book a specific structure, Mr. Guillois created a creative work'.[25]

The protection of several types of compilations has been recognized by French courts: statistical studies,[26] compilations of collective agreements,[27] comparative tables of television audience ratings[28] or even specialized telephone directories[29] and calendars.[30] The French Supreme Court[31] made it clear that labour itself was insufficient[32] and that one had to look at the choice

---

19 CA Paris, 4e ch., 21 March 1989: 142 RIDA 333, 338–39 ('Harrap's' case) [authors' translation].

20 *Ibid.*

21 CA Paris, 1e ch.,14 January 1992: 152 RIDA 198.

22 CA Paris, 4e ch., 28 April 2000: 1/2001 RIDA 314.

23 CA Paris, 4e ch., 23 September 1992: 156 RIDA 224.

24 In the sense of not having been guided by the technique used or standard practices concerning this type of compilation.

25 156 RIDA at 224–5 [authors' translation].

26 TGI Paris, réf. 18 January 1999; Juris-Data no. 043760.

27 *Editions Législatives v Tierry Erhmann et autres*, T.G. I. Lyons, 28 December 1998, (1999) 181 RIDA 325.

28 CA Paris, 1e ch., 22 May 1990: Légipresse 1990, I, at 67.

29 CA Paris, 18 December 1924: DH 1925, at 30.

30 CA Paris, 4e ch., 4e ch., 14 April 1986: D. 1987, somm. P. 152 obs. Colombet.

31 The Civil Supreme Court, namely the *Cour de cassation*. There are other 'supreme courts' in France for administrative and constitutional law.

32 Cass. 1e civ., 2 May 1989: JCP G 1990, II, 21392, note A. Lucas; RIDA 1/1990, at 309 ('Coprosa' case).

of the method used by the author of the compilation.[33] In fact, recognizing that the classical test could not be used for newer types of works such as databases (compilations) and computer software, several French courts have tried to develop a new test or, more precisely, to elevate the classical test to a higher level of abstraction, by answering the following question: what is it that an author does to show her personality through a work? The fairly unanimous answer given by French courts is that it is creative choices that distinguish one work from another and reveal personality.[34] This doctrine was applied by a court denying protection to a database of requests for proposals by governmental authorities that was produced by a newspaper.[35]

Thus in France the modern test is seen to be a subset of the classic test for originality: the modern test of examining creative choices is a way to evaluate whether an author's personality is reflected in a work and hence if the work is original.

Similar though not as completely developed doctrines have been accepted by courts in Belgium,[36] the Netherlands[37] and Switzerland.[38] Swiss copyright scholars Bannelet and Egloff assert that what creates originality are choices made by the author that were not dictated by custom or good practice.[39]

In Belgium, there is authority recognizing copyright originality in functional works, albeit thin, if the author's personality is distinguished. The Supreme Court (*cour de cassation*) acknowledged that a catalog could be original but

---

33 Cass. crim. 18 May 1938: Gaz. Pal. 1938, 2, p. 311; Cass. civ., 27 May 1942: S.1942, 1, 124; and Cass. Com. 17 March 2004: 3/2004 RIDA 263.

34 See Gervais, Daniel (1998) *La Notion d'Œuvre dans la Convention de Berne et en Droit Comparé* 85–86.

35 *Groupe Moniteur et Action Municipal v Observatoire des Marchés Publics*, C.A. Paris, 4e ch., 18 June 1999, (2000) 183 RIDA 316.

36 Cass. civ. 27 April 1989: R.W. 1989–90, at 362; Cass. civ. 25 October 1989; R.W. 1989–90, at 1061; see also Strowel, Alain (1991), 'Rapport belge', in *Copyright and Industrial Property: Congress of the Aegean Sea* II 392; Strowel, Alain (1993), *Droit d'Auteur et Copyright* 420–31.

37 See *Van Dale v Romme* II, HR 1 April 1993, IER 1993 (3) at 82. See also Strowel, *Droit d'Auteur et Copyright, supra* note 36 at 5–26.

38 See Gervais, *supra* note 34 at 87–88; Kummer, Max (1968), *Das Urheberrechtlich Shutzbare Werk* 30; and Bannelet, Denis and Willi Egloff (1994), *Le Nouveau Droit D'auteur: Commentaire De La Loi Federale Sur le Droit d'Auteur et les Droits Voisins* 24.

39 In French, 'règles de l'art'. See also Bannelet and Egloff, *supra* note 38 at 10–24. One leading commentator specifically excludes as a requirement that the author's personality be visible. See Dessemontet, F. (1999), *Le Droit d'Auteur*, at §159.

that the protection would be very thin.[40] Another decision recognized that certain non-descriptive newspaper headlines could also be original, while invoking the classic personality test that a work 'must be original, that is, it must be distinguished by the personality, the distinctive stamp, of its author'.[41]

In the Netherlands, copyright protection has been denied to television program listings, not because of their utilitarian nature per se but because they didn't reflect the author's personality:

> [T]he way in which they are ordered is not sufficient evidence of a personal vision or any originality on the part of their creator. These schedules can therefore not be regarded as works of literature, science or art which are entitled to full copyright protection.[42]

In another Dutch case, this one before the Supreme Court and involving 'kinetic schemes', that is 'representations of a factually existing chemical reaction system', the court again emphasized the subjective personality test, namely whether the scheme bore the 'imprint of the maker'.[43]

Germany, however, is a somewhat different story. Although the standard may not be different, German courts have applied a stricter test. While influenced by Hegelian and Kantian theories, which, especially in Hegel's case, linked creative expression with the formation and deployment of personal autonomy and, therefore, attached great importance to artistic expression, modern German doctrine combines a (mostly subjective) search for individuality (*Individualität*)[44] with the requirement of a minimal threshold of creativity (*Gestaltungshöhe*).[45] In a case involving telephone directories, the Court found the work not to be protected by copyright, even though it followed a complex system of rules:

---

40 *Art Research & Contact v B.*, Cour de Cassation, 11 May 2001, case N° C.00.0391.N, <http://jure.juridat.just.fgov.be/pdfapp/download_blob?idpdf=F-20010511-4>.

41 *Google Inc v Copiepresse SCRL*, Court of First Instance of Brussels, 13 February 2007, 2007 WL 1623283 (RB (Brussels)), [2007] E.C.D.R. 5.

42 *N.V. Holdingmaatschappij de Telegraaf v Nederlandse Omroep Stichting*, Court of Appeal of the Hague, case number 99/165, 30 January 2001, 2001 WL 1676969 (Hof (Den Haag)), [2002] E.C.D.R. 8.

43 *Technip Benelux B.V. v Arie Gerhard Goossens, Hoge Raad*, First Chamber, 24 February 2006, case number C04/250HR. English translation and comment by Quaedvlieg, Antoon A. (2007) 38:5 *International Review of Intellectual Property and Competition Law* 615.

44 See Ulmer, Ernst (1980), *Urheber- und Verlagsrecht* (3rd edn), at 124.

45 See U. Loewenheim (2006), in Shricker, G. (ed), *Urheberrecht Kommentar* (3rd edn), at §20–21.

The personal intellectual creation required for the assumption of a protected literary work can be found in the intellectual formation and structuring of the contents presented or in the particular imaginative form and manner of the collection, classification and arrangement of the material presented. A telephone directory is a work of reference, and the information it contains is, from a copyright point of view, in the public domain, with the result that, given the small scope for individual arrangement, there can a priori be no intellectual creative content in the formation and structure of ideas of the contents reproduced. [C]ompliance with this system of rules does not mean that the ... telephone directories ... can be regarded as individual intellectual creations with the necessary level of creativity. As often in the sorting of large data collections to be reproduced in full, these rules concern less the selection of the data records to be included – the subscribers to be included in the directory are in any event determined in advance – and more the uniformity of the arrangement and presentation. Even if there may be several alternatives, the scope for individual creative arrangement is restricted by the fact that such directories are to a large degree subject to conventions that have developed for alphabetical lists in general and telephone directories in particular ...[46]

In a different case involving computer programs, the Court recalled the *Inkasso* case,[47] which had denied protection to a computer program for lack of originality. According to that previous decision, software originality required that the creative work involved in the 'computer program assumed a clearly outstanding creativity in selection, collation, organization and division of the material and directions compared to the general and average ability'. In noting the adoption of the Computer Programs Directive,[48] the court stated that the originality standard would have to be lowered, at least for software, but failed to elaborate on the revised standard.[49]

A lower requirement was also applied in a case involving maps,[50] and another accepted that headnotes could be original.[51] In such contexts, where

---

46 *Tele-Info-CD*, Decision of the Federal Supreme Court (Bundesgerichtshof), 6 May 1999, case no. I ZR 199/96, <http://lexetius.com/1999,844>, English translation at (2000) 31 *International Review of Industrial Property and Copyrights* (IIC) 1055, 1056.

47 *Inkasso-Programm* (Collection program), IZR 52/83 (1985); 17 IIC 681 (1986); *Computer und Recht* 22. See also Drexl, J. (1995), *What Is Protected in a Computer Program: Copyright Protection in the U.S. and Europe*, IIC Studies, (VCH, Munich).

48 See *infra* note 56.

49 *Buchhaltungsprogramm*, BGH, 14 July 1993, [1993] CR 752-755. Translated in Günther, Andreas and Ulrich Wuermelling, 'Software protection in Germany – Recent court decisions in copyright law', [1995] 11 *Computer Law and Security Report* 12, 13.

50 City Map Collection, Bundesgerichtshof (Federal Supreme Court), 28 May 1998, I ZR 81/96. English translation at (1999) 30:8 *International Review of Intellectual Property and Competition Law* (IIC) 968.

51 *Leitsätze [Headnotes]*. Bundesgerichtshof (Federal Supreme Court), 28 May

factual accuracy is at a premium (for example, in reporting what a judgment stated) or where there is little public interest in providing incentives to deviate from established and familiar formatting conventions (for example, legends on maps), it is more difficult to identify how an author's creative individuality should be assessed and what should be required. Thus, for headnotes, the court drew the line by accepting that concise formulation and structuring of the grounds for the law decision amounted to a creative and individual activity, whereas simply stating the legal problem or a verbatim reproduction without classification would not. In the former situation, there was at least minimal room for choices made by the author.

Courts in Austria also look for the mark of the author's personal intellectual creation, but were willing to recognize that a website of rental properties met the requirement:

> The person creating the work must reveal personal features – in particular through visual design and the conceptual processing. [. . .] The requirement to be made of the character of a database are no higher than for other types of work; quality and aesthetic worth are of no relevance.[52]

The same rule was applied to a website used to offer kitchen design services.[53]

What is strikingly absent in traditional Continental doctrine, whether in Germany, France or elsewhere, is an explicit utilitarian perspective, even though utilitarian considerations may well have informed some of the decisions, in effect lowering the threshold for protection. The equation – If P is protected by authors' rights, then result Q will enhance social welfare – is not commonly found in Europe, in either cases or commentary, at least not explicitly. European legislators, however, seem determined to modernize the notion of originality by giving it more objective characteristics.

2.1.2 Originality in the European Union

Several directives have been adopted by the European Union to regulate various aspects of copyright policy.[54] When adopting directives, which are essen-

---

1998, I ZR 81/96. English translation at (1999) 30:8 *International Review of Intellectual Property and Competition Law* (IIC) 968.

[52] *C-Villas*, Austrian Supreme Court (Oberster Gerichtshof) July 10, 2001, case 4 Ob 155/01. English translation at (2003) 34:2 *International Review of Intellectual Property and Competition Law* (IIC) 223.

[53] *Telering.at*, Oberster Gerichtschof, April 24, 2001, case number 4 Ob 94/01. English translation at (2003) 34:1 *International Review of Intellectual Property and Competition Law* (IIC) 106.

[54] Apart from the Directives mentioned in the following three notes, relevant Directives would include the Directive 98/71/EC of the European Parliament and of the Council of 13 October 1998 on the legal protection of designs, OJ L 289/28,

tially legal instruments addressed at individual EU member States asking them to change their legislation to comply with the directive, a process known as transposition, EU legislators, both Commissioners and members of the European Parliament, are obliged to take account of the interests of all 27 EU member States. In the field of copyright, this includes common law jurisdictions (Ireland and the United Kingdom). Three copyright directives are most important for our purposes, namely the Directive on the legal protection of databases,[55] the Directive on the legal protection of computer programs,[56] and the Directive on the term of protection of copyright.[57]

The Computer Program Directive states that a computer program 'shall be protected if it is original in the sense that it is the *author's own intellectual creation*. No other criteria shall be applied to determine its eligibility for protection'.[58] The Database Directive provides, using similar language but incorporating language closer to Art. 2(5) of the Berne Convention, that 'databases which, by reason of the selection or arrangement of their contents, constitute the author's own intellectual creation shall be protected as such by copyright. No other criteria shall be applied to determine their eligibility for that protection'.[59] Finally, the Term Directive provides that photographs 'which are original in the sense that they are the author's own intellectual

---

28.10.1998; the Directive 2004/48/EC of the European Parliament and of the Council of 29 April 2004 on the enforcement of intellectual property rights, OJ L 157, 30.04.2004; the Directive 2001/29/EC of 22 May 2001 on the harmonisation of certain aspects of copyright and related rights in the information society, OJ L 167/10, 22.06.2001; the Council Directive 92/100/EEC of 19 November 1992 on rental right and lending right and on certain rights related to copyright in the field of intellectual property, OJ L 346/61, 27.11.1992; the Directive 2001/84/EC of the European Parliament and of the Council of 27 September 2001 on the resale right for the benefit of the author of an original work of art, OJ L 272/32, 13.10.2001; the Council Directive 93/83/EEC of 27 September 1993 on the coordination of certain rules concerning copyright and rights related to copyright applicable to satellite broadcasting and cable retransmission, OJ L 248/15, 6.10.1993; and the Council Directive 87/54/EEC of 16 December 1986 on the legal protection of topographies of semiconductor products, OJ L 24/36, 27.01.1987.

[55] Directive 96/9/EC of the European Parliament and of the Council of 11 March 1996 on the legal protection of databases, OJ L 77/20, 27.03.1996 [Database Directive].

[56] Council Directive 91/250/EEC of 14 May 1991 on the legal protection of computer programs, OJ L 122/42, 17.05.1991 [Computer Programs Directive].

[57] Council Directive 93/98/EEC of 29 October 1993 harmonizing the term of protection of copyright and certain related rights, OJ L 290/9, 24.11.1993 [Term Directive].

[58] Computer Programs Directive, *supra* note 56, Art. 1(3). Recital 8 makes it plain that no tests as to the qualitative or aesthetic merits of the program should be applied.

[59] Database Directive, *supra* note 55, Art. 3(1).

creation shall be protected in accordance with Article 1. No other criteria shall be applied to determine their eligibility for protection. Member States may provide for the protection of other photographs.'[60] The last sentence can be explained in that a number of Northern European countries provide protection for non-original photographs, for a shorter term than full copyright.[61] However, Recital 17 of the Term Directive adds the following:

> Whereas the protection of photographs in the Member States is the subject of varying regimes; whereas in order to achieve a sufficient harmonization of the term of protection of photographic works, in particular of those which, due to their artistic or professional character, are of importance within the internal market, it is necessary to define the level of originality required in this Directive; whereas a photographic work within the meaning of the Berne Convention is to be considered *original if it is the author's own intellectual creation reflecting his personality,* no other criteria such as merit or purpose being taken into account ...[62]

Two important points can be made. First, originality is the only criterion that the 27 EU member States are allowed to apply in determining whether content that fits one of the categories of copyright material is protected. Secondly, originality, at least for computer programs, databases and photographs, is present when the work is an author's own intellectual creation.

It has been said that the formulation chosen by European lawmakers was clever because it can be read in two different ways.[63] One can read it as a reflection of the traditional Continental notion based on the personality of the author. Indeed, the term 'personal creation' seems infused with at least some degree of personhood theory. Depending on the linguistic version, that interpretation is reinforced. In French, the creation must be 'propre à son auteur', and the Italian version is to the same effect,[64] while in German it is 'eine eigene geistige Schöpfung ihres Urhebers'. The Spanish is simpler: 'una creación intelectual de su autor'. Recital 17 of the Term Directive is an important argument in support of that thesis.

Another way to interpret the Directive is that the creation is the author's own simply if the author is the originator, that is, if she has not copied. This is closer to the traditional United Kingdom test.[65]

---

60 Term Directive, *supra* note 57, Art. 6.

61 See Institute for Information Law, *The Recasting of Copyright & Related Rights for the Knowledge Economy*, Final Report, Nov. 2006, at 33. Available at <http://www.ivir.nl/publications/other/IViR_Recast_Final_Report_2006.pdf> [*Recasting Report*].

62 Term Directive, *supra* note 57, Recital 17 [emphasis added].

63 Lucas, *supra* note 12, at 85.

64 'una creazione dell'ingegno propria del loro autore'.

65 *Infra* part 2.4.

There is little doubt that the drafters intended to embrace the latter interpretation. In a key preparatory document,[66] one can see that the Commission envisaged a single, low common denominator, in order to protect (European) computer programs and databases:[67]

> In every Member State, to be eligible for copyright protection *stricto sensu* a work must be 'original' in the sense that it is the result of the creator's own intellectual efforts and not itself a copy. But in some jurisdictions, more may be required in certain cases, particularly where works have a utilitarian rather than an aesthetic function. Courts may then find that work lacks sufficient creative merit or is too modest in scope to attract full copyright protection though in some cases this 'small change' (in German, 'kleine Munze') may still be eligible for a lesser form of protection designed to protect the investment of time, manpower and money.[68]

A similar point was made in the Explanatory Memorandum to the Computer Programs Directive,[69] and the EU official who was responsible for copyright policy at the time seems also to have supported this view.[70]

This desire to endorse a single low common denominator is understandable. The Directive was adopted at a time when Europe may have been concerned that too high a standard could hurt its chances of competing in the (then exponentially growing) computer software industry, based on the belief that more copyright protection would help develop a stronger industry. That policy debate was also apparent elsewhere. In the United States, although there was no doubt that copyright applied to software by the time the Computer Programs Directive was adopted, courts were trying to determine the exact scope of protection, which in turn determined the scope of allowable competition.[71]

---

[66] Green Paper on *Copyright and the Challenge of Technology – Copyright Issues Requiring Immediate Action*, COM (88) 172 of 7 June 1988.

[67] Commission first evaluation of Directive 96/9/EC on the legal protection of databases, <http://ec.europa.eu/internal_market/copyright/docs/databases/evaluation_report_en.pdf> at 7–8.

[68] Green Paper, *supra* note 66, §5.6.3.

[69] COM (88) 816, Part II, OJ C 91, 12.4.1989, p. 4 , at 1.3.

[70] Verstrynge, J.-F. (1993), 'Protecting Intellectual Property Rights Within the New Pan-European Framework: Computer Software', in M. Lehmann and C. Tapper (eds), *A Handbook of European Software Law*, 4.

[71] Contrast the protection of 'everything that is not necessary for the purpose or function' of the program in *Whelan Associates, Inc. v Jaslow Dental Laboratory, Inc.*, 797 F. 2d 1222 (3d Cir. 1986) to the abstraction-filtration-comparison test in *Computer Associates International v Altai, Inc.*, 982 F. 2d 693 (2d Cir. 1992) and the refusal to protect menus in *Lotus Development Corp. v Borland International*, 49 F. 3d 807 (1st Cir. 1995).

Indeed, the Computer Programs Directive was 'primarily aimed at reconciling the strict continental test, especially as developed by German courts, with the more generous Anglo-Saxon "skill and labour" standard. According to the Commission, as a result the "droit d'auteur" countries have had to lower their threshold for protection of software, while notably the UK and Ireland have had to raise their standard'.[72] This explains why its drafters would have likely been motivated more by the United Kingdom approach: lowering the standard applied on the Continent at the time seemed like a more appropriate way of achieving the stated policy objective of protecting (more) computer software by copyright.

It is difficult to draw a single conclusion from our analysis of the EU Directives. One could conclude that two standards exist: one for photographs, another for other categories, including software and databases (compilations). One could even conclude that there are three zones of originality, namely skill and labour-based (non-copied) originality for computer programs (and probably then also for databases); a zone with a higher standard based on the mark of the author's personality for photographs; and a third zone which for EU member States remains unregulated. Formally the latter three-zone approach is the one that more closely matches the current letter of EU Directives, but perhaps not their spirit. If asked to consider the appropriate standard of originality, the European Court of Justice is unlikely to adopt the three-zone approach. After all, the Directives were adopted to harmonize the internal market. It would be a strange result indeed if members (the vast majority) who currently have a single standard had to move to a double or triple standard. Yet Recital 17 of the Term Directive should be factored in the equation, as it forms part of EU law.

A solution to harmonize the originality standard may emerge as follows. For all categories of works, based on WIPO's studies on the interpretation of the Berne Convention (and its incorporation in the TRIPS Agreement), a single notion of originality based on creative choices seems to be implied in international copyright law. For functional or utilitarian works such as (most) computer programs and databases, creative choices are those that were not dictated to the author(s) by considerations of efficiency, functionality or applicable standards and practices of the techniques used to program and create the works. For photography, originality follows from similar creative choices, but, as with other artistic media, the choices, the author's '*arbitraire*' in Professor André Lucas' words, will reflect the author's personality, something that is illusory for technical works. Hence, a single standard of originality could be based on creative choices, while acknowledging that how those

72 *Recasting Report*, *supra* note 61, at 37 [internal footnote omitted].

choices are reflected in a particular work, or category of work, may vary depending, inter alia, on the technical nature of the work. This dynamic solution (because the nature of creative choices may evolve as new forms of creation emerge) would also allow modulation of the notion by each member State to reflect possible differences among 'unharmonized' elements of their national legislation. As the Recasting Report notes, 'how the courts interpret the criterion of originality depends on other "local" factors as well, such as the availability of actions in unfair competition. The meaning of the criterion is dynamic, i.e. bound by time, place and local use, which has implications for any attempt to legislate a single standard for all categories of works across the EU.'[73]

2.2 Originality in the United States: *Feist*'s Minimal Creativity

There are many excellent chapters in this volume about *Feist.*[74] The *Feist* standard is also discussed in '*Feist* Goes Global'. It is thus unnecessary to dwell on the standard applied in that case; a short reminder suffices. In *Feist*, a unanimous Court explained that originality requires independent creation plus a modicum of creativity.[75] Because the requirement was distilled from the Constitution's use of the word 'authors' in the Copyright Clause,[76] the requirement was said to be constitutionally mandated.[77] While *Feist* was ostensibly anchored in a number of important precedents, including *Trade-Mark Cases*,[78] and *Burrow-Giles Lithographic Co. v Sarony*,[79] there had been a long-standing split among the Circuits and only the Second, Fifth, Ninth and Eleventh Circuits had openly espoused a notion of originality based on 'creative selection'.[80]

---

73 *Recasting Report*, *supra* note 61, at 38.

74 *Feist*, *supra* note 5.

75 *Feist*, *ibid.* at 346.

76 U.S. Const. Art. 1, s. 8 cl. 8.

77 Whether this limits the powers of Congress or whether Congress could invoke the Commerce Clause to legislate to protect productions that do not result from even a modicum of creativity is beyond the scope of this chapter. However, the question is relevant both for sound recordings (protected as works under US copyright law unlike other countries where they are protected under a separate, 'neighboring' right) and the recent discussions about databases (see Gervais, Daniel (2007), 'The Protection of Databases', 82:3 *Chicago-Kent Law Review* 1101).

78 100 U.S. 82, 25 L.Ed. 550 (1879).

79 111 U.S. 53, 4 S.Ct. 279, 28 L.Ed. 349 (1884).

80 See Lea Meade, Tracy (1994), 'Ex-Post *Feist*: Applications of a Landmark Copyright Decision', 2 *J. Intell. Prop. L.*. 245.

2.3 Originality in Canada: CCH's Exercise of Skill and Judgment

Canada offers a particularly useful perspective for comparative originality studies, as Canada's *Copyright Act* is a hybrid that draws on both the common law and civil law traditions, and at various times and for various types of works it has drawn on both the United Kingdom's industriousness standard and the US *Feist* standard. We also consider the impact that the *CCH* decision may have on other jurisdictions. In 2008, the *New York Times* ran an article[81] on the waning influence of the US Supreme Court and observed that the Supreme Court of Canada is widely cited by other foreign courts now:

> Frederick Schauer, a law professor at the University of Virginia, wrote in a 2000 essay that the Canadian Supreme Court had been particularly influential because 'Canada, unlike the United States, is seen as reflecting an emerging international consensus rather than existing as an outlier'.
>
> In New Zealand, for instance, Canadian decisions were cited far more often than those of any other nation from 1990 to 2006 in civil rights cases, according to a recent study in the *Otago Law Review* in Dunedin, New Zealand.
>
> 'As Canada's judges are, by most accounts, the most judicially activist in the common-law world – the most willing to second-guess the decisions of the elected legislatures – reliance on Canadian precedents will worry some and delight others,' the study's authors wrote.
>
> American precedents were cited about half as often as Canadian ones. 'It is surprising', the authors wrote, 'that American cases are not cited more often, since the United States Bill of Rights precedents can be found on just about any rights issue that comes up'.

This may be prescient for copyright law as well. In a judgment of the India Supreme Court and in a recent oral argument before the Australian High Court,[82] Canada's Supreme Court decision in *CCH* was cited as a dominant precedent, together with *Feist*.

Canada's *Copyright Act* expressly provides that copyright shall subsist in every original work, though there is no statutory definition of 'originality'.[83] In 2004, the Supreme Court of Canada introduced Canada's current originality standard that the work must originate from the author, that is 'be more than a mere copy', and 'must be the product of an author's exercise of skill and judgment' that 'must not be so trivial that it could be characterized as a purely

---

[81] Liptak, Adam (2008), 'US Court is Now Guiding Fewer Nations', 17 September 2008, *New York Times,* <http://www.nytimes.com/2008/09/18/us/18legal.html?pagewanted=all>.

[82] *Eastern Book Company v Modak*, *infra* note 118; *IceTV Pty Limited & Anor v Nine Network Australia Pty Limited,* [2008] HCATrans 356 (transcript, 16 October 2008).

[83] Copyright Act, ss. 2, 5.

mechanical exercise'.[84] Under *CCH*'s 'exercise of skill and judgment' standard, the Court defined *skill* as 'the use of one's knowledge, developed aptitude or practised ability in producing the work', and *judgment* as 'the use of one's capacity for discernment or ability to form an opinion or evaluation by comparing different possible options in producing the work'. As the Court explained, an exercise of skill and judgment will 'necessarily involve intellectual effort'.[85]

Previous to *CCH*, as the Supreme Court of Canada acknowledged, there were effectively two standards for minimal originality thresholds that were being applied by Canadian courts. On one end there was a low standard of sweat of the brow or industriousness, derived from the United Kingdom decision in *University of London Press*, and usually characterized as 'skill, judgment or labour', which required that a work 'originate from' the author in the sense of not having been copied. On the other end, the higher standard reflected the *Feist* test of a modicum of creativity. As in many other jurisdictions, the case that brought the debate over the appropriate copyright originality standard to a head in Canada involved telephone directories. In *Tele-Direct*, the Federal Court of Appeal approvingly cited *Feist*'s creativity requirement and, ruling that 'skill, judgment or labour' is 'conjunctive', declined copyright in the arrangement of data in a yellow pages directory.[86] In the wake of the Federal Court of Appeal's decision, *Tele-Direct* was criticized as straying too far from the traditional United Kingdom standard and too close to the US *Feist* standard.[87] Some suggested the higher originality standard applied only to compilations, with the Federal Court's own Trial Division putting forth that view.[88] After *Tele-Direct* and before the Supreme Court of Canada introduced Canada's current originality standard in 2004, the two originality standards coexisted, with the high standard thought to be limited to factual compilations,

---

84 *CCH*, *supra* note 6, at paras 15–16. The reference to not being mechanical presumably picks up on language from *Feist* that the 'selection and arrangement of facts cannot be so mechanical or routine as to require no creativity whatsoever'. 499 U.S. at 362.

85 *CCH*, *ibid.* at para. 15.

86 *Tele-Direct Publications Inc v American Business Information*, (1997), 76 C.P.R. (3d) 296 (Fed Ct App, 1997), per Décary JA ('It is true that in many of the cases we have been referred to, the expression "skill, judgment *or* labour" has been used to describe the test to be met by a compilation in order to qualify as original and, therefore, to be worthy of copyright protection. It seems to me, however, that whenever "or" was used instead of "and", it was in a conjunctive rather than in a disjunctive way.').

87 Australia's Federal Court of Appeal, for example, declined to follow *Tele-Direct*'s shift to *Feist*: *Desktop Marketing Systems Pty Ltd v Telstra Corp.*, [2002] FCAFC 112.

88 *Hager v ECW Press* (Fed Ct Trial Div, 1998); *Neudorf v Nettwerk Productions*, [2000] B.C.J. No. 1705, 8 C.P.R. (4th) 154, para. 19.

while the traditional labour-based standard adopted from the United Kingdom continued to apply to other works. The confusion was exacerbated by the fact that courts evaluating the copyright of utilitarian or fact-based works in Canada (as in other jurisdictions that adopted the Anglo-standard) used various formulations for the originality standard: 'skill, judgment or labour',[89] 'industry, skill or judgment',[90] 'work, skill, judgment and knowledge',[91] 'industriousness, sweat of the brow',[92] and 'independent research and labour'.[93] The language of the originality standard generally converged around 'skill, judgment or labour', but there were frequent deviations in wording, and discrepancies even within those courts applying a sweat-of-the-brow standard as to whether it was a conjunctive 'and' requiring both skill and labour or a disjunctive 'or' phrasing that would allow the industrious collection of information to qualify for originality.[94]

The Canadian Supreme Court presented *CCH* as a Goldilocks solution, a 'workable yet fair standard' between the 'too low' sweat of the brow standard, which 'shifts the balance…too far in favour of the owner's rights, and fails to allow copyright to protect the public's interest in maximizing the production and dissemination of intellectual works', and the 'too high' 'creativity standard' of *Feist*, which, the Court contended 'implies that something must be novel or non-obvious – concepts more properly associated with patent law than copyright law', even though Justice O'Connor in *Feist* had stated that originality did not require novelty.[95] Although 'intellectual creation' was not explicitly analyzed as part of the hierarchy of originality standards, and only *Feist* and sweat of the brow were contrasted, the Court did suggest that the common law industriousness standard departed from the idea of intellectual creation that was implicit in Berne and that the new standard was more congenial with the civilian jurisdictions' requirement that the author must contribute something intellectual to the work. The Court interestingly interprets that 'something intellectual' as 'namely skill and judgment'; further, by incorpo-

---

89 *Slumber-Magic Adjustable Bed v Sleep-King Adjustable Bed* (1984), 3 C.P.R. (3d) 81 (B.C.S.C.), per McLachlin J (now CJC).

90 *Ibid.*

91 *British Columbia Jockey Club v Standen* (1985), 8 C.P.R. (3d) 283 (B.C.C.A.).

92 *U & R Tax Services Ltd v H & R Block Canada Inc.* (1995), 97 F.T.R. 259, 62 C.P.R. (3d) 257 (Fed. Ct. Trial Div.).

93 *Ibid.*

94 On utilitarian works and the pre-*CCH* originality threshold in Canada, see Scassa, Teresa (2004), 'Originality and Utilitarian Works: The Uneasy Relationship between Copyright Law and Unfair Competition', 1:1&2 *University of Ottawa Law & Technology Journal* 51.

95 *CCH*, *supra* note 6, paras. 17, 24; *Feist*, *supra* note 5, 499 U.S. at 346.

rating the notion of 'comparing different possible options' in the definition of judgment, the concept aligns with the European test of personal choices. Thus, while widening the gap between the new standard of an 'exercise of skill and judgment' and industriousness (or 'skill and labour') the Court effectively aligns the new standard with the civil law 'intellectual contribution'. By treating creativity as a high threshold, one closer to the colloquial sense of creativity than to how it was described in *Feist* or how it has since been applied by the US courts, the Court situates creativity as not only conceptually distinct from intellectual contribution but seemingly higher than intellectual contribution, given that the Court stated it would not 'go as far' as requiring a minimal degree of creativity and yet saw analogies between intellectual contribution and skill and judgment.[96] Whether this *CCH* standard is indeed a middle standard and whether it is situated between 'two extremes' is discussed in Part 4 of this chapter.

Applying the newly crafted standard, the full court unanimously ruled that the headnotes for judicial cases are original, '[e]ven if the summary often contains the same language as the original judicial reasons' because the 'act of choosing which portions to extract and how to arrange them in the summary requires an exercise of skill and judgment'.[97] Likewise, topical indexes were original because knowing which headings to include and distilling the decision down to a pithy summary indicated skill and judgment; conversely, published judicial reasons without editorial additions and which added only basic information and corrected minor grammatical errors were trivial and mechanical changes that did not satisfy originality. It is important to note that, similarly to the civil law standard of personal intellectual creation, the idea of selection and choices played a prominent role in the Court's application of the standard.[98]

The Court associated *CCH*'s originality standard with the explicit public interest statement of copyright purpose that was first elaborated in *Théberge v Galerie d'Art du Petit Champlain*.[99]

---

96 *CCH*, *supra* note 6, at paras. 19–20, 22.

97 *CCH*, *supra* note 6, at para. 31.

98 *CCH*, *supra* note 6, on the case summary: 'act of choosing which portions to extract and how to arrange them in the summary requires an exercise of skill and judgment' (para. 31); on the headnotes: 'authors must select specific elements of the decision and can arrange them in numerous different ways. Making these decisions requires the exercise of skill and judgment… They must also use their capacity for discernment to decide which parts of the judgment warrant inclusion in the headnotes.' (para. 30); on the topical index: 'the author of the index had to make an initial decision as to which cases were authorities' (para. 32).

99 2002 SCC 34.

> [T]he purpose of copyright law was to balance the public interest in promoting the encouragement and dissemination of works of the arts and intellect and obtaining a just reward for the creator. When courts adopt a standard of originality requiring only that something be more than a mere copy or that someone simply show industriousness to ground copyright in a work, they tip the scale in favour of the author's or creator's rights, at the loss of society's interest in maintaining a robust public domain that could help foster future creative innovation. ... By way of contrast, when an author must exercise skill and judgment to ground originality in a work, there is a safeguard against the author being overcompensated for his or her work. This helps ensure that there is room for the public domain to flourish as others are able to produce new works by building on the ideas and information contained in the works of others.[100]

Though the Court had articulated that purpose statement only in 2002, it was quickly entrenched in the high court's jurisprudence. By *Robertson* in 2006, the judgment could iterate that 'This Court has repeatedly held [that is, since 2002] that the overarching purposes of the *Copyright Act* are twofold: promoting the public interest in the encouragement and dissemination of artistic and intellectual works, and justly rewarding the creator of the work.'[101]

2.4 Originality in Common Law Jurisdictions: Skill and Labour and Its Development

England's traditional standard for originality was a Lockean-derived industriousness standard, in which the work must originate from the author and be the product of more than minimal skill and labour. The standard was developed in *University of London Press*, *Walter v Lane*, and *Ladbroke*.[102] This standard has been adopted by Ireland, Australia,[103] New Zealand,[104] Singapore,[105] and

---

100 *CCH, supra* note 6, at para. 23.

101 *Robertson v Thomson Corp.* [2006] 2 S.C.R. 363, 2006 SCC 43, para. 69, citing *Théberge, supra* note 99, at para. 30; *CCH, supra* note 6, at para. 23; and *Society of Composers, Authors and Music Publishers of Canada* ('*SOCAN*') 2004 SCC 45 at para. 40.

102 *University of London Press v University Tutorial Press* [1916] 2 Ch 60, (1916), 86 LJ Ch 107; *Walter v Lane* [1900] AC 539; *Ladbroke (Football) Ltd v William Hill (Football) Ltd* [1964] 1 WLR 273, 287 (HL).

103 *Sands McDougall Pty Ltd v Robinson*, [1917] HCA 14; *Desktop, supra* note 87.

104 *Wham-O Manufacturing Co v Lincoln Industries Ltd*, [1984] 1 NZLR 641, 664; *Henkel KgaA v Holdfast* [2006] NZSC 102 (30 November 2006), <http://www.worldlii.org//cgi-bin/disp.pl/nz/cases/NZSC/2006/102.html?query=Copyright%20and%20originality%20and%20New%20Zealand>, para. 37.

105 See Leong, Susanna H.S. (2002), 'Legal Protection of Factual Compilations and Databases: Re-thinking the Copyright Protection Model in Singapore', 5 *J. World Intell. Prop.* 1047, 1048.

South Africa.[106] Factual compilations and other functional works, however, remain a source of tension when courts apply the industriousness standard. Though most of the Commonwealth jurisdictions remain adherents to the industriousness standard, many cases reveal judicial concerns that skill and labour needs to be applied vigilantly to factual compilations and derivative works to ensure that there is a sufficient contribution by the author. It has proven difficult for courts to, on the one hand, avoid overly expansive copyright when industriousness is applied and, on the other hand, articulate a strict industriousness threshold without incorporating terms associated with other originality standards, such as creativity or personality.

This concern has led some jurisdictions that had used skill and labour to break from that tradition: Canada, as described, has recently replaced that standard with a purportedly higher standard of the exercise of skill and judgment, and India has recently moved away from industriousness to Canada's standard, but with interesting inflections of *Feist*'s minimal creativity. In both instances the supreme courts changed the standard when considering editorial enhancements to law judgments.

In the United Kingdom, there is no statutory definition of originality in the Copyright Designs and Patents Act 1988, except for databases. Section 3A, which was added to transpose the EU's Database Directive into law, provides that databases are original if the selection or arrangement constitutes the author's own intellectual creation.[107] For works that fall outside the scope of EU copyright harmonization, United Kingdom courts continue to apply the skill, labour and judgment standard for originality. Interestingly, the United Kingdom simply incorporated the words of the Database Directive in the copyright statute without an indication of the impact on the definition of originality in other contexts.

An *obiter* statement by Lord Oliver in *Interlego v Tyco* had questioned whether *Walter v Lane*'s skill and labour standard should be applied to copies, averring that '[s]kill, labour or judgment merely in the process of copying

---

106 *University of London Press*, *supra* note 102; *U & R Tax Services*, *supra* note 92.

107 Copyright, Designs And Patents Act 1988, s. 3A, as amended by the Copyright (Databases), Regulations, 18/12/1997, s. 6. Section 3A(2) reads as follows: 'For the purposes of this Part a literary work consisting of a database is original if, and only if, by reason of the selection or arrangement of the contents of the database the database constitutes the author's own intellectual creation.' See also *Report from the Commission to the Council, the European Parliament and the Economic and Social Committee on the implementation and effects of Directive 91/250/EEC on the legal protection of computer programs*, <http://eur-lex.europa.eu/LexUriServ/site/en/com/2000/com2000_0199en01.pdf>.

cannot confer originality'.[108] In *Hyperion Records v Sawkins*, the Court of Appeal considered that question of how the originality of a work intended to be a copy of another should be evaluated, in this case modern performing editions of a late seventeenth-century composer's musical scores that were intended to be as close as possible to the composer's, with the court ruling they did qualify as original musical works.[109] In Lord Jacob's view, the question of originality is one of degree: 'how much skill, labour and judgment in the making of the copy is that of the creator of the copy'. Sawkins 'recreated Lalande's work using a considerable amount of personal judgment. His re-creative work was such as to create something really new using his own original (not merely copied) work'.[110] As with other jurisdictions using the traditional Anglo-standard and facing works on the periphery of originality, such as factual compilations and copies of pre-existing works, skill and labour are shored up by recourse to personality or creativity ('re-creative work' and 'create something really new'). Significantly, the same author was also successful in protecting other performing editions of Lalande's music in litigation before the French courts under the personality test for originality.[111]

In Australia, the principles of originality for compilations are set out in *Desktop Publishing*, a 'whole of universe' telephone directory case in which the Full Court of the Federal Court of Australia endorsed skill and labour and rejected *Feist*:

> [A] compilation will ordinarily be an original literary work for copyright purposes if the compiler has exercised skill, judgment or knowledge in selecting the material for inclusion in the compilation ... or in presenting or arranging the material ... In addition, ... if the compiler has undertaken substantial labour or incurred substantial expense in collecting the information recorded in the compilation.[112]
> [T]here is no principle that the labour and expense of collecting, verifying, recording and assembling (albeit routinely) data to be compiled are irrelevant to, or are incapable of themselves establishing, origination, and therefore originality ...[113]

In 2007, the Federal Court of Australia upheld copyright under the industriousness standard for a factual compilation produced by a television network of its weekly television schedule. The weekly schedules were computer generated from a master programming grid that was entered into a

---

108 *Interlego v Tyco* [1988] RPC 343, at p. 371.

109 *Hyperion Records Ltd v Sawkins* [2005] EWCA Civ 565 (CA), <http://www.bailii.org/cgi-bin/markup.cgi?doc=/ew/cases/EWCA/Civ/2005/565.html>, para. 16.

110 *Ibid.*, at para 86.

111 *Supra* note 15.

112 *Desktop*, *supra* note 87, at para. 409, per Sackville J.

113 *Desktop*, *supra* note 87, at para. 160, per Lindgren J.

computer database. Consistent with *Ladbroke*, the court considered not only the skill and labour of drafting the synopses and selecting and arranging the additional program information but also the ' "antecedent" or "preparatory" skill and labour' of compiling the information, which in this case consisted of the network selecting and arranging television programs to attract viewers to programs in different timeslots and meet competitors' programming.[114] In oral arguments of this case on appeal, the High Court seemed prepared to reconsider those precedents and *CCH* was invoked as a possible benchmark for Australia.[115]

In South Africa, the Supreme Court of Appeal also rejected *Feist*'s standard of minimal creativity and applied the United Kingdom substantial skill, judgment and labour standard to a computer program.[116]

In New Zealand, the Court of Appeal recently addressed a compilation of financial survey data for industry benchmarking. Although the court endorsed the United Kingdom 'sufficient degree of labour, skill, and judgment' standard, in explaining how the standard was satisfied it stressed the survey's 'number of unusual or unique features which clearly result from the expenditure of significant creative effort and skill on the appellant's part'.[117] That is, the unusual and unique features and creative effort were used to measure

---

114 *Nine Network Australia Pty Ltd v IceTV Pty Ltd*, [2007] FCA 1172, <http://www.austlii.edu.au/cgi-bin/sinodisp/au/cases/cth/federal_ct/2007/1172.html?query=FCAFC%202002%20112%20or%202002%20FCAFC%20112>, para. 46; *Ladbroke*, *supra* note 102, at 287–288; *Desktop*, *supra* note 87 ('Despite these qualifications, the course of authority in the United Kingdom and Australia recognises that originality in a factual compilation may lie in the labour and expense involved in collecting the information recorded in the work, as distinct from the "creative" exercise of skill or judgment, or the application of intellectual effort. ... Moreover, much-cited cases ... have rejected the view that, in assessing the originality of a compilation, only skill, judgment or labour associated with the presentation of the compilation (as distinct from skill, judgment or labour at an earlier stage) can be taken into account. ... In assessing whether a factual compilation is an original work, the labour or expense required to collect the information can be taken into account regardless of whether the labour or expense was directly related to the preparation or presentation of the compilation in material form, provided it was for the purpose of producing the compilations ...' paras. 407–409, per Sackville J.)

115 See *supra* note 82.

116 *Haupt t/a Softcopy v Brewers Marketing Intelligence (Pty) Ltd and Others*, [2006] ZASCA 40; 2006 (4) SA 458 (SCA) (29 March 2006), <http://www.saflii.org//cgi-bin/disp.pl/za/cases/ZASCA/2006/40.html?query=copyright%20and%20originality>, para. 35.

117 *University of Waikato v Benchmarking Services Ltd & Anor*, [2004] NZCA 90 (11 June 2004), <http://www.worldlii.org//cgi-bin/disp.pl/nz/cases/NZCA/2004/90.html?query=Copyright%20and%20originality%20and%20New%20Zealand>, paras. 27, 36, 42.

whether the originality standard of sufficient labour, skill and judgment had been satisfied.

Like the Supreme Court of Canada, the Supreme Court of India recently seemed to move away from the skill and labour standard in a case involving the copyright of a compilation of court decisions. In *Eastern Book Company v Modak*, after a lengthy review of copyright originality cases, including English and Indian cases applying skill and labour, *Feist*, and *CCH*, the Court concluded that the:

> principle laid down by the Canadian Court [in CCH] would be applicable in copyright of [a compilation of] … the judgments of the courts which are in the public domain [by statutory provision]. To claim copyright in a compilation, the author must produce the material with exercise of his skill and judgment which may not be creativity in the sense that it is novel or non-obvious, but at the same time it is not a product of merely labour and capital. The derivative work produced by the author must have some distinguishable features and flavour to raw text of the judgments delivered by the court. The trivial variation or inputs put in the judgment would not satisfy the test of copyright of an author.[118]

Under this standard, the publisher's additions of headnotes, editorial notes, and footnotes; designations for whether a judgment was concurring or dissenting; and even changes to the paragraphing to correspond to divisions in the judgment's legal arguments were all original, while minor editorial enhancements to the raw judgments, such as verifying case citations and quotations were not. Interestingly, though it explicitly adopted Canada's *CCH* standard, which is positioned between the creativity and industriousness standards, India's Supreme Court nonetheless re-engages *Feist* by also requiring a minimal degree of creativity. This dual allegiance to *CCH* and *Feist* seems to follow from its requirement that the derivative work have 'some distinguishable features and flavour', by which the court seeks a sign of individuality, and hence creativity.

> No doubt the appellants have collected the material and improved the readability of the judgment by putting inputs in the original text of the judgment by considerable labour and arranged it in their own style, but that does not give the flavour of minimum requirement of creativity. The exercise of the skill and judgment required to produce the work is trivial and is on account of the labour and the capital invested and could be characterized as purely a work which has been brought about by putting some amount of labour by the appellants. … To support copyright, there must be some substantive variation and not merely a trivial variation, not the vari-

---

118 *Eastern Book Company v Modak*, (Supreme Court of India, December 2007), available at: <http://judis.nic.in/>, para. 38.

> ation of the type where limited ways/unique of expression available and an author selects one of them which can be said to be a garden variety. Novelty or invention or innovative idea is not the requirement for protection of copyright but it does require minimal degree of creativity. In our view, the aforesaid inputs put by the appellants in the copy-edited judgments do not touch the standard of creativity required for the copyright.[119]

In applying this blended standard to the paragraphing changes, India's Supreme Court upheld their originality. The paragraphing changes required the 'exercise of the brain work…careful consideration, discernment and choice' and thus 'can be called the work of an author…' These inputs 'require knowledge, sound judgment and legal skill' and 'therefore ha[ve] a flavor of minimum amount of creativity'.[120]

3. ORIGINALITY IN INTERNATIONAL COPYRIGHT TREATIES

The notion of originality was present in the minds of the majority of the drafters of the Berne Convention. A vast majority of those countries that negotiated the Berne Convention belong to the Roman/Civil law tradition of authors' rights. The United States and the United Kingdom, which represented the more economic/utilitarian approach generally attributed to the common law tradition, were also present. However, even in the United States, debates about the role of the author under state common law persisted (this was before the 1909 Act and state common law protection remained, especially for unpublished works[121]). In addition, the US representative, the US Consul at the Swiss Embassy in Berne, was at a disadvantage because he did not attend the first of the three Berne Conferences (1884) at which the groundwork for the future Convention was laid. The initial draft of the Convention was prepared by the Paris-based International Literary Association.[122] The president of the

---

119 *Eastern Book*, *ibid.*, para. 40.

120 *Ibid.*, para. 41.

121 Arnold and Porter *Legislative History*: P.L. 94-553, Copyright Law Revision Studies 29–31 (1961), A&P COPYREV76 Comm. Print 1961 (8J):

> In the United States the rule is now well established that an author or his assignee may have perpetual common law rights in his work unless he publishes it, whereupon the common law rights are terminated. ... Section 2 of title 17, U.S.C. (sec. 2, Act of 1909) provide[d] as follows: 'Nothing in this title shall be construed to annul or limit the right of the author or proprietor of an unpublished work, at common law or in equity, to prevent the copying, publication, or use of such unpublished work without his consent, and to obtain damages therefor.'

122 The predecessor of the modern-day International Literary and Artistic

Association, Louis Ulbach, was a member of the French delegation at the first two Conferences, at which most of the substantive work was done. This should demonstrate the direct impact that the Civil law/authors' rights notion of originality played in the elaboration of the Convention. This is confirmed by the text of Art. 1, which refers to authors, and the many references throughout both the original text and future revisions of the Convention[123] to authors and their economic and moral rights, and to the term being linked to authors' lifetime with no provision for 'corporate' authorship etc.[124]

That said, there is no direct definition of the concept of 'originality' in either the Berne Convention[125] or the TRIPS Agreement.[126] In fact, the requirement that a work be 'original' is not even mentioned. There are, however, several statements in records of diplomatic conferences and committees of experts meeting under the aegis of the World Intellectual Property Organization (WIPO) that confirm the requirement that originality be present, and that this is the only applicable criterion, to the exclusion, for example, of artistic merit or purpose.[127]

The term 'work' itself is only 'defined' officially by the list of categories of works in Art. 2 of the Berne Convention. However, a WIPO Committee of

---

Association (ALAI) which is still active in many countries. The first President of the Association was Victor Hugo, the well-known French author. The key role of the Association is described in the initial letter sent by the Swiss government (Federal Council) on 3 December 1883 to invited governments.

123 The last such revision being the Paris Act (1971).

124 Though specific provisions had to be made for anonymous and pseudonymous works. See Art. 7(3) of the Paris Act (1971).

125 Berne Convention, *supra* note 2.

126 TRIPS Agreement, *supra* note 3. Actually, very few national laws contain such a definition. We studied 93 national laws and found a specific definition of originality in only three national laws, namely Bulgaria, Burkina Faso and Malaysia. See Gervais, *supra* note 34, at 72–76. Indirectly, a definition is contained in the three European Union directives that require that a work be the result of the author's 'own intellectual creation'. See *supra* notes 55–62 and accompanying text; and *Bridgeman Art Library, Ltd. v Corel Corp.*, 36 F. Supp. 2d 191, 195 (S.D.N.Y. 1998).

127 The first statement on originality was made during the Revision Conference of the Berne Convention held at Rome from 7 May to 2 June 1928. The Acts of this conference were originally published only in French (*Actes de la Conférence réunie à Rome du 7 mai au 2 juin 1928* (Berne: Bureau de l'Union internationale pour la protection des oeuvres littéraires et artistiques, 1929)), but WIPO published an English translation of the records of all Berne revision conferences on the occasion of the centenary of the Berne Convention. See WIPO, 1886–1986: *Berne Convention Centenary: 1886–1986* (1986). In the General Report, rapporteur Edoardo Piola Caselli wrote: 'The protection enjoyed by other works of art should be reserved for cinematographic productions which meet the requirements of originality laid down in paragraph (2) [of Article 14]. In order to show clearly that the only requirement concerned here is that of the originality with which every work of the mind must be endowed ....' *Ibid.* at 174.

Experts concluded that this expression was synonymous with 'intellectual creation',[128] and that such creation should contain 'an original structure of ideas or impressions'.[129] The same committee also noted that originality 'was an integral part of the definition of the concept of "work".'[130]

In its memorandum for the meeting of the Committee of Experts, the International Bureau of WIPO explained:

> Although this is not stated explicitly in Article 2(1) [of the Berne Convention], the context in which the words 'work' and 'author' are used in the Convention – closely related to each other – indicates that only those productions are considered works which are intellectual creations (and, consequently, only those persons are considered authors whose intellectual creative activity brings such works into existence). This is the first basic element of the notion of literary and artistic works.

The records of various diplomatic conferences adopting and revising the Berne Convention reflect that the reason why Art. 2(1) of the Convention does not state explicitly that works are intellectual creations is that that element of the notion of works was considered to be evident.[131]

The General Report of the Berne Convention Revision Conference held in Brussels in 1948 specifically states: 'You have not considered it necessary to specify that those works constitute intellectual creations because ... if we are speaking of literary and artistic works, we are already using a term which means we are talking about personal creation or about an intellectual creation within the sphere of letters and the arts.'[132]

---

128 The concept of intellectual creation has been acknowledged as a synonym of work in several international meetings. See Gervais, *supra* note 34, at 45–49.

129 WIPO Committee of Experts on Model Provisions for Legislation in the Field of Copyright, First Session, document CE/MPC/I/3, of 3 March 1989, at 16. (The Committee Report also states, 'Originality [is] part of the definition of "work" and ... a reference to it should be included in Section 2(1) .... The idea of providing a definition of the concept of "work" was, however, opposed by a number of participants; it was felt that that question should rather be left to national legislation and/or to the courts.') *Ibid.*

130 *Ibid.* While international meetings of this nature are not normative in nature, their findings are relevant as doctrinal input and in certain cases may reflect an existing international custom (see Art. 38(1)(b) of the Statute of the International Court of Justice). The history of the Convention was also used extensively by a WTO dispute-settlement panel to interpret provisions of the Convention that were incorporated by reference into the TRIPS Agreement.

131 Draft Model Provisions for Legislation in the Field of Copyright. Memorandum prepared for the WIPO Committee of Experts on Model Provisions for Legislation in the Field of Copyright, document CE/MPC/I/2-III of 20 October 1988, at 10.

132 WIPO, *Berne Convention Centenary: 1886–1986* (1986) at 179.

The Berne Convention itself provides two important hints as to what constitutes an original work. Article 2, when discussing the protection of collections, states that '[c]ollections of literary or artistic works such as encyclopedias and anthologies which, by reason of the selection and arrangement of their contents, constitute intellectual creations shall be protected as such, without prejudice to the copyright in each of the works forming part of such collections'.[133] Again, selection and arrangement are essentially choices that must be creative in order to generate copyright protection; and a creation may be considered 'intellectual' if it fits that description.

The TRIPS Agreement only contains an *a contrario* definition, as it were. For the first time in an international agreement in this field a list of exclusions was agreed upon. In a provision which mirrors § 102(b) of the US Copyright Act, Art. 9(2) of TRIPS states, 'Copyright protection shall extend to expressions and not to ideas, procedures, methods of operation or mathematical concepts as such.' However, while this provision confirms the exclusion of ideas, it does not allow one to draw firm, detailed conclusions about originality, only that it must be 'expressed', that is, objectified so that it *can* be communicated to third parties if the author so wishes.

The WIPO Copyright Treaty (WCT)[134] is also relevant. The WCT, which entered into force on 6 March 2002 and has 67 member countries,[135] echoes Art. 2(5) of the Berne Convention. Article 5 of the WCT provides in part as follows: 'Compilations of data or other material, in any form, which by reason of the selection or arrangement of their contents *constitute intellectual creations* are protected *as such.*' Again this implies that intellectual creation is the applicable threshold, and we know that threshold is referred to as originality in most national legal systems. This recent international instrument thus confirms the link between (at least a modicum of) creativity and the fact that that creativity may be derived from choices such as selection and arrangement. Intellectual creation is, however, a standard that, like *Feist*'s modicum of creativity, is difficult to operationalize, especially in borderline cases such as factual or collective works. It may be that the *CCH* standard of a non-mechanical and non-trivial exercise of skill and judgment would work better as an implementation of the international norm. It certainly seems compatible with it. Put differently, while *Feist* and the creation-based standard is normatively anchored, the *CCH* standard may provide a better implementation in cases where the presence of creativity, as that term is generally understood at least, is not obvious. It is worth noting that the English text of the Convention uses

---

133 Berne Convention, *supra* note 2, Art. 2(5).

134 World Intellectual Property Organization Copyright Treaty, 20 December 1996, S. Treaty Doc. No. 105-17, 36 I.L.M. 65.

135 As of November 2008; see <www.wipo.int>.

the conjunctive phrasing 'selection and arrangement' while the WCT uses the disjunctive 'selection or arrangement'. However, the French text of the Convention, which governs in case of any discrepancy between linguistic versions,[136] uses the disjunctive 'or'.

4. ANALYSIS

As the discussion describes, originality standards are not harmonized internationally. Not only might there be different standards for different categories of works within a country (for example, computer programs, databases, and photographs may have a distinct standard from other works), but different countries might apply the same standard differently in practice (for example, Germany's more rigorous application of the personality test). In this part, we suggest some hypotheses that test the conventional wisdom about the distinctions between originality standards, the hierarchy of originality standards, the significance of the originality standards, and the possibility and desirability of harmonization.

4.1 Hypothesis One: Originality Standards are Constellations not Silos

Originality standards are conventionally presented as four silos of autonomous standards with little overlap and clear conceptual distinctions between jurisdictions. Indeed, the Supreme Court of Canada's characterization of its 'exercise of skill and judgment' standard as a 'workable and appropriate standard' positioned between the 'extremes' of the 'too low' sweat of the brow standard and the 'too high' creativity standard is axiomatic of this premise. Moreover, the lack of harmonization for the originality requirement, which has preserved these separate formulations of originality, underscores the distinctiveness of their objectives and application. However, originality standards are more properly understood as constellations, rather than silos, where the surface differences in wording mask similarities in both concepts and results.

There is a great deal of overlap in results when the different standards are applied to similar facts: ordinarily, a given work that qualifies as original under one standard will also meet the other tests: it will reflect an author's intellectual creation, have a modicum of creativity, show skill and judgment, and originate from the author. Although the wording of the standards might suggest that the results would frequently diverge – industriousness would seem on its face to be much more lenient than intellectual creation or

136 Berne Convention, *supra* note 2, Art. 37(1)(c).

creativity – the judicial application of the standards has narrowed the gap by insisting on a sufficient degree of skill and labour, on one end, and accepting a very low degree of creativity, on the other. As the US Supreme Court took pains to clarify with respect to *Feist*, 'the requisite level of creativity is extremely low; even a slight amount will suffice. The vast majority of works make the grade quite easily, as they possess some creative spark, "no matter how crude, humble or obvious" it might be'.[137] Across the jurisdictions, there are many commonalities that could be said of originality: originality does not require an original form of expression; originality does not require original ideas; originality does not require innovation or novelty; originality is irrespective of aesthetic quality or merit. What England and Wale's Court of Appeal stated recently could be said of any of these jurisdictions regardless of the originality standard that they apply: 'The policy of copyright protection and its limited scope explain why the threshold requirement of an "original" work has been interpreted as not imposing objective standards of novelty, usefulness, inventiveness, aesthetic merit, quality or value.'[138] Thus it is only in unusual contexts, notably utilitarian works, that the different formulations are potentially meaningful.

4.2 Hypothesis Two: Public Policy Through Infringement Analysis Rather Than Copyrightability

Although Canada purportedly increased its standard, relative to 'sweat of the brow', for the public policy of ensuring the appropriate copyright balance, increasingly the originality standard is not where that proper balancing is being guarded. Instead, the judicial trend is to find that the threshold for minimal original copyright has been met and to patrol the public policy objectives through infringement rather than copyrightability; that is, borderline cases are likely to be found original but the scope of protection is thin and another work will have to copy it almost exactly to infringe. As the Supreme Court of New Zealand recently stated, 'The threshold for originality is a low one and it can be material for other purposes how original the work is; that is, how much skill and labour has gone into its creation. In general terms the greater the originality, the wider will be the scope of the protection which copyright affords and vice versa.'[139]

---

137 *Feist, supra* note 5, para. 10, quoting 1 Nimmer, M. and D. Nimmer, *Copyright*, § 1.08[C][1].

138 *Hyperion Records Ltd v Sawkins* (EWCA), *supra* note 109.

139 *Henkel KgaA v Holdfast, supra* note 104, at para. 38.

4.3 Hypothesis Three: Originality Standards Can Deviate From the Assumed Hierarchy

Certainly the four families of originality standards do overlap in result most of the time and are operationally similar for most types of works. Despite the insistent positioning of *CCH* as a middle standard, the catchment for cases where there will be a functional difference between 'exercise of skill and judgment' and creativity (or personal intellectual creation) will be small. The originality standards will usually produce the same results, and this is not surprising because it is only on the margins (for example, compilations of facts, functional works) that the minimal originality threshold is an issue. That being understood as the norm, it is still the exceptions which are most appealing intellectually and best illustrate the nature of each standard. The relatively infrequent occasions in which the standards lead to different conclusions on originality are the most interesting and the most informative, as it is the exceptions on the periphery that prove the rule of the standards' stability and overlap at the center. Two points can be made about these relatively infrequent instances where the originality standards will lead to different results. First, the hierarchy of standards that we followed in Part 2 will usually hold true; that is, it is usually easier to satisfy sweat of the brow than minimal creativity or intellectual creation. But secondly, the hierarchy of standards that we followed in Part 2 is not a necessary result of the standards; that is, in some contexts it may be easier to satisfy minimal creativity than an exercise of skill and judgment.

In Part 2, we followed the traditional hierarchy by sequencing the standards from highest (most rigorous and most difficult to meet) to lowest with the European Union at the upper end of the spectrum, followed by the United States, Canada with its avowedly middle ground, and the United Kingdom industriousness standard at the low end of the spectrum. This hierarchy will hold true for most works where the standards have different results. For functional works (databases or software, for example), it is harder to satisfy standards that emphasize the author's personality than a standard that stresses industriousness.

Courts from outside the US, which may interpret creativity as a significant threshold, but worry (like the US Supreme Court) that sweat of the brow had proved to be too low, have sometimes concluded that a new originality standard needed to be fashioned. The Supreme Court of Canada's design for an originality standard specifically addressed the conundrum of how to protect works in which accuracy is paramount and where creativity in the sense of individual personality is an undesirable aspect (with judicial headnotes being the paradigmatic example). *CCH*'s new originality standard seems designed to set the standard at a threshold where works whose value resides in accuracy could satisfy originality without jeopardizing copyright's purposes (which might occur, for example, if the application of a too generous industriousness standard results in the contents of factual complications being included within copyright's protection). Canada's Supreme Court proceeds from the premise that headnotes are worth protecting but did not, in their view, have the requisite creativity to satisfy the *Feist* standard, and therefore required a new originality standard to be fashioned.

Other examples of types of works for which a *CCH* standard seems to be intended and where it indeed functions as a middle standard are 'whole-of-universe' directories in which the author has also used discretion and judgment to sequence the entries because simple principles of alpha- and chron-ordering are insufficient but where creativity is not desirable. This type of authorial contribution could meet a non-mechanical and non-trivial exercise of skill and judgment more easily than creativity. Similarly, the fraught problem of copies of art works (for example, photographs of paintings or of other photographs) would seem more likely to satisfy skill and judgment than creativity.[140]

In each of these instances, *CCH*'s standard would function as the Supreme Court of Canada envisioned it, as a middle way. Importantly, however, this hierarchy is not a required conclusion of the standards themselves. It is possible to imagine works that would be protected under *Feist* but not under *CCH*; in some cases, albeit rarely, *CCH* may be more rigorous than *Feist*, and especially so if the language of the standards is applied in their colloquial sense. Originality standards do not always fall neatly and consistently in the hierarchy that has been presumed. That is, *CCH* is not *necessarily* a middle standard; it may simply be easier to apply because it focuses on the nature of the choices made by the author, independently of the type of work concerned or indeed any preconceived notion of 'creativity'. *CCH* may thus solve the post-*Feist* quandary of operationalizing the 'modicum of creativity' test.

---

140 See, for example, *ATC Distribution Group Inc. v Whatever It Takes Transmission & Parts Inc.*, 402 F. 3d 700 (6th Cir. 2005) at 30–31:

> A reproduction of a work of art or photograph in a different medium is copyrightable in principle, if it involves 'great skill and originality',... or 'substantial variation, not merely a trivial variation such as might occur in the translation to a different medium'. ... Mere 'sweat of the brow', however, is insufficient to render a copy eligible for copyright protection ... [n]or is the mere demonstration of physical skill or special training. ...The illustrations in ATC's catalog fall far short of the 'substantial variation' required to justify copyright protection. The illustrations were intended to be as accurate as possible in reproducing the parts shown in the photographs on which they were based, a form of slavish copying that is the antithesis of originality.

See also the discussion of copies of pre-existing works in Ginsburg, Jane (2003), 'The Concept of Authorship in Comparative Copyright Law', (2003) 52 *Depaul Law Review* 1063, 1082–1085.

Canada's Supreme Court contended: 'While creative works will by definition be "original" and covered by copyright, creativity is not required to make a work "original".'[141] Yet, this may be *obiter* if the standard is taken to prevail over the interpretation since it does not seem to follow that *by definition* creativity, especially if the term is defined colloquially, will always be an exercise of skill and judgment. Consider, for example, a translator of poetry who has a bad command of the original poem's language, confusing homonyms and cognates for example, but is a gifted stylist: the new poem is an inaccurate and inept translation but an elegant lyrical poem in its own right.[142] An inept translation arguably is not an 'exercise of skill and judgment', though viewed as a poem it is creative, and indeed is more likely to be creative the worse the translation is and the greater the divergence from the first poem. Here *CCH* is arguably operatively higher than *Feist*.

This points to a question that was not addressed by Canada's Supreme Court: an exercise of skill and judgment with respect to *what*? Although the US courts resist making authorial intention a relevant criterion, for Canada's courts it may prove to be difficult to evaluate skill and judgment without considering the author's intention as to the outcome.[143] How should the author who intends a poem to be a translation and not an homage and who fails at the former but succeeds at the latter, be judged with respect to originality? Is 'skill and judgment' to be evaluated according to whether it is *intended* by the author to be a poetic homage or a translation, according to the objective *result* as a translation (or, conversely, as a poem), or considering only the category of the *work* (for example, is it an original literary work)? Given that skill and judgment were defined in *CCH* with reference to knowledge, aptitude, ability, and discernment, inaccuracies would seem to obviate a finding of skill and judgment if the value of the work was primarily with respect to its accuracy but may not be fatal where the value of a work is aesthetic.

Works of 'accidental authorship' – a myopic Mr Magoo who inadvertently paints a masterpiece, for example – also could be anticipated to meet a colloquially defined creativity standard more readily than a skill and judgment standard.[144]

---

141 *CCH*, *supra* note 6, at para. 25.

142 Ezra Pound's translations of Sextus Propertius are an excellent example of this hypothetical. See Judge, Elizabeth F. 'Make It Pound: Translation, Professionalism, and the Right to Propertian Discourse in "Homage to Sextus Propertius",' (Spring 2004) 33:1 *Paideuma* 127–163.

143 On the role of authorial intention, see Nimmer, David (2001), 'Copyright in the Dead Sea Scrolls: Authorship and Originality', 38:1 *Houston Law Review* 1.

144 See *Bell v Catalda*, 191 F. 2d 99, 104–105 (2d Cir. 1951): 'There is evidence that [the mezzotints] were not intended to, and did not, imitate the paintings they reproduced. But even if their substantial departures from the paintings were inadvertent, the

5. CONCLUSION

Feist was certainly a major step forward in forging the normative foundations of the modern notion of originality in copyright law. It sent an unmistakable message: pure labour, or sweat of the brow, does not deserve protection. The social pact requires more, or something else. While the policy underpinnings of *Feist* seemed fairly clear, its definition of originality as being the result of a modicum of creativity posed two problems. One is quantitative in nature: what is a 'modicum'; the other is qualitative: how does one decide what is 'creative'? Courts around the world, many of which found the normative appeal of rejecting copyright protection of pure sweat of the brow productions compelling, have since tried to operationalize the notion of originality. In this chapter, we suggested that the Canadian Supreme Court in *CCH* probably comes the closest to a truly workable standard, one which eschews the colloquial notion of creativity and focuses instead on choices made by the author in the process of creating a new work, and insists that those choices be neither trivial nor mechanical. Other courts could thus follow the example of the *CCH* standard, which prompts courts to look for evidence of a more than minimal number of such choices, to solve both the qualitative and quantitative conundrums posed by *Feist*.

---

copyrights would be valid. A copyist's bad eyesight or defective musculature, or a shock caused by a clap of thunder, may yield sufficiently distinguishable variations. Having hit upon such a variation unintentionally, the "author" may adopt it as his and copyright it' [footnotes omitted].

PART II

The fact: a contested concept

4. Two fallacies about copyrighting factual compilations

Michael Steven Green*

Now let us also take for scrutiny
The homeomeria of Anaxagoras,
So called by Greeks, for which our pauper-speech
Yieldeth no name in the Italian tongue,
Although the thing itself is not o'erhard
For explanation. First, then, when he speaks
Of this homeomeria of things, he thinks
Bones to be sprung from littlest bones minute,
And from minute and littlest flesh all flesh,
And blood created out of drops of blood,
Conceiving gold compact of grains of gold,
And earth concreted out of bits of earth,
Fire made of fires, and water out of waters,
Feigning the like with all the rest of stuff.[1]

The current law on the protection of factual compilations depends upon two fallacies. When these fallacies are recognized and overcome, there is no reason to refuse protection to the factual content of a compilation (as opposed to the compilation's selection and arrangement of facts). Statutory solutions, such as the European Union's 1996 Database Directive[2] and recent proposals in Congress,[3] are unnecessary.

The first fallacy, exemplified in Justice O'Connor opinion in *Feist Publications, Inc. v Rural Telephone Service Co.*, is that facts cannot be copy-

* Thanks to Laura Heymann and to the participants in the 'Feist, Facts, and Functions' symposium at George Washington University Law School for helpful comments on this chapter.

1 Titus Lucretius Carus, *Of the Nature of Things* 31–31 (William Ellery Leonard trans., 1916) (1st Century B.C.).

2 Council Directive 96/9 on the Legal Protection of Databases, art. 7, O.J. (L 77) 20, 25–26.

3 Database and Collections of Information Misappropriations Act, H.R. 3261, 108th Cong. (2003); Collections of Information Antipiracy Act, H.R. 2652, 105th Cong. (1997); Database Investment and Intellectual Property Antipiracy Act of 1996, H.R. 3531, 104th Cong. (1996).

righted because they are not independently created.[4] In the Section I of this chapter, I will argue that once we achieve clarity about what facts are (at least for copyright purposes), O'Connor's argument fails. Facts can be independently created.

That O'Connor's opinion suffers from the first fallacy has largely been recognized in the literature. But the fallacy of division, which can also be found in O'Conner's opinion in *Feist*, has not. This fallacy occurs when one wrongly takes what is true of a whole to be true of all or some of its constituents. (Its converse is the fallacy of composition, which occurs when one wrongly takes what is true of constituents to be true of the whole.) In the passage quoted at the beginning of this chapter, Lucretius accuses the ancient Greek philosopher (and fellow atomist) Anaxagoras of the fallacy of division. A red object, Anaxagoras wrongly assumes, must be composed of atoms that are themselves red; a soft object of atoms that are themselves soft.

Taking what is true of the whole to be true of its parts is not *always* a fallacy. For example, the fact that something takes up space is a reason to think that its parts do as well. In other words, some properties are distributive – that something has the property entails that all or some of its parts have it as well. But not all properties are distributive. Some are emergent.

Consciousness[5] and life,[6] it is often argued, are emergent properties. That we are conscious does not mean that our cells are conscious. That we are alive does not mean that the molecules out of which we are composed are alive. Conversely, one has not shown that we are not conscious or not alive by pointing out that our cells are not conscious or that our molecules are not alive.

Copyrightability, I will argue, is an emergent property. This has been accepted, at least implicitly, in most areas of copyright law. No one thinks that because a novel is copyrightable its individual constituents must be as well. It is recognized that a copyrightable work can emerge from uncopyrightable elements.

Unfortunately, this lesson is forgotten concerning factual compilations. To be sure, courts largely accept that a factual compilation can be copyrightable even though the individual facts out of which it is composed are unprotected.[7]

---

4 *Feist Publications v Rural Tel. Serv. Co.*, 499 U.S. 340, 347–48 (1991).

5 O'Connor, Timothy, 'Emergent Properties', 31 *Am. Phil. Q.* 91 (1994).

6 John Stuart Mill, *A System of Logic*, bk. III, ch. vi., § 1 (8th edn, 1874).

7 Even here, some courts are uncomfortable: '[T]he law of copyrights defies the laws of logic ... since it "affords to the summation of one hundred or one million [individual facts and their unadorned expression] a significant measure of protection" while affording none to the facts themselves.' *Fin. Info., Inc. v Moody's Investors Serv., Inc.*, 751 F.2d 501, 505 (2d Cir. 1984) (quoting Denicola, Robert C., 'Copyright in Collections of Facts: A Theory for the Protection of Nonfiction Literary Works' (1981), 81 *Colum. L. Rev.* 516, 527). The idea that it somehow defies the *laws of logic* that a property of the whole should not be a property of its parts is the fallacy of division.

But the fallacy remains, for they insist upon identifying another component that is copyrightable. Since individual facts cannot be this component, it must be, as Justice O'Connor argued in *Feist*, the compilation's selection and arrangement of facts.[8]

In Section II, I will argue that the *Feist* approach is incoherent, for the copyrightability of a selection and arrangement of a compilation is itself an emergent property. Under the pressure of analysis, a selection and arrangement will dissolve into components – the submethods out of which the selection and arrangement as a whole is composed. Not only will these submethods be uncopyrightable, so will the methods by means of which these submethods are selected and arranged to create an aggregate selection and arrangement. At a sufficiently fine-grained level of analysis, *no* copyrightable component of a selection and arrangement will be identifiable. As a result, the *Feist* approach threatens to deny copyrightability to *all* selections and arrangements and thus to all compilations.

The selection and arrangement of a compilation can be copyrightable only if one sets aside the fallacy of division and looks at the selection and arrangement in the aggregate to determine its copyrightability. But once one has set aside the fallacy of division with respect to a compilation's selection and arrangement, there is no reason not to do the same with respect to its factual content.

My collective fact approach is in keeping with the way that fictional works are treated under copyright law. Although the individual elements out of which a novel's plot, scenes, and characters are composed are unprotected, no one would say that the copyrightable part of a novel is its selection and arrangement of these elements. One determines copyrightability by looking to the collective content of the novel itself – its plot, scenes, and characters. A factual compilation should also be assessed on the basis of whether its collective factual content is copyrightable. I will end the chapter with a brief roadmap for how such a determination should proceed.

I. FACTS CAN BE INDEPENDENTLY CREATED

Imagine that at 2:00 p.m. on 28 September 2007, the one cloud in the sky above Washington, DC looked something like this:

---

8 *Feist*, 499 U.S. at 347–48. See also *Harper & Row Publishers, Inc. v Nation Enters.*, 471 U.S. 539, 556 (1985); 1 Nimmer, Melville B. and Nimmer, David (2006), *Nimmer on Copyright* §§ 2.11[D], 3.03. O'Connor actually spoke of selection, coordination or arrangement. 499 U.S. at 357. For simplicity's sake, I set aside coordination.

Figure 4.1

This cloud is a piece of *reality* that exists in the world independently of human beings and their representations of it.

Let's say that I am the first to see the cloud. I notice that it looks like a poorly drawn dog. In arriving at this belief, I create certain content about the cloud. I can communicate this content in a number of sentences:

> *Sentence 1*: The only cloud in the sky above Washington, DC at 2:00 p.m. on 28 September 2007 looks like a poorly drawn dog.
> *Sentence 2*: The sole visible mass of condensed water droplets in the atmosphere above the capital of the United States at 14:00 on the day after 27 September 2007 resembles a carelessly drafted canine.
> *Sentence 3*: Die einzige Wolke im Himmel über Washington, D.C. am 14:00, 28 September 2007 sieht wie ein schlecht gezeichneter Hund aus.

Each of these sentences communicates (roughly) the same content. Other people can arrive at the same content about the cloud by looking up at it and coming to the same conclusion that I did, or by reading a sentence (like Sentences 1–3) that communicates this content. We can distinguish, therefore, between:

1. the cloud (a piece of *reality*)
2. the *content* I arrived at concerning the cloud, and
3. *sentences* (like Sentences 1, 2, and 3) that communicate this content.

Let us assume that after creating my content, I communicate it in Sentence 1, which I include in a book. What would it mean for me to have a copyright in the *fact* communicated by that sentence? I am not suggesting, of course, that copyright protection would ever apply to an individual fact. I will be arguing for the copyrightability of *collective* facts. But let us assume that the fact *is* copyrightable. What activities would you be legally prevented from engaging in (unless you obtained my consent)?

First of all, you would be prohibited from copying Sentence 1. You could not include that sentence in your works, unless you created it independently, without reliance on my copyrighted work. But you would also largely be prohibited from copying the content communicated by that sentence: You could not include in your works any other sentence (such as Sentence 2 or 3) that communicated the same content – once again, unless you created the content independently. This is true even though Sentences 1–3 share few words in common.

You would not be prohibited, however, from looking up in the sky, arriving at the same content about the cloud that I did, and communicating this content in your own works through a sentence like Sentences 1–3. For in such a case, you would have arrived at the content on your own, not by copying it from my work.

In short, copyrights in facts protect content, not reality. As such, they are like copyrights in fiction. For example, assume that I wrote Sentence 1 in a work of fiction, arriving at its content, not by observing the sky, but simply by making it up. If this content were protected,[9] you would be prohibited not merely from copying Sentence 1, but also from copying the content communicated by that sentence: You could not include any other sentence (such as Sentence 2 or 3) that communicated the same content, unless you arrived at this content on your own.

The primary value that people find in written works, whether of fiction or non-fiction, is the content they communicate. To be sure, content is not the only thing that people are willing to pay for. They also value the way that words are used to communicate content. In the case of some written works, such as poetry, our interest in the manner of communication can be very high. But in general our primary concern is with what written works say – the content they communicate.

Content is often hard to create. This is as true of factual as it is of fictional content. Copyrights can encourage the creation of content by allowing its creators to recoup their production costs. We have a reason, therefore, to think that copyright protection should extend to factual content just as much as it does to fictional content.

But in *Feist*, Justice O'Connor (following Nimmer) argued that facts cannot be given copyright protection because they are not independently created:

> [F]acts do not owe their origin to an act of authorship. The distinction is one between creation and discovery: The first person to find and report a particular fact

---

9 Once again, I am not suggesting that copyright protection would apply to such a small piece of fictional content.

> has not created the fact; he or she has merely discovered its existence. … Census takers, for example, do not 'create' the population figures that emerge from their efforts; in a sense, they copy these figures from the world around them. Census data therefore do not trigger copyright because these data are not 'original' in the constitutional sense. The same is true of all facts – scientific, historical, biographical, and news of the day.[10]

Just about every legal academic who has commented on this argument has been critical, and rightly so.[11] It is simply false to say that my content about the cloud was not authored. The content did not exist until I created it when looking at the cloud.

But some of O'Connor's critics have treated her mistake as dependent upon a philosophical error, namely a commitment to the mind-independence of reality.[12] The truth is, not only is it unclear that a commitment to the mind-independence of reality *is* an error, O'Connor's position does not follow from such a commitment. Assume that the cloud, understood as a piece of reality, is indeed mind-independent. The point remains that there is no content about the cloud until someone starts thinking about it – for example, until I look at the cloud and believe that it resembles a dog.

O'Connor's argument is also mistaken because my content about the cloud is not copied from the cloud the way content is copied from another work in a case of copyright infringement. And it is only if content is copied in the latter sense that the independent creation requirement would not be satisfied. One copies content from another work by figuring out what the content of the work is and then creating a work with the same content. Nothing like this goes on when I observe that the cloud looks like a dog. I don't borrow content from the cloud. The cloud has no content at all – it is not *about* anything.[13] Instead, I create new content by describing what the cloud is like.

---

10 *Feist*, 499 U.S. at 347–348.

11 See, for example, Temin, Marc K. (2006), 'The Irrelevance of Creativity: *Feist*'s Wrong Turn and the Scope of Copyright Protection for Factual Works', 111 *Penn St. L. Rev.* 263; Green, Michael Steven (2003), 'Copyrighting Facts', 78 *Ind. L.J.* 919, 948–49; Durham, Alan L. (2001), 'Speaking of the World: Fact, Opinion and the Originality Standard of Copyright', 33 *Ariz. St. L.J.* 791; Ginsburg, Jane C. (1982), 'Sabotaging and Reconstructing History: A Comment on the Scope of Copyright Protection in the Works of History after *Hoehling v Universal City Studios*', 29 *J. Copyright Soc'y USA* 647, 658; Gordon, Wendy J. (1992), 'Reality as Artifact: From *Feist* to Fair Use', 55 *Law & Contemp. Probs.*, Spring, at 93; Litman, Jessica (1990), 'The Public Domain', 39 *Emory L.J.* 965, 996–97.

12 For example, Gordon, *supra* note 11, at 657–58; Litman, *supra* note 11, at 996–97.

13 It is true that the cloud might be understood as having content, in the sense that it (sort of) represents a dog. But I would borrow that content only if I created something that also represented a dog – for example, if I wrote the word 'dog' or drew a

This is not to say that some sense cannot be drawn out of O'Connor's comments. She might be understood as denying not that factual content is independently created, but that it possesses a minimal degree of creativity. Both independent creation and creativity must be present if a work is to satisfy the 'originality' requirement for copyright. We shall address the question of creativity in Section III. But we can at least set aside the worry that factual content – including the collective factual content of a compilation – is not independently created.

II. THE *FEIST* APPROACH IS INCOHERENT

Under the approach I recommend, the collective factual content communicated by a compilation is copyrightable. One benefit of a collective fact approach is its ability to protect compilations that have no arrangement at all. An example is an electronic database that simply stores facts in a raw form, allowing them to be searched and organized by the consumer. Under *Feist*, the copyrightability of such a compilation will rest, tenuously, on its selection of facts, which may be insufficiently creative to warrant protection.[14] Furthermore, even when a compilation arranges its facts, the primary value of the compilation to consumers will often be the raw facts out of which it is composed, not its arrangement. Most of the value of the compilation can therefore be appropriated by someone who takes its facts and offers a new arrangement.[15]

These worries have motivated the call for *sui generis* protection for factual compilations – that is, protection outside of copyright law. This assumes, however, that the *Feist* approach follows from the underlying principles of copyright law. I will argue that it does not. The *Feist* approach is incoherent.

---

picture of a dog. In writing that the cloud looks like a dog, I am not copying any content that the cloud has.

[14] See, for example, *Database and Collections of Information Misappropriations Act of 2003: Joint Hearing Before the Subcomm. on Courts, the Internet, and Intellectual Prop. of the House Comm. on the Judiciary and the Subcomm. on Commerce, Trade, and Consumer Prot. of the House Comm. on Energy and Commerce*, 108th Cong. (2003) [hereinafter *Hearing*] (statement of Keith Kupferschmid, Vice President of Intellectual Property Policy & Enforcement, Software & Information Industry Association); Nachbar, Thomas B. (2004), 'Intellectual Property and Constitutional Norms', 104 *Colum. L. Rev.* 272, 279-80; Reichman, J.H. and Pamela Samuelson (1997), 'Intellectual Property Rights in Data?', 50 *Vand. L. Rev.* 51, 64–69 (1997).

[15] See for example, *Hearing*, supra note 14; Nachbar, *supra* note 14, at 279–80; Reichman and Samuelson, *supra* note 14, at 67.

Consider *Key Publications v Chinatown Today Publishing Enterprises*.[16] The plaintiff had created a yellow pages directory for the Chinese-American community containing unusual categories such as 'Bean Curd and Bean Sprout Shops'. The Second Circuit held that the selection and arrangement of the directory was sufficiently creative to be protected.[17]

The creation of a selection and arrangement can be divided into a number of decisions. The first is a threshold decision about the type of information to include in the compilation as a whole. For Key, this was the decision to include only businesses in New York City that are of interest to the Chinese-American community.

Clearly this decision is not protectable. The choice of a geographic area (New York) was surely borrowed by Key from other works and so was not independently created. And even if it was not borrowed, the choice involves too little creativity to be copyrightable,[18] or falls on the unprotected idea side of the idea/expression distinction.[19] And the same thing can be said of the focus on businesses that are of interest to the Chinese-American community. Such a principle of selection was probably borrowed by Key or, if it was not borrowed, is unprotected because it is uncreative or an idea. It is not surprising, therefore, that Key did not try to argue that the competing publication infringed Key's copyright because it too was a yellow pages directory for New York's Chinese-American community.

The second type of decision consists of the individual choices to include an entry in the compilation because it satisfies the threshold criteria for inclusion. In Key's case, this would mean including a business's name and phone number because the business is in New York and is of interest to the Chinese-American community.

Here too nothing looks protectable. Each act of inclusion is the communication of a fact, namely that the business is in New York and is of interest to the Chinese-American community. If Key had written a book in which this fact was stated in a declarative sentence, a court would declare without hesitation that both the sentence and the fact it communicates are unprotected.

---

16 *Key Publ'ns, Inc. v Chinatown Today Publ'g Enters., Inc.*, 945 F.2d 509 (2d Cir. 1991).

17 No infringement was found however. *Id.* at 514–17.

18 See *BellSouth Advert. & Publ'g Corp. v Donnelley Info. Publ'g, Inc.*, 999 F.2d 1436, 1441 (11th Cir. 1993).

19 For a discussion of the distinction see *infra* Section III.B. See also 17 U.S.C. § 102(b) (2006) ('In no case does copyright protection for an original work of authorship extend to any idea, procedure, process, system, method of operation, concept, principle, or discovery, regardless of the form in which it is described, explained, illustrated, or embodied in such work.'); *Mazer v Stein*, 347 U.S. 201, 217–18 (1954); *Nichols v Universal Pictures Corp.*, 45 F.2d 119, 121 (2d Cir. 1930).

If the fact communicated by including a business's name and phone number in the compilation is not protected, the only remaining element of the inclusion that could be protected is the *way* in which the fact is communicated. But nothing protectable seems evident here either. Since there are very few methods of communicating the fact that a particular business is in New York and of interest to the Chinese-American community – and one of those few methods is including the business in a compilation devoted to such a community – the merger doctrine would surely apply. Under the merger doctrine, if there are only a few ways of communicating unprotected content, the means of communication must itself be denied protection.[20] Furthermore, even if the merger doctrine did not apply, the individual communicative act involved in this case – namely placing a single business in the book – is surely insufficiently creative to be protected. The act would be no more protected than the individual sentence 'X is in New York and of interest to the Chinese-American community'.[21]

In short, when one looks at an individual act of including a business, nothing looks protectable. Of course, one can argue that the aggregate selection – that is, all the individual decisions to include businesses under the principle of selection considered together – is protected. But since each decision is the communication of a fact, to protect the aggregate selection is to protect a collective fact. One has set aside *Feist's* prohibition on protecting facts.

The Second Circuit was clearly worried about this problem. The defendants emphasized the factual nature of each inclusion, arguing that Key ' "slavishly" included every business about which [it] had information.' But Judge Winter argued that the selection was protectable because Key 'excluded from the directory those businesses [it] did not think would remain open for very long, such as certain insurance brokers, take-out restaurants, and traditional Chinese medical practitioners'.[22]

On the one hand, Winter might be arguing that Key's selection is protectable because it is misleading, that is, because it fails to include businesses that are appropriately included. A perverse set of incentives would be created if facts were denied copyright protection but misinformation received it. Copyright law would systematically encourage authors of factual works to mislead the public, since that would be the only way that the authors could receive protection.[23]

---

20 *Baker v Selden*, 101 U.S. 99, 102–03 (1880).

21 Copyright Office regulations deny copyright registration to '[w]ords and short phrases such as names, titles, and slogans . . . .' 37 C.F.R. § 202.1 (2002); see also *Bell v Blaze Magazine*, 58 U.S.P.Q.2d 1464 (S.D.N.Y. 2001).

22 *Key Publ'ns*, 945 F.2d at 513.

23 In fact, misinformation has also been refused protection, if it is presented by

But presumably the reason that Key excluded these businesses was because the directory would be misleading by including them. Their inclusion would suggest to someone reading the directory some time after its publication that they were still in operation. By including a business Key was aiming at communicating the following fact: This is a currently operating business in New York of interest to the Chinese-American community. So understood, it is hard to see how Winter has shown that facts are not being protected.

Similar problems arise in other cases involving factual compilations. For example, in *Le Book Publications v Black Book Photography*,[24] the plaintiff published a directory of businesses that would be of interest to the fashion, advertising, and visual production industries. It brought a copyright infringement action against Black Book, which published a similar directory. The criterion that Le Book employed when selecting a business from a database of 35,000 possibilities was whether the business 'would be of interest to its audience'.[25] The court argued that the selection of Le Book's compilation was protected, in part because Le Book determined whether a business should be included 'by surveying existing clients, conducting internet research to check "hit rates" on websites, examining portfolios, and reviewing individuals' client lists'.[26]

But it is a fact that a business would be of interest to Le Book's audience. In addition, the information it used to determine this fact also consists of facts. It is a fact that existing clients speak well or ill of a business when surveyed. The hit rate of a business's website is a fact. If Le Book had simply listed all 35,000 businesses, indicating after each whether it was of interest to its audience and the information upon which it relied when coming to this decision, the contents of each entry would surely be denied protection.

Indeed, this very reasoning was used to deny protection to a selection in *BellSouth Advertising & Publications v Donnelley Information Publications*.[27] The Eleventh Circuit found that BellSouth's selection of a geographic and temporal scope for its yellow pages directory was not copyrightable. Furthermore, it rejected BellSouth's contention that its inclusion of particular businesses within its directory was copyrightable because a number of sophis-

---

its author as true. *Silva v MacLaine*, 697 F. Supp. 1423 (E.D. Mich. 1988) (denying protection to plaintiff's account of his Peruvian encounters with an extraterrestrial woman and his theory that astral projection occurs when certain subatomic particles out of which the soul is composed separate from the body, both of which were borrowed by defendant Shirley MacLaine in her book *Out on a Limb*).

24 *Le Book Publ'g, Inc. v Black Book Photography, Inc.*, 418 F. Supp. 2d 305 (S.D.N.Y. 2005).

25 *Id.* at 309.

26 *Id.*

27 *BellSouth*, 999 F.2d 1436.

ticated techniques were used to generate its listings.[28] The court argued, plausibly, that even if a method of discovering facts involves extensive judgment, this does not diminish the factual nature of one's discovery:

> To be sure, BAPCO employed a set of strategies or techniques for discovering this data. Any useful collection of facts, however, will be structured by a number of decisions regarding the optimal manner in which to collect the pertinent data in the most efficient and accurate manner. If this were sufficient, then the protection of copyright would extend to census data, cited in *Feist* as a paradigmatic example of a work that lacks the requisite originality.[29]

It appears that the same point would apply to Key's and Le Book's decisions about which businesses to include in their directories.

Nevertheless, it is common in factual compilation cases for a court to claim that content is protected, even though it is rightly described as factual, because extensive judgment was required for its creation. Sometimes the claim is made not about the factual content communicated by a selection, but about the selected facts themselves. For example, in *CCC Information Services v Maclean Hunter Market Reports*, Judge Leval argued that predictions of the values of average versions of used cars in various regions of the country, which Maclean assembled in its Red Book, were protected. Not only were the selection and arrangement of information in the compilation sufficiently original to satisfy *Feist*, the predictions themselves 'were based not only on a multitude of data sources, but also on professional judgment and expertise' and thus '[were] original creations of Maclean'.[30]

But it is simply false that Maclean's valuations were not facts. That they involved judgment and expertise does not change their factual status. Novel historical and scientific theories have been called facts, and so denied protection, even though they were the product of similar judgment and expertise.[31] Nor does it matter that Maclean's valuations might be false. Outright fantasy has been called fact, and so denied protection, if it was presented as the truth.[32]

The factual nature of Maclean's predictions is particularly evident if a single prediction is considered in isolation. Imagine that another work borrowed only one such prediction. I have no doubt that Leval himself would

---

28 *Id.* at 1441.

29 *Id.*

30 *CCC Info. Servs., Inc. v Maclean Hunter Mkt. Reports, Inc.*, 44 F.3d 61, 67 (2d Cir. 1994).

31 See, for example, *Hoehling v Universal City Studios, Inc.*, 618 F.2d 972 (2d Cir. 1980) (denying protection to an author's novel theory that the airship Hindenburg was destroyed via sabotage).

32 See *supra* note 23.

have described this as the permissible borrowing of a fact. What Leval considers to be protected is, it seems, the collective content of the compilation – that is, the aggregate content of all of the predictions. In effect, Leval adopts the collective fact approach I advocate in this chapter.

Our problem, so far, is this: The choice of a threshold principle of selection for a compilation is unprotected, because it is not independently created, not creative, or an idea. Furthermore, the decision about whether a particular piece of information satisfies that principle is factual, even if it is judgmental. So nothing about a selection looks protected, unless one claims that the aggregate selection is protected, which means adopting the collective fact approach.

Let us now turn to arrangements. The first decision involved in creating an arrangement is determining the categories under which entries are to be placed. In Key's case, it chose its categories – such as 'Bean Curd and Bean Sprout Shops' – because they were of interest to the Chinese-American community. But the selection of a particular category again looks like the communication of a fact. Key chose 'Bean Curd and Bean Sprout Shops' because it is a fact that bean curd and bean sprout shops are of interest to the Chinese-American community. If this fact were communicated as a declarative sentence, not only would the sentence be refused protection, so would the content the sentence communicated. Indeed, even if the choice of a category were not seen as communicating an unprotected fact, each category, considered on its own, would be unprotected because it is not independently created, not creative, or an idea.

The second decision is placing an item under a category. But, once again, this decision communicates a fact. To include a business under the category 'Bean Curd and Bean Sprout Shops' is to state that the business is, in fact, a bean curd or bean sprout shop.

We have run into the same problem with arrangements that we had with selections: Upon analysis an arrangement dissolves into unprotected constituents out of which the aggregate arrangement is composed. What is more, these constituents are often themselves facts. And if they are not, they are not independently created, not creative, or an idea.[33]

The *Feist* approach appears to force one into the awkward position of arguing that what is protected in a factual compilation is not a selection and arrangement, but the means by which the individual unprotected methods of selecting and arranging are themselves selected and arranged to create an

33 Judge Leval recognized this problem: 'It is apparent that virtually any independent creation of the compiler as to selection, coordination, or arrangement will be designed to add to the usefulness or desirability of his compendium for targeted groups of potential customers, and will represent an [unprotected] idea.' *CCC Info. Serv's*, 44 F.3d at 71.

aggregate selection and arrangement. But this merely postpones the inevitable, since this higher-order selection and arrangement itself dissolves under analysis into its own unprotected constituents.

Once again, Judge Winter worried about this problem. If one examines the individual categories in Key's directory in isolation, the arrangement of the directory might look unprotected. His solution is telling: '[T]he individual categories chosen', he argued, 'are irrelevant to our inquiry. Rather, we are concerned with whether the arrangement of the Key Directory, *viewed in the aggregate*, is original'.[34] He recognized that unless the fallacy of division was resisted, no arrangement could be protected. For this reason, he looked at the arrangement as a whole to determine copyrightability.

But why not resist the fallacy even further? If one can look to a collective selection and arrangement, why not look to a collective fact? Indeed because the content of selections and arrangements is largely factual, collective selections and arrangements are collective facts.

Once we have set aside O'Connor's argument that facts are not independently created, the only reason to reject categorically the copyrightability of collective facts is that individual facts do not look copyrightable in isolation. But that is hardly persuasive, since no individual component of any aggregate – whether that aggregate is a collective fact or a collective selection and arrangement – looks copyrightable in isolation.

III. COLLECTIVE FACTS ARE PROTECTABLE

Of course, to say that collective facts can in principle be protected does not mean that they should always be protected. To determine when collective facts are copyrightable, we should apply the same criteria for copyright protection that are applied to fictional content. A collective fact will be protected if it is original (in the sense of being independently created and creative) and expression rather than idea.

A. Originality

The first requirement for protecting fictional content is originality. The originality requirement is commonly taken to involve two criteria. The first is 'independent creation' – the material must be created by the author rather than borrowed from someone else.[35] It is easy to see why the independent creation

---

34 *Key Publ'ns*, 945 F.2d at 514.
35 *Feist*, 499 U.S. at 345.

requirement exists. If an author did not create her work, but simply copied it from another author's or from the public domain, providing her with a property right will do nothing to encourage her to create new works valued by consumers. Instead, it will encourage her to steal. But I have already argued in the first section that a collective fact can be independently created.

1. Distinguishable variation

The second element of originality is the requirement that the material 'possesses at least some minimal degree of creativity'.[36] In fact, it is not clear that creativity is a separate requirement, rather than a consideration that comes into play in determining whether there is independent creation. Imagine that I copy your novel word for word and market it under my own name. I argue, however, that my novel is an independent creation because my name appears on the title page rather than yours. This makes it a new novel, of which I am the author. My argument cannot be rejected without deciding whether, by adding my name, I have done something sufficiently creative to generate a new work.

The 'distinguishable variation' standard for creativity embraces this essential connection between creativity and independent creation.[37] It looks to the work to see whether the author has 'contributed something more than a "merely trivial" variation, something recognizably "his own". Originality in this context "means little more than a prohibition of actual copying".'[38] The standard, in effect, attempts to identify whether there is a work that has been independently created.[39]

Whether there is such a work, however, cannot be determined without appealing to popular preferences and expectations. Imagine that people think an anonymous novel is not worth reading. Knowing in whose voice the novel is presented is absolutely essential to the reading experience. Furthermore, they think that a novel changes dramatically when offered in a different authorial voice. If so, someone who attaches his own name to another author's novel might be creating a new work, since the text of the novel (which consumers

---

36 *Id.*

37 See *Atari Games Corp. v Oman*, 979 F.2d 242, 246 (D.C. Cir. 1992); *Alfred Bell & Co. v Catalda Fine Arts, Inc.*, 191 F.2d 99, 102 (2d Cir. 1951); *Andrews v Guenther Pub. Co.*, 60 F.2d 555, 557 (S.D.N.Y. 1932).

38 *Alfred Bell*, 191 F.2d at 103 (quoting *Bleistein v Donaldson Lithographing Co.*, 188 U.S. 239, 250 (1903)). Judge Posner has recently described the creativity aspect of originality as simply a means of identifying independent creation. *Assessment Technologies of WI, LLC v Wiredata, Inc.*, 350 F.3d 640, 643 (7th Cir. 2003).

39 *Cf.* Ver Steeg, Russ (1993), 'Rethinking Originality', 34 *Wm. & Mary L. Rev.* 801, 877–82 (arguing that the creativity requirement should really be understood as identifying what is a work).

consider worthless on its own) is now offered in a different voice. The public would not think of the borrower as appropriating the other author's work, even if they knew that he had contributed only his name, for they would see the addition of his name as transformative.

Because the distinguishable variation standard is tied to these preferences and expectations, it can be understood as capturing cases in which an author has created something with a value to consumers that is sufficiently greater than the value of its borrowed constituents. It makes sense not to protect works that have very little added value, since the small economic benefits that result from encouraging their protection will be overridden by the transaction and enforcement costs. These costs include borrowers' efforts to identify and contract with copyright holders in order to obtain licenses and the expenses of adjudicating cases of infringement.[40]

But the distinguishable variation standard is influenced by another consideration that is independent of added value, namely the likelihood of parallel independent creation. In *Magic Marketing v Mailing Services of Pittsburgh,* copyright protection was denied on creativity grounds to envelope designs that had bold black strips within which the words 'GIFT CHECK', 'TELEGRAM', and 'PRIORITY MESSAGE' occurred in white letters.[41] It is possible that Magic Marketing did not independently create the designs in which it claimed a copyright. Furthermore, even if it did, it added little of value to borrowed constituents. But there is another reason that its designs are not creative. Other authors are likely to create the same designs. Any author who embarks on a project similar to Magic Marketing's would probably come up with much the same thing.

The likelihood of parallel independent creation both reduces the benefits and increases the costs of protection. The primary benefit of copyright protection is encouraging the creation of new works. But there is less encouragement for works subject to parallel independent creation, for an author will not be able to internalize the full economic value of the works she creates. She will have to share income with other independent creators. As a result, she still may not be able to recoup her production costs. In addition, her incentive to create will be further reduced by the worry that, having created a work, she could be found to have infringed upon some other author's copyright. Although independent creation remains a defense against a suit for infringement, juries routinely rely upon similarity when determining whether copying occurred, and so the chance of such a suit succeeding is significant.

---

40 Green, *supra* note 11, at 933–34.

41 *Magic Marketing, Inc. v Mailing Serv's of Pittsburgh, Inc.*, 634 F. Supp. 769 (W.D. Pa. 1986).

The costs of protection are also increased when parallel independent creation is likely, because the existence of many creators of the same work forces a borrower seeking to insulate himself from an infringement suit to expend a great deal of time and effort tracing the ultimate provenance of the material he borrowed. Furthermore, the enforcement costs will be greater because the fact-finder in an infringement case will have to exclude the possibilities that the defendant came up with the work himself or that the plaintiff copied the work from a third party.[42]

The problem of parallel independent creation is surely the main reason that individual facts have been thought insufficiently 'original' to be protected. Consider Justice O'Connor's claim that '[t]he first person to find and report a particular fact has not created the fact; he or she has merely discovered its existence'.[43] Understood as the claim that factual content is not independently created, she is wrong. But understood as the claim that such content will tend to be created by many people, making the transaction and enforcement costs of protection outweigh its benefits, she is correct. A copyright in a fact about the only cloud above Washington DC is inadvisable, not merely because its value is low, but because other people are likely to arrive at the same fact as well.

It is understandable, therefore, that so much emphasis is placed in factual compilation cases on the judgmental nature of the factual content at issue. The more judgmental content is, the less likely is parallel independent creation. For example, in *Marshall & Swift v BS & A Software*, the court determined that a compilation of estimates of the construction costs of various types of buildings, used by tax assessors for valuing real property, was protectable. Since the format for the compilation was dictated by the Michigan State Tax Commission, which had commissioned the compilation, Marshall & Swift could not claim that the selection and arrangement of the estimates were copyrightable. Nevertheless the court found that the estimates were not facts.[44] Unlike the contents of the white pages in *Feist*, which 'could be discovered and reported by anyone', Marshall and Swift's estimations '[were] not discoverable but [were] unique to it'.[45] In effect, the court limited 'facts' to factual content that has a high likelihood of parallel independent creation.[46]

---

42 Green, *supra* note 11, at 934–35.

43 *Feist*, 499 U.S. at 347–48.

44 *Marshall & Swift v BS & A Software*, 871 F. Supp. 952, 962 (W.D. Mich. 1994).

45 *Id.* at 960 n.12.

46 A similar conclusion was reached in *CDN, Inc. v Kapes*, 197 F.3d 1256 (9th Cir. 1999). In that case, CDN's wholesale prices for coins were considered protected, because it used 'its own judgment and expertise in arriving at that value for the dealers. This process imbues the prices listed with sufficient creativity and originality to make them copyrightable.' *Id.* at 1261.

But there is no reason that a collective fact could not be creative in this sense even if it is composed of individual facts that are not judgmental. Once facts are conjoined, the chance that the collective fact will be replicated is drastically reduced.[47] Indeed, the idea that conjoining uncreative constituents can generate a creative collectivity is relied upon even in cases, like *Marshall & Swift*, that claim that what are being conjoined are judgments and not facts. The court in *Marshall & Swift* would undoubtedly have considered one estimate of construction costs for one type of building to be insufficiently creative to be protected. And yet it concluded that simply by conjoining these uncreative estimates, in a selection and arrangement that was itself borrowed, Marshall & Swift could generate a creative and copyrightable collectivity. The same should be possible concerning collections of less judgmental facts.

2. The creative spark

There is, however, an alternative understanding of creativity. This is the requirement that one's work involve the 'existence of . . . intellectual production, of thought, and conception'.[48] This standard might be understood as looking to the psychological states of the author, without concern for what she produces. But a feeling of creativity is neither necessary nor sufficient for the creativity at issue in copyright. It is not necessary, because creative works can be produced through inadvertence.[49] And it is not sufficient, since one can feel highly creative while producing nothing creative at all.

The standard must instead look to what is produced. So what separates it from distinguishable variation? One possibility is that the standard demands that what is produced show novelty, imagination, or aesthetic merit. I will not repeat in any detail the legitimate criticisms that have been lodged against the creativity standard, so interpreted.[50] Copyright is intended to protect works of authorship. Once protected, it is the marketplace that separates those that have genuine merit from those that don't.

---

[47] To be sure, some collective facts – for example, the collective fact presented in a phone book – are themselves likely to be duplicated by anyone who undertakes the same project. But even in these cases, the difficulty of assembling the facts will reduce the extent to which parallel independent creation is a problem.

[48] *Feist*, 499 U.S. at 347 (quoting *Burrow-Giles Lithographic Co. v Sarony*, 111 U.S. 53, 60 (1884)).

[49] See, for example, *Alfred Bell*, 191 F.2d at 105; *Rockford Map Publ'g, Inc. v Directory Serv. Co. of Colo.*, 768 F.2d 145, 148 (7th Cir. 1985) (holding that copyright can be given to work of an instant).

[50] Gorman, Robert A. (1963), 'Copyright Protection for the Collection and Representation of Facts', 76 *Harv. L. Rev.* 1569, 1603; VerSteeg, Russ (1993), 'Rethinking Originality', 34 *Wm. & Mary L. Rev.* 801, 818–24.

But another problem with the creative spark standard is that it appears to be motivated by the fallacy of division. In looking for a creative *spark* one apparently considers the individual acts of creation by means of which the work as a whole was generated, in order to identify those that added something of sufficient merit. For this reason it does not merely threaten factual compilations, but fictional works as well.

Works of fiction often borrow constituents from other copyrighted works or the public domain. By a constituent I mean not merely a bit of unprotected content, but also unprotected methods of joining bits of content together. Consider, for example, the recent spate of Hollywood movies that set the general plot of a great work of literature in a high school. The first was probably *Clueless*, which set Jane Austen's *Emma* in a high school in Beverly Hills. Then came *10 Things I Hate About You* (*The Taming of the Shrew* in a high school), *Cruel Intentions* (Laclos's *Les Liaisons dangereuses* in a high school), *She's All That* (Shaw's *Pygmalion* in a high school), *O* (*Othello* in a high school), and most recently *She's the Man* (*Twelfth Night* in a high school). Not only did these later works take the tropes of a high school movie from other copyrighted works or the public domain, and the general plot from the target work of literature, they also took the method of putting the two together from *Clueless*.

Indeed, at a sufficiently fine-grained level of analysis, countless constituents of an original work of fiction will appear to be borrowed.[51] We are, after all, not the author of the concepts that we conjoin to create fictional content – nor are we the authors of the methods of conjunction. We learn these things from others. And the remaining bits that might be considered independently created will look uncreative when examined in isolation. We are under the spell of the fallacy of division if we insist that in the act of creating a work some creative spark must be identifiable. Creativity is an emergent property. The simple number of our uncreative acts can result in creativity.[52]

Once we set aside the creative spark standard of creativity in favor of distinguishable variation, many collective facts in compilations can be understood as creative. As we have seen, content is creative under the distinguishable variation standard if it has sufficient value compared to its borrowed constituents and if it is not highly susceptible to parallel independent creation. A collective fact can satisfy both of these requirements. To be sure, creativity will be more likely to the extent that the author borrowed facts widely rather

---

[51] For example Durham, Alan L. (2002), 'The Random Muse: Authorship and Indeterminacy', 44 *Wm. & Mary L. Rev.* 569, 572–73.

[52] See Hughes, Justin (2005), 'Size Matters (or Should) in Copyright Law', 74 *Fordham L. Rev.* 575, 575–80 (arguing that emphasis in copyright protection should not be on originality but on size of protected work).

than from only one work, or created rather than borrowed the individual facts of which the compilation is composed. The judgmental nature of the individual facts created will also be relevant. But we have no reason to categorically refuse to protect collective facts on creativity grounds.

B. Idea and Expression

Even if a collective fact might be understood as original, however, it can still fall on the wrong side of the idea/expression distinction. Indeed, O'Connor offered the distinction as another reason, besides a lack of originality, that facts are not copyrightable: '[C]opyright assures authors the right to their original expression, but encourages others to build freely upon the ideas and information conveyed by a work. This principle, known as the idea/expression or fact/expression dichotomy, applies to all works of authorship'.[53]

1. Ideas as content

The idea/expression distinction has been given a number of different interpretations, however. Sometimes courts and copyright scholars take 'ideas' to refer simply to content (whether factual or fictional) and 'expression' to refer to the means by which this content is communicated (for example, the sentences in the work). It is certainly the case that outside of copyright contexts having an 'idea' often means arriving as some content, and 'expressing' that idea means generating something external to the self (writing, speech, pictures) that communicates the content.

So understood, facts are clearly ideas. Unfortunately so is much fictional content that we would want to protect. Consider the collective content of the novel *Gone with the Wind* – that is, the complete story communicated by that work. Although it is 'idea' in the sense of being content, it is obviously protected by copyright. Borrowing that content and expressing it in a different manner would be a clear case of copyright infringement.

For this reason, 'ideas', as understood in copyright law, cannot be equivalent to content.[54] Some content, such as the collective content of *Gone with the Wind*, is protected expression. Other content, such as the content of a superhero (expressed in countless comic books and movies), is an unprotected idea.

Indeed, if 'ideas' as the term is used in copyright were always content and 'expression' always the content's communication, no expression would be copyrightable.[55] The complete string of words that one finds in any novel communicates a particular collective content about what the characters in that

---

53 *Feist*, 499 U.S. at 349–50.
54 Green, *supra* note 11, at 936–39.
55 *Id.* at 938–39.

novel said and did. If this collective content is an 'idea', then, by the merger doctrine, the complete string of words in the novel must be unprotected as well. According to the merger doctrine, if there are only a few ways of expressing an idea, then the expression itself is denied protection.[56] And there are very few ways to communicate the *exact* collective content of what the characters in the novel said and did. The string of words in the novel is one of the few ways to do it. It would follow, therefore, that this expression is unprotected.

But once it is recognized that some content is idea and some expression, the merger doctrine makes sense. If a means of communication is one of the few ways of conveying unprotected content, then the means cannot be protected either. On the other hand, if a means of communication is one of the few ways of conveying content that is itself protected expression (such as the collective content of a novel), the merger doctrine does not apply.

Because some content can be expression, one cannot argue that a collective fact is an idea simply because it is content. Indeed, collective facts look much like the expressive content of novels, insofar as both are aggregates. If collective facts are unprotected ideas, it must be for a different reason.

2. Ideas as borrowed

At other times, the idea/expression distinction seems a proxy for the independent creation requirement. Landes and Posner offer as examples of ideas a novelist 'combining stock characters and situations (many of which go back to the earliest writings that have survived from antiquity) with his particular choice of words, incidents, and dramatis personae. [The novelist] does not create the stock characters and situations, or buy them.'[57] But if ideas are understood as material that is borrowed, collective facts can be expression, since they can be independently created.

Ideas cannot be equated with borrowed material, however. At some point in the past, stock characters and situations must have been independently created.[58] And stock characters and situations of the future are being created

---

56 *Baker*, 101 U.S. at 102–03.

57 Landes, William M. and Richard A. Posner (1989), 'An Economic Analysis of Copyright Law', 18 *J. Legal Stud.* 325, 349–50. Judge Hand suggests the same in *Nichols v Universal Pictures Corp.*, 45 F.2d 119, 122 (2d Cir. 1930). The characters borrowed in the case were ideas because they were not independently created:

> It is indeed scarcely credible that [the plaintiff] should not have been aware of those stock figures, the low comedy Jew and Irishman. The defendant has not taken from her more than their prototypes have contained for many decades. . . . [T]o generalize her copyright, would allow her to cover what was not original with her.

58 Of course, at a sufficiently fine-grained level of analysis, this might be disputed. But we are considering content that is aggregate enough to be seen as authorable.

today. Despite being independently created, this material is nevertheless idea. The question remains, therefore, whether a collective fact might be an idea even if it is independently created.

3. Ideas as uncreative

Often the refusal to protect independently created ideas sounds similar to the creativity requirement. A primary criterion for distinguishing idea from expression in connection with fiction is abstractness.[59] And abstract material appears uncreative in the sense outlined earlier: It is not very valuable compared to its borrowed constituents and is susceptible to parallel independent creation.

Consider the idea of a superhero. The value of this idea is low compared to its borrowed constituents – certainly less valuable than the more particularized content of an individual superhero, such as Superman. Furthermore, the more abstract material is, the more vulnerable it is to parallel independent creation. The chance of abstract material being independently created by any one person is the sum of that person's chances of independently creating each of the concrete examples that fall under it. For example, my chance of independently creating the idea of a superhero is the sum of the chances of my independently creating each particular superhero – my chance of creating Superman plus my chance of creating Aquaman plus my chance of creating the Green Lantern, and so on. The more abstract material becomes, the more likely it is that more than one author is going to come up with it. And parallel independent creation is, as we have seen, a reason to think that the costs of protection will exceed its benefits.[60]

But, once again, if we understand the refusal to protect ideas as equivalent to the refusal to protect material that is uncreative, collective facts can be protected, since they can be valuable compared to their borrowed constituents and not susceptible to parallel independent creation.

4. Ideas as building-blocks

A further justification for the idea/expression distinction appeals to the important role that ideas can play as components of future works. One worry here is the monopolization costs of a copyright in an idea. If the creator of an idea holds a copyright in it, the idea will be underutilized. The marginal cost of

---

59 *Nichols*, 45 F.2d at 121; *Lotus Dev. Corp. v Paperback Software Int'l*, 740 F. Supp. 37, 60-61 (D. Mass. 1990); Kurtz, Leslie A. (1993), 'Speaking to the Ghost: Idea and Expression in Copyright', 47 *U. Miami L. Rev.* 1221, 1243–51.

60 Green, *supra* note 11, at 942–43.

using it is zero,[61] but the idea's owner will charge more – indeed possibly much more than is necessary to compensate him for his production costs. As a result, many valuable works that could have been made if there were unimpeded access to the idea will not be produced. Furthermore, the monopoly rents enjoyed by the owner of a valuable idea could over-encourage the creation of ideas and motivate inefficient expenditures to capture these rents.

But it is hard to see how worries about monopolization costs can, on their own, justify a categorical refusal to protect ideas. If ideas are valuable components for future works, completely rejecting property rights in them would also have great costs. The refusal to protect ideas reduces the number produced. As a result of such refusal, all the valuable works that depend upon unproduced ideas will also not be produced. The rational response to worries about monopolization costs is to limit the length of copyrights in ideas, not to refuse protection to ideas entirely. This is how monopolization costs concerning copyrights in expression are addressed.

The more likely justification for the categorical refusal to protect ideas is transaction costs. Consider, once again, abstract material in fiction. There is reason to believe that the transaction costs of protecting such material will overwhelm the benefits: The more abstract material is, the more likely it is to be borrowed by many authors. More authors are likely to find the idea of a superhero useful in creating their works than the more concrete character Superman. For this reason, the transaction costs of protection will rise. Each of these many borrowers will have to identify and obtain a license from the owner of the idea. On the other hand, the same abstractness makes the material less valuable to each person doing the borrowing. People would be willing to pay less for the thin idea of a superhero than the rich character of Superman. In short, as fictional material gets more abstract, increasing transaction costs combined with decreasing value to borrowers means that eventually the transaction costs will overwhelm the benefits of protection, making a categorical refusal to protect the proper choice.

---

61 In fact, the marginal cost of the use of a component can be greater than zero, because such use reduces the value of the remaining stock of unrealized works that include the component. For example, the marginal cost of using Superman in pornographic films or commercials in which he endorses hemorrhoid creams would not be zero, for these works would reduce the value of actual and potential Superman-based works. Indeed, since consumers' appreciation of Superman-based works is exhaustible, even works that do not tarnish Superman's image can still reduce the value of Superman-based works that can be produced in the future. Because copyrights allow the owners of existing works to prohibit inefficient use of their components, copyright law could be justified even if it did not encourage the creation of new works at all. *Id.* at 925–26.

Similar reasoning applies to individual facts.[62] Consider the following two facts:

> *Fact 1*: The only cloud in the sky above Washington, DC at 2:00 p.m. on 28 September 2007 looked like a poorly drawn dog.
> Fact 2: The only cloud in the sky above Washington, DC at 2:00 p.m. on 28 September 2007 looked like a poorly drawn dog *and* the only cloud in the sky above New York City at 8:00 a.m. on 14 October 2006 looked like a poorly drawn map of New Hampshire.

Fact 1 is more likely to be borrowed than Fact 2 because the chance of someone being interested in the cloud above a city on one day is greater than the chance of someone being interested in the clouds above two cities on two days. On the other hand, Fact 1 is worth less than Fact 2 because it conveys less useful information.

In short, the more fine-grained facts become, the more likely they are to be borrowed and the less they are worth to borrowers. The result is that as facts become more fine-grained the transaction costs of protection will eventually overwhelm the benefits, and the rational choice will be to refuse to protect them entirely, just as was the case with abstract fictional content. Fine-grained facts are unprotected ideas.

But, by the same reasoning, collective facts are likely to be protectable expression. The more aggregate a fact is, the more valuable it is to borrowers and the fewer borrowers there will be. There is no reason, therefore, to think that the benefits of protecting collective facts will be overwhelmed by transaction costs.

The primary worry that has been expressed about protection for the content of factual compilations concerns the difficulties faced by borrowers who must obtain licenses from the compilations' authors.[63] But this worry is usually expressed in connection with borrowing individual fine-grained facts. The question is entirely different when one speaks of the collective fact of a compilation. Few authors are going to want to use a collective fact, and for these authors its value can justify some substantial transaction costs.

Under the collective fact approach, individual facts would not be protected any more than the individual constituents of a work of fiction are protected under current copyright law. To be sure, drawing the distinction between idea and expression in factual content will be difficult. How large must a collective fact be before it is expression rather than idea?

---

62 *Id.* at 951–52.

63 Zetter, Kim, 'Hands Off! That Fact Is Mine!', *Wired Magazine available at* http://www.wired.com/techbiz/media/news/2004/03/62500 (3 March 2004).

But this difficulty is not a reason to refuse to protect collective facts. After all, no one points to the difficulty in distinguishing between idea and expression with respect to fictional content as a reason to refuse protection to it entirely.

CONCLUSION

The collective fact approach shows greater fidelity than *Feist* to the underlying principles of copyright law. Just as there is no reason to limit protection of fictional works to their selection and arrangement of unprotected constituents, there is no reason to accept the same limitation in connection with factual compilations. In both cases it is aggregate content that should be the focus of inquiry into copyrightability.[64]

Rather than embarking on the uncharted seas of *sui generis* protection, it is better to rely upon the principles of copyright law themselves, which have the flexibility to balance the benefits of copyright protection against the costs. But this will be possible only when our two fallacies are set aside and collective facts are understood as no less deserving of copyright protection than the developed stories or characters of a novel.

64 Adopting the collective fact approach does not mean that proof of infringement will be easy, even if it will be relatively easy to show that the collective fact of a compilation is protected. After all, it is the *collective* fact that is protected. Individual facts can be borrowed at will. Furthermore, the copyright holder must show substantial similarity between his work and the infringing work: That a work borrows a collective fact does not mean that it is substantially similar to, or indeed competes at all with, the compilation from which it borrowed. Finally, borrowing collective facts might be defended as fair use.

5. Speaking of the world: fact, opinion and the originality standard of copyright

Alan L. Durham*

'The world does not speak. Only we do.' So said post-modernist philosopher Richard Rorty.[1] Rorty's epigram occurs in a discussion of truth, mind and language, yet it recalls a persistent problem in copyright law. The world does not speak, but authors speak of the world. When they speak of the world, what do they own by copyright? The question is most difficult in the case of factual works. Whether they are histories, scientific treatises, travel guides or telephone books, such works, in a manner of speaking, hold up a mirror to the world. What is captured in the reflection is attributable, in part, to the author's labor and genius; the world does not, after all, speak for itself. Yet, if the mirror is an accurate one, the truths revealed are properties of the world. The author did not create those truths, and in that sense is not the 'author' of those truths. Hence, if the author's work is copyrighted, to what extent can the author claim those truths as his own, and prevent others, for the duration of the copyright, from reproducing them?

Philosophers might find the mirror analogy naïve, yet it gives us a place to start. Copyright extends to 'original works of authorship fixed in any tangible medium of expression'.[2] Works of authorship may communicate facts, but facts themselves are not copyrightable.[3] If I write, 'In 1970, the population of

---

* Professor of Law, University of Alabama School of Law. J.D. 1988, University of California, Berkeley. I would like to thank the University of Alabama Law School Foundation and Dean Kenneth Randall for their generous support. I am also grateful for the contributions and criticisms of Robert Denicola, Mark Lemley, Wythe Holt, Norman Stein, David Epstein and Dan Filler. Portions of this work were first published at 33 *Arizona St. Law Journal* 791 (2001).

1 Rorty, Richard (1989), *Contingency, Irony, and Solidarity*, p. 6.

2 17 U.S.C. § 102. Works of authorship include, among other things, literary and dramatic works, musical works, pictorial, graphic and sculptural works, motion pictures and other audiovisual works, sound recordings and architecture. Id.

3 See *Feist Publications, Inc. v Rural Telephone Serv. Co.*, 499 U.S. 340, 344–45 (1991) ('That there can be no valid copyright in facts is universally understood.

Princeton, New Jersey, was 12,331',[4] others may reproduce that fact, even if the population is known only because I walked the streets of Princeton, knocking on doors and counting every inhabitant.[5] On the other hand, if I clothe that fact in distinctive rhetoric of my own, I can prevent others from copying my 'expression'.[6] In this way, the law strikes a balance. My language, of which I am truly the 'author', is something I own, but the fact may be reported by others who are obliged only to develop their own 'expression'. In a sense, I own the mirror, not the reflection.

In practice, copyright cases seldom deal with the appropriation of individual facts or the language in which individual facts are expressed. They more often deal with collections of facts, where § 103(a) of the Copyright Act comes into play. Section 103(a) extends copyright protection to 'compilations', defined in § 101 as 'work[s] formed by the collection and assembling of preexisting materials or of data that are selected, coordinated, or arranged *in such a way that the resulting work as a whole constitutes an original work of authorship*'.[7] Because all compilations are 'selected, coordinated or arranged' in some manner,[8] claims based on compilations raise one of the most fundamental questions in copyright law: What constitutes an '*original* work of authorship?'

The Supreme Court addressed this question in the *Feist* case,[9] which considered the copyrightability of a white-pages telephone directory. The compilers of the directory did not invent the numbers; they merely reported the facts. They may have expended considerable labor in assembling those facts, but *Feist* firmly rejected any copyright claim based on their 'sweat of the

---

The most fundamental axiom of copyright law is that "no author may copyright his ideas or the facts he narrates".' (citation omitted)).

4 I borrow this fact, with respect and apologies, from Robert C. Denicola's 'Copyright in Nonfiction Works', 81 *Columbia L. Rev* 516, 524 (1981).

5 See Denicola, *supra* note 4, at 525.

6 See *Feist*, 499 U.S. at 348 ('[I]f the compilation author clothes facts with an original collocation of words, he or she may be able to claim a copyright in this written expression. Others may copy the underlying facts from the publication, but not the precise words used to present them.'). If there are only a few ways to communicate a particular fact, as is perhaps true of this example, even the expression may be denied copyright protection under the doctrine of 'merger'.

7 17 U.S.C. § 101 (emphasis added).

8 Even collections which include every element in a given universe of facts (for example, a telephone number for every resident of a city) are 'selected' in the sense that the author has chosen the boundaries of the universe (for example, the city rather than the county). The author's choice to omit nothing is also a kind of 'selection'. Even a random ordering might be considered an 'arrangement', if it were consciously chosen. Whether such 'selection' and 'arrangement' count for purposes of copyright law depends on how one defines an 'original work of authorship'.

9 *Feist Publications, Inc. v Rural Telephone Serv. Co.*, 499 U.S. 340 (1991).

brow'. Instead, the court imposed the standard of 'originality', which it termed the 'sine qua non of copyright'.[10] An 'original' work, it said, is one 'independently created by the author (as opposed to copied from other works), [which] possesses at least some minimal degree of creativity'.[11] Facts themselves are not 'original', existing independently of their discoverers, but a compilation of facts may be 'original', if the selection, coordination and arrangement of facts exhibits a faint spark of creativity. The court held that the alphabetical arrangement of telephone listings lacked such a spark.

Feist was an important step forward in the treatment of factual works. It ended the debate over whether the industrious collection of facts could itself support a copyright in the collection, and it identified a dose of 'creativity' as an essential element of originality. However, subsequent cases examining other compilations, such as price guides and pitching forms, have exposed a missing term in the *Feist* equation: if originality requires 'creativity', what is 'creativity'? Specifically, if the 'facts' included in a compilation are in part the product of the author's subjective judgment, in contrast to 'hard facts' like telephone numbers, does that element of judgment make the compilation, or even its constituent 'facts', original and copyrightable? If, for example, the *Feist* directory had listed not telephone numbers but life expectancies, and otherwise had maintained the selection, coordination and arrangement of the original directory, would the compilation have been 'original'? Or should copyright law treat differently the kind of creativity involved in estimating a life span and the kind involved in *expressing* any information in a particular manner?

It is not a minor point. Originality is, as the Supreme Court said, the sine qua non of copyright. It separates what can be owned by copyright, for the prolonged period of the life of the author plus 70 years,[12] from what cannot be owned at all, or what can be owned only under the more rigorous standards, and shorter duration, of the patent monopoly. Given the perception of some that intellectual property rights recently have expanded far beyond their proper sphere, this separation is deserving of careful attention. The balance struck in *Feist* seems, in the more recent cases, to have been misunderstood or ignored.

Feist drew the boundary of copyrightable subject matter, or 'original' authorship, between 'creation' and 'discovery'. In factual works – works that describe aspects of the world in which we live – 'creation' generally includes the author's choice of language, arrangement of materials, and selection of

---

10 Id. at 344.

11 Id. at 345.

12 17 U.S.C. § 302(a). The term for anonymous works and works made for hire is 120 years from the date of creation, or 95 years from the date of first publication, whichever expires first. 17 U.S.C. § 302(c).

materials to include or exclude. These are choices made at the author's discretion. They are not imposed by an order found in the world, but reflect the author's judgment as to how and what to communicate to his audience. Together, these choices produce the kind of original 'expression' traditionally protected by copyright. 'Discovery' includes any information about the world communicated through the medium of the author's expression. Sometimes that information is 'original' in the sense that it has never been communicated before, but it is not 'original' in the sense that the author *made* it. If the information is accurate, the author *found* it. Such information, according to *Feist*, belongs to the public.

This distinction has broken down in recent cases, which would characterize as copyrightable subject matter observations that are subjective, uncertain or opinionated, even though they attempt to be, and purport to be, accurate reflections of the world. These cases subvert the *Feist* definition of 'originality' – the 'sine qua non of copyright' – and upset the balance between private ownership and the public domain. Indeed, so few facts are entirely free of subjectivity and opinion, one questions the continuing vitality of *Feist's* prohibition against copyrighting facts. At the very least, the courts have created a significant problem of line drawing, with little theoretical justification. I propose, therefore, a return to the *Feist* standard of copyrightable 'originality', with the understanding that even subjective facts are not subject to copyright protection. To the extent that public policy demands a reward for the compilers of such facts (and that may or may not be the case), new legislation must be crafted that strikes the right balance to advance the public interest. The long duration and low thresholds of copyright may be appropriate for traditional 'expression', but quite inappropriate for facts, no matter how 'opinionated'.

In Part I of this chapter, I review the perennial tensions in copyright law born of the effort to separate copyrightable expression from uncopyrightable ideas, discoveries and procedures. Any effort to define copyrightable originality in the context of 'opinionated' factual works must conform to, or at least co-exist with, the traditional framework discussed in this section. In Part II, I examine *Feist* and other cases dealing with the concept of originality. I have organized this section according to the kinds of works examined – from directories, which afford little room for opinion except in the choice of material to include, to works which speculate about the past, predict the future or deliberately mislead. These cases provide a number of perspectives on a common problem; namely, how can one separate what is original to the author, and copyrightable, from what the author merely discovers in the world, when the author's work is the product of a complex interaction between creation and observation. In Part III, I propose a refinement, or re-affirmation, of the *Feist* standard of originality, to permit copyright protection for individual ways of communicating facts, while denying copyright protection to facts themselves, even when they are 'opinionated' facts. If we follow the contrary path suggested by the recent cases, we may give to authors who speak of the world too much of the world of which they speak.

I. CONUNDRUMS AND DICHOTOMIES

Like other fields of intellectual property law, the law of copyright is characterized, to a large extent, by the balancing and tension of opposing principles. Much of the conflict, or equipoise, of these principles can be traced to Article I, Section 8, Clause 8 of the United States Constitution, which is the source of congressional authority to enact both patent and copyright laws. It provides Congress the power '[t]o promote the Progress of Science and useful Arts, by securing for limited Times to Authors and Inventors the exclusive Right to their respective Writings and Discoveries'. Historians and legal scholars find in this sentence two parallel threads – one relevant to patent law ('[t]o promote the Progress of . . . useful Arts, by securing for limited times to . . . Inventors the exclusive Right to their . . . Discoveries') and the other relevant to copyright law ('[t]o promote the Progress of Science . . . by securing for limited times to Authors . . . the exclusive Right to their . . . Writings').[13] 'Science', in the eighteenth century, meant knowledge or learning, rather than the narrower field of inquiry to which 'science' refers today.[14]

As made explicit in the copyright laws, the 'exclusive Right to their . . . Writings' includes the rights of authors to reproduce, distribute, perform or adapt their works.[15] These exclusive rights advance the progress of knowledge by ensuring that authors will reap the financial reward of their efforts, and consequently will have an incentive to undertake such efforts in the first place.[16] Compared to other means by which governments could encourage progress, such as prizes to worthy authors, the exclusive rights model has the advantages of simplicity, efficiency and self-regulation.[17] Yet the constitution

---

[13] See Walterscheid, Edward C. (1998), *To Promote the Progress of the Useful Arts: American Patent Law and Administration*, 1798–1836, at 60–61; Lutz, Karl B. (1960), 'Patents and Science: A Clarification of the Patent Clause of the U.S. Constitution', 18 *Geo. Wash. L. Rev*. 50, 51.

[14] See Lutz, *supra* note 13, at 51 ('The word "science", which comes from the Latin *scire*, "to know", at the writing of the Constitution meant learning in general.'); Seidel, Arthur H. (1966), 'The Constitution and a Standard of Patentability', 48 *J. Pat. Off. Soc'y* 5, 11 (1966).

[15] See 17 U.S.C. § 106.

[16] See *Harper & Row v Nation Enterprises*, 471 U.S. 539, 564 (1985).

[17] In other words, the authors whose efforts are, in the judgment of the marketplace, most worthy will be most richly compensated.

holds that authors' rights can endure only for 'limited times,'[18] and the stated purpose of 'promot[ing] the Progress of Science' implicitly disallows any grant of rights hostile to that purpose. One might suppose that the strongest rights inevitably 'promote the Progress' most effectively, but the copyright laws, like the 'limited times' provision in the constitution itself, reflect an understanding that the most effective policy lies in a middle ground, where authors' rights are strong enough to provide the required incentive, but not so strong that the public – the intended beneficiary of the intellectual property laws[19] – is denied the greatest possible enjoyment, and productive use, of authors' labors.[20]

The built-in tensions between ownership and access, incentive and enjoyment, underlie certain 'dichotomies' which are fundamental to the subject matter of copyright. These include the idea/expression dichotomy and the fact/expression dichotomy. A third, for the sake of uniformity, I will call the process/expression dichotomy, although it is not generally expressed in those terms. Each of these dichotomies has some bearing on the question of 'originality', so I will discuss them in turn in the following subsections, relying in large part on the seminal cases still cited by courts and academics.

A. The Idea/Expression Dichotomy

The idea/expression dichotomy has its statutory basis in § 102(b) of the Copyright Act, which provides that '[i]n no case does copyright protection for an original work of authorship extend to any idea . . . regardless of the form in which it is described, explained, illustrated, or embodied in such work'.[21] The task of identifying an 'idea' and distinguishing it from the protectable elements of a work of authorship has been left to the courts. In *Nichols v Universal Pictures Corp.*,[22] decided in 1930, Judge Learned Hand said nearly all that can be said. His remarks laid down the analytical framework still employed today, while candidly admitting its shortcomings. The plaintiff had written a play, entitled 'Abie's Irish Rose', which concerned the romance of a Jewish boy and a Catholic girl – a match opposed by their respective families, but ending in a

---

[18] See *Graham v John Deere Co.*, 383 U.S. 1, 5 (1966) (referring to the parallel patent language as 'both a grant of power and a limitation').

[19] See *Harper & Row*, 471 U.S. at 546 (' "The monopoly created by copyright . . . rewards the individual author in order to benefit the public".' (citation omitted)).

[20] The principle of 'fair use', for example, circumscribes the rights of authors by allowing their works to be reproduced without permission under limited circumstances. See 17 U.S.C. § 107.

[21] Section 102(b) also denies copyright protection to 'any . . . procedure, process, system, method of operation, concept, principle, or discovery'.

[22] 45 F.2d 119 (2d Cir. 1930).

happy reconciliation. The defendant's motion picture, 'The Cohens and the Kellys', told a similar tale, but in this instance the genders were reversed and a stolen fortune played a significant role in the plot. The works were similar in outline, but differed in many details. The question was whether the works shared anything more than unprotectable 'ideas'.[23]

One might say that texts employing different language have nothing in common but ideas. To use a short example, if the sentence 'Attorneys enjoy stamp collecting' is changed to 'Lawyers like philately', one could argue that the 'expression' has changed because the words have changed; perhaps nothing remains but the 'idea' of associating a certain profession with a certain hobby. Judge Hand held that copyright protection cannot be limited to specific language: 'It is of course essential to any protection of literary property . . . that the right cannot be limited to the text, else a plagiarist would escape by immaterial variations.'[24]

To call such protection 'essential' may be an overstatement,[25] but copyright that could be avoided by minor changes would be of limited value. On the other hand, if copyright does not extend to ideas, there must be some way for a second author to convey the same ideas as a first author without liability for infringement. Judge Hand saw the problem in terms of the varying 'levels of abstraction' in which a work can be characterized:

> Upon any work, and especially upon a play, a great number of patterns of increasing generality will fit equally well, as more and more of the incident is left out. The last may perhaps be no more than the most general statement of what the play is about, and at times might consist only of its title; but there is a point in this series of abstractions where they are no longer protected, since otherwise the playwright could prevent the use of his 'ideas', to which, apart from their expression, his property is never extended . . .[26]

The difference between unprotectable 'ideas' and protectable 'expression' is one of specificity. If works are similar only at a general level, they share only ideas; if they are similar at a more specific level, though not necessarily the level of precise wording,[27] they may share expression. This is more a way

---

23 Judge Hand assumed, for the sake of argument, that copying had occurred. See id. at 120.

24 Id. at 121.

25 Copyright 'limited literally to the text' would protect authors against the easiest and least expensive forms of plagiarism, such as reproduction by a photocopier. It would not stop 'plagiarists' who took pains to re-phrase the original work. If the latter sort of copying were permitted, presumably the author's expectation of financial recovery would be so undermined that the 'Progress of Science' would be hindered.

26 45 F.2d at 121.

27 Or the equivalent level of expression for non-textual works.

of formulating the problem than it is a solution,[28] and Judge Hand admitted that the boundary between idea and expression can never been drawn with certainty.[29] Still, he had little difficulty finding the similarities between 'Abie's Irish Rose' and 'The Cohens and the Kellys' so general that they could not be considered similarities of expression.[30]

Today the work scrutinized under the 'levels of abstraction' microscope is as likely to be a computer program as a play,[31] yet the line between idea and expression still eludes precise definition. In the case of a dramatic work, the broad outlines of a story are likely to be considered its 'idea'. More specific plot twists or elements of character development may be considered 'expression' protected from copying.[32] Although distinguishing idea and expression sounds like a metaphysical issue, it is characterized more commonly as a matter of policy, based upon what best promotes the 'Progress of Science'. Ultimately, 'idea' is whatever a court regards as so general that it belongs in the public domain; 'expression' is whatever remains.[33] Courts are guided more by intuition than by rigorous analysis, and as Learned Hand confessed late in his career, the decisions are inevitably '*ad hoc*'.[34]

Nichols also discusses the position of authors as unwitting contributors to the public domain. 'Abie's Irish Rose' may have contained original ideas, and those ideas, rather than any particular expression, may have been the

---

28 As Judge Easterbrook observed, '[s]ometimes called the "abstractions test", Hand's insight is not a "test" at all. It is a clever way to pose the difficulties that require courts to avoid either extreme of the continuum of generality. It does little to help resolve a given case . . . .' *Nash v CBS, Inc.*, 899 F.2d 1537, 1540 (7th Cir. 1990).

29 'Nobody has ever been able to fix that boundary, and nobody ever can.' *Nichols*, 45 F.2d at 121.

30 Id. at 121–122.

31 See, for example, *Computer Associates Int'l, Inc. v Altai, Inc.*, 982 F.2d 693, 703-707 (2d Cir. 1992) (applying an idea/expression analysis to copyrighted computer programs); *Apple Computer, Inc. v Franklin Computer Corp.*, 714 F.2d 1240, 1252–1254 (9th Cir. 1983).

32 For example, in *Sheldon v Metro-Goldwyn Pictures Corp.*, 81 F.2d 49 (2d Cir. 1936), Judge Hand found copyright infringement in the duplication of various incidents in a tale of murder.

33 See *Herbert Rosenthal Jewelry Corp. v Kalpakian*, 446 F.2d 738, 742 (9th Cir. 1971) ('The guiding consideration in drawing the line is the preservation of the balance between competition and protection reflected in the patent and copyright laws. What is basically at stake is the extent of the copyright owner's monopoly – from how large an area of activity did Congress intend to allow the copyright owner to exclude others?'); see also *Apple v Franklin*, 714 F.2d at 1253.

34 *Peter Pan Fabrics, Inc. v Martin Weiner Corp.*, 274 F.2d 487, 489 (2d Cir. 1960); see also *Herbert Rosenthal*, 446 F.2d at 742 ('At least in close cases, one may suspect, the classification the court selects may simply state the result reached rather than the reason for it.').

source of whatever success the play achieved. Although Judge Hand doubted whether the ideas *were* original, he held it 'immaterial'.[35] 'Though the plaintiff discovered the vein [of ideas], she could not keep it to herself.'[36] Her copyright protected her expression, but 'not . . . everything that might be drawn from her play; its content went to some extent into the public domain'.[37] As Judge Easterbrook observed 60 years later, the consignment of ideas to the public domain is a part of the balancing of opposing interests that advances, or is intended to advance, the progress of knowledge. To include ideas within the ambit of copyright might encourage original thinking, but it would hinder the process by which authors build upon the work of their predecessors.

> Intellectual (and artistic) progress is possible only if each author builds on the work of others. No one invents even a tiny fraction of the ideas that make up our cultural heritage. Once a work has been written and published, any rule requiring people to compensate the author slows progress in literature and art, making useful expressions 'too expensive', forcing authors to re-invent the wheel, and so on. Every work uses scraps of thought from thousands of predecessors, far too many to compensate even if the legal system were frictionless, which it isn't.[38]

The trick is to encourage a first author, without too much discouraging a second.[39] The idea/expression dichotomy is one means of striking that balance.

An important addendum to the idea/expression dichotomy is the concept of 'merger', discussed in *Herbert Rosenthal Jewelry Corp. v Kalpakian*.[40] Sometimes an 'idea' can be expressed in only a small number of ways. In *Herbert Rosenthal*, the court found that to be true of the plaintiff's idea of a jewel-encrusted pin in the shape of a bee. The plaintiff (or, at any rate, plaintiff's counsel) could not suggest any ways in which the same idea could be expressed without the result being substantially similar to the plaintiff's expression.[41] In this circumstance, idea and expression are 'inseparable',[42] and if the expression were to be protected by copyright, the idea of the jeweled bee pin would be locked up as well. 'When the "idea" and its "expression" are thus inseparable, copying the "expression" will not be barred, since protecting

---

35 45 F.2d at 122.
36 Id.
37 Id.
38 *Nash v CBS, Inc.*, 899 F.2d 1537, 1540 (7th Cir. 1990).
39 See Id. at 1541.
40 446 F.2d 738 (9th Cir. 1971).
41 Id. at 740.
42 Id. at 742.

the "expression" in such circumstances would confer a monopoly of the "idea" upon the copyright owner . . . .'[43]

B. The Fact/Expression Dichotomy and the Concept of 'Originality'

The fact/expression dichotomy is in many respects similar to the idea/expression dichotomy, and courts sometimes treat the two as a unitary principle.[44] Both are concerned with identifying and protecting only an author's 'expression', and both find support in § 102(b) of the Copyright Act.[45] But there are important differences to consider. First, as already discussed, the line between idea and expression is one of specificity. As authors work out the details of their conceptions, their efforts pass imperceptibly from unprotected idea to protected expression. This is not true of the fact/expression dichotomy. Facts cannot be copyrighted, no matter how detailed, arcane or even trivial they may be. Second, the line between idea and expression lies primarily, if not exclusively, within the abstract realm of intellect. Without straying too far into Rorty's territory, both idea and expression seem products of the mind.[46] The line between fact and expression lies, or purports to lie, between the mind and the world – that is, between what is *created* by the author and what is, at most, *discovered* by the author. This distinction promises a more concrete boundary between fact and expression than between idea and expression.

The fact/expression dichotomy is closely tied to the concept of 'originality'. Section 102(a) defines the subject matter of copyright as '*original* works of authorship . . .' In *Feist*, the Supreme Court held that 'originality' is also a constitutional requirement, linked to the 'crucial terms "authors" and "writings" ' in Article 1, Section 8.[47] For its analysis of the originality requirement and, by extension, of the fact/expression dichotomy, the *Feist* court turned to

---

43 Id. See also *Morrissey v Procter & Gamble Co.*, 379 F.2d 675, 678-79 (1st Cir. 1967).

44 See, for example, *Feist*, 499 U.S. at 349–50.

45 'Section 102(b) is universally understood to prohibit any copyright in facts.' Id. at 356. That prohibition lies in the reference to 'discover[ies]': 'In no case does copyright protection for an original work of authorship extend to any . . . discovery, regardless of the form in which it is described, explained, illustrated, or embodied in such work.'

46 One could argue that some ideas exist independent of the human mind. For example, perhaps the 'idea' of the Pythagorean theorem would still exist, in some sense, even if there were no human mathematicians to appreciate it. These philosophical quandaries of the tree-falls-in-the-forest variety can be short-circuited simply by categorizing as 'fact', rather than 'idea', any property of the world that may be discovered, but is not created, by an author.

47 *Feist*, 449 U.S. at 340.

another seminal copyright case – *Burrows-Giles Lithographic Co. v Sarony*, decided in 1884.[48]

The work at issue in *Burrows-Giles* was a photograph of Oscar Wilde, which the defendant had reproduced and offered for sale in thousands of copies. The photograph shows Wilde seated in a contemplative pose, his head propped against his left hand while his right hand clutches a book. He is dressed in what appears to be a velvet coat and knee breeches, and plush draperies cover his chair. The defendant argued that a photograph is not subject to copyright because it is not the 'writing' of an 'author', as the constitution requires, but a 'reproduction on paper of the exact features of some natural object or of some person'.[49] The Court found the constitutional question 'not free from difficulty',[50] but ultimately held that photographs can be copyrightable works. In part, the Court extrapolated from the treatment previously given to maps and charts. While they are usually intended to reflect the facts of the world rather than their author's fancy, maps and charts were included in the subject matter of copyright in the act passed by the First Congress.[51] More importantly, the Court found that photographers are properly considered 'authors'. An 'author', said the court, is 'he to whom anything owes its origin; originator; maker; one who completes a work of science or literature.'[52] Similarly, a 'writing' does not mean only words on paper, but properly includes other means, such as printing and engraving, 'by which the ideas in the mind of the author are given visible expression'.[53] If Congress (up to that time) had not explicitly included photography in the list of works subject to copyright, it was probably only because photography had not been invented when the statute was enacted.[54]

The 'difficulties' lay in the argument that a photograph, unlike a painting or even a map, is not the product of an artist's skill, but a mechanical reproduction of the scene laid before the camera's lens:

> [I]t is said that an engraving, a painting, a print, does embody the intellectual conception of its author, in which there is novelty, invention, originality, and therefore comes within the purpose of the Constitution in securing its exclusive use or sale to its author, while the photograph is the mere mechanical reproduction of the physical features or outlines of some object animate or inanimate, and involves no originality of thought or any novelty in the intellectual operation connected with its

---

48 111 U.S. 53 (1884).
49 Id. at 56.
50 Id.
51 See Id. at 56–57.
52 Id. at 57–58.
53 Id. at 58.
54 Id.

> visible reproduction in shape of a picture. . . . It is simply the manual operation, by the use of . . . instruments and preparations, of transferring to the plate the visible representation of some existing object, the accuracy of this representation being its highest merit.[55]

In other words, Oscar Wilde at a particular time on a particular day had looked just as depicted in the photograph. His image was recorded on paper by a mechanical process, but the photographer was not the 'author' of the scene.

The Court disagreed. The photograph, it held, was an expression of the photographer's 'own original mental conception', given 'visible form by posing the said Oscar Wilde in front of the camera, selecting and arranging the costume, draperies, and other various accessories in said photograph, arranging the subject so as to present graceful outlines, arranging and disposing the light and shade, [and] suggesting and evoking the desired expression'.[56] By stage-managing the scene the photographer had become the 'author' of the photograph; the act of authorship was not triggering the shutter, but setting up the shot. The resulting photograph was 'the product of plaintiff's intellectual invention'.[57]

Subsequent cases have also relied on photographers' exercise of creative discretion in terms of arranging, selecting or framing a scene, as well as in such technical matters as the choice of lenses, film and developing techniques, to supply the necessary elements of 'authorship' and 'originality'.[58] In an era when photography is universally accepted as an art form, and the differences between an Ansel Adams landscape and an amateur's snapshot are readily apparent,[59] the status of photographs as copyrightable works could pass unquestioned. Still, the idea that authorship can be found in the manipulation of the 'facts' recorded in the work – such as the 'fact' of how Oscar Wilde posed in a chair at a particular moment – is a curious one. In a sense, manip-

---

55 Id. 58–59.

56 Id. at 60.

57 Id.

58 See, for example, *Los Angeles News Service v Tullo*, 973 F.2d 791, 794 (9th Cir. 1992). In *Los Angeles News*, the court held that 'raw' news footage of disaster scenes met the standard of originality, based on testimony regarding 'the initial decisions about the newsworthiness of the events and how best to tell the stories succinctly and effectively; the selections of camera lenses, angles and exposures; the choices of the heights and directions from which to tape and what portions of the events to film and for how long.' Id. The camera operator compared herself to an artist: ' "I use a paintbrush. I use the camera to tell a story." ' Id.

59 The amateur's snapshot is no less copyrightable than the artist's photograph. Even the least sophisticated photographer makes choices that influence the outcome, and courts are unwilling to base decisions of copyrightability on their perceptions of artistic merit.

ulating the scene to produce a photographic image is similar to manipulating daubs of paint to produce a portrait on canvas. Both translate the author's vision into a medium of communication. On the other hand, the former changes the scene portrayed in the work of authorship, not just the representation of that scene in a medium of expression, somewhat blurring the line between author and subject, or medium and message.[60]

In any event, the *Burrows-Giles* definition of 'author' as 'he to whom anything owes its origin' has played a leading role in the development of the fact/expression dichotomy. In *Feist*, the court described this 'originality' requirement as 'the touchstone of copyright protection'[61] and 'the very premise of copyright law'.[62] As the court explained:

> No one may claim originality as to facts. . . . This is because facts do not owe their origin to an act of authorship. The distinction is one between creation and discovery: The first person to find and report a particular fact has not created the fact; he or she has merely discovered its existence. To borrow from *Burrow-Giles*, one who discovers a fact is not its 'maker' or 'originator.' . . . The discoverer merely finds and records. . . . Census takers, for example, do not 'create' the population figures that emerge from their efforts; in a sense, they copy these figures from the world around them. . . . Census data therefore do not trigger copyright because these data are not 'original' in the constitutional sense. . . . The same is true of all facts – scientific, historical, biographical, and news of the day. They may not be copyrighted and are part of the public domain available to every person.[63]

On its face, the distinction seems obvious and relatively easy to apply. Authors are truly 'authors' of the expression they use to communicate facts; such expression has its 'origin' in an authors' thought processes. Authors do not create the facts, and cannot claim that the facts they report are 'original' in that sense. If I report the population of Princeton New Jersey as 12,331 – a figure I may have discovered but did not create – others may reproduce that fact. They may not reproduce my individual manner of expressing that fact,[64] which does 'owe its origin' to me. As the *Feist* court went on to explain, compilations of facts raise more difficult issues. Even though each fact in a

---

60 See *Natkin v Winfrey*, 56 USPQ2d 1594, 1600 (N. D. Ill. 2000) (rejecting claim by the producers of the Oprah Winfrey show that they were co-authors of photographs depicting Winfrey on the set, holding that the elements the producers contributed – such as Winfrey, her facial expressions, her attire and the staging of the show – are not copyrightable).

61 499 U.S. at 347.

62 Id. (quoting *Miller v Universal City Studios, Inc.*, 650 F.2d 1365, 1368 (5th Cir. 1981)).

63 Id. (citations omitted).

64 Unless there are so few ways to express the fact that the doctrine of 'merger' applies, as it would in the idea/expression context.

compilation, considered individually, is uncopyrightable, the collection of facts may be copyrightable. This is so because the 'selection, coordination, and arrangement' of the facts may introduce an element of expression which does 'owe its origin' to the author.

Although originality is essential to the copyrightability of a work of authorship, the amount of originality required is very modest. In the words of one court, 'only a dash of it will do'.[65] Originality does not require any measure of talent. The humblest doodle is as 'original', in the sense of 'owing its origin' to its creator, as the most sophisticated work of art.[66] Nor does 'originality' require novelty. Unlike a patent, which can be denied or held invalid if the claimed invention already existed in the 'prior art',[67] a valid copyright can subsist in a work that is indistinguishable from other works that preceded it, so long as it was not copied from its predecessors.[68]

The Supreme Court set the low threshold of originality in *Bleistein v Donaldson Lithographic Co.*,[69] where the parties (and members of the court) debated the copyrightability of a set of circus posters. Justice Harlan, in dissent, argued that a mere advertisement with scant artistic qualities should have no copyright protection.[70] The majority held otherwise, largely based on the unsuitability of courts to judge aesthetic merit.[71] The court observed that even the least of artistic creations, and those that most faithfully depict 'actual . . . visible things', reflect something of the author's personality:

> The copy is the personal reaction of an individual upon nature. Personality always contains something unique. It expresses its singularity even in handwriting, and a very modest grade of art has in it something irreducible, which is one man's alone. That something he may copyright . . .[72]

---

65 *Rogers*, 960 F.2d at 307. See also *Feist*, 499 U.S. at 358 (referring to the 'minimal level' of creativity required by the 'not particularly stringent' requirement of originality).

66 See *American Dental Assoc. v Delta Dental Plans Assoc.*, 126 F.3d 977 (7th Cir. 1997) ('Term papers by college sophomores are as much within the domain of copyright as Saul Bellow's latest novel.').

67 See 35 U.S.C. § 102.

68 The usual hypothetical involves a poet whose verse happens to be identical to Keat's 'Ode on a Grecian Urn', even though not copied from the earlier poem. See *Sheldon,* 81 F.2d at 54. In theory, the second poet could claim a copyright for *his* poem. Id. Of course, the poet would have a difficult time persuading anyone of the poem's originality, and potential infringers would argue that they had copied from Keats, not from his successor.

69 188 U.S. 239 (1903).

70 Id. at 253.

71 Id. at 251–52.

72 Id. at 250. Subsequent cases set the threshold of originality so low that it might be satisfied in spite of the author's best efforts to be *un*original. For example, in

C. The Process/Expression Dichotomy

The last of the dichotomies is what I will call the 'process/expression dichotomy', which distinguishes between a process (for example, a method of preparing a crème brulé) and a work of authorship describing that process (for example, a cookbook recipe for crème brulé). Generally speaking, the process/expression dichotomy separates useful procedures that are, at best, patentable from writings that are potentially copyrightable. The doctrine can be traced to the seminal case of *Baker v Selden*.[73] Selden devised an improved double-entry system of bookkeeping, which he explained in a book containing examples of the required forms. Baker made and used account books based on essentially the same system, leading to charges of copyright infringement. A book explaining an accounting method may be copyrighted,[74] but the court noted the 'clear distinction between the book, as such, and the art which it is intended to illustrate'.[75]

> The same distinction may be predicated of every other art as well as that of book-keeping. A treatise on the composition and use of medicines, be they old or new; on the construction and use of ploughs, or watches, or churns; or on the mixture and application of colors for painting or dyeing; or on the mode of drawing lines to produce the effect of perspective, – would be the subject of copyright; but no one would contend that the copyright of the treatise would give the exclusive right to the art or manufacture described therein. . . To give to the author of the book an exclusive property in the art described therein, when no examination of its novelty has ever been officially made, would be a surprise and a fraud upon the public.[76]

The inventor of a useful process must seek exclusive rights to that process through the patent system,[77] and if the inventor publishes a book explaining the process, without obtaining a patent, the process itself is 'given to the

---

Alfred Bell & Co. v Catalda Fine Arts, 191 F.2d 99 (2d Cir. 1951), the court determined that carefully reproduced mezzotints of old masters were sufficiently 'original' to be copyrighted. 'All that is needed to satisfy both the Constitution and the statute is that the "author" contributed something more than a "merely trivial" variation, something "recognizeably his own". Originality in this context "means little more than a prohibition of actual copying". No matter how poor artistically the "author's" addition, it is enough if it be his own.' Id. at 102–103 (citations omitted). The court found that the mezzotints had ' "originated" with those who made them', and it credited evidence that the reproductions did not, and were not intended to, precisely imitate the original paintings. Id. at 104–105.

73 101 U.S. 99 (1879).

74 Id. at 101–102.

75 Id. at 102.

76 Id.

77 Id.

public'.[78] Moreover, if the process cannot be used without the reproduction of written materials (as was the case with Selden's forms), then the materials 'are to be considered as necessary incidents to the art, and given therewith to the public . . . for the purpose of practical application'.[79]

The court found the distinction between the explanation of a process and the process itself 'so evident, that it requires hardly any argument to support it'.[80] Although the distinction is less evident today, when computer programs are included within the subject matter of copyright,[81] the principle of *Baker v Selden* is still important.[82] As the court observed, 'the very object of publishing a book on science or the useful arts is to communicate to the world the useful knowledge which it contains', and that object 'would be frustrated if the knowledge could not be used without incurring the guilt of piracy of the book'.[83] Since an author's motivation might be making money for himself rather than communicating knowledge to the public, it would be more accurate to say that the object of the copyright laws is to benefit the public by the dissemination of knowledge. If publishing a description of a process allowed the author to monopolize that process, the public would benefit little from the publication. Should a monopoly be warranted as a means of encouraging invention, then it should be obtained through the patent system, which provides for rigorous examination, a shorter term than copyright, and strict standards of novelty and non-obviousness.

An issue not discussed in *Baker v Selden* is originality. Both Selden's system and his description of it seem to fall within the broad *Burrows-Giles* definition of originality, since both 'had their origin' in Selden's mind. He did not 'copy' his system from the world around him, as a census taker might be said to 'copy' population statistics.[84] Nevertheless, the court's recognition of separate realms of creativity with separate systems of reward – patents for innovations in the useful arts, copyrights for original means of expression – bears on the question of originality in factual works, particularly when the works purport to be 'useful' in ways generally associated with patentable inventions.

---

78 Id. at 103.

79 Id.

80 Id. at 102.

81 A computer program is both a detailed description of a process and a necessary means for carrying it out.

82 The principle of *Baker v Selden* is now embodied in § 102(b) of the Copyright Act, which provides that '[i]n no case does copyright protection for an original work of authorship extend to any idea procedure, process, system, method of operation, concept, principle, or discovery, regardless of the form in which it is described, explained, illustrated, or embodied in such work.'

83 101 U.S. at 103.

84 See *Feist*, 499 U.S. at 347; Denicola, *supra* note 4, at 525.

II. FACTS, LIES AND SPECULATION

The *Feist* case marked an attempt to reconcile two opposing principles of copyright law, each with 'an impeccable pedigree':[85] 'The first is that facts are not copyrightable; the other, that compilations of facts generally are.'[86] As long as the compilation is nothing more than a compendium of data, as could be said of the telephone book at issue in *Feist*,[87] the two propositions may seem incompatible. As the court said, '[c]ommon sense tells us that 100 uncopyrightable facts do not magically change their status when gathered together in one place'.[88] Yet properties can be found in a collection that are absent in its individual components. A symphony is more than the notes of the scale; the character of the symphony depends on how those notes are combined. Similarly, the qualities of a novel depend on how the author puts together words that might be found in any dictionary. When notes or words are assembled in works of authorship, the whole means much more, and has far greater claims to originality, than any of its component parts. In the same way, a collection of facts may include dimensions of authorship entirely lacking in any isolated fact.

That circumstance is reflected in the Copyright Act, which denies protection to facts,[89] but includes within the subject matter of copyright 'compilations'[90] wherein 'preexisting materials or . . . data . . . are selected, coordinated, or arranged in such a way that the resulting work as a whole constitutes an original work of authorship'.[91] Facts are not born in the mind of an author and are not 'original' in that sense, but the selection of facts for a particular compilation, and the manner in which those facts are organized and presented, may be as creative as any other product of an author's taste, judgment or imagination. According to *Feist*, it is here one finds the 'originality' necessary for a factual compilation to be copyrighted as a work of authorship.[92]

Because copyright extends only to those 'original' aspects of a compilation and not to the facts themselves, the protection afforded to a factual compilation is inevitably 'thin'.[93] A subsequent author may borrow freely from a

---

85 *Feist*, 499 U.S. at 344.

86 Id.

87 Narrative works, such as histories or biographies, can be described as 'compilations of facts', but they are usually so rich in language that it is easier to distinguish between the facts themselves and the expression used to communicate them.

88 499 U.S. at 345.

89 Through the reference in § 102(b) to 'discoveries'.

90 See 17 U.S.C. § 103(a).

91 17 U.S.C. § 101.

92 See *Feist*, 499 U.S. at 348.

93 Id. at 349.

factual compilation, so long as there is no copying of the first author's original 'selection, coordination or arrangement'.[94] That result might seem 'unfair' because 'much of the fruit of the compiler's labor may be used without compensation', but it is, according to *Feist*, the very 'essence of copyright',[95] and what the constitution itself requires:

> The primary objective of copyright is not to reward the labor of authors, but 'to promote the Progress of Science and useful Arts.' . . . To this end, copyright assures authors the right to their original expression, but encourages others to build freely upon the ideas and information conveyed by a work. . . . This principle, known as the idea/expression or fact/expression dichotomy, applies to all works of authorship. As applied to a factual compilation, assuming the absence of original written expression, only the compiler's selection and arrangement may be protected; the raw facts may be copied at will. This result is neither unfair nor unfortunate. It is the means by which copyright advances the progress of science and art.[96]

In the remainder of Section II, I review how courts have dealt with factual or pseudo-factual compilations[97] of various kinds. Some of these compilations, like the directories discussed in Section II.A, present rather unambiguous facts in rather obvious ways. Others, such as the works of conjecture and prediction discussed in Sections II.C–E, are based on the authors' more speculative notions of reality. In their various ways, these works present a common problem: when a work conveys, or purports to convey, information about the world beyond the inner workings of the author's imagination, what aspects of the work are properly subject to copyright, and what aspects, through the operation of the dichotomies already discussed, are properly given over to the public domain?

---

[94] See Id. On the other hand, infringement requires only that the selection, coordination and arrangement be substantially similar; they need not be identical. See *Key Publications, Inc. v Chinatown Today Publishing Enterprises, Inc.*, 945 F.2d 509, 514 (2d Cir. 1991) (although copyright in compilations is 'thin', 'we do not believe it is anorexic').

[95] *Feist*, 499 U.S. at 349 (citation omitted).

[96] Id. at 349–50 (citations omitted). Relying solely on the incentive theory of copyright, the court rejected any award of rights to fact compilers to compensate for their labors, or 'sweat of the brow'. See Id., 499 U.S. at 354 ('Without a doubt, the "sweat of the brow" doctrine flouted basic copyright principles.').

[97] I use 'compilation' here in a general sense, to mean any work or authorship in which facts are assembled. In some cases, such as telephone directories, any original authorship would have to reside in the selection, coordination and arrangement of facts, since the form allows few opportunities for the creative use of language. In works such as histories and biographies, language is a much larger part of the author's creative contribution.

A. Directories

Although the *Feist* court resolved to its satisfaction the abstract dilemma of copyrightable compilations of *un*copyrightable facts, it still had to determine whether a white-pages telephone directory met the standard of a copyrightable compilation. Section 101 does not say that *all* factual compilations are entitled to copyright, but only those wherein the facts are 'selected, coordinated, or arranged *in such a way* that the resulting work as a whole constitutes an original work of authorship',[98] This suggests that the facts included in some compilations may be 'selected, coordinated, or arranged' in a manner that does *not* produce an 'original work of authorship'.

To require a high degree of artistry in the selection or arrangement of facts would be inconsistent with the low threshold of originality established in *Bleistein* and other cases. *Feist* reaffirms that the requirements of originality are, in fact, minimal:

> [T]he originality requirement is not particularly stringent. A compiler may settle upon a selection or arrangement that others have used; novelty is not required. Originality requires only that the author make the selection or arrangement independently (i.e., without copying that selection or arrangement from another work), and that it display some minimal level of creativity.[99]

While 'the vast majority of compilations will pass this test', there is still 'a narrow category of works in which the creative spark is utterly lacking or so trivial as to be virtually nonexistent'.[100] In a copyrightable compilation, 'the selection and arrangement of facts cannot be so mechanical or routine as to require no creativity whatsoever'.[101] The court found the selection and organization of materials in the alphabetically-ordered white pages directory so routine as to be utterly lacking in creativity, thereby disqualifying the directory as a copyrightable work of authorship.[102]

A number of other directories have been tested under the *Feist* standard of originality. In *Key Publications, Inc. v Chinatown Today Publishing Enterprises, Inc.*,[103] the Second Circuit considered whether a 'Chinese yellow pages' telephone directory met the standard of originality. Whereas the *Feist* white pages directory had merely listed telephone subscribers in alphabetical order, the *Key* directory, like other yellow pages directories, listed businesses

---

98 17 U.S.C. § 101 (emphasis added).
99 *Feist,* 499 U.S. at 358.
100 Id. at 359.
101 Id. at 362.
102 Id.
103 945 F.2d 509 (2d Cir. 1991).

by category. In this case, the businesses and categories had been chosen with regard to the needs and interests of the Chinese community. The directory, for example, included listings under the category of 'Bean Curd and Bean Sprout Shops'.[104] Although the court found no infringement, it did find the directory sufficiently original to be copyrighted. In contrast to the directory in *Feist*, where every telephone subscriber in the area had been included, the Chinese directory included only those businesses that the compiler, in the exercise of her judgment, considered most appropriate for her audience:

> In assembling the directory, Ms. Wang had to select from a multitude of businesses in New York and elsewhere those of greatest interest to her audience – the New York City Chinese-American community. . . . Ms. Wang testified that she excluded from the directory those businesses she did not think would remain open for very long, such as certain insurance brokers, take-out restaurants, and traditional Chinese medical practitioners.[105]

The choice of categories to include and how they should be named also required the exercise of creativity.[106] These acts of selection and judgment were found sufficient to render the compilation 'original'.[107]

In *BellSouth Advertising & Pub. Corp. v Donnelley Information Pub.*,[108] the Eleventh Circuit considered a more conventional yellow pages and found its 'selection, coordination and arrangement' lacking in originality. Although businesses were organized by category, the court held those categories to be 'entirely typical' of yellow pages directories,[109] or, in the characterization of *Feist*, ' "not only unoriginal, [but] practically inevitable." '[110] The choice of which businesses to list under which categories had been based, in significant part, on the preferences of customers and their willingness to pay, and so could not be considered an 'original' selection.[111] The plaintiff had employed distinctive and creative marketing techniques, which ultimately influenced the contents of the directory, but the court characterized these marketing techniques as 'not acts of authorship, but techniques for the discovery of facts'.[112] To find 'originality' in such techniques, however innovative, would contradict the *Feist* distinction between 'creation' and 'discovery'.[113]

---

104 Id.
105 Id.
106 Id. at 514.
107 Id.
108 999 F.2d 1436 (11th Cir. 1993) (*en banc*).
109 Id. at 1442 (citation omitted).
110 Id. (quoting *Feist*, 499 U.S. at 363).
111 Id. at 1444.
112 Id.
113 Id.

> By employing its sales strategies, [plaintiff] discovered that certain subscribers describe their businesses in a particular fashion and were willing to pay for a certain number of listings under certain available business descriptions. To be sure, [plaintiff] employed a set of strategies or techniques for discovering this data. Any useful collection of facts, however, will be structured by a number of decisions regarding the optimal manner in which to collect the pertinent data in the most efficient and accurate manner. If this were sufficient, then the protection of copyright would extend to census data, cited in *Feist* as a paradigmatic example of a work that lacks the requisite originality. . . . Just as the Copyright Act does not protect 'industrious collection', it affords no shelter to the resourceful, efficient, or creative collector. . . . The protection of copyright must inhere in a creatively original selection of facts to be reported and not in the creative means used to discover those facts.[114]

In other words, it is not enough for the author of a factual compilation to be clever; rather, the author must be clever (or, at least, minimally creative) in the presentation of the facts, if the compilation is to be considered 'original'.

One of the most difficult of the directory cases is *Warren Publications, Inc. v Microdos Data Corp.*,[115] also from the Eleventh Circuit. The work at issue was a directory of cable television systems,[116] 'system' defined by Warren as 'an entity offering subscribers in one or more communities the same cable services for the same price'.[117] The directory included a section for each state, and within each section a listing of communities in that state, arranged alphabetically. Because many of the systems served multiple communities, and listing the same information under the heading of each community would have been duplicative, Warren listed the pertinent information for each system only under the heading of the 'principal' community, with cross-references under the heading of the other communities.[118] The 'principal' communities were selected by the operators of each cable system.[119] The district court granted partial summary judgment, holding Warren's organization sufficiently 'original' to merit copyright protection under *Feist*.[120] The Eleventh Circuit reversed.

As to the 'selection' of the information presented, the court found that Warren had included *all* of the communities of which it was aware.[121] In that

---

114 Id. (citations omitted).

115 115 F.3d 1509 (11th Cir. 1997).

116 The directory contained 'extensive information on cable systems, including, inter alia, the name, address, and telephone number of the cable system operator, the number of subscribers, the channels offered, the price of service, and the types of equipment used.' Id. at 1512.

117 Id. at 1517.

118 Id. at 1512.

119 See Id. at 1517, 1519.

120 See Id. at 1511.

121 Id. at 1518.

respect, the directory was closer to the all-inclusive listing held unoriginal in *Feist* than the more selective listing in *Key*.[122] The selection of the 'principal communities' was also unavailing, since that selection had been made by the cable system operators, rather than Warren.[123] Consequently, Warren's best claim of 'originality' lay in its general plan of organizing information by principal communities, rather than in some other fashion. The court dismissed that argument as well, holding that if Warren's plan of organizing data was a 'system', as the district court had termed it, then permitting Warren exclusive rights to that 'system' would contradict § 102(b) of the Copyright Act.[124] Even if Warren's plan was not a 'system' within the meaning of the statute, its *usefulness* denied it the status of an 'original' creation. The court described Warren's decision to use 'principal communities' as a decision 'to make the [directory] commercially useful',[125] and held that '[t]he mere discovery of an organizing principle which is dictated by the market is not sufficient to establish creativity'.[126] In terms of the line drawn in *Feist*, a system of organization that serves the needs of the market is a 'discovery' rather than a 'creation'.[127]

The majority's decision prompted a strong dissent by three judges, who argued that Warren had made a series of choices regarding the presentation of the cable system information, which in aggregate were sufficiently creative to meet the low threshold of originality.

> The acts of selection carried out by Warren were a stream of events, beginning with its choice of the facts it wanted and the construct of a functional methodology in which to develop and present them. The use of a geographic name for each cable system, and the choice of the names of principal communities as identifiers, and the decision on a particular name, were not isolated acts of selection like Athena springing full grown from the brow of Zeus, or a decision made by a snap of someone's fingers, or a mechanical decision from a single telephone call, or by numerous calls. They were parts of the stream of acts of selection . . . . This court does not, however, refer to Warren's exercise of judgment in creating this structure of selection and in choosing the facts to be reported and how to report them. Yet these acts of selection are independent expressions of the author, part of the overall 'work of authorship'. This court does not hold them to be unoriginal or non-creative. Instead, it ignores them and treats this case as turning on the single fact of the source of information about principal communities. This trivializes what this case is about.[128]

---

122 Id. at 1518–19.
123 Id. at 1519.
124 Id. at 1517. Section 102(b) prohibits the extension of copyright to 'any idea, procedure, process, system, method of operation, concept, principle, or discovery'.
125 Id. at 1518.
126 Id. at 1520 n.31.
127 See Id.
128 Id. at 1527–28 (Godbold, J., dissenting).

Warren is a difficult case because it raises questions under each of the 'dichotomies' discussed in Section I. Organizing information by principal communities undoubtedly serves a useful function, at least in reducing the bulk of the directory, so one might conclude, under *Baker v Selden*, that such a practical system should be beyond the scope of copyright. On the other hand, the author of the directory in *Key* based her selections on what she considered most 'useful' to her audience, as would the authors of most factual compilations. To deny copyright to any 'selection, coordination or arrangement' of facts which is useful would deny copyright to most factual compilations, contrary to the clear intentions of *Feist*,[129] or would, at the very least, provide the authors of such works with perverse incentives. Application of the fact/expression dichotomy is equally problematic. The identity of the principal community in each system might be considered a 'fact', even if based on the opinion of the system operators. It is more difficult to characterize Warren's organizational scheme itself as a 'fact'. The majority appears to treat it as a fact, because it best suits the needs of the market, and is therefore, in some sense, 'discoverable'. But one can argue that organizational schemes are always imposed on the world, rather than discovered in it, so they are 'creations' more than they are 'discoveries'. These issues arise more explicitly in the case of taxonomies, discussed in Section II.B.

Perhaps the best way to analyze the facts of *Warren* is under the rubric of the idea/expression dichotomy. The dissent characterizes Warren's directory as the product of a series of choices, beginning with the 'choice of facts it wanted'.[130] One could say that Warren's first choice was to produce a directory of cable systems, rather than a directory of Italian restaurants or internet websites. However, many of Warren's more general choices must have been choices of ideas to pursue, rather than choices of how to express those ideas. As already discussed, the line between idea and expression is a difficult one to draw, and depends primarily on the court's intuitive understanding of the most fruitful competitive balance. Given what are likely to be a limited number of reasonable ways in which to organize a cable system directory, it would be reasonable to treat Warren's organizing principle as an unprotectable idea, thereby circumventing the more difficult to apply fact/expression and process/expression dichotomies.

B. Taxonomies

The issues hinted at in *Warren* were more squarely presented in *American*

---

129 See *Feist*, 499 U.S. at 344 (describing as a 'well-established proposition' the principle that 'compilations of facts generally are [copyrightable]').

130 115 F.3d at 1527.

Dental Ass'n v Delta Dental Plans Assoc.,[131] which concerned the copyrightability of 'taxonomies'. A 'taxonomy' is a system of grouping and describing differing objects or phenomena.[132] A taxonomy of baseball cards might group them by manufacturer, then by year, by team, by player position and so on, so that any card could be classified – for example, Topps/1989/Yankees/Outfielders. In *American Dental*, the taxonomy took the form of a uniform 'Code on Dental Procedures and Nomenclature', devised for convenience in billing and insurance processing. The code grouped procedures by type and included a number and brief description for each – for example, '04267 "guided tissue regeneration – nonresorbable barrier, per site, per tooth (includes membrane removal)".'[133] The defendant, Delta Dental, claimed the right to reprint modified versions of the code, without the permission of the Code's author, the American Dental Association.[134]

The District Court considered the element of 'creativity' required of an original work of authorship,[135] and found that it involved a measure of 'imagination'.[136] 'Imagination' it defined as ' "the power which the mind has of forming concepts beyond those derived from external objects".'[137] The concept of a horse, said the court, is not imaginative because horses exist in the world and are observable through the senses.[138] Even the concept of a unicorn is not particularly imaginative, since examples 'exist in literature and art'.[139] A horse with *three* horns would be truly imaginative, because until the court 'made it up just now', such an animal 'probably . . . existed in neither nature nor art'.[140] To limit 'imagination', and hence 'creativity', to '[o]nly the fantastic, the yet unimagined' would, however, 'have the practical effect of excluding the great bulk of materials submitted for copyright protection'.[141]

---

131 126 F.3d 977 (7th Cir. 1997).

132 Or, in the definition provided by Webster's Third International Dictionary – 'the systematic distinguishing, ordering, and naming of type groups within a subject field'.

133 See *American Dental,* 126 F.3d at 977.

134 See Id. at 977–78.

135 See *American Dental Ass'n v Delta Dental Plans Assoc.*, 39 USPQ2d 1715, 1720 (N.D. Ill. 1996).

136 'Imagination is the standard touchstone of creativity.' Id.

137 Id. at 1721 (quoting 7 O.E.D. 669). An alternative definition of 'imagination' would limit it to ' "the creative faculty of the mind in its highest aspect; the power of framing new and striking intellectual conceptions; poetic genius".' Id. The court acknowledged that '[i]f copyrightability were dependent on qualities of poetic genius, the body of material suitable for copyright would be slim indeed'. Id.

138 Id.

139 Id.

140 Id.

141 Id.

Hence the court proposed a novel (one could even say 'imaginative') analysis for testing the originality of less fanciful works.

> Perhaps it is better to think about creativity (and therefore imagination) as that element which remains when form is separated from function. In other words, isolating the merely useful (i.e., those things which are solely about function) from those things which are useful plus something else (i.e., those things which can be appreciated for some quality aside from their utility). This paradigm essentially boils down to a distinction between means and ends. Is the material merely a means to some end, or is it an end in itself?
>
> Consider a lamp. A lamp's primary function is to provide light; thus it may be said to be the means (bulb, switch, electricity) to a particular end (illumination). But a lamp may also be an end in itself – an object that can stand on its own after its utility is factored out – as may be seen in the multicolored leaded-glass mosaic lamps designed by Louis Comfort Tiffany, which provide a degree of aesthetic pleasure aside from their illuminative capacities. A Tiffany lamp exemplifies what I mean when I say 'useful plus'. Remove the 'useful', and some 'plus' remains. That remaining 'plus' is the creative, imaginative component deserving of copyright protection. If, on the other hand, nothing remains after the 'useful' is taken away – if the primary function is removed from the form – the work is devoid of even that modicum of creativity required for protection, and hence is uncopyrightable.[142]

The court called its approach a 'means/ends analysis'.[143] It borrows, to some extent, from the analysis applied to 'useful articles',[144] which are copyrightable if, but only if, the 'design incorporates pictorial, graphic, or sculptural features that can be identified separately from, and are capable of existing independently of, the utilitarian aspects of the article'.[145] In the version the court proposed for literary works, one would ask whether the work merely served a function, or whether it could be appreciated on its own account. An entirely functional work would fail the test of creativity. Moreover, 'if the *primary purpose* of a factual compilation is not to entertain, express, incite, inform, educate, etc., but these effects occur anyway, they may be considered simply noncreative byproducts of the work's main purpose of accomplishing a specific task'.[146]

---

142 Id.

143 Id.

144 'A "useful article" is an article having an intrinsic utilitarian function that is not merely to portray the appearance of the article or to convey information.' 17 U.S.C. § 101.

145 Id. Since 'separability' may be *conceptual* rather than physical, the copyright analysis of useful articles can be particularly vexing. See *Brandir Int'l, Inc. v Cascade Pacific Lumber Co.*, 834 F.2d 1142 (2d Cir. 1987); *Barry Kieselstein-Cord v Accessories by Pearl, Inc.*, 632 F.2d 989 (2d Cir. 1980).

146 39 USPQ2d at 1722 (emphasis added). The court characterized its means/ends analysis as a 'refined shortcut' of the analysis suggested in *Feist*. Id. Yet the court's

The court offered a standard eye chart as an example of a work lacking in originality, applying the court's means/ends distinction: 'Remove the function, and the creative component of the form is negligible; there is no imaginative "plus" that reasonably warrants copyright protection'.[147] Turning its means/ends analysis to the code of dental procedures, the court found no creativity: 'The primary purpose behind the Code is administrative convenience: making billing easier for dentists, their clients, and insurance companies . . . The Code is intended solely as the means to an end (administrative efficiency), not an end in and of itself.'[148] The kind of aesthetic 'plus' that makes a Tiffany lamp more than a light source is not to be found in the Code.[149]

On appeal, the Seventh Circuit rejected the district court's analysis. As urged by the American Medical Association, the American National Standards Institute, the Underwriter Laboratories and similar groups,[150] the court held that taxonomies, useful or not, are creative efforts worthy of copyright. Just as a scientist may copyright a description of the world (though not the facts *per se*), '[s]o too with a taxonomy – of butterflies, legal citations, or dental procedures'.[151]

> Classification is a creative endeavor. Butterflies may be grouped by their color, or the shape of their wings, or their feeding or breeding habits, or their habitats, or the attributes of their caterpillars, or the sequence of their DNA; each scheme of classification could be expressed in multiple ways. Dental procedures could be classified by complexity, or by the tools necessary to perform them, or by the parts of the mouth involved, or by the anesthesia employed, or in any of a dozen different ways. The Code's descriptions don't 'merge with the facts' any more than a scientific description of butterfly attributes is part of a butterfly. . . . There can be multiple, and equally original, biographies of the same person's life, and multiple original taxonomies of a field of knowledge.[152]

A taxonomy is a 'creation', not a 'discovery'; to paraphrase Rorty, 'The world is not organized. Only we are.' To some extent a taxonomy must

---

denial of copyright to works having a utilitarian 'primary purpose' seems contrary to the supposition of *Feist* that the vast majority of factual compilations are copyrightable, as well as the long tradition of copyrighting maps and charts, the 'primary purpose' of which is seldom aesthetic. In addition to its means/ends analysis, the court also applied what it deemed a conventional *Feist* analysis of selection, coordination and arrangement and still found the Code lacking in originality. See Id.

147 Id.
148 Id. at 1723.
149 Id.
150 See *American Dental,* 126 F.3d at 978.
151 Id. at 979.
152 Id.

conform to reality, or it would poorly serve its admittedly utilitarian purpose.[153] However, reality still leaves taxonomers with ample freedom to organize and describe the world in individual and creative ways. With respect to the Code:

> Number 04267 reads 'guided tissue regeneration – nonresorbable barrier, per site, per tooth' but could have read 'regeneration of tissue, guided by nonresorbable barrier, one site and tooth per entry'. Or 'use of barrier to guide regeneration of tissue, without regard to the number of sites per tooth and whether or not the barrier is resorbable'. The first variation is linguistic, the second substantive; in each case the decision to use the actual description is original to the ADA, not knuckling under to an order imposed on language by some 'fact' about dental procedures. Blood is shed in the ADA's committees about which description is preferable.[154]

A taxonomy, in the Seventh Circuit's view, is not a 'compilation of bits and pieces of "reality",'[155] but a *description* of reality. Like other descriptions of reality (histories, biographies, maps or scientific treatises), taxonomies are original and copyrightable, at least as long as other descriptions of reality serve equally well.

C. Conjecture

The fact/expression dichotomy is easiest to apply when the fact is reasonably objective – such as the population of Princeton, New Jersey in 1970. A fact of that nature depends to some extent on the person who reports it, since one census taker may be more accurate than another, or may define 'population', 'Princeton' or '1970' in a different manner. However, there are still truths about the population of Princeton, New Jersey which may owe their discovery, but do not 'owe their origin', to the census taker. Those truths are not subject to copyright, though an author's manner of expressing them may be.

The harder cases are those in which the 'fact' is really a theory. Even if the theory is presented as truth, it may be based as much on the author's imagination as it is on independently verifiable data. One could more plausibly argue that a theory 'owes its origin' to the author, but at least with respect to historical accounts, courts have treated conjecture in the same manner as 'hard facts'. In *Hoehling v Universal City Studios, Inc.*,[156] the plaintiff devised a

---

153 See *American Dental,* 126 F.3d at 978 ('No one would read the ADA's Code for pleasure; it was designed and is used for business (for records of patients' dental history or making insurance claims) rather than aesthetic purposes.').

154 Id. at 979.

155 See Id. at 980.

156 618 F.2d 972 (2d Cir. 1980).

theory that the Hindenburg dirigible had been sabotaged by a crewman named Eric Spehl. That theory, which was the product of extensive research but also some speculation, served as the framework for the plaintiff's written account, entitled 'Who Destroyed the Hindenburg?' Ten years later, a second author produced a more literary retelling of the same events, employing the same theory as to the saboteur.[157] Universal Studios adapted the latter book for a motion picture.

Although the sabotage theory was novel, the court denied it any copyright protection:

> [T]he protection afforded the copyright holder has never extended to history, be it documented fact or explanatory hypothesis. The rationale for this doctrine is that the cause of knowledge is best served when history is the common property of all, and each generation remains free to draw upon the discoveries and insights of the past. Accordingly, the scope of copyright in historical accounts is narrow indeed, embracing no more than the author's original expression of particular facts and theories already in the public domain.[158]

The court feared the 'chilling effect' that would ensue if authors of histories were not given 'broad latitude' to make use of theories and interpretations advanced by their predecessors.[159]

In a similar case,[160] the Seventh Circuit denied an author exclusive rights to his theory that gangster John Dillinger survived long after his supposed demise. That theory, first advanced in books published by the plaintiff, rested on discrepancies in the generally-accepted accounts of Dillinger's death by gunfire in 1934. An episode of CBS's Simon and Simon television series toyed with the same premise. In an opinion by Judge Easterbrook, the court noted that intellectual advancement requires authors to 'build[] on the work of others', and it refused to treat the Dillinger theory differently merely because it was novel and speculative.

> Nash does not portray The Dillinger Dossier and its companion works as fiction . . . which makes all the difference. The inventor of Sherlock Holmes controls that character's fate while the copyright lasts; the first person to conclude that Dillinger survived does not get dibs on history. If Dillinger survived, that fact is available to all. Nash's rights lie in his expression: in his words, in his arrangement of facts (his deployment of narration interspersed with interviews, for example), but not in the naked 'truth'.[161]

---

157 See Id. at 975–76.
158 Id. at 974.
159 *Hoehling*, 618 F.2d at 978.
160 *Nash v CBS, Inc.*, 899 F.2d 1537 (7th Cir. 1990).
161 Id. at 1541.

If an author presents a theory as fact, it is perhaps only reasonable to treat it as a fact, however improbable it may be. Taking the author at his word also relieves the court of the burden of deciding whether a theory is true, or merely a product of the author's imagination.[162]

D. Matters of Opinion

Some propositions are either true or false. Although the truth may never be known, and forgetting for the moment the quantum-physics limbo endured by Shroedinger's cat, we can be confident that John Dillinger either did or did not die in 1934, and Eric Spehl either did or did not sabotage the Hindenburg. We cannot say, in the same way, that 'Ozymandius' is or is not a great poem; that is a matter of taste, not a matter of fact. Selections based on an author's taste have been treated as protectable expression.

In *Eckes v Card Prices Update*,[163] the Second Circuit held a baseball card price guide to be an original work of authorship. With entries for approximately 18,000 cards, the Eckes guide was 'a comprehensive listing of baseball cards manufactured . . . from 1909 to 1979'.[164] The author, James Beckett, selected 5000 of those cards as 'premium' cards commanding a correspondingly premium price.[165] In distinguishing between the 'premium' and the 'common', Beckett 'rel[ied] on his extensive knowledge of trading in baseball cards and his background in statistics'.[166] The defendant's guide, styled a price 'update', listed separately only premium cards, but those cards were the same 5000 selected in the Eckes guide.[167] The defendant also duplicated some of the prices, pictures, and mistakes in the original.[168] Conceding that '[c]opyright law and compilations are uneasy bedfellows',[169] the court held that the 'selection' of premium cards in the Eckes guide merited copyright

---

162 See *Hoehling*, 618 F.2d at 979 ('The cases in this circuit . . . make clear that factual information is in the public domain. . . . Each appellee had the right to "avail himself of the facts contained" in Hoehling's book and to "use such information, *whether correct or incorrect*, in his own literary work".'' (emphasis added, citations omitted)).

163 736 F.2d 859 (2d Cir. 1984).

164 Id. at 860.

165 '[T]hey are considered particularly valuable because of the player featured on the card, e.g., a hall of famer, a rookie of the year, or because of the team on which he plays, or because of some characteristic of the card itself, such as an imperfection or the scarcity of the card.' Id.

166 Id.

167 Id. at 860–61.

168 Id. at 861.

169 Id. at 862.

protection.[170] The court concluded that Beckett 'exercised selection, creativity and judgment in choosing among the 18,000 or so different baseball cards in order to determine which were the 5000 premium cards'.[171]

Eckes is noteworthy in two respects. First, the court refers to Beckett's creative 'selection' of premium cards, echoing the language of the Copyright Act which defines a 'compilation' as 'a work formed by the collection and assembling of preexisting materials or of data that are *selected*, coordinated, or arranged in such a way that the resulting work as a whole constitutes an original work of authorship'.[172] The definition would apply to collections such as 'Favorite Poems' or 'Healthy Recipes', where authors exercise their creativity by choosing what to include. Beckett's guide, however, seems to have been a comprehensive one, listing *all* baseball cards produced in a given period.[173] Beckett did not 'select' certain cards for inclusion in the guide, but rather 'selected' certain cards as worthy of 'premium' status. It is not self evident that this is the kind of 'selection' contemplated in the statute.[174] On the other hand, if the question is one of *creativity*, whether Beckett excluded common cards from the collection or merely labeled them as such seems to make no difference.

Second, if Beckett had selected as 'premium' cards those which gave him the greatest pleasure, or if in some other way he had employed entirely subjective criteria, one could easily say that the selection 'owes its origin' to the author. But Beckett's selection of 'premium' cards was determined in part by the marketplace – hence the need to exercise his 'extensive knowledge of trading in baseball cards and his background in statistics'.[175] Market price is a factor largely external to Beckett;[176] consequently, one could question whether his selection was 'original' in the copyright sense. An accurate assessment of the market no doubt requires judgment and experience, and the results may be speculative, but the same considerations apply to theories of history which, as we have seen, have been held lacking in originality. Still, the result in *Eckes* may be correct. If baseball cards command a range of prices, as one assumes they do, Beckett must have drawn the line between 'premium' and 'common'

---

170 Id. at 862–63.
171 Id. at 863.
172 17 U.S.C. § 101 (emphasis added).
173 See *Eckes*, 736 F.2d at 860.
174 Possibly Beckett's identification of premium cards should be considered a matter of 'coordination' or 'arrangement', rather than 'selection'.
175 *Eckes*, 736 F.2d at 860.
176 A price guide may influence prices in the marketplace, but it seems to have been Beckett's intention to report market conditions rather than to determine them.

somewhat arbitrarily.[177] If so, one could argue that even if card prices are facts external to Beckett, the distinction between 'premium' and 'common' 'has its origins' with Beckett. Because a different distinction might have made the guide less useful or appealing, it is also a choice related to form and presentation as well as content.

Later cases adopting the result of *Eckes* seem oblivious to its difficulties. The Second Circuit considered the copyrightability of the Red Book guide to used car prices in *CCC Information Services, Inc. v Maclean Hunter Market Reports, Inc.*[178] The defendant duplicated large portions of the Red Book data in its own database,[179] but the district court found that the car prices were not 'original': 'While Maclean Hunter [the author of the Red Book] may have been first to discover and report this material, the material does not "owe its origin" to Maclean Hunter.'[180] The appellate court reversed. The figures in the Red Book, it observed, are not historical market prices but 'predictions, based on a wide variety of information sources and . . . professional judgment'.[181] Because the numbers were based on 'judgment and expertise', they must be considered 'original creations'.[182]

In several respects, *CCC* is more troubling than *Eckes*. In *Eckes*, the sharp division of cards into 'common' and 'premium' is a device that has no precise analog in the marketplace, and thus can be considered the author's 'original' creation. In contrast, in *CCC* the court suggests that the prices themselves, which presumably are as close to reality as the authors could make them, are 'original' because they are estimates. Many facts can only be estimated. It is difficult to imagine a court holding an estimated value of gravity to be a figure protected by copyright, even if some 'judgment and expertise' went into its formulation.[183] *CCC* also strains the concept of 'selection', as it is used in the definition of 'compilation'. The authors of the Red Book 'selected' their prices by choosing them from a multitude of possibilities, but this is not selection in the sense of determining which materials to include in a collection and which to omit. If § 101 referred to data 'selected, coordinated, arranged *or devised*

177 If the choice were arbitrary to the extent of randomness, there would be some authority for holding it unoriginal. See *Toro Co. v R&R Products Co.*, 787 F.2d 1208, 1213 (8th Cir. 1986).

178 44 F.3d 61 (2d Cir. 1994).

179 Id. at 64. The defendant sometimes used the Red Book data as is, and sometimes averaged its prices with those listed in the similar Bluebook. Id.

180 Id. at 67.

181 Id. at 63.

182 Id. at 67.

183 Such 'judgment and expertise' might come into play, for example, if scientists discounted the values produced by certain experiments which, according to their 'judgment and expertise', were prone to error.

in such a way that the resulting work as a whole constitutes an original work of authorship', one could make a better case that estimated prices are 'original'.

The court argues that information such as the Red Book prices must be protected or the public welfare will suffer:

> Compilations that devise new and useful selections and arrangements of information unquestionably contribute to public knowledge by providing cheaper, easier, and better organized access to information. Without financial incentives, creators of such useful compilations might direct their energies elsewhere, depriving the public of their creations and impeding the advancement of learning.[184]

Identical reasoning could be applied to fact gathering. Facts unquestionably contribute to public knowledge, and if facts are not subject to copyright those who gather them may 'direct their energies elsewhere'. Yet the Supreme Court has held unequivocally, either in spite of the Constitution's concern for the public welfare or because of it, that facts are not 'original' and are not copyrightable. The same could be said of estimated facts, and with much the same justifications. Furthermore, in addressing the argument that estimated prices are 'ideas' rather than the expression of ideas, the court overstates its case when it warns that 'if CCC's argument prevails . . . virtually nothing will remain of the protection accorded by the statute to compilations, notwithstanding the express command of the copyright statute'.[185] Something would remain – namely, the protection of any original 'selection, coordination and arrangement' of prices. The author might not consider that protection enough, but it would prevent at least the easiest and most mechanical duplication of creatively presented information. In fact, the Red Book itself may have included such creativity, since it estimated prices by geographic regions, the selection of which may have been as arbitrary as the distinction between 'common' and 'premium' cards in *Eckes*.[186] However, any case that could be made for creative presentation is lost in the court's insistence that the facts themselves are protectable, because they are 'infused with opinion'.[187]

The Ninth Circuit reached similar conclusions in *CDN Inc. v Kapes*,[188] where the copyrighted works were lists of estimated wholesale coin prices. Here the issues were presented even more starkly:

---

184 *CCC*, 44 F.3d at 66.
185 Id. at 70.
186 See Id. at 67.
187 See Id. at 72-73.
188 197 F.3d 1256 (9th Cir. 1999).

> Whether CDN's selection and arrangement of the price lists is sufficiently original to merit protection is not at issue here. CDN does not allege that Kapes copied the entire lists, as the alleged infringer had in *Feist*. Rather, the issue in this case is whether the prices themselves are sufficiently original as compilations to sustain a copyright.[189]

At the 'heart of the case' lay '[t]he distinction between facts and non-facts, and between discovery and creation'.[190] 'Discoverable facts', the court admitted, 'are not copyrightable'.[191] Coin prices, on the other hand, are not historical facts based on actual transactions, but values derived by 'using [the authors'] judgment to distill and extrapolate from factual data'.[192] The faint spark of creativity demanded by *Feist* 'glows in CDN's prices, which are compilations of data chosen and weighed with creativity and judgment'.[193]

The district court characterized each CDN price as a ' "best guess" as to what the current "bid" and "ask" price should be'.[194] Similarly, the Ninth Circuit described the prices as whatever the authors, 'in their best judgment', thought would 'represent[] the value of [the] item as closely as possible'.[195] The court's language suggests that there is a true price for each coin which the authors sought to approximate, presumably with some success. But because the methodology was imperfect, and dependent on 'judgment and expertise', the court held the CDN prices sufficiently creative and original to be copyrighted.[196] The implications are far-reaching. Any reported facts that depend on judgment and approximation – crowd estimates, the age of antiquities, weather forecasts and medical diagnoses, to name just a few – could be considered copyrightable subject matter by the Ninth Circuit's reasoning.

One could argue that a collection of estimates, such as a price list, should be treated differently than any particular estimate, perhaps because of the Copyright Act's explicit protection of 'compilations'.[197] However, once the estimates are judged original in themselves, and not because of the manner in which they are selected or arranged, one faces the common sense observation in *Feist* that '100 uncopyrightable facts do not magically change their status when gathered together in one place'.[198] More plausibly, one could argue that

---

189 Id. at 1259.
190 Id.
191 Id.
192 Id. at 1261.
193 Id. at 1260.
194 Id.
195 Id. at 1261.
196 See Id. at 1260.
197 See 17 U.S.C. § 103.
198 499 U.S. at 345.

a price is not like other facts. Perhaps there is no such thing as a 'true' coin price, or an 'actual value', since price and value are always dependent on the changing and sometimes arbitrary desires of buyers and sellers. Perhaps the pretense of assigning a price to a coin is more fiction than fact. But whatever merits that line of argument might have, the Ninth Circuit did not rely upon it.

Finally, one might characterize the CDN coin prices as a vehicle for *presenting* complex data. In other, less controversial cases, courts have held that a particularly useful or concise presentation of facts is original and worthy of copyright protection. For example, in *U.S. Payphone, Inc. v Executives Unlimited, Inc.*,[199] the Fourth Circuit held copyrightable a publication distilling complicated public domain payphone tariff information into a convenient one-page-per-state format.[200] *CDN* suggests that coin price lists serve a similar function:

> If CDN merely listed historical facts of actual transactions, the guides would be long, cumbersome, and of little use to anyone. Dealers looking through such data would have to use their own judgment and expertise to estimate the value of a coin. What CDN has done is to use its own judgment and expertise in arriving at that value for the dealers.[201]

In a sense, the CDN price lists condense complicated data into something briefer and more useful, but the same could be said of the product of any research. Anyone interested in the fate of the Hindenburg would find the theory of Eric Spehl's sabotage more convenient than the stack of evidence from which it was derived. Just as the sabotage theory is more than a concise summary of the evidence, the CDN prices are more than a distillation of price data. They are the authors' best estimates of what the coins are actually worth.

E. Predictions

Predicting the future is, inevitably, an art 'infused with opinion'. Price guides can be described as predictions,[202] or as reflections, however imperfect, of the current state of the marketplace. Other copyrighted works are more explicitly concerned with future events. Because few things are as useful as accurately predicting the future, such works raise difficult issues under the idea/expression, fact/expression *and* process/expression dichotomies.

---

199 18 USPQ2d 2049 (4th Cir. 1991).

200 Id. at 2050.

201 *CDN*, 197 F.3d at 1261.

202 They are predictions in the sense of guessing what sellers will demand, and what buyers will pay, for a particular item. See *CCC*, 44 F.3d at 63.

Not long after the Supreme Court decided *Feist*, the Second Circuit, in *Kregos v Associated Press*,[203] addressed the copyrightability of a 'pitching form' listing baseball player statistics. Although other pitching forms predated Kregos' form, his was the first to list nine categories of data concerning the previous performances of the pitchers matched for an upcoming game.[204] The defendant, Associated Press, published a pitching form virtually identical to Kregos' form.[205] The district court granted summary judgment for AP, holding, among other things, that Kregos' selection of statistics lacked originality, and that the idea of the form had merged with its expression.[206] The Second Circuit reversed, drawing parallels between Kregos' selection of statistics and Eckes' selection of 'premium' baseball cards:

> The universe of known facts available only from inspection of box scores of prior games is considerably greater than nine, though perhaps not as great as the quantity of 18,000 cards in Eckes. For example, Kregos could have selected past performances from any number of recent starts, instead of using the three most recent starts. And he could have chosen to include strikeouts, walks, balks, or hit batters. By consulting play-by-play accounts of games, instead of box scores, he could have counted various items such as the number of innings in which the side was retired in order, or in which no runner advanced as far as second base. Or he could have focused on performance under pressure by computing the percentage of innings in which a runner scored out of total innings in which a runner reached second base, and he could have chosen to calculate this statistic for any number of recent starts. In short, there are at least scores of available statistics about pitching performance available to be calculated from the underlying data and therefore thousands of combinations of data that a selector can choose to include in a pitching form.[207]

Since Kregos had chosen his nine statistics from a wealth of possibilities, the court found his selection 'creative' in the sense required by *Feist*.

Of course, it was no accident that Kregos' form reported earned run averages rather than hot dog sales; Kregos evidently considered these nine statistics to be the most useful for picking a winner.[208] Yet the court did not regard

---

203 937 F.2d 700 (2d Cir. 1991).

204 See Id. at 702. The categories included the pitchers' won/lost records and earned run averages for the entire season; their won/lost records, innings pitched and earned run averages for the entire season, against the opposing team at the site of the game; and their won/lost records, innings pitched, earned run averages and men-on-base averages for their last three starts. See Id.

205 See Id.

206 See Id.

207 Id. at 704.

208 '[Kregos] is doing more than simply saying that he holds the opinion that his nine performance characteristics are the most pertinent. He implies that his selections have some utility in predicting outcomes.' Id. at 707.

the selection as an 'idea'. 'Every compiler of facts has the idea that his particular selection of facts is useful', the court observed. 'If the compiler's idea is identified at that low level of abstraction above the particular selection of facts the compiler has made, then merger of idea and expression is automatic'.[209] Similarly, Kregos' form was something more (or something less) than a 'system' for predicting outcomes.[210] The form reported 'facts that [Kregos thought] newspaper readers should consider in making their own predictions of outcomes', but it did not do the work for them.[211] Kregos did not 'weight the nine statistics, much less provide a method for comparing the aggregate value of one pitcher's statistics against that of the opposing pitcher in order to predict an outcome'.[212] He had simply 'compiled facts, or at least categories of facts'.[213]

The court 'confess[ed] . . . some unease', given the potential for monopolizing an idea by copyrighting a particular selection of data.[214] A doctor, for example, might publish a list of symptoms used to diagnose a disease. Even if other symptoms could be selected for the same purpose, there would be 'a substantial question' of copyrightability;[215] the selection of symptoms might represent the 'idea' of diagnosis based on those particular symptoms, which could be expressed only in that list.[216] That concern did not prevail here, apparently because Kregos' selection of statistics involved 'taste and personal opinion',[217] and did not, without further analysis, predict any future outcome.[218] The court described a 'continuum spanning matters of pure taste to matters of predictive analysis', and held Kregos' selection of statistics near enough to the 'taste' end of the spectrum to avoid any question of monopolizing a useful idea.[219]

Judge Sweet, writing in dissent, struggled to distinguish between the majority's medical diagnosis example and the predictive function of Kregos' statis-

---

209 Id. at 706.

210 See 17 U.S.C. § 102(b) ('In no case does copyright protection for an original work of authorship extend to any . . . *system* . . . regardless of the form in which it is described, explained, illustrated, or embodied in such work.' (emphasis added)).

211 *Kregos*, 937 F.2d at 706.

212 Id. 'Like the compilers of horse racing statistics, Kregos has been content to select categories of data that he obviously believes have some predictive power, but has left it to all sports page readers to make their own judgments as to the likely outcomes from the sets of data he has selected.' Id. at 707.

213 Id. at 706.

214 Id. at 707.

215 Id.

216 Id.

217 Id.

218 Id.

219 Id.

tics: 'In both cases, the creators have conceived very precise "ideas" concerning the significant data which ought to be considered in predicting a given result, and those ideas can be expressed only by identifying the relevant data.'[220] Even if medicine is 'more socially beneficial than a system for estimating sports odds', the distinction, argued Judge Sweet, 'does not offer a basis for denying copyright protection to one while granting it to another'.[221] Nor could one argue that diagnosis is 'more "scientific" and less "creative" than handicapping a baseball game. No doubt many people, including both doctors and those who make their living, either legally or illegally, in the sports gambling profession, would dispute such a claim.'[222] Finally, Judge Sweet regarded the majority's reasoning as inconsistent with the process/expression dichotomy of *Baker v Selden*: 'In my opinion, Kregos' form constitutes an explanation of his preferred system of handicapping baseball games, and he seeks to use his copyright here to prevent others from practicing that system.'[223]

Other critical observations can be added to those of Judge Sweet. First, it is curious that the incompleteness of Kregos' system – that is, his failure to suggest how the statistics he identified should be used – leads to the conclusion that the statistics can be reserved to Kregos as his exclusive property. Apparently, if Kregos had described a specific method of using these statistics to predict an outcome, the court would have held that method uncopyrightable. Yet, the very incompleteness of Kregos' system leads to a broader monopoly; not just one method, but *any* method of using Kregos' statistics, would be preempted by his copyright. Kregos' system is both less useful and more all-encompassing than a more complete system which the court would have committed to the public domain.

Second, one can question whether the court has properly imagined a 'continuum' between opposite poles of 'pure taste' and 'matters of predictive analysis'.[224] Many selections based on 'pure taste' have nothing to do with prediction, other than the prediction that readers will benefit from the selection.

---

220 Id. at 711 (Sweet J., dissenting in part).

221 Id. Distinguishing between different fields of endeavor based on their 'social benefits' might cause discomfort similar to what would be experienced if courts took on the role of art critics. Further, to discount the value of a particular set of statistics would be, in most cases, to reject the judgment of both plaintiff and defendant, each of whom evidently regarded the statistics as worthy of publication. On the other hand, if the boundary between idea and expression is just a pragmatic one designed to promote healthy competition, one cannot entirely dismiss the notion of case-specific line drawing in which courts take into account, among other things, the likely impact on society.

222 Id. at 711 n.12 (Sweet J., dissenting in part).

223 Id. at 713.

224 Id. at 707.

A collection of 'Amazing Facts About Alabama', for example, predicts no outcome external to the reader's experience of the work. The court seems to intend, rather, a distinction between highly speculative prediction (perhaps so speculative as to be defensible only on the arbitrary grounds of 'taste') and more reliable, systematic or 'scientific' prediction. As Judge Sweet observes, it is difficult to draw such distinctions, given the manner in which art and science combine in most attempts to predict the future.

Finally, the court is so intent on denying that idea and expression have merged, a concern pertinent only to the idea/expression dichotomy, that the court misses the separate concerns raised by the fact/expression and process/expression dichotomies. If Kregos' list of statistics reflects a fact about the game of baseball – that there is a correlation between pitchers' relative performances in these areas and their likelihood of winning the next game – then it should make no difference whether there are other such correlations to be discovered. Similarly, to the extent that Kregos' form is necessary to use any system based on those statistics to predict the outcome of a game, it should make no difference that other systems, using other statistics, could be used instead. Although there are many systems of bookkeeping, under *Baker v Selden* no one system can be monopolized by copyright.

Equally troubling is *Compaq Computer Corp. v Procom Technology, Inc.*,[225] decided by a district court in Texas. Compaq developed software for warning a network administrator when disk drive failure could be imminent. The timing of a 'prefailure warning' – a warning based on a likelihood of failure, rather than an actual problem – depended on five parameters selected and monitored by Compaq. The intention was to allow disk drives nearing the end of their life cycles to be replaced before they actually failed.[226] In order to make its own products compatible with the Compaq software, Procom copied onto its disk drives data representing Compaq's 'threshold values' for the five failure-predicting parameters.[227] Compaq filed suit, arguing that the threshold values were copyrighted.

As in *Kregos*, the court held the values 'original' because of the many choices available to their 'author':

> Compaq had to determine both the number and the particular parameters which it would monitor . . . . In addition, Compaq had to decide upon the appropriate threshold value for each of the five parameters selected. In selecting the threshold value, Compaq had to consider the point at which the drive would actually fail and then

225 908 F. Supp. 1409 (S.D. Tex. 1995).
226 See Id. at 1415.
227 See Id. at 1416.

> select a threshold that would be reached before actual failure. However, Compaq did not want to set the prefailure point too early in the life of the drive, otherwise Compaq would incur unnecessary expenses [under its warranty program].[228]

Compaq could have chosen to monitor other parameters, or could have used different threshold values for the same parameters.[229] The selections, the court noted, were 'based on both engineering and business related judgments',[230] and they 'reflect the requisite degree of creativity and judgment necessary to [copyright the] compilation'.[231]

In addition, the court held that Compaq's threshold values were not facts because they were not, like telephone numbers, 'empirically verifiable'.[232] They were, instead, the 'result of a decision making process', and 'more a prediction than a fact'.[233] Compaq's selection amounted to a 'business decision as to the point in the life of the drive that Compaq is willing to replace it under its warranty program',[234] or even an 'express[ion of] opinion' regarding when a drive should be replaced.[235] Other companies could express their own opinions by choosing different thresholds.[236]

Applying copyright rules to data 'understood' only by a machine[237] is frequently problematic, but both Congress and the courts have determined that such data may be within the scope of copyright.[238] Deferring to that precedent, the threshold values recorded on Compaq's disk drives should be no less copyrightable than the same values would be if printed in a user's manual for the benefit of a system administrator. Nevertheless, the question remains whether those values, wherever they appear, are an 'original' work of authorship.

As in *Kregos*, the court concentrates on the problem of merger of idea and expression, and solves it by finding that the author selected from a wide range

---

228 Id. at 1415.
229 See Id. at 1418.
230 Id. at 1415.
231 Id. at 1418.
232 Id.
233 Id.
234 Id.
235 See Id. at 1419.
236 See Id.
237 Procom itself did not understand what the threshold data represented; it knew only that the data had to be on its disk drives if they were to be compatible with the Compaq system. See Id. at 1416.
238 See 17 U.S.C. § 101 (defining a 'computer program' as 'a set of statements or instructions to be used directly or indirectly in a computer in order to bring about a certain result', and, by implication, including such programs within the subject matter of copyright); *Apple Computer,* 714 F.2d at 1249 (a computer program is copyrightable as a 'literary work', even when embodied in virtually unreadable object code).

of available choices. The court pre-empts the fact/expression dichotomy by holding the threshold values an expression of 'opinion', rather than a statement of fact, a characterization which, presumably, also disposes of the process/expression dichotomy. But the outcome is unsatisfying. What Compaq achieved was, in effect, a monopoly on its insights into disk drive operation and business planning. The former, especially, might be characterized as discoveries, rather than creative expression. The point at which a disk drive will fail is a fact, as is the relationship of any given set of parameters to the life expectancy of the drive. Even if one can only guess at those facts, it is unsettling to make Compaq's educated 'best guess' the subject of exclusive rights through *copyright*, rather than, perhaps, the patent monopoly, which is devised with such useful ingenuity in mind. However worthy Compaq's achievement, can it really be appropriate to treat the insights of an engineer (or a warranty-minding accountant) on a par with those of the author whose selection of poetry effectively communicates a mood? Is this what *Feist* meant by 'creativity?'

III. RESTORING THE FEISTIAN BARGAIN

The recent cases imply a new copyright dichotomy, separating not fact and expression but *fact and opinion*, or, perhaps more accurately, 'hard facts' and 'soft facts'.[239] Hard facts are objective, unoriginal and in the public domain; soft facts are subjective, original and copyrightable. Plausible as it may at first appear, the distinction between public domain hard facts and copyrightable soft facts has serious flaws.

A. Distinguishing Fact and Opinion

Hard facts and soft facts differ only in objectivity. A telephone number is a hard fact because the correct number is the correct number, regardless of the point of view of the person who reports it. The telephone number for the White House switchboard is (202) 456–1414. Unless I have it wrong, nothing about that fact 'owes its origin' to me. On the other hand, if I assign a value of $16.09 to a 1924 Denver Mint buffalo nickel in fine condition, that value may owe a great deal to me. Perhaps no other person would attribute precisely that price to that coin. Other judgments and other experiences could lead to other prices,

239 I use 'hard facts' to refer to information, like telephone numbers, which is relatively certain and independent of any point of view, and 'soft facts' to refer to information, like price forecasts, which is relatively uncertain and 'infused with opinion'.

some of which might be closer to the mean than others, but none of which could be truly described as right or wrong. Nothing in the world 'out there' compels the choice of exactly $16.09. Hence, the courts might describe me as the 'author' of that coin price and, at least in the aggregate, might consider my prices susceptible to copyright.

While the example suggests a clear distinction between uncopyrightable hard facts and copyrightable soft facts, it is a distinction that in practice is difficult to maintain. Indeed, one wonders whether there are enough hard facts to preserve the principle of *Feist* that facts in general are uncopyrightable, or whether the subjectivity exception would overwhelm the rule. Few facts are entirely objective. Even as colorless a fact as 'In 1970, the population of Princeton, New Jersey, was 12,331', owes something to its author. The person who collects and reports that information has an idea of Princeton, New Jersey as a distinct political or geographic entity, and 1970 as a distinct division of time. These are conventional ideas, but ones derived from human thought and culture rather than imposed by the world. Other elements built into this fact are more personal. Census takers may have differing ideas of 'population'. Some may include, or exclude, tourists, college students, the homeless, legal or illegal aliens, people who only worked in Princeton, or people who lived in Princeton for only a portion of the year. Some may calculate the population based on persons living in Princeton on 1 January 1970 or 31 December 1970. Some may take an average. The choice of methodology is, in some sense, a matter of 'opinion'. This is not to suggest that the reported population is nothing more than the census taker's fantasy, or that one figure cannot be more accurate than another, but any census data is, at least, the product of objective reality *and* subjective decisions rendered by the census taker. One can imagine a census taker reciting the methodological choices reflected in his data, just as photographers recite the choices of lens, film, lighting and so forth that led to their individual renderings of a scene.

Philosophers would be particularly reluctant to recognize a category of objectively ascertainable facts, many philosophers, particularly of the post-modern school, insisting that truth itself is a social construct.[240] That is not to say that there is no world 'out there',[241] rather that the world does not 'split[] itself up, on its own initiative, into sentence-shaped chunks called facts'.[242]

---

240 See Anderson, Walter Truett (ed.), *The Truth About Truth: De-confusing and Re-constructing the Postmodern World*, p. 8.

241 Although Jaques Derrida famously declared 'il n'y a pas de hors-texte' – 'there is nothing outside of the text' – there are probably few philosophers who would deny the existence of a 'real world', even when they question our capacity to grasp it. See Id. at 8, 89.

242 Rorty, *supra* note 1, at 5.

What we call 'facts', philosophers argue, are 'the product of a highly creative interaction between human minds and the cosmos'.[243] By constraining the questions we ask of the world, such subjective elements as personality and culture influence the answers we find. Benjamin Whorf, for example, argued that much of our perception of the world is determined by language.[244] As Whorf observed:

> We dissect nature along lines laid down by our native languages. The categories and types that we isolate from the world of phenomena we do not find there because they stare every observer in the face; on the contrary, the world is presented in a kaleidoscopic flux of impressions which has to be organized by our minds – and this means largely by the linguistic systems in our minds. We cut nature up, organize it into concepts, and ascribe significances as we do, largely because we are parties to an agreement to organize it in this way – an agreement that holds throughout our speech community and is codified in the patterns of our language.[245]

Because of such language constraints, even the truths of science cannot be entirely objective. '[N]o individual is free to describe nature with absolute impartiality but is constrained to certain modes of interpretation even while he thinks himself most free.' [246] If the public domain facts discussed in *Feist* are only those uncorrupted by the author's point of view, *Feist* is a much less significant case than most have supposed.

One might expect distinctions to break down in the rarified atmosphere of philosophy, but even on the most practical level nagging questions remain. If the application of 'judgment and expertise' makes the prediction of a used car price an 'original creation', why not a meteorologist's forecast, a physician's diagnosis or an archaeologist's interpretation of an artifact? Why not an historian's theory on the sabotage of the Hindenburg or the demise of John Dillinger? Is a controversial theory of physics any less 'infused with opinion'

---

243 Anderson, *supra* note 240, at 8.

244 See Whorf, Benjamin Lee (1956), *Language, Thought and Reality*, at 213. Whorf's best-known example involves Eskimos and snow; Eskimos perceive differences in snow because they have the vocabulary to describe each variety of snow distinctly, whereas, to the inhabitants of more temperate regions, snow is snow. See Id. at 216.

245 Id. at 213.

246 Id. at 214. Whorf rejected the notion of a 'universe that can be "found" independently by all intelligent observers, whether they speak Chinese or Choctaw,' which perhaps undercuts the distinction between creation and discovery associated with the fact/expression dichotomy. Whorf still does not suggest that truth is entirely personal. He suggests, rather, that perceptions of truth are different in different communities, speaking different languages. Within any particular community, it would appear that truths could be 'discovered' rather than 'created', at least so far as to justify treating those truths as common property rather than as the property of their 'author'.

than a car price? If so, how much less 'infused' must it be before it enters the realm of the unprotectable?

Debates among scientists are commonplace, even when the scientists are evaluating the same information. For example, astronomer David Black contends that all of the extra-solar planets so far discovered are actually mis-identified stars.[247] Most astronomers, viewing the same data, strongly disagree. Independent researchers from Tel Aviv University agree with Black that most of the identified planets are mis-identified stars, with two exceptions.[248] Given the present state of knowledge, anyone's list of genuine extra-solar planets is bound to be speculative, and to a degree personal. The controversy over the Martian meteorite, said by *some* scientists to contain evidence of life, is a further example of 'opinionated' science.[249]

One might conclude that most beliefs – even many we confidently label facts – are personal and subjective, hence 'creative' and copyrightable, yet we cannot go so far without largely, or even entirely, abandoning what the *Feist* court called 'the most fundamental axiom of copyright law'.[250] Instead, we are driven to the contrary conclusion: if subjectivity is an attribute of all facts, one cannot rely upon it, unless in indeterminate matters of degree, to identify a limited category of 'opinionated' facts which are subject to copyright.

The soft facts distinction also runs contrary to the various dichotomies that traditionally define the subject matter of copyright. One engineer's (or accountant's) 'opinion' that an aging disk drive should be replaced today rather than tomorrow may fairly be characterized as an idea about disk drive maintenance (or good business practices) rather than the expression of an idea. *Compaq* rejects that argument because '[t]here are numerous ways that a drive supplier may express its opinion as to when it should replace its disk drive'.[251] Perhaps – but only if each disk drive manufacturer has a different opinion or, in effect, a different idea. At best, the *Compaq* approach to the idea/expression quandary begs the question; one must *assume* that Compaq's 'idea' lies at a higher level of abstraction than its particular choice of parameters before one can conclude that the 'idea' is capable of various expressions. The same is true of the *Kregos* list of baseball statistics and the prices quoted in the *CCC* and *CDN* guides.

The process/expression dichotomy is also a concern. Compaq's system can be described as a method, or system, for predicting the failure of disk drives,

---

247 See 'Lost Worlds', *Scientific American* (Jan. 2001) at 21–22.

248 Id.

249 See 'Searching for Life in a Martian Meteorite: A Seesaw of Results', *Science News*, Vol. 150 p. 380 (14 December 1986).

250 *Feist*, 499 U.S. at 344–45 ('The most fundamental axiom of copyright law is that "no author may copyright his ideas or the facts that he narrates".' (citation omitted)).

251 *Compaq*, 908 F. Supp. at 1419.

or at any rate, for optimizing the timing of their replacement. Such a method, if it is non-obvious, is a candidate for patent protection, particularly now that 'methods of doing business' have been recognized as patentable subject matter.[252] Certainly it would be useful enough to satisfy the patent law requirement of 'utility'.[253] Hence, Compaq's attempt to protect its parameters as copyrightable 'expression', no less than Selden's attempt to protect his book-keeping form, seems an intrusion into the territory of patent law, without the relatively short duration of monopoly, rigorous examination and disclosure quid pro quo that patent law demands. Every inventor may have a different 'opinion' regarding the optimal invention, but the product of an inventor's labors is still the stuff of patents, not copyrights.

Finally, and most importantly, it is difficult to justify the exclusion of soft facts from so fundamental a concept as the fact/expression dichotomy. However opinionated or subject to error a soft fact may be, it reflects, or purports to reflect, an external reality which 'do[es] not owe [its] origin to an act of authorship'[254] – a discovery, not a creation. Compaq did not create the physical laws or business considerations that make disk drive replacement at a particular time more or less optimal. Kregos did not create the statistical relationships implied by his choice of baseball statistics. Except to the extent that their works are self-fulfilling prophecies, the authors of price guides do not create the demand for certain cars or coins. How, then, can we justify locking up such 'un-original' insights in the long-lasting monopoly of copyright?

Policy considerations add very little. While it is true that opinion-infused facts are valuable and that their 'authors' should be encouraged, hard facts are also valuable, and those who discover them likewise should be encouraged. Nevertheless, copyright law forbids a property interest in hard facts, favoring public access over incentives. Perhaps soft facts, because they are more speculative, are in some sense less useful than hard facts, so their authors' exercise of dominion withholds less from the public domain.[255] Yet if soft facts are less in demand than hard facts, one could argue that encouraging their production through monopoly is proportionately less justified. Any differences between

---

252 See *State Street Bank & Trust Co. v Signature Financial Gp.*, 149 F.3d 1368, 1375 (Fed. Cir. 1998).

253 See 35 U.S.C. § 101 (patents awarded to inventors of 'any new and useful process, machine, manufacture, or composition of matter').

254 *Feist*, 499 U.S. at 347.

255 See Gorman, Robert A. (1982), 'Fact or Fancy? The Implications for Copyright', 29 *J. Copyright Soc'y* 560, 572–73 ('Permitting a monopoly against copying (even in modestly embellished form) one's list of the fifty most liveable cities in America will, because of the very subjectivity involved in the compilation, not likely deprive the public of quite as significant information as when the compilation is mechanical, streamlined, and exhaustive.').

hard facts and soft facts, at least in terms of their contributions to society, appear on both sides of the copyright equation and seemingly cancel out.

B. *Feist* Revisited

On any question of copyright as it applies to factual works, *Feist* is the pre-eminent authority. Predictably, the later 'soft facts' decisions[256] make reference to *Feist*, particularly in emphasizing the low *threshold* of originality – phrased in *Feist* in terms of a 'minimal level' of creativity,[257] a 'not particularly stringent' requirement,[258] or a 'creative spark'.[259] Perhaps, however, they pay too little heed to *Feist*'s observations on the *nature* of originality. *Feist* strongly suggests that, in the case of factual works, 'originality' or 'creativity' lies only in the manner of presentation. In discussing the copyrightability of compilations, the court states: 'Facts are never original, so the compilation author can claim originality, if at all, *only in the way the facts are presented.*'[260] The way for the author to exhibit such originality is primarily through the selection, coordination and arrangement of the materials.[261]

Feist does not hold that a spark of creativity at any stage of the production of a written work suffices to make that work 'original'. On the contrary, by rejecting copyright protection for collections of facts based on the labors of the fact gatherer – the so-called 'sweat of the brow' – *Feist* impliedly rejects creativity in fact gathering as a relevant consideration. No matter how clever the research techniques behind the telephone directory, and no matter how indispensable they were to its contents, it is highly unlikely that the *Feist* court would have considered such creativity sufficient. As subsequent cases have observed, crediting originality in fact-gathering techniques, as opposed to fact-expressing techniques, would contradict the *Feist* distinction between creation and discovery. For the same reason, the *Feist* court almost certainly would not have recognized creativity in *formulating* facts – whether characterized as

---

256 For example, *CDN*, 197 F.3d at 1259; *CCC*, 44 F.3d at 65.

257 *Feist,* 499 U.S. at 358.

258 Id.

259 Id. at 359.

260 Id. at 358 (emphasis added). In other instances the court similarly focuses on creativity in presentation or expression, as opposed to creativity in substance. See, for example, Id. at 348 ('Factual compilations . . . may possess the requisite originality. The compilation author typically chooses which facts to include, in what order to place them, and how to arrange the collected data so that they may be used effectively by readers. These choices as to selection and arrangement, so long as they are made independently by the compiler and entail a minimal degree of creativity, are sufficiently original that Congress may protect such compilations through the copyright laws.').

261 Id. at 358.

judgment, experience or opinion – as a source of copyrightable originality. Originality in formulating facts, like originality in gathering facts, is creativity that precedes expression, rather than being a part of it. It may allow an author to convey a truer picture of the world, but that truth is not of the author's making, and cannot belong to the author by copyright.

C. A Suggested Approach

The approach to factual works that is most consistent with *Feist* is to seek out originality only in expression or presentation. Original language, or an original arrangement of materials, should be subject to copyright, at least as long as alternative means exist to express the same facts. What should not be subject to copyright is anything that reflects, or purports to reflect, a truth about the world external to the author and his works. Such truths, whether they are presented uncorrupt and unarguable or through the fallible lens of opinion, should become a part of the public domain, just as an author's ideas become a part of the public domain.

Collections of facts, like the directories considered in *Feist*, should be held copyrightable, as long as the selection, coordination and/or arrangement of facts is minimally creative, and as long as other selections, coordinations and arrangements can serve equally well. Coordination and arrangement are, in most cases, matters of presentation rather than substance. Coin prices are precisely the same, whether they are organized by value, by type of coin, or by the year the coins were minted, and no matter how various lists are cross-referenced. Such choices are not constrained by any circumstance external to the work. 'Selection' must be looked at more carefully. One could say that the author of a coin price guide 'selects' $16.09 as the price of a coin, instead of $16.08 or $16.10. Such selection is more than a matter of presentation, at least to the extent that it represents the author's best guess as to what the coin's value *actually is*. Similarly, a musicologist's list of all authentic pieces by J. S. Bach, based as it may be on the musicologist's golden ear and subjective judgment, purports to reflect a truth about Bach that would exist, and did exist, independently of its author. Other musicologists should be privileged to reproduce that list, just as they could reproduce newly-discovered facts about Bach's personal relationships or financial condition. Any other result contradicts *Feist*.

Some 'selections' are matters of presentation and do qualify as creative expression. The map maker who chooses to include some streets but not others is making a choice as to the most convenient way, or most aesthetically pleasing way, to present a subset of the available information. Only if the selection reflected an external circumstance not of the author's making (for example, the map illustrated all interstate highways but no lesser roads) could the selection be held to embody information about the world that belongs in the public domain.

Other 'selections' are less obviously matters of presentation, but equally reflect the author's taste and imagination, rather than the discoverable world. An example can be found in *Worth v Selchow & Righter.*[262] The plaintiff, Fred L. Worth, compiled a two-volume work he called 'The Complete Unabridged Super Trivia Encyclopedia'. Based on information derived from books, films and television shows, each book included 6000 items, arranged alphabetically by subject matter headings.[263] Worth's goal was to collect and present 'interesting and trivial facts' as well as 'facts that are difficult to find'.[264] Worth charged that the creators of the board game 'Trivial Pursuit' had appropriated many of their questions and answers from the materials collected in his books. He lost the case because the court found the works lacking in substantial similarity, but the originality of Worth's compilation is indisputable. Although the individual facts he reported were discoveries, the selection was Worth's creation. It owed nothing to the world external to Worth's individual taste and imagination.

This kind of creativity can be recognized in factual works, and protected by copyright, without doing violence to the separation of fact and expression, or creation and discovery. The creativity exhibited in the CDN coin prices, the car prices collected in the Red Book, or the Compaq parameters, is a different matter. These are 'selected' for their perceived fidelity to a reality 'out there'. There is creativity in the sense that subjective judgments have been brought to bear; only these authors, with their individual experiences and opinions, could produce exactly these works. To that extent, the works 'owe their origin' to their authors. But their judgments, subjective or not, are directed at a reality beyond themselves and their individual beliefs.

The place to draw the copyright line is not between objective and subjective accounts of the world, but between what one could call reporting and taste. The musicologist's collection of *authentic* pieces by Bach is an example of the former, however tentative, even individual, a report it may be. A collection of *favorite* pieces by Bach is an example of the latter, based on the author's aesthetic perceptions rather than any discoverable property of the world.[265] Such a collection fits far better within the framework of copyright

---

262 827 F.2d 569 (9th Cir. 1987).

263 See Id. at 570.

264 Id.

265 See Ginsburg, Jane C. (1992), 'No "Sweat?" Copyright and Other Protection of Works of Information after *Feist v Rural Telephone*', 92 *Columbia L. Rev*. 338, 345 ('*Feist* does not challenge or undermine the long-standing principle that a subjective selection of information, such as the "best" baseball players or the most socially promi-

than the collection of 'authentic' pieces by Bach, even if the latter is based upon highly subjective judgments regarding what sounds, or does not sound, genuine.

Where aesthetics are concerned there is no such thing as a 'fact'. Critics can debate the merits of a film, musical composition or restaurant without ever reaching a definite conclusion, because there is no external reality that makes an aesthetic opinion true or false. Usually a list of the 100 'best' of anything does not purport to reflect a fact, other than the author's feelings; to treat such opinion as copyrightable content does not take anything of 'the real world' into the realm of property. It is just conceivable, however unlikely, that the author of a price guide could defend his prices as nothing more than expressions of taste. That, however, should be the issue, not whether the prices are uncertain or opinionated. To be sure, there will be some cases where it is difficult to separate taste from highly opinionated facts. Gorman's example of the 'fifty most liveable cities in America', is an example. But if the line drawing is difficult at least it conforms with the fundamental principles of copyright laid down in *Feist*, and in many cases the distinction can be resolved by looking at what the author purports to offer – a personal reaction or a truth about the world.

IV. CONCLUSION

One can argue, with some force, that facts should be subject to intellectual property rights;[266] perhaps not exclusive rights that would bar the rediscovery and use of facts by independent researchers, but at least rights that would prevent the appropriation of labor, and imagination, by copying.[267] Such rights might encourage more research, and more publication of data, to the benefit of everyone. But the law should be consistent. If, as the Supreme Court held in

---

nent families, satisfies the minimal creativity standard.'). I disagree with Ginsburg, to some extent. The principles of *Feist* do undermine the potential copyrightability of any such selection, to the extent that the selection purports to mimic some aspect of the external world. If the 'best' baseball players and the most 'prominent' families are nothing more than expressions of personal taste, then *Feist* would not stand in the way of copyright.

266 Such rights were the subject of bills in the 106th Congress. See 'Collections of Information Antipiracy Act' (H.R. 354, 106th Congress, 1st Session) and 'Consumer and Investor Access to Information Act of 1999' (H.R. 1858, 106th Congress, 1st Session).

267 Professor Denicola argued, prior to the *Feist* decision, that the public's interest in access to information is largely protected if later authors can collect the same facts from the same sources as prior authors, without actually copying from those prior authors. See Denicola, *supra* note 4, at 541.

Feist, facts are not copyrightable, soft facts should not be excepted without both sound reasons and a principled methodology for drawing the distinction. More importantly, if any kind of fact is to be made property, it should be only after a thorough examination of the policies at stake, and a thorough consideration of the appropriate measure of protection. It may well be that the optimal balance between access and incentives for facts, even opinionated facts, would be struck at a much shorter duration of monopoly than the-life-of-the-author-plus-70-years term that Congress has recently found appropriate for copyrightable expression. Until *Feist* is overruled, those who 'speak of the world' must allow their observations, like their ideas, to become a 'part of the public domain available to every person',[268] reserving to themselves only their manner of expression, of which they are genuinely the 'author.'

ADDENDUM: OPINIONATED FACTS AND THE ABSENCE OF AUTHORIAL CONSTRAINT

The preceding text, in expanded form, first appeared in 2001, in Volume 33, Number 3 of the *Arizona State Law Journal*. Afterwards I published two additional articles discussing authorship, originality and creativity: 'The Random Muse: Authorship and Indeterminacy',[269] and 'Copyright and Information Theory: Toward and Alternative Model of Authorship'.[270] The opportunity to participate in George Washington University's 2007 copyright symposium on factual and functional works led me to consider how these three articles fit together, and specifically whether my later thoughts on authorship contradict my earlier impressions. I will take this opportunity to supply a general reconciliation.

'The Random Muse' examined indeterminate rather than factual works, but it too was an attempt to come to grips with the meaning of 'authorship'. Indeterminate works include some that are highly utilitarian – like parts lists composed of randomly-assigned numbers – and some with only artistic aspirations – like the aleatory music of John Cage, who often used random processes such as coin-tosses in the composition of his music. Courts have sometimes implied that a copyrightable work of 'authorship' must reflect human personality or intellectual labor, something that chance works fail to do. The most famous statement to the contrary, albeit in *dicta*, appears in *Alfred Bell v Catalda Fine Arts, Inc.*,[271] which considered whether mezzotint engravings of

268 *Feist*, 499 U.S. at 347 (citations omitted).
269 44 *William & Mary L. Rev*. 569 (2002).
270 2004 *BYU L. Rev*. 69 (2004).
271 191 F.2d 99 (2d Cir. 1951).

public-domain artworks were 'original' enough to be copyrighted. Determining that the mezzotints did include enough 'distinguishable variations', the court remarked that even an inadvertent fault in copying might constitute 'authorship': 'A copyist's bad eyesight or defective musculature, or a shock caused by clap of thunder, may yield sufficiently distinguishable variations. Having hit upon such a variation unintentionally, the "author" may adopt it as his and copyright it.'[272]

A random process certainly produces an 'original' work in the sense that it was not copied from other works of authorship, or even from 'the world' outside of the work itself. But does it possess the spark of 'creativity' required by *Feist*? I argued that 'creativity' might be defined as the influence of some peculiarly human quality, or, like 'originality', it might only exclude that which had been copied.[273] A randomly-organized telephone directory (if one can imagine such a thing), would not be creative in the first sense, but it would be creative in the second.

I offered several arguments in favor of considering randomly-organized or indeterminate works as copyrightable works of authorship. One is that such works are inherently unique, so that infringing works – which have to be *copied* from the copyrighted original – can be readily identified. This may be one of the reasons for the originality requirement itself. Second, I argued that a definition of originality dependent on the qualities of the work, rather than the circumstances of its origin, seems more consistent with a copyright system, like ours, designed to serve the public. In contrast, requiring the imprint of human labor or personality would fit better with a system of copyright emphasizing the natural rights of authors. Third, I observed that treating indeterminate expression as copyrightable would serve the goals of the idea/expression and fact/expression dichotomies. Indeterminate expression can be made the subject of exclusive rights without harm to the public because it is inexhaustible in a way that facts and ideas are not. Finally, I noted that a system of copyright de-emphasizing the human qualities of the author would match current theories of literary criticism, which have marginalized, if not debunked, the 'romantic' idea of authorship as the communication of meaning from the mind and soul of an author-genius.

---

272 Id. at 105–05.

273 The *Feist* telephone directory was 'original' in the narrow, or 'technical[]', sense that it did not exist until its 'authors' made it. However, it embodied the union of telephone numbers 'copied from the world' and a scheme of organization copied from other alphabetized lists. Even the idea of alphabetizing the telephone directory had been copied from other telephone directories. In that sense, the 'authors' of the Feist director created nothing – something the court acknowledges in calling it 'garden-variety' and 'practically inevitable'.

In the next article, I took these ideas even further by considering the relation between some fundamental ideas in copyright and the teachings of the branch of mathematics known as information theory. In a nutshell, information theory tells us that information is a function of *dis*order. This is a perplexing notion because we expect information to equate with meaning. Conveying meaning requires order; random messages, inevitably, are gibberish. But in a specialized sense the random string is the most information-laden message of all.

When a message has structure and patterns, the recipient can fill in any gaps with some confidence. The patterns allow the recipient to guess at the missing pieces. When that is the case, the message can be compressed into a denser format by omitting the unnecessary parts. The message that cannot be compressed is the random string, because no element of that message can be predicted in advance. In order to reproduce a message consisting of random elements, each and every element must be transmitted accurately. To a communications engineer, that means that the random string is dense with information. One way to put it is that the information in a message is inversely related to the constraints imposed on its composition – including the constraints imposed by pattern or meaning.

Copyright law also deals with freedom from constraint. If one can express a fact or an idea in only a limited number of ways, the merger of idea and expression, or fact and expression, rules out copyright. I proposed a model of authorship in which originality – like information in information theory – means unconstrained selection from an array of possible forms of expression. The *Feist* telephone directory was not original because the facts in the world and the existing system of alphabetizing dictated the form of the work in every respect. On the other hand, a randomly-organized directory would be highly original, even though it did not exhibit human personality or intellectual labor. Random organizations are original because they are distinctive, inexhaustible, and as free as possible from any manner of constraint.

The question I now face is whether this conception of originality is consistent with my former skepticism toward the copyrightability of opinionated facts. Opinionated factual compilations – which may include coin prices in a price guide, baseball statistics used to predict the outcome of games, or disk drive parameters indicating imminent mechanical failure – are said to be original and creative because they are colored by judgments and experiences individual to the author. Certainly there is an aspect to such compilations that is *internal*, and therefore unpredictable from anyone else's perspective. Furthermore, every expert who compiled a list of opinionated facts would likely produce something different and distinctive. If, like indeterminate works, compilations of opinionated facts are distinctive, inexhaustible, free of external constraint – in a way, random – must I concede that, under my proposed model of authorship, they are original and copyrightable? I would still say no, but I would have to invoke different considerations of copyright policy to justify my conclusion.

Copyright law exists to promote the progress of knowledge and cultural development, for the ultimate benefit of the public. Copyright protects the investments of authors – investments in labor or capital – to ensure that they have adequate incentives to create. If it were legal to photocopy and distribute the latest Harry Potter adventure, author J. K. Rowling could expect much diminished returns. On the other hand, the public interest forbids copyright protections so strict as to prevent any competition with established authors. Other writers can borrow Rowling's successful *idea* for a book about young wizards, so long as they steer clear of Rowling's expression. But, if other authors wish to compete in that market, they must be prepared to invest as she did in their own individualized expression; rather than take the simple expedient of photocopying Rowling's text, they must also burn the midnight oil thinking of plot twists, dialogue, intriguing characters and so forth. Similarly, composers wishing to write music similar to John Cage's (assuming that Cage's works are copyrightable) would be expected to busy themselves with dice and star atlases, just as Cage had done. The result is enhanced investment in, and enhanced production of, alternative forms of expression – a result that seems entirely consistent with the goals of copyright.

Now let us imagine how one would compete with 'authors' who had used their judgment and experience to compile opinionated lists of parameters predictive of disk drive failure, assuming that courts treated the contents of those lists as copyrightable subject matter. To produce a similar list, one would have to study engineering, conduct tests on disk drives, examine business considerations, and so forth. All of these are worthy endeavors, but are they the kinds of investments that copyright law expects to be duplicated by every author? *Feist* strongly suggests that they are not. Historians must find new ways to express the facts, but they need not re-discover the facts themselves. Compilers of telephone directories must devise their own systems of organization (if the directory from which they take their information is not organized in the 'inevitable' fashion of the *Feist* directory), but need not hire census takers to knock on every door. Requiring that kind of duplicated investment would, if anything, inhibit the availability of competing forms of expression. Investments in fact gathering are not the kinds of investments protected by copyright, and neither are investments in the study of engineering, coin prices or baseball.

In short, the lack of constraint characteristic of opinionated facts is a point in favor of exclusive rights; one need not worry about exhaustion of the resource. However, it is not enough to justify extending copyright protection to such facts. Copyrights for indeterminate works would encourage investments in expression – or, if 'expression' suggests a communication of meaning that is missing from indeterminate works, at least investments in presentation. Copyrights for opinionated facts, in contrast, would hinder the development of new forms of expression, all for the sake of protecting precisely the kinds of investments that *Feist* held beyond the purview of copyright.

6. Created facts and their awkward place in copyright law

Justin Hughes*

The writ of copyright reaches all *original expression*, a phrase that contains the two principal boundaries of copyright's realm. On one side, copyright law protects only expression, never ideas – no matter how imaginative those ideas are. On the other side, faithfully retype nineteenth century poems to your heart's content, but you will not get a copyright – because the expression you have produced is not original.

It is equally black letter law that facts are outside the realm of copyright because they similarly fail the originality requirement. As the Supreme Court told us in the 1991 *Feist v Rural Telephone* case, 'facts do not owe their origin to an act of authorship'[1] and, therefore, they will always fail the minimal creativity requirement of copyright law. The unanimous *Feist* opinion says little as to the nature of facts, but it is clear that the Justices view a 'fact' as something we discover, as something that might happen to us, not something that originates with us. A person might experience a fact; she does not create it.

The problem with the *Feist* analysis is that it is wrong – and that error has produced a decade of distortion in copyright doctrine. *Feist* is wrong because many facts clearly owe their origin to discrete acts of human originality. These human-created facts function in the social discourse no differently than the temperature in downtown Chicago on a particular date or the frequency with

* Professor of Law, Cardozo School of Law, Director Intellectual Property Law Program. The author thanks Robert Brauneis, David Dolinko, Michael Madison, David McGowan, David Nimmer, Pam Samuelson, Clyde Spillenger, Eugene Volokh, Clark Wolf, and Leif Wenar for helpful comments at different stages of this article's long gestation; the article benefited more recently from discussions at talks and conferences at Santa Clara University, UC Berkeley, and George Washington University. The author also thanks Taylor Ball, Shelley Cobos, Jesse Fox, David Morrison, and Wendy Wang for their research assistance. The remaining shortcomings are the exclusive intellectual property of the author. Email: Justin@justinhughes.net. This chapter is a modified and abridged version of Hughes, Justin (2007), 'Created Facts and the Flawed Ontology of Copyright Law', 83 *Notre Dame L. Rev.* 43.

1 499 U.S. 340 (1991).

which 'Old Faithful' erupts in Yellowstone Park. Indeed, the facts most unimpeachably *discovered* – ice core depths in Antarctica, planets orbiting distant stars, new species of animals – are often less important to your daily life than many facts that are human-created – such as the credit rating that Equifax gives you or the valuation your insurer gives your car after an accident.

This chapter explores the strange world of 'created facts', a world in which the expressive work brings the very facts themselves into existence. There are two incompatible characteristics of these situations: first, if the copyright incentive is needed to produce the expression, copyright is also needed for the facts to exist. Secondly, if the expression really produces facts, then one of copyright's core principles – the 'merger' doctrine – is likely to denude the expression of any protection. To avoid this second outcome, the discussion below proposes that we modestly amend how the merger doctrine works.

As an initial matter, Part I places facts in their historical and epistemological context, showing how copyright law – and the legal system generally – adheres to a view of facts that is out of synch with much philosophy and social theory. But accepting 'facts' as an inevitable construct of the legal system, Part II then explores how facts can arise in social life, following the work of philosopher John Searle. Parts III, IV, and V turn to the case law that has been percolating around three kinds of facts created by original expression: respectively, when people name things; when people create evaluations, judgments, or opinions that become widely accepted as true; and when private individuals create expression which becomes law. We will see that until quite recently courts have been unwilling to recognize that these original expressions produce 'facts' because, per *Feist*, such recognition would largely destroy any copyright protection.

Part VI explores further how expressive works can produce 'facts' as real – much more real for most of us – than the temperatures on the Martian surface or what we know happened from the fossil record.[2] Having established that the

---

[2] Different commentators have analyzed some of these cases in different ways. Lawrence Cunningham has discussed some of these cases as the integration of private expression into *public law*. See Cunningham, Lawrence A. (2005), 'Private Standards in Public Law: Copyright, Lawmaking and the Case of Accounting', 104 *Mich L. Rev.* 291. Dennis Karjala has approached some of these cases recognizing the establishment of copyright over taxonomic systems. See Karjala, Dennis (2003), 'Distinguishing Patent and Copyright Subject Matter', 35 *Conn. L. Rev*. 439. Pam Samuelson has critiqued some of these cases as establishing copyright over standards. See Samuelson, Pamela (2007), 'Questioning Copyright In Standards', 47 *B.C. L. Rev*. 193. I have separately criticized some of these cases for creating independent copyright protection over 'microworks'. See Hughes, Justin (2005), 'Size Matters (or Should) in Copyright Law', 74 *Fordham L. Rev.* 575 [hereinafter *Size Matters*]. But the emphasis here is on the fact-creating characteristic of these expressive works.

copyrighted works discussed in these cases produce facts, the question arises whether copyright's merger doctrine eliminates the copyright protection – a result that is both seemingly harsh and seemingly necessary. Part VII considers fair use, implied licenses, and merger doctrines as limiting principles for copyright protection in such works. I propose a recalibration of the merger doctrine borrowing from antitrust's 'essential facilities' doctrine to produce a result that makes the created facts accessible without eliminating the copyright incentive that leads to the facts' very creation.

I. *FEIST*, FACTS, AND EXPRESSIONS OF FACTS

The 1991 *Feist Publications v Rural Telephone Service* case[3] is now synonymous with the proposition that facts are outside the gamut of copyright protection. The defendant, Feist Publications, had sought to create a regional telephone directory for northwest Kansas. To that end, Feist had copied entries from Rural Telephone's white pages telephone without authorization – over 1300 entries verbatim and an additional 3600 entries in part. Rural Telephone sued for copyright infringement.

Interestingly, the word 'fact' does not appear in the Court's description of the disputants' activities. The Court characterizes Rural as refusing 'to license its listings'; tells us that Feist verified 'the data reported by Rural'; and even describes its own action as '[w]e granted certiorari . . . to determine whether the copyright in Rural's directory protects the names, towns, and telephone numbers copied by Feist'.[4] It is only when Justice O'Connor turns to doctrine – and the very moment she turns to doctrine – that we are told that the case involves the interaction of two fundamental propositions of copyright law: 'The first is that facts are not copyrightable; the other, that compilations of facts generally are.'[5]

But what are these facts? Perhaps the only important thing the Court tells us about the nature of facts is that they are discovered, not created:

> facts do not owe their origin to an act of authorship. The distinction is one between creation and discovery: The first person to find and report a particular fact has not created the fact; he or she has merely discovered its existence. To borrow from *Burrow-Giles*, one who discovers a fact is not its 'maker' or 'originator'.[6]

---

3 499 U.S. 340 (1991).

4 Id. at 343–44.

5 Id. at 345.

6 Id. at 347 (citing *Burrow-Giles Lithographic Co. v Sarony*, 111 U.S. 53, 58 (1884)).

Exemplary of how facts are discovered, the *Feist* Court described how 'Census takers . . . do not "create" the population figures that emerge from their efforts' because these facts are 'figures from the world around them'.[7] It follows that the one unifying characteristic of 'all facts – scientific, historical, biographical, and news of the day' is that they 'are not "original" in the constitutional sense'.[8] In other words, if facts are always discovered, then they always lack originality; if they always lack originality, then they are always beyond the ambit of copyright. This unanimous decision,[9] cast at the constitutional level when it could have been easily decided at the statutory level,[10] had a powerful impact on copyright law, both here and abroad.

Philosophically, the Feistian view of facts as 'out there', waiting to be discovered (and capable of being discovered) is *realism*, a realism that is basic to our entire legal system.[11] The view of facts laid out in *Feist* could be drawn right from criminal law, negligence doctrine, jury instructions, and the deference appellate courts have for triers of fact.[12] Our legal system requires a notion of facts as having what W.V.O. Quine described as 'unvarnished objectivity . . . a

---

7 Id. Because 'facts are never original', id. at 358, the *Feist* Court concluded that 'the only conceivable expression is the manner in which the compiler has selected and arranged the facts'. Id. at 349.

8 Id.

9 See, for example, Hamilton, Marci A. (2000), 'Copyright at the Supreme Court: A Jurisprudence of Deference', 47 *J. Copyright. Soc'y. U.S.A.* 317, 321 (discussing the rarity of unanimous decisions in copyright).

10 The Court could have achieved the same result at the statutory level, and much of Justice O'Connor's opinion is devoted to the conclusion that purely factual works are not 'original works' under the statute. *Feist*, 499 U.S. at 354–59. Some scholars identify 17 U.S.C. § 102(b)'s prohibition on copyright in 'discoveries' as the prohibition on copyright in facts. See 1 Nimmer, Melville B. and Nimmer, David (2007), *Nimmer on Copyright* § 2.11[A], at 2-178.9 ('The current Act has codified the rule precluding copyright in facts by providing that its protection does not extend to any "discovery" '.) But § 102(b)'s preclusion of any 'discovery' from copyright protection may refer to patentable inventions, not facts. Justice O'Connor does not pin her statutory interpretation on the word 'discovery', but rather says only that '[s]ection 102(b) is universally understood to prohibit any copyright in facts'. *Feist*, 499 U.S. at 356.

11 Simon Blackburn describes realism as holding the view that statements 'describe the world; they answer to or represent (independent) facts of a particular kind . . . These facts are discovered, not created, and they have their own "ontological" and "metaphysical" natures, about which reflection can inform us' 'the facts or aspects of the world that make commitments true or false be "mind independent", or not of our own making.' Blackburn, Simon (2005), *Truth: A Guide* 117–118.

12 See, for example, Kerr, Orin S. (2000), 'Rethinking Patent Law in the Administrative State', 42 *William & Mary L. Rev.* 127, 145 ('Questions of fact describe the state of affairs in the world, such as the time of day when an event occurred or the temperature at a particular time in a particular place.')

certain accessibility to observation . . . and the hint of bruteness'.[13] This is precisely what Los Angeles police Sgt Joe Friday meant on *Dragnet* whenever he implored female witnesses to provide 'Just the facts, ma'am'. In just this spirit, the *Feist* court understood 'wholly factual information' to be 'raw data'.[14]

A. A Very Short History of Facts

Our judicial system's foundation on fact-finding is a reflection of the long development of the fact in science, commerce, and public policy. Scholars have studied how late seventeenth and then eighteenth century thinkers sought to emphasize the need for observational particulars, for separating theory from the collection of observational data, and for privileging these 'facts' until they became, in Mary Poovey's apt description, 'the epistemological unit that organizes most of the knowledge projects of the past four centuries'.[15] This observable fact that is 'out there' became foundational for empiricism, for the kind of public policy debates that took hold in the West in the eighteenth century, and, arguably, for democratic self-governance itself. This is because cleaving observed particulars from (apparently more) theoretical arguments allowed learned men to agree on something, while they disagreed strenuously on issues of theory, method, ideology, or policy.[16] Broadly understood, most of us adhere most of the time to this 'extra-lingual' or 'mind independent' view of facts, at least to the degree that there is *something* out there to which an expression of fact corresponds. In this 'correspondence theory' true statements are statements which correspond to real world facts; facts are states of the

---

13 Quine, Willard Van Orman (1960), *Word and Object* 247. In this common understanding of facts, 'facts are what make sentences true'. Id. Simon Blackburn characterizes this as the 'absolutist' view of truth – which seems a good characterization of what law aims for. Of it, he says 'We like plain, unvarnished objective fact, and we like it open, transparent, and unfiltered.' Blackburn, *supra* note 11 at xv.

14 *Feist*, 499 U.S. at 345.

15 Poovey, Mary (1998), *The History of the Modern Fact* xiii; see also Daston, Lorraine (1991), 'Baconian Facts, Academic Civility, and the Prehistory of Objectivity', 8 *Annals of Scholarship*, nos. 3–4, 337; Daston, Lorraine (November 1992), 'Objectivity and the Escape from Perspective', 22 *Social Studies of Science* 597; Dear, Peter (1995), *Discipline and Experience: The Mathematical Way in the Scientific Revolution*. Poovey refers to this scholarship as 'historical epistemology', supra at 7.

16 Poovey, *supra* note 15 at 111 (noting that seventeenth and eighteenth century English writers and scholars argued that facts were separable 'from both theory and method in order to decrease the likelihood of civil dispute'). See also Arendt, Hannah (1968), *Between Past and Future* 259–260 (describing how the 'fact-finder' – witness or reporter – needs to be outside the community debating issues and differing in opinions).

world.[17] 'Santa Claus lives at the North Pole' is not a true statement because it does not correspond to any fact (state of the world), but 'Santa Claus is commonly depicted as living at the North Pole' is a true statement of fact because it corresponds to the contents of innumerable films, books, and holiday displays.

B. Two Worldviews Without Facts

This neat worldview was always subject to doubt and caveat, but came under increasing attack in the twentieth century. While a law review chapter is not the place to review these schools of thought, a general sense of the intellectual topography helps place copyright's ontology in context.

The first main line of critique has been against the fact/value distinction itself, that is to question whether there are any facts [or truths] independent of our theories. As Hilary Putnam puts it '[p]erception is not innocent; it is an exercise of our concepts'[18] or as Jose Ortega y Gasset wrote '[r]eality is not a datum, not something given or bestowed, but a construction which man makes out of the given thing'.[19]

Of course, all this sits quite uncomfortably with the law's reliance on 'facts' and, yet again, *Feist* provides a simple example whose complexity was overlooked by the Court. When Census workers gather information on literacy, occupations, and incomes of respondents, these are facts created by humans in the regular course of living – and 'discovered' subsequently by other humans. But when the Census enumerators start compiling facts about race, things become murkier. The abiding debates about Census racial categories show that racial facts are very much constructed by our judgments about categories.[20] Similarly, when the 1920 Census reported that 51.2 per

---

17 See, for example, Nozick, Robert (1993), *The Nature of Rationality* 107–114 ('Reasons and Facts'); Searle, J.R. (1995), *The Construction of Social Reality* 199–226 ('Truth and Correspondence') [hereinafter Social Reality]. See also Lowe, E.J. (1995), 'Fact', in Honderich, Ted (ed), *The Oxford Companion to Philosophy* ('A fact is, traditionally, the worldly correlate of a true proposition, a state of affairs whose obtaining makes that proposition true.'). Blackburn, *supra* note 11 at 56 ('This is the idea that truth can be understood and explained in terms of correspondence with the facts. It is not merely the idea that "true" means "corresponds with the facts"; this may be a harmless synonym. . . . But for the phrase to work as a philosophical explanation of truth, more is needed. It is needed that "corresponds" means something on its own and "facts" are identifiable in some special way, and then we can put them together and see correspondence with the facts as a special kinds of success.')

18 See Putnam, Hilary (2002), *The Collapse of the Fact/Value Dichotomy and Other Essays* 15.

19 Gasset, Jose Ortega y (1958), *Man and Crisis* 13 (Mildred Adams, trans.).

20 Over the history of the Census, it has offered at least 26 different racial or ethnic characterizations for respondents. In recent times, the process left many people

cent of the American population was living in urban areas,[21] it sounds like a pretty hard-boiled fact until you learn that the Census Bureau decided that anyone in a town with over 2500 inhabitants was an 'urban' dweller[22] – an evaluation quite different from what we might make today.

The second, more radical critique of the traditional correspondence theory comes from a number of twentieth century philosophers who have reasoned that facts are *only* linguistic elements[23] and that our notion of a 'fact' should be reduced to that of a true statement (and effectively eliminated). As Quine succinctly observed, '[i]n ordinary usage "fact" often occurs where we could without loss say "true sentence" or . . . "true proposition".'[24] The reduction of 'facts' to true statements led many philosophers to conclude that the nature of facts is an ancillary issue – if an issue at all – for inquiries into the nature of truth and knowledge.[25] As Colin McGinn writes of his own epistemological views, '[t]o explain the concept of truth we therefore do not need to appeal to obscure relations of correspondence and dubious entities called facts'.[26]

---

feeling that they were pigeonholed, that is that their racial status (the actual reality about their race) was not accurately captured. See Gurza, Agustin, *In Search of a Census Pigeonhole*, *L.A. Times*, 1999 July 6 [national edition], at A10, col. 1.

21 Shaffer, Helen B. (1969), 'Population Profile of the United States', Boeckel, Richard M. and William B. Dickinson (eds), in *Editorial Research Reports on the Urban Environment* 1, 12 (Congressional Quarterly, Inc.) ('The 1920 census was first to tip the balance with 51.2 per cent counted as city dwellers.').

22 Anderson, Margo J. (1988), *The American Census: A Social History* 134.

23 For example, in the 1950s, P.F. Strawson advanced the view that 'facts' were linguistic elements. Strawson thought that in order to specify a fact, in order to answer the question 'which fact?' one would have to have a true statement already. Strawson, P.F. (1950), 'Truth', 34 *Proceedings of the Aristotelian Society*, reprinted in Pitcher (ed.), (1964) *Truth*. Strawson believed that facts were linguistic in that 'facts are what statements (when true) state; they are not what statements are about' Id. at 38.

24 Quine, Willard Van Orman (1960), *Word and Object* 247. Of course, for many philosophers a 'true sentence' and a 'true proposition' differ in that propositions are non-linguistic entities expressed by sentences. In that view, 'it rains' and 'il pleut' express the same proposition. Frege held to a view of this sort, defining a fact as 'a thought [gedanke] that is true'. Frege, Gottlob (1967), 'The Thought' in Strawson, P.F. (ed), in *Philosophical Logic* 35 (Oxford). Here 'gedanke' seems to mean proposition, not a mental state – a point that Frege clarifies later on the page. My thanks to David Dolinko for this clarification.

25 See, for example, Quine, *supra* note 24 (in *passim*); Bonjour, Laurence (1985), *The Structure of Empirical Knowledge* (dealing very little with 'facts' in its analysis of knowledge). See also Quine,Willard Van Orman (1987), *Quiddities* 213 [hereinafter Quiddities] ('The world is full of things, variously related, but what, in addition to all that, are facts? . . . . The true sentence "Snow is white" is true if and only if it is a fact that snow is white. Now we have worked the fact, factitious fiction that it is, into a corner where we can deal it the coup de grace. The combination "it is a fact that" is vacuous and can be dropped; "It is a fact that snow is white" can be reduced to "Snow is white".').

26 McGinn, Colin (2003), *The Making of a Philosopher* 93.

C. What Courts Say about Facts and Expressions of Facts

Among these three possibilities – the facts being 'out there', facts arising from subjective perspectives, and facts being nothing more than true statements – it seems pretty clear that the legal system adheres to a correspondence theory: the facts are out there, quite separate from subjective viewpoints. Yet if lawyers, judges, and jurors hold to a correspondence theory of facts, there is a certain lack of rigor in any judicial pronouncement that 'facts are not copyrightable',[27] that 'there can be no valid copyright in facts',[28] or that 'no author may copyright . . . the facts he narrates',[29] If a fact is 'out there' in the world, then quite typically it is not 'fixed in a tangible medium'. That it rained in Chicago last night, that Ella Fitzgerald played a concert at Deutschlandhalle, Berlin on 13 February 1960,[30] that you said 'I love you' to someone yesterday – none of these facts 'out there' are fixed at all. (There may be fixed, historical recordations of the facts, but it is not the recordations which make the facts facts). That the wingspan of a Boeing 767-400 aircraft is 51.9 meters[31] or that the Todai-ji temple in Nara, Japan is the largest wood structure in the world are facts that are 'fixed' in a sense, although not as traditionally understood in copyright law. In other words, if facts are out there, then broadly speaking, they are not even in the ballpark of copyright.

By the lights of the correspondence theory, what judges and legal scholars are actually discussing are *representations* or *statements* of facts. Occasionally, judicial opinions capture this point precisely. Thus, Judge Roney on the Fifth Circuit wrote that it is 'well settled that copyright protection extends only to the author's *expression of facts* and not to the *facts* themselves'[32] and Judge Easterbrook on the Seventh Circuit noted that 'core equations, such as the famous E=mc2, *express* "facts".'[33]

---

27 *Feist Publ'ns, Inc. v Rural Tel. Serv. Co.*, 499 U.S. 340, 344 (1991).

28 Id.

29 Id. at 345 (quoting *Harper & Row, Publishers, Inc. v Nation Enters.*, 471 U.S. 539, 556 (1985)).

30 Ella Fitzgerald, *Mack the Knife – The Complete Ella in Berlin* (Verve Records, 1960).

31 Boeing, *767 Family: Technical Characteristics, Boeing 767-400ER*, http://www.boeing.com/commercial/767family/pf/pf_400prod.html (last visited 22 October 2007).

32 *Miller v Universal City Studios, Inc.*, 650 F.2d 1365, 1368 (5th Cir 1981); see also *Feist*, 499 U.S. at 348 ('Others may copy the underlying facts from [a] publication, but not the precise words used to present them.')

33 *Am. Dental Ass'n v Delta Dental Plans Ass'n*, 126 F.3d 977, 979 (7th Cir. 1997) (emphasis added).

On the other hand, when a distinguished judge or scholar just says *facts* are not protected by copyright law, he or she is engaged in a form of shorthand that is more than just imprecision. It is a subconscious application of copyright's merger doctrine. With most ideas, there seem to be many ways to express each idea, so that cleaving expression and idea is relatively easy. But facts are a different matter. Cleaving the fact and its expression is not so easy because 'generally speaking, there are few ways of depicting, rendering, or expressing facts'.[34] This is particularly true with quantitative conclusions. With any fact or idea expressed in Hindu-Arabic numbers, the idea or fact seems inextricably 'merged' with its expression because there is no other reasonable way to express the idea/fact.[35] Loose discussion that 'facts' are not protected by copyright inadvertently points to the 'tightness' between facts (out there) and the expression of facts. Consider this statement from *Feist:*

> Thus, if the compilation author clothes facts with an original collocation of words, he or she may be able to claim a copyright in this written expression. Others may copy the underlying facts from the publication, but not the precise words used to present them. Where the compilation author adds no written expression but rather lets the facts speak for themselves, the expressive element is more elusive.[36]

Under this standard, when I write '*That first morning in February on the Park Avenue, the temperature nudged just above freezing and stuck there*' I have 'clothed' a fact in protectable 'expression'. But imagine my journal instead showing the following:

> 1 February 2004, morning – Park Avenue – 33 degrees F

For Justice O'Connor, the expression here was 'elusive'. But it is not elusive at all. There is 'expression' – words fixed on paper – probably unoriginal, but expression nonetheless. The tightness between fact and statement of fact is summarized well by philosopher John Searle:

---

34 *Skinder-Strauss Associates v Massachusetts Continuing Legal Education, Inc*., 914 F. Supp 665, 672–73 (D. Mass. 1995).

35 At least not in this time and culture. See Crosby, Alfred (1997), *The Measure of Reality* (describing the gradual triumph of Hindu-Arabic numbers over Roman numbers as western European societies became increasingly sophisticated in mathematics and commerce); Seife, Charles (2000), *Zero: The Biography of a Dangerous Idea* 67–81 (same). Of course, as discussed above, in a few cases the idea and its expression in Hindu-Arabic number seem *less* merged, that is where a temperature can be expressed in Fahrenheit or Centigrade (or Kelvin), or where the Super Bowl designation is common in either Roman or Hindu-Arabic numbers.

36 *Feist*, 499 U.S. at 348–49.

> Because statements determine their own truth conditions and because the term 'fact' refers to that in virtue of which statements are true, the canonical way to specify the fact is the same as the way to specify the statement, by stating it.[37]

If we substitute the copyright term 'expression' for the philosopher's 'statement', we have a succinct rendering of the problem in copyright law: the canonical way to specify the fact is the same as the way to specify the expression of the fact, that is by expressing it.

II. HUMAN FACTS – HISTORICAL, SOCIAL, CREATED

The *Feist* characterization of facts fits well with the geographic facts explorers discovered when mapping the coast of the New World or with the discovery of when and where a particular animal died (leaving behind fossil remains).[38] These are features of the world that are 'intrinsic to nature'.[39] Contrast these with the height of the Chrysler Building or a Mayan temple, the itinerary of a political candidate or of a soccer mom – these facts are the result of human agency. Among such 'human facts', some facts result from the cumulative, uncoordinated actions of humans (for example the population of Los Angeles on 4 July 2007) and some result from the intentional actions of individual people or coordinated groups of people (for example who wrote the script for the film *L.A. Confidential*). For either kinds of human fact, some seem to become permanent, independent features of the world. As Lawrence Friedman writes, '[n]o doubt the average person in France or Italy thinks there is something quite specific about French or Italian nationality; that these are clear-cut categories of the world, as real as mountains and rivers; and that somehow the nation was always meant to be'.[40] Of course, divisions among nationalities are facts created by all kinds of human interactions over years. On the other hand, street names and street addresses are facts created by an identifiable individual or individuals. As Wendy Gordon writes, 'one's address does not cease to be a fact upon a showing that the name of one's street originated in the fancy of a housing developer'.[41]

---

37 Social Reality, *supra* note 17 at 219.

38 For discussions of the fossil record, see generally Gould, Stephen Jay (1989), *Wonderful Life: The Burgess Shale and the Nature of History*; Morris, Simon Conway (1998), *The Crucible of Creation* 53–56.

39 Social Reality, *supra* note 17 at 9.

40 Friedman, Lawrence (1999), *The Horizontal Society* 82–83.

41 Gordon, Wendy (1992), 'On Owning Information: Intellectual Property and the Restitutionary Impulse', 78 *Va. L. Rev.* 149, 281, n. 21. The mini-taxonomy of facts in these paragraphs does not correspond to the classic distinctions that have been devel-

This immediately puts us in a position to see how things are much more complicated than the *Feist* opinion suggests. With street addresses collected in the Census, some human(s) create the facts and another human collects them – there is both creation and 'discovery'. And when a local telephone company publishes a telephone directory, it collects some human facts that pre-existed (customer names) and other facts that it itself created (the phone numbers). The person who is publishing the expressions of the telephone number facts seems to be the same person who 'created' those facts.[42] The same could even be said of what our legal system calls 'mixed questions of law and fact', that is where the raw facts are admitted (the car plowed into the storefront; X was driving the car) and the 'issue is whether the facts satisfy the statutory standard'[43] (X was negligent). When the court makes such a determination and certifies its opinion for publication, the entity publishing the expression (the opinion) is the same person who 'created' the fact (X was negligent).

A. The 'Created Fact' as a Kind of Human Fact

Still this does not yet focus on the 'created fact' problem. For one thing, the telephone company probably created the telephone number well before it published the expression of the telephone number. For another thing, the telephone company would have created the telephone numbers even if there was to be no telephone book; telephone numbers are necessary for telephone switching equipment to work. Unlisted telephone numbers are created – and are 'facts' – even if they are never publicly expressed.

So, let us draw one further distinction. Most human facts are 'side effects' of human activity – as in the Ella Fitzgerald concert, 'I love you', and Los Angeles population examples. Contrast this with human facts that result from an act that was the *intentional creation of information qua information* through the *intentional creation of expression qua expression*. I will call these 'created facts' or 'authored facts'. For example, computer modeling and simulation

---

oped in philosophy, such as the concept of a 'brute fact' or a 'social fact'. For the classic formulation of the former, see Anscombe, G.E.M. (1958), 'On Brute Facts', 18 *Analysis* (no. 3). A 'brute fact' is also used more generally to describe the terminus of a series of explanations that is itself not further reducible. Haldane, John (2005), 'Brute Fact', *The Oxford Companion to Philosophy*, available at Oxford Reference Online. For a classic theory of social facts separate from Searle, see Durkheim, E. (2005), *The Rules of Sociological Method* 50–60 (Steven Lukes (ed.), W.D. Halls (trans).

42 At least for those local service customers whose telephone companies print their own telephone books. The process of creating the number may, of course, still lack originality. See Nimmer, David (2001), 'Copyright in the Dead Sea Scrolls', 38 *Houston L. Rev.* 1, 97–98 (noting that the telephone numbers were not antecedent facts, but still can lack originality).

43 *Pullman-Standard v Swint*, 456 U.S. 273, 289 n. 19 (1982).

now generate much of our social science and public policy data. Numbers for current population counts, traffic flows, or economic levels are treated as facts although they are often numbers extrapolated from sampling (real Feistian observational facts) combined with human guesses/judgments/opinions.[44] Complex computer simulations that provide estimates of pre-historic animal migration patterns or dispersal patterns for explosive devices that have never been constructed give us datapoints that are 'created', but which we treat as facts.[45] But created facts need not be so esoteric, as we will see in Parts III, IV, and V.

B. Facts, Values, and Social Reality

The 'factness' of the original expression at issue in the copyright cases discussed below comports with John Searle's broader project of showing how social reality relates to the rest of reality, that is how some facts arise from human agreement.[46] Searle's basic thesis is that 'there are portions of the real world, *objective facts in the world*, that are only facts by human agreement'.[47] Searle analyzes this human agreement, that is the establishment of social conventions, as what he calls 'collective intentionality'.[48]

Institutions, occupations, membership in groups, our particular jobs, our familial relations and status – are all established by social conventions which require representations, language, and – almost always – fixed expressions. A basic characteristic of these 'social facts' is that they are language-dependent (for our purposes, we could say 'expression dependent'). In Searle's proposal, a social fact depends on mental representations which, in turn, require expressive communication among persons. As Searle notes, 'marriages and money, unlike mountains and atoms, do not exist independently of all representations'.[49] The representations (or expressions) constitute communication

---

44 An example of this is the 'Transportation Analysis Simulation System' [TRANSIMS] developed at Los Alamos National Laboratory. TRANSIMS 'extrapolates US Census data to create a synthetic population, which is assigned activities – such as driving to work – based on diaries kept by selected residents of the studied area. TRANSIMS then factors in transit-system constraints and simulates traffic flow.' Verge, *Wired*, January 2001, at 236; see also Kolata, Gina, 'Why Some Numbers Are Only Very Good Guesses', *New York Times,* 11 March 2001, § 4, at WK5 (describing the reason for the estimating process in the census).

45 Poovey makes a similar observation and calls such datapoints 'a post-modern variant of the fact'. Poovey, *supra* note 15, at 2–3.

46 *Social Reality*, *supra* note 17 at 1–6; Searle, John R. (1969), *Speech Acts*, 50–53 [hereinafter *Speech Acts*].

47 *Social Reality*, *supra* note 17 at 1 (emphasis added).

48 Id. at 26, 122.

49 Id. at 190. For Searle, 'a fact is language independent if that very fact requires no linguistic elements for its existence'. Id. at 61.

among people; when that communication leads to collective acceptance of the new, additional reality, we have a 'social fact'.[50] Thus, Searle's overall project is to show how additional, human-created, intention-laden reality gets overlaid on top of 'brute' reality, producing different sorts of facts through social agreement. Those commonly accepted facts are distinct from all the beliefs, theories, opinions, and ideas on which we differ *and we know we differ*.[51] This distinction between such 'facts' and opinions is commonplace, but as Robert Post says in the context of defamation law, 'it is also deeply obscure, and it has proved resistant to most analytic attempts at clarification'.[52] More or less unnoticed, this is a deep and fundamental problem in the series of cases we now consider.

III. THE PROTECTION OF NAMING FACTS

When an individual or group gives a name to something – and that name sticks – we have perhaps the most basic of social facts. When Augustine and Mary Ball Washington named their first child 'George', when Spanish settlers called their encampment 'El Pueblo de Nuestra Senora la Reyna de los Angeles del Rio Porciuncula' [shortened by an early tourist board to *Los Angeles*], or when Apple researchers dubbed one of their projects 'Carl Sagan'[53] each of these acts produced a social fact. These acts of naming can have great importance (as in *Malvinas* versus *Falklands* or as with new corporate names like *Verizon* or *Exxon*).

In the face of this importance, copyright law has a long-standing rule that '[w]ords and short phrases such as names, titles, and slogans' are not copy-

---

50 See id. at 111 (describing the 'primitive logical operation' by which institutional reality is created).

51 This connects nicely with Robert Post's argument that a public discourse of the kind protected by the First Amendment is characterized by discourse across ethnic, religious, and social communities which requires agreement on certain things, but not all things. 'The conduct of public discourse', Post wrote, 'requires persons to share standards, but not the kind of standards that fuse them into a [single] community.' Post, Robert C. (1990), 'The Constitutional Concept of Public Discourse: Outrageous Opinion, Democratic Deliberations and *Hustler Magazine v Falwell*', 103 *Harv. L. Rev.* 603, 636. Post further makes a persuasive argument that 'facts' as the Court has described them in defamation law are things on which we can *expect* agreement or 'convergence'. Id. at 657–658.

52 Id. at 649–650.

53 See *Sagan v Apple Computer, Inc.*, 874 F. Supp. 1072 (C.D. Cal. 1994) (Apple had given a development project the internal name 'Carl Sagan', but when this fact was publicized Sagan demanded his name not be used. Apple technicians changed the project's code name to 'Butt Head Astronomer'.)

rightable.[54] Elsewhere, I have discussed reasons for this bar, including how adequate incentives for these short expressions are already provided by markets, law (trademark law), and non-economic motives.[55] But another ground to justify the bar on copyrighted names and titles is that they function as social facts in which the fact and expression are always merged. You cannot say 'X is called Y' without expressing Y. And having names for things – both general and proper names – is fundamental to communicating any other facts.[56] To name something is to establish a fact,[57] and yet there is no sensible way to argue that these are acts of 'discovery' unless we are prepared to reduce all creativity to an act of discovery.[58] However, this bar against copyrighting names has been threatened by disputes involving what are basically designation systems. Let us consider three such cases.

A. The AMA and ADA Cases

Beginning in the 1960s, the American Medical Association developed a coding system for medical procedures, the *Physicians' Current Procedure Terminology* ('CPT').[59] The CPT gives five digit codes to various medical

---

54 37 C.F.R. 202.1(a) (2007) (indicating that 'words and short phrases such as names, titles, and slogans; familiar symbols or designs; mere variations of typographic ornamentation, lettering or coloring; mere listing of ingredients or contents' are not copyrightable).

55 *Size Matters, supra* note 2, at 610–19.

56 So, it is no wonder that in Genesis Adam names all the animals even before Eve is created. Genesis 2:19 (King James) ('And out of the ground the Lord God formed every beast of the field, and every fowl of the air; and brought them unto Adam to see what he would call them: and whatsoever Adam called every living creature, that was the name thereof.') My thanks to David Nimmer for this interesting point.

57 Naming as establishment of a social fact has the same structure as government declarations. Searle gives the example of money: '[w]hen the Treasury says it is legal tender, they are declaring it to be legal tender, not announcing an empirical fact that it already is legal tender.' *Social Reality, supra* note 17, at 55. Naming one's child, one's pet, or one's new car part has the same structure; by convention, we agree that you are entitled to declare the name of this thing.

58 The 'discovery' notion of creativity pops up repeatedly, particularly in regards to great art. For example, Einstein is said to have characterized Mozart's music as 'so pure that it seemed to have been ever-present in the universe, waiting to be discovered by the master'. Miller, Arthur I. (2006), 'A Genius Finds Inspiration in the Music of Another', *New York Times*, 31 January, at F3. In Orhan Pamuk's novel *Snow*, the main character believes that the better poems he is writing 'always seem[] to come from outside, from far away' (p. 122); see also Hughes, Justin (1998), 'The Personality Interest of Artists and Inventors in Intellectual Property', 16 *Cardozo Arts & Ent. L. J.* 81, 142–46; Quiddities, *supra* note 25, at 39.

59 *Practice Mgmt. Info. Corp. v Am. Med. Ass'n*, 121 F.3d 516, 517 (9th Cir. 1997), amended by 133 F.3d 1140 (9th Cir. 1998).

procedures. For example, '92950' designates 'cardiopulmonary resuscitation'. A decade later, the Department of Health and Human Services sensibly adopted the CPT for use in the Medicaid program.[60]

In *Practice Management Information Corp. v American Medical Association*,[61] Practice Management challenged AMA's copyright in the CPT. It first argued that the AMA forfeited the CPT copyright when it allowed the CPT to be integrated into Medicaid regulations. The Ninth Circuit disagreed, concluding, first, that the incentive structure was different: while 'judges' salaries provide[d] adequate incentive to write opinions . . . [the] copyrightability of the CPT provides the economic incentive for the AMA to produce and maintain the CPT'.[62] As to due process concerns about availability of the legally mandated codes, the appellate panel concluded that there was no evidence that the AMA had foreclosed public access to the codes and that there were adequate, less draconian tools to ensure such access.[63]

The appellate panel ultimately ruled for Practice Management on the ground that the AMA had 'misused' its copyright by obtaining a commitment from the federal authorities to use the CPT designations *exclusively* for Medicaid forms. That conclusion prevented the panel from applying any fine-toothed analysis to the issue of *what* was protected by the copyright over the CPT. That job was taken up by Judge Easterbrook in the contemporaneous and curiously parallel *American Dental Association v Delta Dental Plans Association.*[64]

Just as the AMA had created the CPT, the American Dental Association had created the *Code on Dental Procedures and Nomenclature* ('ADA Code') – a taxonomy in which each dental procedure has [a] a long description, [b] a short description, and [c] a number designation.[65] Delta Dental published the *Universal Coding and Nomenclature* which 'include[d] most of the numbering system and short descriptions from the ADA's Code.'[66] When the ADA

---

60 Id. at 518; see also Cal. Code Regs. tit. 22, § 51050 (2007) ('HCPCS [Health Care Financing Administration's Common Procedure Coding System] consists of the Physicians' Current Procedural Terminology (CPT) ... To the extent not elsewhere adopted in these regulations, HCPCS, and each of its subsequent updates, is herein incorporated by reference into these regulations.').

61 121 F. 3d 516 (9th Cir. 1997).

62 Id. at 518. The court pointed out the increasing trend of governments, on cost savings grounds, to rely on 'model' codes and statutes written by non-governmental entities, which would lend a note of irony to any holding that such privately-created works should lose their copyright protection on adoption. Id. at 518–19 nn. 4–5.

63 Id. at 519.

64 126 F.3d 977 (7th Cir. 1997).

65 Id.

66 Id.

sued, the district court concluded that the ADA Code was not copyrightable subject matter, reasoning that the ADA Code was only a 'useful' taxonomy and, therefore, lacked the modicum of creativity necessary for copyright.

Judge Easterbrook rejected this reasoning, pointing to the many useful works (software, architectural drawings, maps) protected by copyright law[67] and opining that '[c]lassification is a creative endeavor'.[68] He concluded that the long descriptions in the ADA Code were unquestionably copyrightable; and that the 'original long descriptions make the work as a whole copyrightable'[69] – two vanilla-plain conclusions. Judge Easterbrook's analysis then moved in a much more troubling direction, opining that 'even the short descriptions and the numbers are original works of authorship'.[70] Notice that he says 'works'; the ADA numbers were, in effect, *names* for dental procedures and Easterbrook's language here suggests that each name merits independent copyright protection.[71] But the important point is to see that copyright is being recognized either in a set of names or in individual names and that these names function as facts as surely as street addresses – they are the only practical way to refer to the particular medical and dental procedures just as your home address is the only practical way to refer to the particular place where you live. In both of these cases, the taxonomies produce facts.

B. *Southco, Inc. v Kanebridge Corporation*[72]

Southco manufactured hardware, including a line of fasteners. Each of its fastener models was designated with a nine digit number in which different digits 'denote[d] functional characteristics of each product, for example, installation type, thread size, recess type (phillips or slotted), grip length, type of material and knob finish'.[73] The Southco numbering system had become, to some degree, an industry standard.[74] Nonetheless, there was no evidence that

---

67 Id. at 978–79.

68 Id. at 979.

69 Id.

70 Id. This statement, implying individual 'work' status for each number actually appears in the opinion before the more general and less worrisome conclusion that 'all three elements of the [ADA] Code – numbers, short descriptions, and long descriptions, are copyrightable subject matter'. Id.

71 Other language in the opinion throws some doubt on this suggestion. For further discussion and criticism, see *Size Matters* supra note 2, at 577.

72 2000 U.S. Dist. LEXIS 112; 53 U.S.P.Q.2D (BNA) 1490; Copy. L. Rep. (CCH) P28,020 (E.D. Pa. 2000), *rev'd,* 258 F.3d 148 (3rd Cir. 2001).

73 Id. at *2.

74 Id. at *9; see *Southco, Inc. v Kanebridge Corp.*, 258 F.3d 148, 150 (3d Cir. 2001).

Southco had ever licensed the numbering system to third parties and no evidence that it had developed the numbering system with a mind to marketing it as such.

The defendant Kanebridge published comparison charts showing Southco part numbers with their counterpart Kanebridge part numbers.[75] On occasion, Kanebridge also labeled its parts with Southco numbers. Southco alleged that Kanebridge had 'copied some or all' of 51 particular part numbers from a Southco handbook which contained over 1000 discrete part numbers.[76] Initially, the district court granted a preliminary injunction against Kanebridge, concluding that 'Southco [was] likely to succeed in establishing that its product identification numbers are copyrightable' (notice, again, the plural) and that Kanebridge could be liable for copying 'Southco's numbering *system'*.[77]

It took three trips to the Third Circuit,[78] but eventually an *en banc* opinion written by now Justice Alito put to rest the claim that individual numbers designating (naming) parts could be individually copyrighted. The *en banc* '*Southco III*' decision[79] announced that Southco's part numbers were not copyrightable for two separate reasons: (a) 'the Southco product numbers are not "original" because each number is rigidly dictated by the rules of the Southco [numbering] system';[80] and (b) '[t]he Southco part numbers are also excluded from copyright protection because they are analogous to short phrases or the titles of works'.[81] Although the Court of Appeals recognized that the part numbers were 'analogous to . . . titles', none of the parties pursued

---

[75] *Southco,* 258 F. 3d at 150.

[76] 2000 U.S. Dist. LEXIS 112 at *3, *13. The 'copied' Southco numbers came either from a Southco 'Handbook' or a 'Supplement' to one of the company Handbooks. Id. at *3.

[77] Id. at *13 (emphasis added). In prior part number cases, courts had concluded that the taxonomies lacked originality because of randomness. *Toro Co. v R & R Products Co.*, 787 F.2d 1208, 1213 (8th Cir. 1986) (holding that there was no copyright in part numbers because the numbering system was 'arbitrary and random', as opposed to a system that used symbols according to a meaningful pattern); *Mitel, Inc. v Iqtel, Inc.,* 124 F.3d 1366, 1373–74 (10th Cir. 1997) ('Mitel's arbitrary selection of a combination of three or four numbers required de minimis creative effort, Mitel's own witness testified to the arbitrariness of the command codes ... We agree with the district court that the random and arbitrary use of numbers in the public domain does not evince enough originality to distinguish authorship').

[78] For the first two decisions on appeal, see *Southco, Inc. v Kanebridge Corporation*, 258 F.3d 148 (3d Cir. 2001); *Southco, Inc. v Kanebridge Corp.* (*Southco II*), 324 F.3d 190, 196 (3d Cir. 2003).

[79] *Southco, Inc. v Kanebridge Corp.*, 390 F.3d 276 (3d Cir. 2004) (*en banc*).

[80] Id. at 282.

[81] Id. at 285. Interestingly, three Third Circuit judges (Becker, McKee, and Smith) did not join this portion of the *en banc* decision. See id. at 277 n*.

the obvious next step: if these part names had become industry standards: the names were social facts – facts by common agreement just as that green rectangular paper is commonly agreed to be a 20 dollar bill – that had become basic to carrying out non-expressive activities.

IV. THE PROTECTION OF EVALUATIVE FACTS

While the drift toward protecting names was stopped in the Third Circuit, eerily similar trends have not yet been abated in the Second and Ninth circuits. In these cases, private parties have made evaluations – qualitative or quantitative – and courts have intimated that such original evaluations may be individually protected under copyright law. Obviously 'evaluations' and 'designations' overlap to some degree; the CPT and ADA Codes were also 'evaluative' in their many taxonomic decisions. As with designations, the evaluations in the cases below can become so widely accepted and so relied upon for substantial non-expressive activities that they become social facts.

A. *CCC Information Services v Maclean Hunter*[82]

Maclean Hunter published (and still publishes) the well-known 'Red Book', listing used car valuations for different parts of the United States. These valuations were 'the editors' projections of the values for the next six weeks of "average" versions of most of the used cars (up to seven years old) sold in that region'.[83] The court recognized that the Red Book was one of two 'leading valuation book[s],' so much so that some state laws mandated the use of valuations from both books in calculating required insurance payments for loss of a vehicle.[84] The defendant CCC Information Services distributed an online database of used car valuations to its customers by 'loading major portions of the Red Book onto its computer network and republishing Red Book information in various forms to its customers'.[85] The trial court found that 'numerous Red Book customers ha[d] canceled their subscriptions, opting instead to purchase CCC's services'.[86]

---

82 44 F.3d 61 (2d Cir. 1994), *cert. denied*, 516 U.S. 817 (1995).

83 Id. at 63.

84 Id. at 64 (discussing the National Automobile Dealers' Association's 'Blue Book' and that 'the laws of certain states use th[e] average figure [from the two books] as minimum for insurance payments upon the "total loss" of a vehicle.').

85 Id.

86 Id.

Nonetheless the trial court granted summary judgment for CCC, finding that the valuations were unprotectable facts or, alternatively, expressions of ideas which had merged with the underlying ideas. The Second Circuit reversed, reasoning that the selection and arrangement of the Red Book was protectable, that the Red Book numbers were themselves protectable expression, and that merger did not apply. As a first step, the court found sufficient originality in the selection and arrangement of the Red Book's valuations. Judge Leval found that originality was expressed in the particular regions into which Maclean had divided the country, implying that the selection of regions was 'original' because it produces inaccurate car values: 'In furnishing a single number to cover vast regions that undoubtedly contain innumerable variations, the Red Book expresses a loose judgment that values are more likely to group together within a defined region than without. The number produced is necessarily both approximate and original.'[87] The court also pointed to other 'selection' decisions that appeared to manifest originality, including Maclean's 'selection of the number of model years to be included in the compilation' (seven years) and 'the selection and manner of presentation of optional features for inclusion'.[88] This reasoning that choices that do not seem to be dictated by extrinsic considerations are *original* is, again, straightforward copyright doctrine,[89] although Leval's connection – that such choices will produce inaccurate evaluations – is more candid than usual.

But were the Red Book valuations, as the trial court thought, (expressions of) 'facts'?[90] Judge Leval quickly and correctly concluded that the items in the Red Book were not Feistian facts because the Red Book entries were 'predictions based not only on a multitude of data sources, but also on professional judgment and expertise'.[91] As such, '[t]he valuations themselves [were] original creations of Maclean'.[92]

---

87 Id. at 67.

88 Id. Judge Leval also considered that 'the adjustment of mileage by 5,000 mile increments (as opposed to using some other breakpoint and interval)' was a creative choice, but this seems wrong. Five thousand and/or ten thousand mile increments seems like an unoriginal, pedestrian choice.

89 See, for example, *Eckes v Card Price Update*, 736 F.2d 859, 862 (2d Cir. 1984); see generally Hughes, Justin (1998), 'The Personality Interest of Artists and Inventors in Intellectual Property', 16 *Cardozo Arts & Ent. L. J.* 81, 114 (reasoning that '[s]omething will be considered "creative" only when it appears to come from neither a purely mechanical process, nor a purely random one.')

90 The trial court also called them 'interpretations of facts'. *Maclean Hunter*, 44 F.3d at 64.

91 Id. at 67.

92 Id.

By honing to the Feistian definition, Leval avoided addressing how people use these numeric valuations as *facts*: the car salesman tells you that your car is 'worth *X* dollars' or the state insurance adjuster says its replacement value is *Y*. But even while rejecting the 'factness' of these values, Leval recognized that the Red Book entries were nonetheless subject to an argument that they were the only way of expressing the authors' idea of the value of a particular vehicle, and therefore merged with the idea.

Leval's direct rebuttal was a standard tactic: identify the 'idea' as being at a more abstract level, that of *making some valuation* of a particular used car, the idea is not *this particular valuation*. Judge Leval realized that this was not particularly satisfying reasoning and presented a more practical way to avoid the merger doctrine's 'not easily rebutted' implications: a two-level hierarchy of ideas. The first level is comprised of 'building block' ideas and the second of 'ideas of [a] weaker category, infused with opinion'.[93] The court reasoned that protection of the expressions of opinion-infused ideas can be tolerated because restricting access to such expressions 'will not inflict injury on the opportunity for public debate, nor restrict access to the kind of idea that illuminates our understanding of the phenomena that surround us or of useful processes to solve our problems.'[94] On this utilitarian calculus, the court held that the merger doctrine should be 'withheld' from application to Maclean Hunter's valuations.

B. *CDN, Inc. v Kenneth A. Kapes*[95]

The immediate sequel to *Maclean Hunter* was the Ninth Circuit's 1999 decision in *CDN, Inc. v Kenneth A. Kapes*. In *Kapes*, the plaintiff published the *Coin Dealer Newsletter*, a weekly publication that 'include[d wholesale] prices for virtually all [United States] collectible coins and [was] used extensively by dealers'.[96] Defendant Kapes operated an internet web page that provided retail prices for many collectible coins,[97] derived from the CDN wholesale prices by consistent application of a simple 'mark-up algorithm'. The Ninth Circuit panel, in agreement with the district court, concluded that the CDN wholesale coin prices were the result of 'a process that involves using [the editors'] judgment to distill and extrapolate from factual data'.[98] Whereas the numbers in the *Feist* telephone book lacked any creative spark,

93 Id. at 73.
94 Id.
95 197 F.3d 1256 (9th Cir. 1999).
96 Id. at 1258.
97 Id. at 1257.
98 Id. at 1261.

the Ninth Circuit panel was clear that '[t]his spark glows in CDN's prices, which are compilations of data chosen and weighed with creativity and judgment'.[99]

After a succinct exposition of the merger doctrine, the court concludes simply that 'accepting the [merger] principle in all cases would eviscerate the protection of the copyright law',[100] the same basic conclusion as in *Maclean Hunter*. Yet rather than attempting to maintain the separation of unprotectible idea and protectable expression, as *Maclean Hunter* does, the court (a) implicitly says that the prices are ideas and (b) explicitly says that copyright law sometimes protects ideas: 'CDN does not, nor could it, claim protection for its idea of creating a wholesale price guide, *but it can use the copyright laws to protect its idea of what those prices are*.'[101] Even treating this language concerning copyright protecting ideas as dicta, *CDN* broadened the scope of protection for such judgments/evaluations by extending the protection to *derivatives* from the plaintiff's evaluations, not just reproducing the *expressions* of the plaintiff's evaluations. While *CDN* seems like a fairly bare-knuckled application of anti-misappropriation sentiments without sufficient concern for the integrity of copyright doctrine,[102] in another sense *CDN* did not aggravate the 'created facts' problem beyond *Maclean Hunter*. There was no evidence that the CDN wholesale prices were mandated for use in law and there was less evidence that the CDN prices had become *de facto* industry standards than the evaluations in *Maclean Hunter*. It would take a few more years before another case again brought the *Maclean Hunter* analysis under scrutiny.

C. *NYMEX v IntercontinentalExchange*[103]

That case came in 2006 and was brought by the New York Mercantile Exchange ('NYMEX'), the world's largest exchange for the trading of commodity futures contracts and an entity regulated by the Commodity

---

99 Id. at 1260. As with *Maclean Hunter* and *Delta Dental*, this is regrettable dicta suggesting that *single* prices in the respective publications would count as independently protectable 'works'. *Size Matters, supra* note 2 at 592–595.

100 *Kapes*, 197 F.3d at 1261.

101 Id. at 1262 (emphasis added).

102 See, for example, Karjala, *supra* note 2, at 480. ('It is evident that *CDN* simply uses anti-misappropriation notions to force the defendant to do its own work in determining the value estimates rather than to protect the creative selection or arrangement of compiled data, paying only lip service to *Feist's* elimination of the sweat of the brow basis for copyright originality.')

103 *N.Y. Mercantile Exch., Inc. v IntercontinentalExchange, Inc.*, 389 F. Supp. 2d 527 (S.D.N.Y. 2005), *aff'd*, 497 F.3d 108 (2d Cir. 2007).

Futures Trading Commission ('CFTC'). People trading NYMEX futures contracts ('members') must deposit an initial margin deposit – a performance bond – to cover any losses they suffer. As explained by the district court:

> On each day on which a futures contract remains open and unexpired, the amount of the required margin deposit changes as the price of the underlying commodity – and thus the value of the contract – changes. These changes in the value of the contract are determined by reference to the end-of-day 'settlement prices' for the futures contract.[104]

The parties disputed how much judgment and creativity went into these settlement prices, although there was no dispute that they are not actual prices of single transactions and that the daily settlement prices are established by a NYMEX 'committee'.

IntercontinentalExchange ('ICE') has its own over-the-counter futures contracts on two popular NYMEX commodities and each day ICE relies on the NYMEX settlement prices for the processing of the ICE futures contracts.[105] NYMEX claimed that this activity violated its copyright in the settlement prices. When ICE sought declaratory judgment against NYMEX on the copyright issue, NYMEX 'urged the Court to consider a NYMEX settlement price as a "creative copyrightable work" ' – a result that follows unsurprisingly from Judge Leval's reasoning in *Maclean Hunter* (as well as Easterbrook's reasoning in *Delta Dental*). NYMEX conceded that 'market participants often provide that the parties will refer to a NYMEX settlement price to serve as the final settlement price in OTC [over-the-counter] contracts'.[106] At the same time, NYMEX counsel expressly argued that '[w]hat is done with [a settlement price], what we permit to be done with it', had no bearing on it becoming a fact – an argument obviously at odds with the claims made here about the nature of social facts.

The district court found that the settlement prices were facts,[107] but it is clear that Judge Koeltl understood he was treading in an uncharted quadrant of the *Feist* universe. One passage in the opinion adopts a page from Searle's theory on why the prices are (social) facts:

---

104 Id. at 530.

105 Id. at 533 ('According to ICE, an OTC swap is generally defined as an agreement whereby a floating price is exchanged for a fixed price over a specified period, thus allowing a buyer or seller of energy products to "lock in" a specific price and avoid the risk of floating prices. The financial purpose of an OTC transaction, therefore, is usually the same as the financial purpose of a NYMEX transaction.').

106 Id. at 541.

107 Id. ('The argument that NYMEX settlement prices do not embody facts is without merit.')

> NYMEX prices are widely publicized and used as benchmarks by market participants. NYMEX settlement prices are thus real-world facts used by commodities traders to value their open positions and trigger margin calls or market reductions.[108]

Judge Koeltl then found that the facts and expression of facts have merged, but carefully hedges his bets throughout the opinion, framing the problem also as one of 'idea' and expression having merged.[109]

In August 2007, the Second Circuit affirmed the lower court on merger grounds only.[110] Viewing the NYMEX Committee's activities, the court pointed to the *Feist* example of census-takers (as discoverers of fact) and noted that '[w]hile the line between creation and discovery is often clear-cut, we recognize that it is a difficult line to draw in this case'.[111] This left the originality – hence copyrightability – question unresolved. Similarly, while the appellate panel noted how the settlement prices are treated after their creation as facts,[112] it did so as almost an estoppel point against NYMEX – and without any recognition, as in the *Veeck* case discussed below, of the 'created facts' doctrinal dilemma.

While *NYMEX* seemed to test the basic soundness of *Maclean Hunter*, the court avoided directly confronting its own precedent – and *CDN v Kapes* – in a couple of ways. First, the court noted that *Maclean Hunter's* statement that '[t]he valuations themselves are original creations' was 'arguably dicta' unnecessary to the decision because the defendant had copied the entire compilation.[113] Secondly, the court distinguished the NYMEX evaluative process from the *Maclean Hunter* evaluative process on the grounds that NYMEX attempts to establish/reconstruct *past* facts while the prices in *Maclean Hunter* and *CDN* were judgments as to future events. Of course, reconciling application of the merger doctrine in *Maclean Hunter, CDN v Kapes,* and *NYMEX* this way required more or less treating the NYMEX settlement prices as discov-

---

108 Id. at 542; see also id. at 543 ('NYMEX settlement prices are a matter of basic market fact, and therefore, they are not copyrightable.')

109 See id. at 541.

110 *N.Y. Mercantile Exch., Inc. v IntercontinentalExchange, Inc.*, 497 F.3d 109, 116–18 (2d Cir. 2007).

111 Id. at 114.

112 Id. at 115 n.6 ('While NYMEX now argues that settlement prices are merely opinions, we note that NYMEX itself treats the prices as news of the day. . . . NYMEX also provides the prices to newspapers which publish them alongside other market facts.').

113 Id. at 115 n. 6. ('[I]n *CCC* a subscriber could not rely solely on the Red Book in valuing any particular used car. Similarly, *CDN Inc. v Kapes* . . . is distinguishable because the prices for collectible coins in that case were estimates, not discovered market facts.') (citations omitted).

ered facts – something the court said it was not deciding. The court also appeared to distinguish application of merger on the grounds that used car or collector coin values would not apply *directly* to any particular used car or coin. In contrast, even if the NYMEX settlement price was 'created', once the settlement price exists it *is* the 'fair market value for each NYMEX contract' and 'any dissension [from that number] would be exceptionally narrow'.[114] Of course, that is an unsatisfactory way to distinguish the *NYMEX* ruling from *Maclean Hunter*: dissension from the Red Book used car values may also be 'exceptionally narrow', particularly on insurance compensation where the Red Book is mandated as the valuation authority. Finally, the Court of Appeals distinguished *Maclean Hunter* from the *NYMEX* case on policy grounds that have heretofore only obliquely been stated in merger doctrine: whether or not the putative copyright holder needed the incentive of copyright to produce the work.[115] We will return to that theme in Part VII.

V. LEGAL FACTS – WHEN PRIVATE PERSONS AUTHOR LAWS

Dating back to the 1834 *Wheaton v Peters* and 1888 *Banks v Manchester* decisions,[116] it has been black letter American copyright doctrine that expressions of law cannot be copyrighted. One rationale is that the public 'authors' the law, not particular judges or legislators.[117] Another is that the incentive of copyright is unneeded because the expression of judges, as employees of the state, has already been bought and paid for by the citizenry (a kind of public work-for-hire doctrine, if you will). A third reason is a pure due process requirement of open access to the law: 'the whole work done by judges constitutes the authentic exposition and interpretation of the law, which, binding every citizen, is free for publication to all . . .'[118]

But this bar to copyright in law has been attacked on the flanks in cases concerning privately-developed 'model codes' that are adopted into law. These

114 *N.Y. Mercantile Exch.*, 83 U.S.P.Q.2d (BNA) at 1615.

115 After discussing the incentive function of copyright, particularly in respect of Maclean Hunter, the court noted 'NYMEX needs no such incentives here'. Id.

116 *Wheaton v Peters*, 33 U.S. (8 Pet.) 591 (1834); *Banks v Manchester*, 128 U.S. 244 (1888).

117 As the majority noted in *Wheaton*, 'It may be proper to remark that the court are unanimously of opinion, that no reporter has or can have any copyright in the written opinions delivered by this court; and that the judges thereof cannot confer on any reporter any such right.' *Wheaton*, 33 U.S. (8 Pet.) at 668.

118 *Banks*, 128 U.S. at 253.

model codes are usually the result of an intense, quasi-private deliberative process by a professional body that then claims copyright in the final expression of the model code. At the moment the code is completed (and not yet adopted as law), the copyright claim is as unremarkable as a movie studio claiming copyright in a big budget picture on which hundreds of people worked. Only a couple of courts have confronted the problems that begin when the model code is adopted whole cloth as law. In the most recent of these controversies, the federal courts have finally recognized that when a privately-written code is adopted as law, the private expression becomes 'in one sense, a "fact" '[119] and that these 'codes are "facts" under copyright law.'[120]

A. *BOCA v Code Technology, Inc.*

The First Circuit was the first to wade into this thicket in the 1980 *Building Officials and Code Administration v Code Technology, Inc.* decision.[121] The private Building Officials and Code Administration (BOCA) had developed and published a model building code; it copyrighted the code and then 'encourage[d], through a licensing program, public authorities such as states to adopt the BOCA Code'. After Massachusetts adopted the BOCA code with some minor modifications,[122] BOCA published it as the *Commonwealth of Massachusetts State Building Code*; it appears that there was no official state publication of the state building code.[123] When the defendant, Code Technology (CT), sought to publish its own edition of the Massachusetts code, BOCA sued and the trial court granted a preliminary injunction.

After reviewing the case law on copyright in law from *Wheaton* and *Banks* forward, the First Circuit reversed the injunctive relief. The appellate panel concluded that it was 'far from persuaded that BOCA's virtual authorship of the Massachusetts building code entitles it to enforce a copyright monopoly over when, where, and how the [code] is to be reproduced and made publicly available', but 'stopped short . . . of ruling definitely on the underlying legal issues'.[124]

119 'The global enactment of a code does make that code the law of the enacting municipality and hence, in one sense, a "fact".' *Veeck v S. Bldg. Code Cong. Int'l, Inc.* (*Veeck I*), 241 F.3d 398, 408, n. 49 (5th Cir. 2001), *rev'd en banc* (*Veeck II*), 293 F.3d 791 (5th Cir. 2002).

120 *Veeck II*, 293 F. 3d at 801.

121 628 F.2d 730 (1st Cir. 1980).

122 Id. at 732.

123 Id.

124 Id. The First Circuit left open the possibility that BOCA could persuade the trial court that its copyright in the model code should lead to damages. Id. at 736.

B. *Veeck v Southern Building Code Congress*

Twenty years later, the Fifth Circuit gave a much more thorough treatment of this problem in the *Veeck v Southern Building Code Congress* case,[125] concluding that privately drafted codes adopted as law had, indeed, become 'facts'. The non-profit Southern Building Code Congress International (SBCCI) was formed in 1940 with its primary mission being to 'develop, promote, and promulgate model building codes'.[126] Along with many other municipalities, the Texas towns of Savoy and Anna had adopted versions of a SBCCI code as their own. When Peter Veeck posted the town building codes on his non-commercial website promoting north Texas, SBCCI sued for copyright infringement.

The trial court granted summary judgment on Veeck's infringement of the SBCCI copyright, a result the Court of Appeals initially affirmed (*Veeck I*). Rehearing *en banc* produced a strong split among the Fifth Circuit judges, with a majority finding both that the *Wheaton/Banks* reasoning required that Veeck have unfettered access to the law[127] and that 'the codes are "facts" under copyright law'.[128] As to the first of these two grounds, until *Veeck II* due process/access claims in these cases had been diffused through an understanding that the *minimum* due process need is for people to *know* the laws, not for people to *republish* the laws.[129]

Of course, the ability of third parties to republish a code can be linked with increased general access, but not all of the situations in these disputes lend themselves to that kind of analysis. In *BOCA,* for example, the plaintiff sold

---

125 241 F.3d 398 (5th Cir. 2001), *rev'd en banc,* 293 F.3d 791 (5th Cir. 2002).

126 *Veeck II*, 293 F.3d at 793.

127 Id. at 799–800. The majority disagreed that *Wheaton* and *Banks* embodied the pecuniary/incentives argument that judges 'do not need the "incentives" that copyright affords in order to write opinions.' Id. at 797. Instead the majority viewed the *Banks* holding as based on 'a "metaphorical concept of citizen authorship" together with the need for citizens to have free access to the laws'. Id. at 799.

128 Id. at 801.

129 For example, the *Practice Management* panel focused on the *access* side of a work being 'available':

> There is no evidence that anyone wishing to use the CPT has any difficulty obtaining access to it. Practice Management is not a potential user denied access to the CPT, but a putative copier wishing to share in the AMA's statutory monopoly. Practice Management does not assert the AMA has restricted access to users or intends to do so in the future.

Practice Mgmt. Info. Corp. v Am. Med. Ass'n, 121 F.3d 516, 520 (9th Cir. 1997). Thus, the *Practice Management* court addressed the access issue and did not opine on the other half of *Banks* – that the law be 'free for publication to all'. *Banks*, 128 U.S. at 253.

copies of its *Commonwealth of Massachusetts State Building Code (3d ed.)* for $22 each while the defendant was selling an edition that included the state code and other materials for $35 – hardly an increase in accessibility. It is only with the Internet-based cases – *Maclean Hunter* and *Veeck* – that 'free for publication' obviously increases access.

The second ground for the *Veeck II* holding was a clear endorsement of the thesis of this chapter. In ruling that 'the codes are "facts" under copyright law' the *en banc* majority reasoned: 'It should be obvious that for copyright purposes, laws are "facts": the U.S. Constitution is a fact; the Federal Tax Code and its regulations are facts; the Texas Uniform Commercial Code is a fact.'[130]

With this result, the majority reasonably felt compelled to distinguish the building codes which had 'become law' from things 'the law requires citizens to consult . . . in the process of fulfilling their obligations', like the Red Book valuations or CPT medical codes.[131] This is the same distinction that Lawrence Cunningham draws between 'strong' (or 'semi-strong') and 'soft' adoption into the law[132] – and the reason I do not consider evaluation cases like *Practice Management* to be true 'legal fact' situations. But the *en banc* dissent rightly criticized this line-drawing and, as I will argue in the next section, it is a distinction without much difference: the legal codes, the CPT, and the Red Book car valuations are all social facts in the Searlean sense. The groupings here (of naming, evaluative, and legal facts) have been for convenience; the key issue is status as a social fact. The argument then becomes that a law is a (social) fact that can be expressed in only one or a very limited number of ways, producing merger of expressive work and fact.[133]

While the due process argument can be limited as the courts in *Practice Management* and *Veeck I* limited it (access means 'access' and use, not reproduction), the traditional merger doctrine cannot be so limited. If there is merger of expression and fact, the copyright disappears, raising a colorable claim that the government decision to integrate or reference the privately-created work produces a compensable 'taking'.[134] Part VI aims to convince

---

130 *Veeck II*, 293 F.3d at 801. This gave a ringing endorsement to Judge Little's dissent in *Veeck I*. Judge Little had recognized that 'there is merit to Veeck's argument that once enacted, the codes do become a fact or idea, in that there is only one accurate way to express an enacted law. . . By its very nature, an enacted law enters the public realm as a concrete, definite fact/idea.' *Veeck I*, 241 F.3d at 415 (Little, dissenting).

131 *Veeck II*, 293 F.3d. at 804 – 805.

132 Cunningham, *supra* note 2, at 293.

133 *Veeck I*, 241 F.3d at 407. As the *Veeck I* panel feared, 'the adoption of SBCCI's codes into law was a transformative event that instantly denuded the work of copyright protection'. Id.

134 *Practice Mgmt. Info. Corp. v Am. Med. Ass'n*, 121 F.3d 516, 520 (9th Cir.

the reader that this radical conclusion is warranted in the sense that these are facts; Part VII aims to convince the reader that this radical conclusion can be avoided by judicious recalibration of the merger doctrine to take account of situations in which creation of the expression entails creation of the facts.

VI. BUT ARE THESE 'FACTS'? AND, IF SO, WHAT HAPPENS?

In *Maclean Hunter,* Judge Leval announced a new distinction between 'building block' and opinion 'infused' ideas,[135] shielding expressions of the latter from copyright's merger doctrine. In a 1999 speech, Judge Jon Newman offered the same distinction, but inadvertently admitted that this device allows copyright to protect ideas:

> . . . for copyright purposes, simply labeling an aggregation of facts as an idea does not help decide whether a particular aggregation is protectable. All ideas are not created equal. The unprotected category includes those that are undertaken to advance the understanding of phenomena or the solution of problems, while the protectable category includes those that reflect the author's taste and opinion.[136]

To use Judge Leval's language, the problem with each Red Book car valuation is that it is both an opinion-infused idea *and* a necessary building block for lots of further human activity. To use Judge Newman's distinction, car valuations both 'reflect the author's . . . opinion' and are 'undertaken to advance . . . the solution of problems'. Used coin prices, restaurant ratings, medical procedure designations, 'settlement prices', and privately-drafted model laws may be (initially) very much matters of opinion, but opinions systematically undertaken/formulated to solve problems.

Of course, that does not mean that these designations, evaluations, and privately-drafted laws are facts in our copyright doctrine, let alone in our metaphysics. But anyone who wants to deny 'factness' to designations, evaluations, and privately-drafted laws has to reconsider all types of facts established through social institutions. Just as we may question whether a 2005 Chevy Malibu is really worth $10,250 or a 'Henry Hub natural gas futures

---

1997) (quoting *CCC Info. Serv., Inc. v Maclean Hunter Mkt. Reports, Inc.*, 44 F.3d 61, 74 (2d Cir. 1994)), amended by 133 F.3d 1140 (9th Cir. 1998); see also Cotter, Thomas F. (1998), 'Do Federal Uses of Intellectual Property Implicate the Fifth Amendment?', 50 *Fla. L. Rev.* 529.

135 *Maclean Hunter*, 44 F.3d at 72–73.

136 Newman, Jon O. (1999), 'New Lyrics for an Old Melody: The Idea/Expression Dichotomy in the Computer Age', 17 *Cardozo Arts & Ent. L.J.* 691, 698 (footnote omitted).

contract is worth $25',[137] we can ask the same question – in the same philosophical tone of voice – about *any* social fact. John Searle raises just the same objection to all social facts as we might make to a state's bond rating or a used car valuation:

> Our sense that there is an element of magic, a conjuring trick, a sleight of hand in the creation of institutional facts out of brute facts derives from the nonphysical, non-causal character of the relation of the X and Y terms . . . .In our toughest metaphysical moods, we want to ask 'But is an X really a Y?' For example, are these bits of paper really money? . . . Is making certain noises at a ceremony really getting married? . . . Surely when you get down to brass tacks, these are not real facts.[138]

Searle's answer is that a social fact arises when (a) someone declares or states that such and such is the case, and (b) it becomes widely accepted that such and such is the case. That green, rectangular piece of paper is $20 because the US Treasury declares it to be[139] and we all accept that.[140]

Similarly, a designation – whether an airplane type ('787') or a person ('Rock Hudson'[141]) – is only treated as a fact when it is widely accepted by the relevant community. The same is true with credit ratings[142] and other numeric evaluations. In the *CDN* case, CDN was alleged to have promoted its wholesale coin prices as facts[143] – a charge also leveled against NYMEX.[144] And if those used coin values were widely accepted, CDN was right to do so. Widespread acceptance may take time, but social facts can also arise abruptly. Indeed, the example Searle gives of social facts arising abruptly is 'legislation being passed' or 'authorities changing the rules of the game'[145] – just as the

---

137 *N.Y. Mercantile Exch., Inc. v IntercontinentalExchange, Inc.*, 497 F.3d 109, 117 (2d Cir. 2007).

138 *Social Reality*, *supra* note 17, at 45.

139 As Searle observes, 'When the Treasury says [this piece of paper] is legal tender, they are declaring it to be legal tender, not announcing an empirical fact that it already is legal tender.' Id. at 55.

140 See id. at 112 ('We have nothing but the ability to impose a status, and with it a function, by collective agreement or acceptance.')

141 Born Roy Sherer. See Boykin, Keith (2006), *Beyond the Down Low* 71.

142 For example, there has never been any doubt that credit ratings are 'customer information of a financial institution' under 15 U.S.C. § 6827(2) (2000), defined as '[a]ny information maintained by or for a financial institution which is derived from the relationship between the financial institution and a customer of the financial institution and is identified with the customer'. Id.

143 *CDN Inc. v Kapes*, 197 F.3d 1256, 1262 (9th Cir. 1999).

144 *N.Y. Mercantile Exch., Inc. v IntercontinentalExchange, Inc.*, 497 F.3d 109, 115 n.6 (2d Cir. 2007).

145 *Social Reality*, *supra* note 17, at 125.

Veeck en banc majority understood. But even in those cases there must be acceptance (or at least not general, active rejection) by the society.

A. Fact or Fiction?

One might ask how all this relates to the 'facts' created by works of literature. Indeed, the only American court to use the phrase 'created facts' did so in relation to 'facts' within a fictional storyline[146] and it is fair to say that well-known literary or artistic narratives establish widely-known, socially-accepted details, that is that Ahab lost a leg to the white whale;[147] that ground control lost contact with Major Tom;[148] that Bruce Wayne is Batman[149] – as surely as Peter Parker is Spider Man;[150] that Marge is married to Homer – as surely as Wilma is married to Fred.[151] To consider the widely-known, socially-accepted nature of these details, conduct a thought-experiment: if there had been no footnotes in this paragraph would you have known these things to be 'true?' And yet, as Jeanette Winterson says, '[t]he truth of fiction is not the truth of railway tables'.[152]

I have repeatedly said that the created fact cases above generate designations, evaluations, and propositions that are necessary for further activity, expressive and non-expressive. It is tempting to say that this distinguishes them from facts in a fictional storyline because elements of fiction are rarely needed for *non-expressive activity*. You might need *Star Trek* for your 'Slash' stories – this is the whole 'recoding' debate in copyright scholarship[153] – but

---

146 See *Castle Rock Entm't, Inc. v Carol Publ'g Group, Inc.*, 150 F.3d 132, 139 (2d Cir. 1998) (recognizing that the 'original, protected expression' at issue – character and event details from the television series Seinfeld – were 'created facts'.). Scholars who have used the phrase 'created facts' are few too, but include Karjala, supra note 2, at 477.

147 Melville, Herman (1851), *Moby Dick*.

148 David Bowie, *Space Oddity*, on *Space Oddity* (Philips 1969).

149 One could cite literally thousands of sources for this, but although Bob Kane created Batman in the 1930s, my favorite is Miller, Frank and Klaus Janson (1986), *The Dark Knight Returns*.

150 Spider-Man first in appeared in 15 *Amazing Fantasy* (August, 1962) and is the subject of three blockbuster films from Sony Pictures creatively titled *Spider-Man* (Columbia Pictures 2002), *Spider-Man 2* (Columbia Pictures 2004), and *Spider-Man 3* (Columbia Pictures 2007).

151 *The Flintstones* (ABC television broadcast 1960–66).

152 Winterson, Jeanette, *Art Objects* 54 (1995).

153 See for example, Litman, Jessica (1990), 'The Public Domain', 39 *Emory L.J.* 965, 1007; Boyle, James (1992), 'A Theory of Law and Information: Copyright, Spleens, Blackmail and Insider Trading', 80 *Cal. L. Rev.* 1413; Jaszi, Peter (1992), 'On the Author Effect: Contemporary Copyright and Collective Creativity', 10 *Cardozo*

you do not need any details from Faulkner or *Star Wars* to sell your used car, get reimbursed for medical services rendered, or engage in construction as a line of work. Not only do people *rely* upon authored designations, evaluations, and laws for subsequent non-expressive activity, but we normatively accept and expect such reliance across the board; we believe that such reliance is (nearly?) always useful. In contrast, undue reliance on details from popular film and television to manifest the expressive activities of one's life is often considered sub-optimal: Margaret Jane Radin might say this is not 'human flourishing';[154] William Shatner might tell Trekkers to 'get a life'.[155] For good reason, we might not want to treat these details of literature as facts.[156]

Of course, even if utility can distinguish the created facts in designations, evaluations, model laws, etc. from the details created in literature and the arts, utility should not be an indicator of 'factness' or truth-status. As Simon Blackburn notes '[t]ruth has rights and privileges of its own, and they are not just the same as utility';[157] indeed, when it comes to utility, 'in many circumstances an adaptive illusion will do just as well as truth'.[158]

For one who adheres to the correspondence theory of truth, the difference between these created fact cases here and 'fictional facts' is, in some sense, where the fact is 'located'. If someone says 'Is Marge really the wife of Homer?' we are likely to disabuse them of the notion that Marge and Homer are real, living people with something like 'Marge is really the wife of Homer on the *Simpsons* show'. In contrast, the CPT codes, the Red Book valuations, and the building code of Savoy, Texas take on a life outside the expressive work where they first appear. Fictional facts can be inconsistent – they do not have to 'cohere' because they are understood to be located within and only within the expressive work.[159]

Arts & Ent. L.J. 293; Coombe, Rosemary J. (1992), 'Author/izing the Celebrity: Publicity Rights, Postmodern Politics, and Unauthorized Genders', 10 *Cardozo Arts & Ent. L.J.* 365. Aoki, Keith (1993), 'Adrift in the Intertext: Authorship and Audience "Recoding Rights",' 68 *Chi.-Kent L. Rev.* 805; Tushnet, Rebecca (1997), 'Legal Fictions: Copyright, Fan Fiction, and a New Common Law', 17 *Loy. L.A. Ent. L. J.* 651; Hughes, Justin (1999), '"Recoding" Intellectual Property and Overlooked Audiences', 77 *Tex. L. Rev.* 923, 926.

154 See Radin, Margaret Jane (1996), *Contested Commodities* 79–102.

155 Shatner, William with Chris Kreski (1999), *Get a Life!*. The title comes, as Amazon says, from Shatner '[p]oking fun at *Star Trek's* gung-ho fans and conventions in a now infamous *Saturday Night Live* sketch . . .' Amazon.com, Book Review of Get a Life!, http://www.amazon.com/Life-Star-Trek-William-Shatner/dp/0671021311 (last visited 22 October 2007).

156 My thanks to David McGowan for this observation.

157 Blackburn, *supra* note 11, at 9.

158 Id. at 105 (discussing Nietzsche).

159 As Blackburn writes about believing something to be true:

A belief is given its identity by what it excludes. A fiction is not. We can happily

B. Facts, Utility, and Processes

In keeping with what I have just said, it is tempting to focus on the functional aspect or 'essentiality' of created facts. As with many other social facts, in a created fact situation the expression becomes important, if not essential, to functional, non-expressive activities in the society.[160] Just as that rectangular green paper being a $20 bill has functional implications, credit ratings, economic valuations, estimates of material strength, and designations (particularly those in classificatory taxonomies) are all used by people to do things – purchase cars, trade baseball cards, build buildings, decide where to eat, order the right size and kind of parts, etc. Private expression integrated into the law is the most straightforward example of expressions becoming essential to functional activities. If the law is precise – that the walls of two-storied wood frame buildings must have 2″ by 4″ studs that are centered at 16″ or closer – then access to the expression is necessary for non-expressive activity (construction).

But the analysis here is quite different from Lawrence Cunningham's analysis of these cases as private expression being integrated into *public law*.[161] The argument here focuses on *expression becoming fact* – of which

---

> read one story about a fictional character, and then a different story, without finding it necessary to reconcile them. True, aficionados can get very shirty if in one story it is said that the hero has fair hair and in the next story he is said to have black hair, but that is because they are trying to join the two stories together, which they don't have to do. Whereas if the stories were histories of one actual man, they would have to be reconciled.

Blackburn, *supra* note 11, at 192.

160 Defining what is 'functional' or 'utilitarian' has plagued jurists – as well as scholars for some time. For example, in *Computer Associates International, Inc. v Altai, Inc.*, 982 F.2d 693 (2d Cir. 1992), in trying to identify the 'functional', Judge Walker compared the Humpty Dumpty story to a recipe for scrambled eggs by saying the latter is 'a more process oriented text'. Id. at 704. A recipe, of course, is aimed at a non-expressive human activity.

161 Professor Cunningham distinguishes between 'weak', 'semi-strong', and 'strong' adoption of private expression into public law. His paradigmatic examples are 'ex ante government designation of the standard setter as an officially recognized body' ('strong'), Cunningham *supra* note 2, at 293; standards 'incorporated into law after creation' by a private entity ('semi-strong'), id.; and adoption through 'passing reference in legal materials' ('weak'). Id. He posits that access to the expression is most needed in cases of 'strong' adoption, less with 'semi-strong', and even less with 'weak'. Id. I do not find that this tripartite division adequately captures the important differences and similarities among the ways private expression is adopted into law. For example, he says that with 'strong form' adoption the 'distinguishing feature' is that the privately-generated expressions 'constitute the fabric of that law', id. at 299, but that is apparently true of the semi-strong too. Cunningham posits an inverse relationship between how much people need access to these codes and how much copyright incen-

expression becoming law (Cunningham's concern) is just one form. Indeed, in *Practice Management, Delta Dental, Maclean Hunter*, and *Veeck* the private expression was adopted (one way or another) into law because it was already widely agreed upon as the standard. Governments adopt existing, privately-created standards not just to avoid (the cost of) reinventing the wheel: they adopt existing, privately-created standards because those standards already have legitimacy and social reference. A cardiopulmonary resuscitation had already become a 92950 by the time Medicaid adopted the AMA taxonomy; the value of your 10-year-old, driven-only-on-Sundays sedan had already become whatever value the Red Book said it was when the values were adopted by reference into state insurance laws.

Social facts are like standardized industry practices, particularly as to a social fact's existence being conditioned on widespread acceptance in the society or relevant portion of the society. It is easy to see that some protocols – like the generally accepted accounting principles (GAAP) become both social facts and 'methods of operation': it becomes impossible to do the process (accounting) without the expression. It is not as obvious how a used car valuation or a parts designation can be an uncopyrightable 'process', but there is some parallelism: once it is widely accepted, a designation (like '787' or 'Rock Hudson') is a social convention – a communication standard, so to speak. Like technical or industry standards, it becomes the only reasonable way to do something – in this case, the only reasonable way to refer to *X* is using *X*'s name. So it might be possible to subsume the recognition of created facts into recognition of expressions which become communication 'protocols' that are necessary for non-expressive activity.

Nonetheless, as long as we subscribe to facts and a correspondence theory of truth (in the way our legal system generally does), the designation and evaluation cases discussed above feel like something more than communication protocols. In these cases, original expression becomes the basis for universally accepted propositions of the form 'this is X', 'that is Y', 'A is B' that seem to have truth values. These are social facts generated directly from what copyright calls 'original expression' and from what copyright calls 'authors'. That is the created facts problem – and the gaping hole in the *Feistian* scheme of things.

The problem is that an honest assessment that these evaluations, judgments, and designations produce social facts can lead to blunt application of the merger doctrine – and, thereby, eliminate any possible copyright incentive. To understand this, we have to recognize that the merger doctrine works differently with what we call 'ideas' and what we call facts.

---

tive is needed to produce, that is the more access is needed, the less copyright incentive is needed. Id. at 299–300. This might be generally right, but this appears to be an empirical question that deserves careful attention.

The merger doctrine is notoriously malleable. With ideas, the doctrine's indeterminacy comes from trying to apply an either/or dichotomy – with draconian implications – to a multi-layered world. Resting on top of any given expression, there is, metaphorically, a stack of increasingly abstract ideas. At the bottom of the stack, there may be a *least* abstract, most precise idea expressible only in the words chosen – if that were the 'idea' in merger doctrine, there would be no copyright.[162] At the other end, one can always find an idea so abstract that there is definitely no merger. For example, the original brain-in-a-vat science fiction story, 'Donovan's Brain', became, according to its author, 'the acknowledged basis for three movies, as well as perhaps 50 more that appropriated the basic idea'.[163] Distinguishing between the three films and the 50 films makes sense to us because we know that the reference to a 'basic idea' is a reference to a *highly abstracted, very general* idea. It is the same notion that Judge Hand presented in saying that a filmmaker would not infringe a stage play if they used 'only the more general patterns' of the play.[164]

But notions of the 'basic idea' or the 'general pattern' are not useful when it comes to facts and expressions of facts. We would not say that the expression of a specific temperature reading in Chicago at noon on 4 May 2007 (say, '63 degrees F') is protectable because, after all, it does not propertize the *basic idea* of a temperature in Chicago at noon on 4 May 2007 (or of a temperature in Chicago, more generally). There is something irrelevant about this kind of reasoning: we are not concerned about more abstract levels when it comes to facts. An *abstract fact* is a classification, a theory, a law of nature, that is that there will be a *temperature* in Chicago on 4 May 2007. This is what is so dissatisfying about Judge Leval's comment in *Maclean Hunter* that the plaintiff's 'ideas' were general ideas of used car valuations – and why the same argument did not fly in *NYMEX*. What matters to us are the precise valuations.[165] Those precise valuations are social facts; the social facts and the expression of those facts are merged.

In many cases – as in *Feist* – drawing a distinction between facts and

---

162 Cf. Wiley Jr., John Shephard (1991), 'Copyright at the School of Patent', 58 *U. Chi. L. Rev.* 119, 123 (suggesting that if copyright law protected only the literal expression of an idea, then every admitted copier would have a defense).

163 Martin, Douglas, 'Curt Siodmak Dies at 98; Created Modern "Wolf Man" ', *New York Times,* 19 November 2000, § 1, at 56.

164 *Sheldon v Metro-Goldwyn Pictures Corp.*, 81 F.2d 49, 54 (2d Cir. 1936).

165 And, similarly, this is what seems so irrelevant about the *Veeck I* court telling us that 'there are at least two other sets of building codes that currently compete with SBCCI's'. *Veeck v S. Bldg. Code Cong. Int'l, Inc.* (Veeck I), 241 F.3d 398, 407 (5th Cir. 2001), *rev'd en banc*, 293 F.3d 791 (5th Cir. 2002).

expression of facts is an extra, pointless step. Facts are always unprotected and, at least in databases, there is almost always merger between them and their expressions. That is what produces the bind with created facts. After *Feist*, if a court recognizes that the expressions in a non-fictional database are as much expression of facts as the phone numbers in *Feist*, the merger doctrine proceeds swiftly and surely to denude the work of any copyright protection beyond selection and arrangement.

VII. PRESERVING INCENTIVES WHEN INCENTIVES ARE NEEDED

As post-industrial economic development proceeds, valuable non-fictional databases filled with evaluations, judgments, and designations (and business models based on these databases) will only proliferate, as will the likely disputes about who controls the contents and how. If being honest about 'facts' means the merger doctrine will knock out copyright protection for many of these works, is that a problem? Arguably yes, for a discrete subset of these information products. For such products, we will need to find ways to curb and/or probably recalibrate the merger doctrine. To that end, let's consider what kinds of 'created fact works' may need the incentive of copyright and what limiting doctrines of copyright can be brought to bear in balancing the need to have incentives for the expression with the need to access to the facts created by the expression.

A. Determining Where Incentives are Needed

In considering whether the copyright incentive is needed, we must recognize that many facts will be 'created' by people for non-economic incentives, such as a sense of civic or professional duty. Within the economic realm, we should also distinguish between economic incentives dependent on copyright and other economic incentives. Without delving into the minefield about whether such determinations should affect copyright protection more broadly (there are lots of reasons to think they shouldn't), let us consider these issues in relation to the eight cases discussed above.

The most obvious of the cases are *Southco* and *NYMEX*. For-profit Southco had a strong business incentive to give designations to its parts – indeed, it could not carry on a parts-selling business without doing so. No copyright protection is needed for that economic incentive to remain stable. The *NYMEX* litigation also seems a simple case because [a] preparation of the settlement prices is mandatory for NYMEX to carry on its business and [b] disclosure of the prices is legally required for NYMEX to be in that business.[166] In contrast, *Maclean Hunter* seems at the other extreme: its for-profit business was producing and selling the expression, not to mention that substantial numbers of its customers were migrating to the cheaper service that the defendant was able to offer by freely copying Maclean Hunter's expressions. This persuasive distinction clearly animated the Second Circuit decision in *NYMEX*: after recognizing the fear 13 years earlier that without copyright Maclean Hunter 'might direct their energies elsewhere, depriving the public of their creations', the court concluded that 'NYMEX needs no such incentives'.[167]

The rest of the cases seem to fall somewhere between *Maclean Hunter* and *NYMEX*, potentially pointing for the need to make careful determinations whether the copyright incentive is needed in situations involving 'created fact' works. In *Practice Management* and *Delta Dental*, the courts expressly concluded that the copyright holder needed the incentive of copyright, but the status of each as a non-profit, professional association raises the legitimate issue of whether that was really true. The non-profit status hardly settles the issue – non-profit organizations can certainly depend on publication sales for their operations;[168] in *Veeck* this precise point was contested among the various opinions.[169] The status of the group as a professional association – intent on rendering beneficial services to the profession – seems a stronger argument for why the copyright incentive is not needed. Further along this spectrum, the case against copyright incentive being genuinely needed seems even stronger when the 'author' is a professional association intent on getting its expression enacted into law (as in *BOCA*); at that point, professional prestige and public service seem to be the driving forces. This was an important argument for the *Veeck* majority.[170]

---

166 See *N.Y. Mercantile Exch., Inc. v IntercontinentalExchange, Inc.*, 497 F.3d 109, 110 (2d Cir. 2007).

167 *N.Y. Mercantile Exch.*, 497 F.3d at 118 (quoting *Maclean Hunter*, 44 F.3d at 66 (2d Cir. 1994)).

168 The finances are often hard to figure out. For example, roughly 18 per cent of the revenues of the American Institute of Certified Public Accountants (AICPA) come from sales of accounting standards. *Am. Inst. of Certified Pub. Accountants, 2002–2003 Annual Report 17* (2003). But Professor Cunningham discusses how the AICPA sales operation sustained losses in the early 2000s. Cunningham, *supra* note 2, at 320.

169 In *Veeck*, the majority characterized the evidence that copyright revenues were needed as 'self-serving affidavits from [SBCCI] officers and employees' and 'perhaps proof that 40% of its revenue' came from selling copies of its model codes. *Veeck v S. Bldg. Code Cong. Int'l, Inc.* (*Veeck II*), 293 F.3d 791, 805 n.21 (5th Cir. 2002) (*en banc*).

170 See id. at 805; Cunningham, *supra* note 2, at 297, 304.

In these types of cases, perhaps district courts need to do a more thorough job developing evidence of the copyright holder's business model – presumably they would do so if they knew that the way in which they were to apply the merger doctrine turned on whether copyright was needed to bring the expression (and, hence, the facts) into existence.

B. Fair Uses, Implying Licenses, and Recalibrating Merger Doctrine

If there remains a kernel of situations where the copyright incentive seems quite important for production of the expression and, therefore, the facts, what are we to make of copyright's limiting principles in such situations? Before turning to the merger doctrine – and how it sweeps too broadly in *Maclean Hunter* type situations – let us consider what happens with fair use and the doctrine of implied licenses when we understand these works as 'factual works'.

1. Fair use and implied licenses for created fact works

Concluding that a copyrighted work is principally a (created) factual work affects the fair use analysis because 'the scope of fair use is greater with respect to factual than non-factual works'.[171] Mechanically, a determination that a plaintiff's work is a created fact work would impact the fair use analysis principally through the second factor.[172] In *Harper & Row v Nation Enterprises*, the Court told us that this factor, the nature of the copyrighted work, recognizes 'a greater need to disseminate factual works than works of fiction or fantasy'.[173] The Court quoted Professor Gorman approvingly for the notion that '[t]he extent to which one must permit expressive language to be copied, in order to assure dissemination of the underlying facts, will thus vary from case to case'.[174] With created fact works of the sort considered in this chapter, the expression is probably the only way to 'assure dissemination of

---

171 *New Era Publications, Int'l v Carol Publ'g Group*, 904 F.2d 152, 157 (2d Cir. 1990); see also *Stewart v Abend*, 495 U.S. 207, 237 (1990) ('In general, fair use is more likely to be found in factual works than in fictional works.'); *American Geophysical Union v Texaco*, 37 F.3d 881, 893 (2d Cir. 1994) (adopting the same reasoning).

172 See 17 U.S.C. § 107(2). The first factor, 'the purpose and character of the [defendant's] use', see id. at §107(1), is sufficiently open-ended that we could include 'for compliance with the law' as a characteristic of the circumstances that should weigh in the defendant's favor. But this effect on the fair use analysis is not directly related to understanding the expressive works as producing facts.

173 *Harper & Row, Publishers, Inc. v Nation Enterprises*, 471 U.S. 539, 563 (1985).

174 Id. (quoting Gorman, Robert (1982), 'Fact or Fancy? The Implications for Copyright', 29 *J. Copyright Soc'y U.S.A.* 560, 563).

the underlying facts'. Thus, one could argue that the fair use doctrine, by itself, would permit extensive copying of a created facts work. This could cover the activities of the defendants in *Southco, CDN,* and perhaps *NYMEX.*

On the other hand, in many of these opinions with grand propositions about access to factual works – *Harper & Row, American Geophysical* – fair use is *not* found. This is probably because the fourth fair use factor – effect on the plaintiff's market – has been both doctrinally and descriptively dominant.[175] If that is correct, it suggests that wholesale copying as in *Maclean Hunter, Delta Dental, Veeck,* and *BOCA* – or as was sought in *Practice Management* – would not be tolerated under fair use.[176] In contrast, the implied license doctrine may both cover the most important created fact cases and prompt a certain amount of self-selection on the question of copyright incentives.

As the name indicates, implied licenses in copyright may be inferred from words or conduct.[177] The model code cases seem particularly apt for this treatment: once the model code is written, the professional association effectively 'hands it over' to the government knowing that the government will reproduce and distribute the expression. In the case law, these are paradigmatic indicators of an implied license,[178] particularly 'the delivery of the copyrighted material without warning that its further use would constitute copyright infringement'.[179]

---

175 Beebe, Barton (2008), 'An Empirical Study of Copyright Fair Use Options, 1978–2005', ('Correlation and regression analyses reveal the surprising extent to which the outcomes of the first and especially the fourth factors appear to drive the outcome of the test'), 156 *U. Pa. L. Rev.* 549, 555.

176 The Nimmer treatise reasons that adoption of a private work into law may enlarge the range of private copying which is protected by the fair use doctrine, but should not immunize a commercial publisher who wants to compete with the copyright owner, since this would 'prove destructive of the copyright interest in encouraging creativity in connection with the increasing trend toward state and federal adoption of model codes'. 1 *Nimmer on Copyright* § 5.12 [A] at 5-92 to -93.

177 Id. at §10.03[A][7] at 10-49 ('[N]onexclusive licenses may . . . be granted orally, or may even be implied from conduct').

178 See, for example, *Effects Assoc., Inc. v Cohen*, 908 F.2d 555, 558 (9th Cir. 1990) ('Effects created a work at defendant's request and handed it over, intending that defendant copy and distribute it.'); *I.A.E., Inc. v Shaver*, 74 F.3d 768, 776 (7th Cir. 1996) ('In the case before us, as in *Effects,* Mr. Shaver created a work at Joint Venture's request and handed it over, intending Joint Venture to copy and distribute it for the Airport Project.')

179 *Effects*, 908 F.2d at 559, n. 6. When an entity 'encourage[d], through a licensing program, public authorities such as states to adopt' its model code, *Bldg. Officials & Code Adm'rs v Code Tech., Inc.*, 628 F.2d 730, 732 (1st Cir. 1980), the only alternative to the association anticipating the widespread reproduction of the adopted law would be the unsavory scenario in which the association planned to charge monopoly rents after state adoption. See id. at 732–35. In other words, the state adoption was like the state awarding a supply contract, except that the citizens, instead of the state coffers, pay directly for the state's supply of 'law'.

Further, it is reasonable to think that the association's agreement – or lack of objection – to integration of its model code into law grants an implied license for derivative works, that is amendment and modification of the code.[180]

A tantalizingly similar case where implied license through government use might have been inferred is the 2000 *SmithKline Beecham v Watson Pharmaceutical* case, in which SmithKline sued a generic drug manufacturer for copying SmithKline's copyrighted labels and user guides, despite the generic drug manufacturer being *required* to copy the materials by the Food & Drug Administration.[181] Although the defendant raised the issue of implied license, the court decided that the Hatch-Waxman Act directly obviated the copyright claim without need to pass through implied license or fair use analyses.[182] Not satisfied with its strict legal analysis – and in keeping with the discussion here – the court engaged in a substantial analysis that SmithKline did not need copyright incentive for the preparation of the labels, user's guide, etc.[183]

Such an implied license seems obviously to cover government and government authorized publishers – and it is not difficult to extend to other publishers based on it being widely understood that 'law' may be freely copied.[184] The implied license argument reasonably extends to situations like *NYMEX* (and *SmithKline*) where both the expression and its publication were legally required to engage in an otherwise lucrative business.[185] But the implied

180 *Gracen v Bradford Exch.*, 698 F.2d 300, 303 (7th Cir. 1983) (indicating that a contest to prepare derivative works was the basis for an implied nonexclusive license to contestants).

181 *SmithKline Beecham Consumer Healthcare, L.P. v Watson Pharms.*, 211 F.3d 21 (2d Cir. 2000). Although there was some back and forth between Watson and the FDA, in its final determination 'the FDA "determined that Watson had to copy verbatim substantially all of the text used in the SmithKline" user's guide.' Id. at 24 (quoting *SmithKline Beecham Consumer Healthcare, L.P. v Watson Pharms., Inc.*, No. 99 Civ. 9214, 1999 WL 1243894, at *4 (S.D.N.Y. 22 December 1999)).

182 *SmithKline*, 211 F.3d at 25 ('[T]he Hatch-Waxman amendments to the FFDCA not only permit but require producers of generic drugs to use the same labeling as was approved for, and is used in, the sale of the pioneer drug . . . [T]he FDA's requirement that Watson use much of SmithKline's label precludes a copyright infringement action . . . [W]e need not address either the fair use or implied license defenses.')

183 Id. at 28–29.

184 On the theory that 'there is ample support for the proposition that implied license scope in general is determined by considering the reasonable expectations of the parties in view of all of the circumstances, including the parties' conduct'. Janis, Mark D. (1999), 'A Tale of the Apocryphal Axe: Repair, Reconstruction, and the Implied License in Intellectual Property Law', 58 *Md. L. Rev.* 423, 502.

185 Although it is fair to ask what would happen if a professional association then tried to withdraw its implied license. See *Jacob Maxwell, Inc. v Veeck*, 110 F.3d 749, 753 (11th Cir. 1997) (withdrawal of implied license after use of song for several months).

license argument seems to have little traction with cases like *Maclean Hunter*, *CDN*, and *Southco* – in which the putative copyright holder did no single act to 'hand over' their copyrighted work. To extend the doctrine to those situations would really involve either some kind of laches or acquiescence argument (more familiar to trademark law) or a kind of the-value-is-the-public's-investment argument that has surfaced in scholarship,[186] but has not been well-formulated in jurisprudence.[187]

2. Recalibrating the merger doctrine for created fact works

When the merger doctrine is applied to ideas, a central issue is the choice of level of abstraction; but as I said earlier, with things that strike us as 'facts', the ability to slide up and down the scale of abstractness disappears. If copyright, like other forms of property, should satisfy the criterion of leaving 'enough and as good for others',[188] then access to the precise facts seems necessary. Yet assuming that some economic incentive was needed for creation of the expressions (which created the facts) if the merger doctrine

---

186 Litman, Jessica (1999), 'Breakfast with Batman: The Public Interest in the Advertising Age', 108 *Yale L. J.* 1717, 1730). One might also interpret Rochelle Dreyfuss' argument about expressive genericity along these lines. Dreyfuss, Rochelle Cooper (1990), 'Expressive Genericity: Trademarks as Language in the Pepsi Generation', 65 *Notre Dame L. Rev*. 397, 407.

187 One of the best known efforts might be Judge Boudin's concurrence in *Lotus Development Corp. v Borland International*, 49 F.3d 807, 821 (1st Cir. 1995) ('But if a better spreadsheet comes along, it is hard to see why customers who have learned the Lotus menu and devised macros for it should remain captives of Lotus because of an investment in learning made by the users and not by Lotus'), *aff'd by an equally divided court*, 516 U.S. 233 (1996).

188 This condition was famously identified by (is now identified with) John Locke. See Locke, J. (1690), 'Second Treatise of Government', § § 27–33, in Laslett, P. (1963) (rev. ed), *Two Treatises of Government*. Across the spectrum of modern political philosophy, there is widespread recognition that any adequate theory of property – or just distribution of goods – will contain some version of the condition. See, for example, Nozick, Robert (1978), *Anarchy, State and Utopia* 181 (interpreting the 'enough and as good requirement' as a principle meant 'to ensure that the situation of others is not worsened' by the appropriation of property from the commons); Singer, Peter (2002), *One World – The Ethics of Globalization* 27–30 (contending that the enough and as good proviso plays a key role in the just distribution of the world's natural resources). See also Otsuka, Michael (2003), *Libertarianism Without Inequality* 22–29 (endorsing the 'enough and as good' principle); Schmidtz, David, 'The Institution of Property', 11 *Soc. Phil. & Pol'y* 42, 44–50 (Summer 1994). Many believe that Locke's proviso, stricto senso, is a sufficient condition, while a more general, harm-based version of the proviso is a necessary condition. See Waldron, Jeremy (1979), 'Enough and as Good Left for Others', 29 *Phil. Q.* 319, 320; Wolf, Clark (1995), 'Contemporary Property Rights, Lockean Provisos, and the Interests of Future Generations', 104 *Ethics* 791, 795–99. Nozick's reinterpretation can be taken this way.

strips away the copyright protection, we will destroy the incentive for the creation of the next iteration of the Red Book or the CDN Coin Dealer – the very thing that brought the facts into existence.

The resolution of this problem lies in understanding the temporal difference. The merger doctrine comes into play *ex post facto* when recognizing that property rights stemming from some *existing work* would make ideas and/or facts unavailable to the broader society. In contrast, the incentive rationale of copyright comes into play *ex ante* when *failure* to recognize (or make a commitment to recognize) property rights stemming from some *yet to exist work* would make expressions unavailable to the broader society. The two can be reconciled with a simple presumption: that facts and expressions of fact should not be found to have merged if *ex ante* knowledge of the merger doctrine applying to the *expression* would have prevented creation of the *facts* at issue. In other words, we must ask two questions. First, is the project of bringing the expression into existence also *a project that brings the fact into existence*? Secondly, does this project of bringing the expression into existence need the incentive provided by the copyright system? If the answer to both these two questions is 'yes', then in the absence of copyright incentives there will be neither expressions nor facts to have 'merged'. The question is how we might recalibrate the merger doctrine to deal with – and not completely eliminate copyright in – situations where the incentive of copyright is needed to generate the *facts*. There may be profitable insights from comparing merger doctrine with the 'essential facilities' doctrine in antitrust law. Although often used by the courts,[189] the essential facilities doctrine is much maligned in antitrust scholarship;[190] its status has been further complicated by the Supreme

[189] The doctrine has been applied most cleanly to expensive infrastructure which is not utilized to one hundred per cent capacity by the defendant, that is electric transmission lines, natural gas pipelines, and sports stadiums. See, for example, *Otter Tail Power Company v United States*, 410 U.S. 366 (1973) (electric transmission lines); *Woods Exploration and Producing Co. v ALCOA*, 438 F.2d 1286 (5th Cir. 1971), *cert. denied*, 404 U.S. 1047 (1972) (natural gas pipelines); *Fishman v Wirtz*, 807 F.2d 520 (7th Cir. 1986) (professional sports arena); *Hecht v Pro-Football, Inc.*, 570 F.2d 982 (D.C. Cir. 1977) (professional football stadium).

[190] See, for example, 3A Areeda, Phillip E. and Herbert Hovenkamp (1996), *Antitrust Law* ¶ 771b at 174 (viewing the doctrine as 'inconsistent with antitrust's goals'); Reiffen, David and Andrew N. Kleit (1990), 'Terminal Rail-road Revisited: Foreclosure of an Essential Facility or Simple Horizontal Monopoly?', 33 *J.L. & Econ.* 419, 420–21 ('[E]conomic theory suggest[s] that there is no need for an essential facilities doctrine. . .'); Downie, Gordon and Laura MacGregor (2000), 'Essential Facilities and Utility Networks', in MacGregor, Prosser, and Villiers (eds) (2000), *Regulation and Markets Beyond 2000* 19, 38 ('[t]he essential facilities doctrine takes competition law to the very limits of its legitimate scope, and possibly across the order into regulation').

Court's 2004 refusal to either embrace or kill the doctrine.[191] In that context, I propose the essential facilities doctrine only as a lens through which we might rethink the merger doctrine as a kind of 'essential expression doctrine'. While there are arguably a couple of American cases applying the essential facilities doctrine to information works broadly understood,[192] neither the similarity between the merger and essential facilities doctrine[193] nor application of the essential facilities doctrine to copyrighted works has been explored in American legal literature.[194]

The essential facilities cases involving unilateral action (§2 of the Sherman Act) typically involve a vertically-integrated defendant who controls an input for some downstream market in which the defendant has or could have monopoly power.[195] As formulated in the Seventh Circuit's 1983 opinion in *MCI Communications Corp. v A.T.& T*, successful assertion of the essential facilities doctrine requires four elements:

---

[191] See *Verizon Communications, Inc. v Law Offices of Curtis V. Trinko*, 540 U.S. 398, 411 (2004) ('We have never recognized [the "essential facilities"] doctrine and we find no need either to recognize it or to repudiate it here.').

[192] One case, *Alaska Airlines v United Airlines*, 948 F.2d 536 (9th Cir. 1991), arguably comes close because the computerized reservation systems at issue – United's 'Apollo' and American's 'Sabre' systems – were, in part, elaborate, constantly updated databases. Those databases, however, probably fell outside post-*Feist* American copyright law. Id. at 542–46; see also *Intergraph Corp. v Intel Corp.*, 3 F. Supp.2d 1255, 1278 (N.D. Ala. 1998) (finding that '[r]easonable and timely access to critical business information . . . is an essential facility'), *vacated*, 195 F.3d 1346 (Fed. Cir. 1999).

[193] See, for example, Wagner, Dana R. (2000), 'The Keepers of the Gates: Intellectual Property, Antitrust, and Regulatory Implications of Systems Technology', 51 *Hastings L.J.* 1073, 1122–1124 (identifying the two doctrines as two distinct 'possible doctrinal foundations' for creating liability for systems technology industries that fail to license or open their technology, but not identifying the similarity or identity of the two doctrines).

[194] Exceptions are McGowan, David (1996), 'Regulating Competition in the Information Age: Computer Software as an Essential Facility Under the Sherman Act', 18 *Hastings Comm. & Ent. L.J.* 771 (in the context of network effects); Carrier, Michael A. (2006), 'Of *Trinko*, Tea Leaves, and Intellectual Property', 31 *J. Corp. L.* 357, 361; Carrier, Michael A. (2006), 'Refusals to License Intellectual Property After *Trinko*', 55 *DePaul Law Review* 1191; McGowan, David (1996), 'Regulating Competition in the Information Age: Computer Software as an Essential Facility Under the Sherman Act', 18 *Hastings Comm. & Ent. L.J.* 771, 841–49 (1996) (discussing the essential facilities doctrine in the context of network effects); Menell, Peter S. (1987), 'Tailoring Legal Protection for Computer Software', 39 *Stan. L. Rev.* 1329, 1366–67 (applying an essential facilities approach to compulsory licensing for innovative operating system features that become widely established); Reichenberger, Melanie J. (2006), 'Note, The Role of Compulsory Licensing in Unilateral Refusals to Deal: Have the United States and European Approaches Grown Further Apart After IMS?', 31 *J. Corp. L.* 549, 558–65.

[195] See, for example, 3A Areeda and Hovenkamp, supra note 190, ¶ 771a at 172.

1. that the defendant controls an upstream facility or resource that is essential to competition in the market where the defendant has (or could have) monopoly power;
2. that competitor(s) cannot practically or reasonably replicate the facility;
3. that the defendant denies use of the facility to the competitor(s); and
4. that granting access is feasible [and economically rational but for maintenance of the monopoly] because granting access would not disrupt the monopolist's own use of the facility.[196]

Each of these requirements can have some resonance for copyright cases. For example, a requirement differentiating between upstream and downstream markets mirrors, in some respects, a strongly intuitive concern in fair use doctrine – the distinction between primary and ancillary markets: copyright scholars have focused much of their turn-of-the-century angst on the issue of how derivative works should be freed (or freer) of the upstream works from which they are derived.

But it is the second and fourth criteria of the essential facilities doctrine that should interest us with 'created fact' works. The second criterion in the essential facility checklist is that 'the competitors of the monopolist are unable to duplicate the facility'.[197] As the Areeda and Hovenkamp treatise points out in the context of antitrust law,

> [t]he essential facility claim is about the duty to deal of a monopolist who is able to supply an input for itself in a fashion that is so superior over anything else available that others cannot succeed unless they can access that firm's input as well. For this reason a strict conception of objectively measured 'essentiality' is critical for any rational essential facility doctrine . . .[198]

When expressions have taken on the glow of institutional facts because of integration into binding law, the case of essentiality seems straightforward. The Medicare/Medicaid programs would not permit a physician to seek reimbursement with any other procedure designations; a person whose car is totaled must use the Red Book number in seeking an insurance recovery. Although quite critical of the essential facilities doctrine in antitrust law, even Professor Areeda recognized that 'the strongest claims of essentiality' include

---

196 708 F.2d 1081, 1132 (7th Cir. 1983), *cert. denied*, 464 U.S. 891 (1983); *accord, Ferguson v Greater Pocatello Chamber of Commerce*, 848 F.2d 976, 983 (9th Cir. 1988); *City of Malden v Union Elec. Co.*, 887 F.2d 157, 160 (8th Cir. 1989).

197 Ferguson, 848 F.2d at 983.

198 3A Areeda and Hovenkamp, supra note 190, ¶ 771a at 172; see also Areeda, 'The "Essential Facilities" Doctrine: An Epithet in Need of Limiting Principles', 56 *Antitrust L. J.* 841, 847–53 (1989).

resources 'whose duplication is forbidden by law'.[199] That is exactly the situation in the *BOCA, Veeck, Maclean Hunter,* and *Practice Management* cases.

For expressions which have taken on the glow of social facts as a matter of convention – *CDN, Southco* – the case for essentiality is substantial, but not as strong. Still, if we have concluded that an author's creations have become social facts or institutional facts in the Searlean sense, then generally speaking the expression of those social facts will be necessary, unique, and irreplaceable as to a range of activities distinct from the author's primary market. 'Factness' *is* essentiality in a society that places the emphasis on public discourse that ours does.

But it is the fourth requirement of the essential facilities doctrine which provides the most interesting payoff in how to apply the merger doctrine to created fact works. The fourth requirement of the essential facility doctrine is 'the feasibility of providing the facility'[200] to others without undermining the defendant's own commercial activities. At first blush, it appears that this fourth element is *automatically* satisfied with intellectual property: the public goods nature of information works means that the copyright owner will *always* be able to 'provide' the information facility while continuing to use the expression themselves.

But the situation is more complicated if we think, again, about *ex ante* and *ex post facto* perspectives. If the fourth requirement is that the property owner must be able to continue to enjoy use of the facility, then we should ask: *will the defendant, over the long term, be able to continue to use the created fact work for its own commercial activities?* And this is the key difference of eliminating exclusive rights in traditional merger analysis and what an essential facilities analysis would produce: a kind of compulsory license.

We have posited that in *some* situations *ex ante* knowledge of the merger doctrine applying to the *expression of facts* would have prevented creation of the *facts* at issue. In other words, if the publishers of the Red Book or the *Coin Dealer Newsletter* knew, in advance, that the merger doctrine would allow people to freely copy their publications, they 'might direct their energies elsewhere, depriving the public of their creations'[201] – and, thereby, depriving the

199 3A Areeda and Hovenkamp, supra note 190, ¶ 773 at 199. But the Areeda and Hovenkamp treatise also notes that 'when duplication is prohibited by law, forced sharing may be as well', citing patent law. Id. at 196 n. 2. While the federal government's adoption of the CPT codes for Medicaid payments did not 'forbid' the development of alternative codes, it does make such development pointless or, more strongly, it makes it impossible to develop a competitor facility.

200 See *MCI*, 708 F.2d at 1081, 1133.

201 *CCC Info. Servs., Inc. v Maclean Hunter Mkt. Reports, Inc.*, 44 F.3d 61, 66 (2d Cir. 1994).

public of the (created) facts. In other words, the traditional merger doctrine might eliminate the next iteration of the 'facility' – both for the producer of the work and for those who benefited (temporarily) from the merger doctrine. In antitrust law the essential facilities doctrine certainly does *not* require the defendant to give away access to the facility *so as to cause decline, waste, or destruction of the facility.*[202] So, where we determine that the incentive structure of copyright is genuinely needed to generate the (created) facts, then our modified merger doctrine should require the producer of the created fact work to license the work on reasonable, non-discriminatory, and still profitable terms. Since merger is a judge-created doctrine, there is no ban to grafting onto it compelled licensing in these rare situations of created fact works for which the economic incentive of copyright has been judged necessary for creation of the work. This comports with a small, but growing body of intellectual property case law including the Ninth Circuit's 1988 *Abend v MCA* decision,[203] the Supreme Court's 1995 *Campbell v Acuff-Rose* decision,[204] and the Court's recent 2006 *eBay v MercExchange* decision:[205] cases that, as many commentators have noted, constitute the germ of a case-by-case, judicially-imposed compulsory licensing system.[206]

---

202 Cf. Areeda, supra note 199, at 850, where Areeda points out that in the context of MCI, no court would order interconnection if it would harm the incumbent's facilities. Some uses might do that to a work.

203 863 F.2d 1465 (9th Cir. 1988). The compulsory license nature of the court's decision is made clear by the remand instructions that, in calculating the plaintiff's portion of defendant's profits, 'the district court must recognize' that 'the tremendous success' of the film was 'attributable in significant measure to . . . Grace Kelly and James Stewart – and the brilliant directing of Alfred Hitchcock.' Id. at 1478. The court clearly of the mind that the plaintiff would take far less than 100 per cent of the studio's profit from the film. Id. at 1480.

204 510 U.S. 569, 578, n. 10 (1994) (the goals of the copyright law 'are not always best served by automatically granting injunctive relief when [defendants] are found to have gone beyond the bounds of fair use.').

205 126 S. Ct. 1837, 1838–41 (2006) (concluding that injunctive relief in patent law is not automatic, but follows equitable considerations).

206 Gordon, Wendy J. (1994), 'Assertive Modesty: An Economics of Intangibles', 94 *Colum. L. Rev.* 2579, 2588 n. 41 (Citing *Campbell* and noting '[t]oday, judges are more open to exploring liability-rule avenues in copyright litigation'; Haemmerli, Alice (2006), 'Take It, It's Mine: Illicit Transfers of Copyright by Operation of Law', 63 *Wash & Lee L. Rev.* 1011, 1020 ('In these cases, one could say that the court's refusal to grant injunctive relief for copyright infringement effectively results in a compulsory license in favor of the defendant'); Karjala, *supra* note 2 at 524 ('If fair use were a reliable form of compulsory license, it could be an important counterweight to a copyright in functional works. Its use in this fashion, however, has little foundation other than a footnote in the Supreme Court's decision in Campbell'); McClimon, Timothy J. (1986), 'Denial of Preliminary Injunction in Copyright Infringement Cases: An Emerging Judicially Crafted Compulsory License', 10 *Colum.-VLAJ.L. & Arts* 277.

While a situation like *Abend v MCA* leaves the damage level to the judge's intuitions, decisions concerning the created fact works discussed above need not be so *ad hoc*. Created fact works are typically *iterated* works – works that are continually updated and for which any one edition has a limited shelf-life of value. The Red Book and Coin Dealer Newsletter have extremely short shelf lives; the CPT, the ADA Nomenclature, and the model legal codes are more stable, but a party using the code is ill-advised not to have a complete, up-to-date set. Thus, when a judge determines that 'essential expression' should be made available to third parties, a price can be set that ensures that the copyright owner continues to keep the information facility in 'good repair', so to speak – not much differently than the owner of a bridge or power lines deserving adequate returns under the essential facilities doctrine to maintain the physical facilities.

In the occasional circumstances when this proposal will come into play, it is still subject to the same criticism that the Court recently leveled against any court-enforced sharing: that it forces courts to identify the 'proper price . . . and other terms of dealing – a role for which they are ill-suited'.[207] If there is no visible market failure in, say, the used car or collector coin markets, why attempt this market intervention? The answer comes in more or less summarizing the project here: (a) we generally make copyright available for these sorts of expressive works to avoid one sort of market failure; and (b) we have identified one limited set of situations (*Maclean Hunter*-like cases) where the intervention of copyright does seem needed to ensure that the market is supplied with the expression *and* the facts; (c) we have strong *non*-market reasons – related to democratic self-governance – for wanting to make 'facts' available to all; yet (d) application of our usual doctrinal tool – merger – will negate 'b' and, thereby, kill off the facts. The most reasonable course in these rare circumstances is to 'dial back', not turn off, the incentive of copyright.

CONCLUSION

In the thirteenth century, St. Bonaventure called the scribes of his time 'compilers and weavers of approved opinions',[208] an apt description for the activities – and resulting works – of companies like Maclean Hunter and non-profit associations like the AMA, ADA, BOCA, and SBCCI. Sometimes

---

[207] See *Verizon Commc'ns, Inc. v Law Offices of Curtis V. Trinko*, LLP, 540 U.S. 398, 408 (2004) ('Enforced sharing also requires antitrust courts to act as central planners, identifying the proper price, quantity, and other terms of dealing – a role for which they are ill-suited').

[208] Strayer, Joseph R. (ed) (11th ed. 1988) *Dictionary of the Middle Ages* 56.

privately-generated opinions become so widely 'approved' that they become necessary for subsequent expressive and non-expressive activities. Based on such wide-spread – often legally-mandated – use these 'opinions' become woven into the social fabric as facts, as or more significant to our lives than facts of nature. When an author's intentional act of creating the *expression* produces the *social fact*, I call the results 'created facts'.

The *Feist* decision's definition of 'facts' and its understanding of their unprotected nature fails to capture how created facts arise in our social reality. Copyrighted works can generate social facts via many avenues: the ones described in this chapter have been evaluations, designations, and model provisions that become essential for others to use in subsequent expressive and non-expressive activities. As our economy produces more and more 'information products', valuable non-fictional databases filled with evaluations, judgments, and designations will proliferate. Similarly, government reliance on privately-created model codes 'reflects a governmental off-balance sheet financing strategy'[209] and is not going to abate at a time when the public fisc is strained (if there ever was a time when it was not).

Skillful jurists like Judges Leval and Newman deftly avoided the 'facts' issue in the years immediately following *Feist,* but courts are now starting to recognize that expressions created by identifiable individuals produce social facts. The problem is that if we admit that these works generate 'facts', the merger doctrine seems to lead – almost inextricably – to elimination of the copyright in the works involved. This chapter suggests that the merger doctrine should be applied differently in created fact situations depending on whether the copyright incentive was truly needed for production of the created facts work. Where no copyright incentive was needed, the merger doctrine can be applied traditionally – as in situations like *Southco* – because those lists or designations would be created even if the creator knew that the results would not be protectable under copyright. But the merger doctrine should not apply to eliminate copyright when the *ex ante* elimination of copyright's incentive for yet-to-be-created *expressions of fact* would prevent the social facts themselves from ever coming into existence. *Maclean Hunter* and *CDN* probably fit this description. Instead, in such circumstances – as infrequent as they may be – the merger doctrine should produce a compulsory license/sharing result, as the essential facilities doctrine does. Instead of doctrine-distorting machinations to withhold application of the merger doctrine, we should apply it in a sensible way that does not destroy the future flow of *both* expressions of facts and the facts themselves.

---

209 Cunningham, *supra* note 2, at 330.

7. Copyright and convergence: a pragmatic perspective

David McGowan*

To describe Justice Sandra Day O'Connor, scholars typically reach for such words as centrist, moderate, pragmatic,[1] Burkean, or minimalist.[2] She is supposed to have developed a 'split-the-difference' jurisprudence,[3] which allowed her to occupy the 'middle ground' on issues before the Court.[4] Critics said she employed 'balancing tests only she could apply'.[5] A critic grasping for something nice to say actually restates the account: At least 'she decided the particular, and often sensitive, case before her'.[6] An admirer counters with a defense of her 'down-to-earth realism'.[7]

Such a consensus makes Justice O'Connor's opinions an appealing if imperfect ground for considering the relationship between pragmatism and the law.[8] Though few in number, Justice O'Connor's copyright opinions are at

---

* My thanks to Wendy Gordon, Mark Lemley, Glynn Lunney, Miranda McGowan, and Lisa Ramsey for excellent comments. Remaining mistakes are my fault.

1 Biskupic, Joan (2008), 'The Alito/O'Connor Switch', 35 *Pepp. L. Rev*. 495, 496.

2 Sunstein, Cass (2006), 'Burkean Minimalism', 105 *Mich. L. Rev.* 353, 361. Sunstein uses 'Burkean minimalism' as one phrase to describe the style of judges among whom he counts Justice O'Connor, but each part of the phrase has some significance, so I break them apart in the text.

3 Basiak, Jr., John F. (2007), 'The Roberts Court and the Future of Substantive Due Process: The Demise of "Split the Difference"Jurisprudence?', 28 *Whittier L. Rev.* 861.

4 Colker, Ruth (2007), 'Justice Sandra Day O'Connor's Friends', 68 *Ohio State L.J.* 517, 543.

5 Kmiec, Douglas W. (2007), 'The Rule of Law and Roberts's Revolution of Restraint', 34 *Pepp. L. Rev*. 495, 497.

6 Id. at 497 (complimenting Justice O'Connor for at least being better than Justice Kennedy).

7 Joyce, Craig (1006), 'Afterword: Lazy B and the Nation's Court: Pragmatism in the Service of Principle', 119 *Harv. L. Rev.* 1257, 1268.

8 Imperfect because Justice O'Connor was not as self-consciously pragmatic as, say, Richard Posner, for example, Posner, Richard A. (2008), *How Judges Think*,

odds with these descriptions of her work. They are particularly hard to square with the claim that she judged pragmatically.[9]

Many descriptions of Justice O'Connor seem to equate pragmatism with difference splitting. I do not endorse that equation, but it is worth noting that her copyright opinions do not satisfy even this very crude conception of pragmatic judging. Leaving aside *Stewart v Abend*[10] as presenting too narrow and technical an issue for generalization, Justice O'Connor wrote two important copyright opinions.

Harper & Row Publishers, Inc. v Nation Enterprises,[11] affirmed liability for *The Nation* magazine's pre-publication excerpting of Gerald Ford's memoirs. Although I agree with the result and much of her analysis, Justice O'Connor's opinion dealt tersely with the competing traditions and values in the case, and she emphasized the right of first publication implied by the Copyright Act to such an extent that Congress amended the statute's fair use provision to ameliorate the opinion's effects.[12] The result in *Harper & Row* can be defended on pragmatic grounds,[13] but it is not a poster case for pragmatism.

The other opinion, and my subject here, was *Feist Publications, Inc. v Rural Telephone Service Company, Inc.*[14] *Feist* held that a standard 'white pages' telephone directory was not within the subject matter of copyright. The case could have been decided easily on statutory grounds,[15] but Justice

Chapter 9, and because a theoretical commitment to pragmatism (or utilitarianism, or whatever) does not entail the practice of that commitment in all cases. A pragmatist may, for pragmatic reasons, be a formalist in adjudicating certain issues. For example, Posner, Richard A. (1998), 'Pragmatic Adjudication', in Dickstein, M. (ed.), *The Revival of Pragmatism* 236.

[9] For the contrary view, see Aoki, Keith (2007), 'Balancing Act: Reflections on Justice O'Connor's Intellectual Property Jurisprudence', 44 *Hous. L. Rev.* 965, 993–997. I believe Aoki makes a stronger case for balancing with regard to Justice O'Connor's patent and trademark opinions. As this chapter shows, however, I think balancing is only one aspect of pragmatism, which I think of more as a disposition, an 'attitude of mind', than a technique. (For the quotation, see Peirce, C.S. (1998), 'What Pragmatism Is', in 2 *The Essential Peirce* 340.

[10] 495 U.S. 207 (1990).

[11] 471 U.S. 539 (1985).

[12] 17 U.S.C. §107 (amended in 1992 to add a last sentence: 'The fact that a work is unpublished shall not itself bar a finding of fair use if such finding is made upon consideration of all the above factors').

[13] The ability to introduce a work into the market is important to getting the most out of the work, and *Harper & Row* was right to emphasize that fact, though perhaps not in quite the way it did.

[14] 499 U.S. 340 (1991).

[15] The principle of compilation was not original to Rural, and thus was excluded from protection by s.103(b) of the act. The numbers themselves serve as names, and therefore would not have been protected under the analysis of Part III, *infra*.

O'Connor invoked the Constitution to impose requirements for copyrightability not found in the constitutional text.[16] Repudiating the 'sweat of the brow' doctrine, the Court held the need to cover the cost of expression is not a basis for copyright protection; a dash of creativity is needed, too. Justice O'Connor also undertook to define the nature of facts, authorship, and originality. She did so casually, with an ease implying something less than full engagement with these subjects.[17]

Feist and *Harper & Row* are as much at odds with each other as with the notion of Justice O'Connor as a difference-splitter. *Harper & Row* exalted the incentive effects of copyright; it was 'the engine of free expression'.[18] *Feist* said nothing in favor of the incentive argument at all,[19] and the Court's repudiation of cost recovery as a basis for copyright pointed the other way. In *Harper & Row* copyright was about free speech and cost recovery. In *Feist* it was about free riding.[20] In scholarly debates over copyright, the two stand close to the ends of the continuum of views on protection. Minimalists cite *Feist* and distinguish *Harper & Row*; maximalists do the opposite.

As I said, though, difference splitting is not a good definition of pragmatism, so to say Justice O'Connor's was not much of a difference splitter in copyright cases is only to clear away some rhetorical clutter. In this chapter I use *Feist* to think about what it would mean to take a pragmatic approach to originality, authorship, and facts.

Rather than difference splitting, I take as the touchstone of pragmatic analysis of these topics a comment from the early work of Charles Sanders Peirce. Speaking of the relation between scientific inquiry and truth (and, by extension, the relationship between inquiry and fact), Peirce wrote: '[t]he opinion which is fated to be ultimately agreed to by all who investigate is what we mean by the truth, and the object represented in this opinion is the real. That is the way I would explain reality.'[21]

---

16 United States Constitution Article 1 sec. 8, clause 8. Indeed, the Court showed much greater interest in the Nimmer treatise than in the language or history of the Constitution.

17 An invocation, ironically, that may have been necessary in part because of her own overly broad language in *Harper & Row*, in which she wrote '[c]reation of a nonfiction work, even a compilation of pure fact, entails originality'. 471 U.S. at 547. 'Entails' is wrong, which is the holding of *Feist*.

18 471 U.S. at 558.

19 See Ginsburg, Jane C. (1992), 'No "Sweat"? Copyright and Other Protection of Works of Information After *Feist v Rural Telephone*', 92 *Colum. L. Rev.* 338, 350.

20 499 U.S. at 349.

21 Peirce, Charles Sanders (1992), 'How to Make Our Ideas Clear', in 1 *The Essential Peirce* 139. A similar thought is expressed in Peirce, 'The Fixation of Belief',

This conception was part of Peirce's efforts to reconcile scientific thought with the fact that people must do the thinking even about the external world, which we may take as the paradigm case for Justice O'Connor's un-authored facts. This conception of truth, and thus facts, as the product of practices and understandings that force observers to converge on a conclusion, provides an interesting perspective on what it means to treat something as a fact, and thus not original, for purposes of copyright law. (Peirce's comment has obvious echoes in the work of Thomas Kuhn,[22] and, more recently, Deirdre McCloskey's work on the rhetoric of economics,[23] and these echoes also have implications for pragmatic analysis of copyright, but that is for another day.)

My thesis here is that there is a relationship between social forces that produce convergence of opinion regarding some thing and the usefulness of variety in expression about that thing. Where convergence of opinion and understanding is fated, variation at that level is, by hypothesis, impossible. Variation in expressing understandings may be possible, but will be constrained, and may be undesirable. Where variation is possible, it may be desirable to promote it.

I argue that this relationship, not abstract notions of originality or 'fact', should guide copyright policy in cases such as *Feist*. Granting exclusive rights in expression encourages variation in expression by discouraging reproduction. Denying such rights encourages reproduction and decreases variation.[24] Courts therefore should think about the probability that social conventions and practices will tend to force convergence in the apprehension of some object, and the degree to which such convergence implies convergence in expression as well. In general, the more convergence is expected and useful, the warier courts should be about extending rights. The less convergence is expected and

in id. at 120. The quotation was written in 1878. Compare Peirce's later statement, written in 1905: 'That which any true proposition asserts is *real*, in the sense of being as it is regardless of what you or I may think about it.' 'What Pragmatism Is' in (1998) 2 *The Essential Peirce* 343. On the other hand, compare Holmes: 'All I mean by truth is the path I have to travel.' Letter of Oliver Wendell Holmes, Jr. to Alice Stopford Green, 1 October 1901, quoted in Posner, Richard A. (2003), *Law Pragmatism and Democracy* 8 n.12. Obviously the quotation I focus on here is just one strand of pragmatic thought concerning truth, and it may be part of what Judge Posner has in mind as a strand he rejects, Posner, Richard A. (2003), *Law, Pragmatism, and Democracy* 10. I use this strand because the language points the way to thinking about social conventions that imply convergence in expressive behavior, which is relevant to some of my examples, and because I think by itself this comment is compatible with other aspects of pragmatic thinking about truth.

22 Kuhn, Thomas S. (1962), *The Structure of Scientific Revolutions*.

23 McCloskey, Deirdre N. (1998), *The Rhetoric of Economics* (2nd edn).

24 See McGowan, David (2004), 'Why the First Amendment Cannot Dictate Copyright Policy', 65 *U. Pitt. L. Rev.* 281.

useful, the more courts should consider promoting variation by extending rights.

I defend this thesis by examining *Feist* and three types of cases to which Justice O'Connor's opinion might apply. The first type deals with video images of spontaneous news events.[25] My examples are Abraham Zapruder's tape of the Kennedy assassination,[26] George Holliday's tape of the beating of Rodney King, and Robert Tur's aerial footage of the beating of Reginald Denny in the riots following the trial of the officers who beat King. The second type of case involves the conventions of naming, as exemplified in cases concerning the reproduction of part numbers. The third type of case deals with price lists for cars and coins.

Courts refuse to demand *Feist*-like originality in the first type of case. Courts get the second type of case right, even though *Feist's* framework impedes analysis. Courts get the third type of case right, too, by giving only lip service to *Feist*. That it is usefully ignored in two of my three classes, and is a hindrance to clear thinking in the third, provides the gist of my claim that *Feist* cannot be considered a pragmatic opinion.

More practically, the conclusion of this analysis is that cost recovery – the 'sweat of the brow' doctrine – is alive and well, though living under various assumed names. That it lives on is a good thing; that it must live in hiding is bad. My analysis implies that copyright protection should be withheld when (1) variation in expression reduces the usefulness of expression; and (2) the party seeking protection does not sink costs for the purpose of creating expression.

---

[25] I emphasize 'spontaneous' events to distinguish such images from the case of a photographer who may take his or her time with a subject, waiting for the right light or juxtaposition of images. Cf *Mannion v Coors Brewing Co.*, 377 F.Supp. 2d 444, 453–55 (S.D.N.Y. 2005). In *Mannion* Judge Kaplan suggested that originality may inhere in timing of photograph, using as examples photographs of a street scene in New York, a salmon appearing to jump into a bear's mouth, and Eisenstadt's picture of a sailor kissing a woman on VJ day. The last two examples would fit my definition of spontaneous; in the first the timing of the image would be controlled by the photographer's imagination rather than the presentation of an obvious and fleeting occurrence.

[26] Zapruder's tape pre-dates *Feist* of course. My claim is that courts would have rejected an originality argument regarding Zapruder's tape even in a post-*Feist* world. One court has argued that litigation over Zapruder's film 'is not a proper point of reference in determining the copyright of a photograph'. *SHL Imaging, Inc. v Artisan House, Inc.*, 117 F. Supp. 2d 301, 310 n.3 (S.D. N.Y. 2000). The court reasoned that the 'copyrightability of an audiovisual work is analyzed in accord with the definition of audiovisual works in the Copyright Act'. Id. That is true, and means creativity may inhere in the relation of images to one another or to sounds, *Atari Games Corp. v Oman*, 979 F.2d 242, 244–45 (D.C. Cir. 1992), but the point is not relevant here.

These conditions are met with respect to some forms of naming, as when a parts manufacturer designates its products with part numbers. Neither condition is met for works of fiction, such as novels or video games. Those are easy cases. The hard cases occur where the first condition may be met – it may be hard to tell – but the second is not. Contrary to what is probably the consensus among copyright scholars, I believe copyright should extend to this middle case, and should not be diluted into a liability rule unless unusual economic facts favor such dilution.

I.

The Constitution empowers Congress to secure to 'authors' the exclusive rights to their 'writings'.[27] *Feist* elaborates on this language in several famous propositions: 'Authors' are persons who originate expression. Originate means two things: the author created the writing, rather than copied it, and the writing is to some degree creative.[28]

The creativity hurdle is 'extremely low'.[29] A work must posses only 'some creative spark, "no matter how crude, humble or obvious" it might be'.[30] The writing must be 'founded in the creative powers of the mind'[31] so that it displays 'the stamp of the author's originality'.[32] Originality, so understood, is the *sine qua non* of copyright;[33] it 'is a constitutional requirement'.[34]

The cases the Court cited for its originality analysis did not support it very well.[35] *The Trade-Mark Cases*[36] held that Congress's power to grant to authors exclusive rights in their writings did not include the power to protect trademarks. The Court said 'originality is required' for copyright, and that only works 'founded in the creative powers of the mind' were eligible,[37] but these remarks were meant to distinguish copyright from the source-identifying function of trademarks. The Court thought trademarks often consisted of 'something already in existence' which took on new meaning through use as a mark,

---

27 U.S. Const. Art. I §8, cl.8.
28 499 U.S. at 345.
29 Id.
30 *Feist*, quoting 1 Nimmer, M. and D. Nimmer, *Copyright* §1.08[C][1] (1990).
31 *Feist*, quoting *The Trade-Mark Cases*, 100 U.S. 82, 94 (1879).
32 *Feist* quoting *Harper & Row Pubs, Inc. v Nation Enters*, 471 U.S. 539, 546 (1985).
33 *Feist*, 499 U.S. at 345.
34 Id.
35 Ginsburg, *supra* note 19, at 374.
36 100 U.S. 82 (1879).
37 Id. at 94.

while copyrighted works were by definition new because they originated with their authors.[38] New expression need not be creative, however, so the Court's distinction survives even without a creativity requirement.[39]

The second case, *Burrow-Giles Lithographic Co. v Sarony,*[40] held that a highly stylized photograph of Oscar Wilde was proper copyright subject matter. The Court said 'the existence of those facts of originality, of intellectual production, of thought, and conception on the part of the author' had to be shown to justify copyright protection.[41] None of these terms necessarily requires creativity rather than industry. The Court's initial definition of author – 'he to whom anything owes its origin; originator; maker' – does not require creativity, either. As we will see, the *Burrow Giles* Court gave a hint that it might require creativity in a different case, but the Court explicitly refrained from deciding hypothetical issues, and the *Feist* Court did not rely on that portion of the opinion.

Low as the originality hurdle is, *Feist* held that facts cannot clear it. They have no authors: '[t]he distinction is one between creation and discovery: the first person to find and report a particular fact has not created the fact; he or she has merely discovered its existence.' The Court explained with an unfortunate example:

> Census-takers, for example, do not 'create' the population figures that emerge from their efforts; in a sense, they copy these figures from the world around them. Census data therefore do not trigger copyright because these data are not 'original' in the constitutional sense. The same is true of all facts – scientific, historical, biographical, and news of the day. 'They may not be copyrighted and are part of the public domain available to every person.'[42]

Scholars were quick to notice that the Court's discussion of facts was muddled. It is wrong to say that census data are copied from nature.[43] Persons exist in nature, but the categories and counts of the census do not. They are the product of human choice and intervention. To copy nature would be to clone. This criticism may be generalized: A fact and its expression are different

---

38 Id. The court did not elaborate on how pre-existing things functioned as marks. Presumably it had in mind secondary meaning associated with such things as a person's name or a descriptive phrase.

39 The court was also wrong to presume that the selection of a mark cannot be creative, but that is a different issue.

40 111 U.S. 53 (1884).

41 Id. at 60.

42 499 U.S. at 347.

43 For example, Green, Michael Steven (2003), 'Copyrighting Facts', 78 *Ind. L.J.* 919; Gordon, Wendy (1992), 'Reality As Artifact: From *Feist* to Fair Use', 55 *Law & Contemp. Probs* 93.

things. $E=MC^2$ expresses a fact.[44] If the equation is not copyrightable, it is because application of the merger doctrine merges the expression into the fact to deny protection, not because the two were never separate.[45]

The Court used these propositions to resolve what it saw as a tension between the rule that facts are not subject to copyright and the rule that compilations of them may be.[46] That could have been done without reference to creativity: The defendant did not originate in any sense the alphabetical arrangement of a phone book. But the reference to creativity was not just superfluous. It misleads analysis in two directions. In some cases in which copyright protection is useful, creativity is undesirable, and perhaps impossible. In some cases where copyright is counterproductive, creativity is possible but irrelevant.

II.

Much has been written about *Feist* as applied to databases, telephone books, price lists, and the like, but the logic of the opinion is not limited to such works. By grounding its propositions in the Constitution, the Court extended its reasoning to anything copyright might cover.

In this Part, I argue that *Feist's* logic implies that video recordings of spontaneous news events should receive no copyright protection. My aim is not to deprive such works of copyright (though that would be a fair extension of my argument). It is instead to examine *Feist*'s logic from the perspective of a 'speech' case in the sense of the freedom of speech, rather than the type of expression at issue in *Feist*, which is instrumental to something other than deliberation and debate.

A.

Justice O'Connor's reference to 'copying nature' is at least intelligible, if still wrong, with respect to video recordings of spontaneous news events. Many famous tapes involve nothing that deserves to be called creative at all, even in a trivial, *Feist*-ian sense. I mentioned earlier three examples that, I claim, should fail the *Feist* test: the Zapruder film, Holliday's tape of the beating of Rodney King, and Robert Tur's aerial footage of the beating of Reginald Denny.

---

44 *American Dental Ass'n v Delta Dental Plans Ass'n*, 126 F.3d 977, 979 (7th Cir. 1997) (Easterbrook, J.).

45 Id.

46 Id.

Burrow-Giles is relevant to this claim. The defendants in that case argued that Congress did not have the power to extend copyright to photographs. The Court found the question 'not free from difficulty'.[47] It held that photographs qualified as 'writings' by analogizing them to maps, charts, and engravings, which had long been statutory subject matter (and, in the case of maps and charts, were included as subject matter by the first Congress).[48]

The Court did not make a similar categorical ruling on the question of authorship. It had 'no doubt that the constitution is broad enough to cover an act authorizing copyright of photographs, so far as they are representatives of original intellectual conceptions of the author'.[49] It then responded to the defendant's specific objection in a more qualified way:

> It is said that an engraving, a painting, a print, does embody the intellectual conception of its author, in which there is novelty, invention, originality, and therefore comes within the purpose of the constitution in securing its exclusive use or sale to its author, while a photograph is the mere mechanical reproduction of the physical features or outlines of some object, animate or inanimate, and involves no originality of thought or any novelty in the intellectual operation connected with its visible reproduction in shape of a picture. . . It is simply the manual operation, by the use of these instruments and preparations, of transferring to the plate the visible representation of some existing object, *the accuracy of this representation being its highest merit. This may be true in regard to the ordinary production of a photograph, and that in such case a copyright is no protection. On the question as thus stated we decide nothing.*[50]

The Court distinguished Sarony's highly stylized photograph of Wilde from ordinary photographs that aimed mostly for 'accuracy of representation'. It relied on district court findings that the picture was 'entirely' the result of Sarony's mental conception, which included posing Wilde, selecting his clothes, arranging the background, setting the lighting, and suggesting and evoking the expression he desired.[51] The *Burrow-Giles* Court did not require this level of involvement as some minimum of originality, but this is what Justice Miller had in mind in writing the language quoted in *Feist*.

The scope of exclusion left open in *Burrow-Giles* was narrowed by rhetoric in *Bleistein v Donaldson Lithographing Co.*,[52] in which Justice Holmes held that advertisements for a circus were within the subject matter of copyright. Holmes wrote that the ads were subject to copyright even if they 'had been

---

47 111 U.S. at 56.
48 Id. at 57.
49 Id. at 58.
50 Id. at 59 (emphasis added).
51 Id.
52 188 U.S. 239, 251 (1903).

drawn from the life'.[53] A contrary holding 'would mean that a portrait by Velasquez or Whistler was common property because others might try their hand on the same face'.[54]

Holmes's conclusion does not follow from his premise. As in *Burrow Giles,* it would depend on what had been added to nature in the first representation. To invoke artists famous for their style is to negate the inference he drew. But Holmes's point was broader:

> the copy is the personal reaction of an individual upon nature. Personality always contains something unique. It expresses its singularity even in handwriting, and a very modest grade of art has in it something irreducible, which is one man's alone. That something he may copyright unless there is a restriction in the words of the act.[55]

Holmes also cautioned that '[i]t would be a dangerous undertaking for persons trained only to the law to constitute themselves final judges of the worth of pictorial illustrations, outside of the narrowest and most obvious limits'.[56]

There is something appealing in Holmes's claim that expression is irreducibly individual. But it seems odd to say that handwriting is inherently expressive in a sense relevant to copyright. The compilation in *Feist* would be no more protectible if hand-written; it would only be less useful. And the point dissolves when we move from great artists conveying impressions by hand to bystanders pointing a camera and pressing a button. Handwriting may be individual, and so may videotaping, but the former point does not imply the latter.

Holmes's caution against judges deciding cases based on their own tastes, though no doubt well taken as a general matter, cannot be read to imply that judges must not think about the works at issue in copyright cases. The originality question raised in *Burrow-Giles* asks where the content of a work came from – the author or somewhere else – not whether it is any good.[57] Probably that is why the 'narrow and obvious limits' language took on a life of its own, as authorizing some level of scrutiny. It appears in *Feist* in support the Court's test for creativity: Whether 'the creative spark is utterly lacking or so trivial as to be virtually nonexistent'.[58]

---

53 Id. at 249.

54 Id. at 249.

55 Id. at 250.

56 Id.

57 In any event, having gone so far, Holmes retreated to more conventional analysis, in keeping with *Burrow-Giles*: 'in their ensemble and in all their details, in their design and particular combinations of figures, lines, and colors, are the original work of the plaintiffs' designer'. Id.

58 499 U.S. at 345.

Thus, *Bleistein* does not answer the question *Burrow-Giles* left open. A comparatively recent case took the hint of *Burrow-Giles*, however, to deny protection to photographs of public domain art works. The plaintiff in *The Bridgeman Art Library, Ltd. v Corel Corp.*,[59] photographed or commissioned photographs of famous works of art. It turned the pictures into transparencies it then digitized. It alleged the defendant had copied the transparencies into its own digital images.[60]

The district court found Bridgeman's transparencies were not original within the meaning of the Copyright Act. Relying on *Burrow-Giles's* open question and the Nimmer treatise, the court held that '"slavish copying", although doubtless requiring technical skill and effort, does not qualify.'[61] The opinion is a bit unsatisfying; the court also held that originality may inhere in 'lighting, angle, selection of film and camera . . . and almost any other variant involved' in taking a picture, but did not explain why these elements are negated by 'slavish' copying. Even the slavish copier has to choose the camera, film, lighting, and angle that present the most slavish effect.[62]

Judge Kaplan's main point is clear enough, though: Where the goal is to present as nearly as possible an unmediated reproduction, effort toward that end counts as skill, not originality, which requires some creative spark. At least two of my three examples of spontaneous video recording fail that test, if it is to be taken seriously at all. George Holliday's tape of the beating of Rodney

---

59 36 F. Supp. 2d 191 (S.D.N.Y. 1999).

60 *The Bridgeman Art Library, Ltd. v Corel Corp.*, 25 F. Supp. 2d 421, 423-24 (S.D.N.Y. 1998).

61 36 F. Supp. 2d at 197. To rebut the plaintiff's reliance on *Graves Case* (1869), L.R. 4 Q.B. 715, which dealt with the copyrightability of photographs of engravings, Judge Kaplan cited Laddie, Hugh, Peter Prescott and Mary Vitoria (1995), *The Modern Law of Copyright and Designs* §3.56 at 238. The Laddie treatise endorsed three types of photographic originality: originality in technique, such as 'angle of shot, light and shade, exposure' and the like; originality in the 'creation of the scene to be photographed' (which was present in *Burrow Giles*), and, lastly, that 'a person may create a worthwhile photograph by being in the right place at the right time. Here his merit consists of capturing and recording a scene unlikely to recur, e.g., a battle between an elephant and a tiger.' 36 F. Supp. 2d at 198. The third category substitutes the notion of a 'worthwhile' photograph for that of an 'original' photograph, a very sensible move but one inconsistent with *Feist*-ian notions of creativity.

62 Cf *SHL Imaging, Inc. v Artisan House, Inc.*, 117 F. Supp. 2d 301, 310 n.3 (S.D. N.Y. 2000) (commercial photographs of mirrored picture frames were original). Judge Kaplan himself later made precisely this point, holding that 'Decisions about film, camera, and lens, for example, often bear on whether an image is original. But the fact that a photographer made such choices does not alone make the image original. "Sweat of the brow" is not the touchstone of copyright. Protection derives from the features of the work itself, not the effort that goes into it.' *Mannion v Coors Brewing Co.*, 377 F.Supp. 2d 445, 450 (S.D.N.Y. 2005).

King is the clearest case. He did not even choose a location for his camera; he just happened to have a balcony with a view.[63] After that, his choices were limited to focusing the camera and following the action, to the extent his balcony permitted.

Zapruder arrived early to get a clear view of President Kennedy's motorcade, and chose to climb up on a concrete abutment,[64] but it would be pointless to treat that as creativity. Anyone wanting to see the motorcade would have had to find a clear field of view and would have done what he did. Zapruder's choices were determined by the physical layout of the area, not his aesthetic sense.[65]

My third example feels like a closer case because it involves professionals and because running a helicopter news service is costly. But though Robert Tur and his camera operator, Marika Gerrard, had the idea to launch such a service, neither that idea nor an aerial perspective as such is proper subject matter. Nor, I submit, is there *necessarily* a creative spark in expression produced by the desire to get the clearest close-up possible.

This point can be seen in *Los Angeles News Service v Tullo*,[66] which rejected a *Feist*-based originality challenge to videotape of spontaneous news events. L.A. News sued a video recording service for taping and distributing footage Tur and Gerrard shot of a train wreck and a plane crash. The defendant argued that the raw footage (as opposed to edited or transformed footage) was not original. The Ninth Circuit disagreed.

The *Tullo* Court said *Burrow Giles* had 'rejected a similar argument more than 100 years ago', though it also acknowledged that the Court did not claim to rule on all photographs.[67] But the Court thought *Bleistein* answered the question *Burrow Giles* left open, a position Learned Hand had taken in *Jewelers' Circular Publishing Co. v Keystone Publishing Co.*[68]

Jewelers' Circular Publishing Company posed a good test for *Bleistein.* The pictures at issue were still photographs of trademarks (the pictures were incorporated in a directory of jewelers). Hand thought 'no photograph, however simple, can be unaffected by the personal influence of the author, and no two will be absolutely alike'.[69] But Hand did not rest on the point because

---

63 Cannon, Lou (1999), *Official Negligence* 21.

64 http://mcadams.posc.mu.edu/russ/testimony/zapruder.htm.

65 In a case about software, the point would be obvious. For example, *Computer Associates, International, Inc. v Altai, Inc.*, 982 F.2d 693, 708 (2d Cir. 1992).

66 973 F.2d 791 (9th Cir. 1992).

67 Id. at 972.

68 274 F. 932 (S.D.N.Y. 1921), *aff'd* 281 F. 83 (2d Cir. 1922).

69 Id. at 934. On its face, the claim seems implausible: Let one person set a tripod and camera and let five photographers press a button and there will be no difference among the pictures owing to the button-pressing. One might argue that original-

he thought the Copyright Act of 1909 protected pictures 'without regard to the degree of "personality" which enters into them'. He felt '[t]he suggestion that the Constitution might not include all photographs seems to me overstrained'.[70]

As *The Bridgeman Art Library* shows, *Feist* explicitly repudiated this latter point of *Jewelers' Circular Publishing*. The *Feist* Court saw Hand's opinion as one source of the 'sweat of the brow' doctrine it rejected.[71] *Feist's* repudiation seemed to matter little to the Ninth Circuit in *Tullo*, however. The court quoted Hand in the text of its opinion, and quoted the Nimmer treatise elaborating on Hand, while disposing of *Feist* with a footnote saying its decision did not rest on 'sweat of the brow' reasoning.[72]

Tullo illustrates an important point: One can always find some decisions made in the course of producing a work and declare that originality inheres in them. That is what the *Tullo* court did. The opinion cites Tur and Gerrard's testimony that they decided what was newsworthy[73] and chose camera lenses, exposures, and angles, as well as the height and direction to film from.[74] Gerrard (the camera operator) testified she was 'an artist. I use a paintbrush. I use the camera to tell a story'.[75]

The hyperbole in this testimony shows the weakness in the claim. Had Gerrard used a paintbrush, there would have been no originality issue at all. She was not an author in the sense of Sarony composing the Wilde photograph. She had nothing to do with planes crashing, trains wrecking, or mobs beating truck drivers. She did not control the action, the setting, the available light, or anything else about such events. They did not start, stop, or proceed at her command.[76]

Nor should we take too seriously the claim that they decide what is newsworthy. If they film for money they film to satisfy demand regarding what counts as 'news', and that determination is influenced strongly, probably in many cases dictated, by social tastes and expectations they may satisfy but do not create. (I will return to this point later.)

---

ity inhered in the set-up, as Tur and Gerrard did in *L.A. News*, but even that undercuts Hand's claim, and has problems of its own, as discussed in the text.

70 Id.

71 499 U.S. at 352.

72 973 F.2d at 794.

73 Which might be relevant for a compilation but would not be relevant for any given work, which would itself have to display originality.

74 973 F.2d at 794.

75 Id.

76 Unlike, say, Ansel Adams, Gerrard could not wait until the light or other circumstances created the image she wished to express. She recorded actions determined by others without reference to her vision.

That leaves lens and exposure selection and camera position as possible sources of creativity. As to those variables, however, the *Tullo* Court cited no evidence that the tapes evidenced creativity rather than skill. The Court provided no reason to think that Gerrard's choices were different in any creative way from those any skilled camera operator would have made. Her choices may have produced clear pictures focused as closely as circumstances would allow. But 'clear and close' conveys no 'stamp of the author's originality', as *Harper & Row* requires.[77]

More importantly, and, I think, decisive for my claim, is that the *absence* of such choices would not undercut Gerrard's claim to copyright protection. Suppose Gerrard saw some tragedy while riding in a car, and that she jumped out and photographed it with whatever lens she had on her camera, without checking the exposure, and with no ability to pick a spot to film from. (Suppose, in other words, she was George Holliday.) Or suppose a news service covers a war zone by placing a camera in a location, turning it on, and then leaving it there while the bullets and bombs fly, monitoring the feed for as long as the camera lasts.

Under the prevailing interpretation of *Feist*, Gerard would have rights in her picture, and the news service would have rights in its remote feed. At some point, we will have an iconic picture taken with a phone camera that gives its owner no choices to speak of at all; courts will still grant the owner rights. Grant that, and the rhetoric of cases such as *Tullo* means nothing.

It follows that the choices the court pointed to as the source of originality were in fact window-dressing.[78] Neither the way they were made nor whether they were made mattered to the originality analysis. Such decisions are unrelated to the actual decision to grant rights, and, in all likelihood, unrelated to the benefits of the footage as well.

The truth of the matter is that the originality requirement does not apply to camera operators such as Gerrard. Thus a question: Why not?

III.

The examples of Zapruder, Holliday, and Tur are in one sense consistent with Justice O'Connor's notion of copying reality, but in another sense they contradict her as much as any other work. Zapruder taped the Kennedy assassination, but his tape was not the assassination itself. One may refer to

---

77 471 U.S. at 547.

78 Cf Burk, Dan (2007), 'Method and Madness in Copyright Law', 2007 *Utah L. Rev.* 587, 593–97 (noting that courts tie protection to the method of producing expression, and in particular to choices (real or contrived) in that method).

the assassination, which is the fact, without ever having seen Zapruder's representation.

Even so, these tapes feel different from fictional works or highly stylized representations such as Sarony's pictures of Wilde. What comprises this feeling of difference? In this Part I want to argue that there is less to the difference than one might think. The key is the possibility that variation in expression might make it more valuable.

A.

I want to begin my argument by suggesting a continuum of expression. The continuum depicts the degree to which social conventions shape our understanding of expression. At one end, the highly creative, we can place fictional works. These are comparatively unconstrained; indeed fiction can be understood as constituted by conventions that act to 'suspend the normal operation of the rules relating to illocutionary acts in the world'.[79] Anything goes in theory, even if in fact much fiction is conventional in every sense of the word.

Toward the middle of the continuum, we can place works that strive to depict un-intermediated reality. Zapruder, Holliday, and Tur are here.[80] These works present themselves as conforming to conventions that signal to a reader or viewer that a 'fact' is being asserted or represented. (More on this point shortly.) Somewhat farther down the line I will place predicted prices for things like cars and coins, and (it is important to keep this separate) lists of such prices.[81] These are subject to a subset of the conventions and standards we rely on in interpreting a statement as one of fact. At the end I will place names. These could be the names of persons, or part numbers,[82] or numbers designating dental[83] or medical procedures.[84] These are subject to conventions of naming, which have more to do with stipulation than representation.[85]

---

79 Searle, John R. (1979), *Expression and Meaning* 67.

80 And Bleistein and Sarony are in between them and fiction.

81 *CCC Info. Servs v Maclean Hunter Market Reports, Inc.*, 44 F.3d 61 (2d Cir. 1994) (cars); *CDN Inc. v Kenneth A. Kapes*, 197 F.3d 1256 (9th Cir. 1999) (coins).

82 *ATC Distribution Group, Inc. v Whatever It Takes Transmissions & Parts, Inc.*, 402 F.3d 700 (6th cir. 2005) (part numbers); *Southco, Inc. v Kanebridge Corp.*, 258 F.3d 148 (3rd Cir. 2001) (*en banc*); *Mitel, Inc. v Iqtel, Inc.*, 124 F.3d 1366, 1373–74 (10th Cir. 1997).

83 *American Dental Ass'n v Delta Dental Plans Ass'n*, 126 F.3d 977 (7th Cir. 1997) (Easterbrook, J.).

84 *Practice Management Information Corp. v American Medical Association,* 121 F. 3d 516 (9th Cir. 1997).

85 Obviously one could include on the continuum such 'functional' works as maps, charts, and architectural plans, but for present purposes it does not matter if these works rest with prices and price lists on the continuum.

1.

Let's begin with names. Names are not within the subject matter of copyright. That is not because they are not creative – Dweezil and Moon Unit Zappa refute such a charge – nor because they are unimportant. Conventional (and perfectly sound) reasoning would exclude names on the ground that words and short phrases are not copyright subject matter.[86]

The conventional analysis is conclusory, but it can be defended on substantive grounds. Justin Hughes offers one such defense: names 'function as social facts in which the fact and expression are always merged'.[87] This approach provides reasoning rather than an assertion about short phrases. According to Hughes, 'You cannot say "X is called Y" without expressing Y',[88] therefore you cannot copyright 'Y'.

I agree with Hughes but I would amend this argument slightly and cast it in terms of efficiency. Though you cannot say: 'X is called Y' without saying 'Y', you can describe Y without using 'Y' in the description. You can specify Y's height, weight, color of eyes, and so on, perhaps even Y's blood type and genetic information, until you have singled Y out.[89] This possibility shows that 'Y' simply designates a particular person, and thus is no more Y herself than a picture of a mountain is a mountain. But what would be the point requiring such a description? Why not just say: 'Y'?[90]

Hughes is right to refer to naming as a social convention in the sense John Searle uses that idea in his book *The Construction of Social Reality*.[91] Searle points out that most social interaction relies on or invokes things we treat as facts not because they exist regardless of human intervention (as mountains and rivers do) but because there is enough agreement among some relevant set of persons to confer on them a status that people experience as a fact. My $20 bill is a $20 bill because, and only so long as, there is a sufficient level of agreement among people with whom I deal to treat it as a $20 bill.[92]

---

86 37 C.F.R. 202.1(a).

87 Hughes, Justin (2007), '*Created Facts and the Flawed Ontology of Copyright* Law', 83 *Notre Dame L. Rev.* 43, 63.

88 Id.

89 Cf *CDN, Inc. v Kapes*, 197 F.3d 1256, 1261 (9th Cir. 1997) (noting that coin values could be expressed other than as estimated prices, but at cost: 'if CDN merely listed historical facts of actual transactions, the guides would be long, cumbersome, and of little use to anyone'.).

90 Compare Holmes on names. Holmes, Jr., Oliver Wendell (1899), 'The Theory of Legal Interpretation', 12 *Harv. L. Rev.* 417, 418 ('By the theory of our language, while other words may mean different things, a proper name means one person or one thing and no other').

91 Searle, John R. (1995), *The Construction of Social Reality*.

92 'Sufficient' is going to be judged in practical terms. Some people deny that

Money is not necessary to exchange just as names are not necessary to the designation of persons. Everything could be done by barter. As with using extensive descriptions instead of names, however, the costs (in terms of foregone efficiencies) would be extremely high and nothing would be gained in return.

Extensive description is not the only way to get around the problem that to say Y's name is to say 'Y'. Instead of extensive description, we could simply use multiple names, as we in fact use multiple currencies around the world. Y's parents could call Y 'Susan', and, to avoid infringement, I could call her 'Kate' (on the assumption that variations on Susan would be barred as derivative works).

The problem with this option points to the most persuasive reason to exclude names from copyright protection. To grant exclusive rights is to encourage variation in expression. Variation lessens the usefulness of the convention of naming (that is, the usefulness of a name is, in at least a rough, non-linear sense, inversely related to the number of names for the same object).[93] We don't want to encourage the multiplying of names to avoid infringement, so we avoid the problem by not extending protection in the first place.

2.

This point can be seen clearly in the part numbers cases.[94] The paradigm case involves one firm that assigns numbers to parts it makes and compiles those numbers in a catalog customers use to order parts. A second firm sells parts in competition with the first. The second firm reproduces the first firm's part numbers to make it easier for consumers to order the part they want.

Assigning numbers to parts reduces transaction costs. The copied numbers

---

paper money is money. They are wrong, and their dissent does not affect the status of the paper in my pocket. The point at which paper becomes money will depend on the facts, but the fraction of potential transactions it can be used for is the place to look to make that determination.

93 One person may have several names in the sense of a nickname among friends or coworkers, a pet name used by partners or children, and so on. So long as these are essentially complementary to the person's 'real' name (the fallback by which they are most widely recognized in society), they do little or no harm. They could cause harm if they disable the real name without superceding it. (A superceding nickname becomes the 'real name', as with 'Babe' Ruth.)

94 Other paradigm cases include maps and charts, included in pictorial, graphic or sculptural works under 17 U.S.C. §101, whose usefulness is obviously inversely related to their creativity in displaying natural features, though they may be more useful if loaded up with non-natural features, such as a scheme for designating different types of buildings.

facilitate competition by lowering consumer information costs.[95] To require extensive description (type and size of screw, and so on) or a new set of names would impede understanding, and thus competition, with no corresponding benefit. Refusing to extend copyright to either the part numbers or compilations of them (catalogues) implements the policy decision that uniformity is better than variation. Such a decision acknowledges that part numbers are a by-product of parts production rather than the object of production, and that parts competition will be more robust if parts may be freely named.[96]

Feist's focus on creativity provides a perverse incentive for firms to come up with creative names in order to secure rights that would impede competition. Plaintiffs in the part number cases tend to emphasize the choices they made in adopting names.[97] The opinion that discusses such a claim most extensively rejects it on the ground that creativity inhered in the choice of an uncopyrightable system, which then automatically generated numbers.[98] My analysis here suggests that point is collateral; copyright should not extend even if a firm exercised deliberate creativity in naming parts.

It is important to note that the undesirability of variation is a function of the conventions of naming, and the usefulness of names, not of market power or some sense that a particular set of names has become an industry standard, as Hughes at one point may be read to suggest.[99] Variation is no more desirable in names that are not industry standards than it is in names that are. It is the conventions of naming that matter, not the market share of a name or set of names. I return to this point in Part V.

Naming people and parts is an example of the use of social conventions and practices to force (or fate, if you prefer) convergence. When we understand that a term is meant to be a name, we understand that it designates particularly; the name is a focal point forcing convergence on a single person or object.

---

95 The parts cases therefore resemble the finding in *Lotus v Borland* that a user interface was not copyrightable subject matter. *Lotus Development Corp. v Borland Int'l, Inc.*, 49 F.3d 807 (1st Cir. 1995).

96 Hughes recognizes this point when he says names are the only *practical* way to refer to things such as dental procedures. Hughes, *supra* note 87 at 65.

97 For example, *Southco, Inc. v Kanebridge Corp.*, 390 F.3d 276, 281 (3d Cir. 2004) (*en banc*).

98 Id. at 283.

99 Id. at 66 (discussing *Southco* and suggesting that the court should have followed its logic further: 'if these part names had become industry standards: the names were social facts by common agreement just as that green rectangular paper is commonly agreed to be a $20 dollar bill – that had become basic to carrying out non-expressive activities.'). I read this passage as relating to Hughes's subsequent invocation of the essential facilities doctrine rather than as an interpretation of Searle or the conventions of naming.

When I refer to Barack Obama, you know to whom I am referring, and vice versa. If I use a more common name – John McCain, say – so long as you know I am using it as a name, you understand that the purpose of the expression is to designate, which entails convergence. If we use the same name to refer to different things – the two ships *Peerless* – we consider our exchange infelicitous precisely because we intended convergence but failed to achieve it.[100]

B.

The undesirability of variation provides a satisfactory explanation for the uncopyrightability of names, and it also provides such an explanation for the copyrightability of fiction. Variation in fiction is presumably desirable, or at least better than ceaseless repetition. Extending rights to authors whose works are original (even in the thinnest sense of not being copied) provides an incentive to other authors to come up with something new.

The situation is murkier toward the middle of my continuum. To understand the problems it helps to think about what makes an assertion one of fact rather than fiction or opinion. Defamation law is a good place to start. Defamation plaintiffs must plead and prove the defendant made a false statement of fact about them.[101]

What makes a statement factual, as opposed to opinion or something else? The answer is not obvious. Some statements that do not seem like factual assertions do make such assertions. To say 'Professor X drinks like a fish' is not to say Professor X drinks as a fish drinks, but it is to say Professor X: (1) drinks (2) alcohol; (3) excessively.[102] And some expressions that take the form of a factual statement are not. The assertions of characters in a fictional work, for example, are factual in form but they are not assertions of fact in either a legally relevant sense or in common usage.

Here is an example of what I mean. Eloise is the heroine of a children's book about a little girl who lives and runs amok in the Plaza Hotel in New York. In one scene in this book, Eloise encounters the hotel manager; his name

---

100 Lisa Ramsey raised with me the nice question of how my convergence analysis would apply to slogans, most of which are excluded from subject matter as short phrases. To the extent slogans designate, serving trademark-like functions, the naming analysis applies. To the extent they serve expressive functions unrelated to a source, the naming analysis does not apply. The practical question would then be whether anything would be gained by extending rights to such slogans, to allow someone to manage its meaning to the extent possible, and whether the gains would be worth the cost.

101 *Philadelphia Newspapers, Inc. v Hepps*, 475 U.S. 767 (1986).

102 The example is taken from Post, Robert C. (1990), 'The Constitutional Concept of Public Discourse', *103 Harv. L. Rev.* 601, 652 n.265.

is Mr Salomone. On the cover of the book, Eloise stands on a chair and writes 'Eloise' in pink lipstick on the mirror before her.[103] A parody of the book, *Eloise Returns*, had a 26-year-old Eloise still living in the Plaza. On the cover of this book, Eloise is shown as having covered the room with graffiti; on the mirror she has written: 'Mr Salomone was a child molester'.[104]

Though the authors of *Eloise Returns* did not know it, Alphonse Salomone was in fact the manager of the Plaza Hotel for many years. He sued the parodists for libel. The authors moved to dismiss the complaint on the ground that *Eloise Returns* was – literally – a joke, and a joke about a fictional work at that. The trial court denied the motion. Humor, it said, 'may well be a defense to a suit in libel, but the mere assertion that a statement was meant to be funny does not automatically absolve the utterer. Humor is intensely subjective.'[105] Noting that precedent warned judges against construing literature by reference to their own values (shades of Justice Holmes in *Bleistein*), the court concluded:

> whether a matter is harmless humor or cruel and vicious derision is peculiarly a judgmental question. . . Just as questions of what is truth, what is reasonable, or what is obscene are left to the collective judgment of a group of laymen serving on a jury, so the question of whether a particular statement is non-actionable humor or compensable libel should appropriately be left to the judgment of a jury.[106]

The court was wrong, I think, and it is instructive to specify why it was wrong. One problem is that neither of the interpretations the court mentioned – harmless humor or derision – requires that a jury find an assertion of fact about Salomone, which is what the defamation tort requires.

More fundamentally, however, the court was wrong because *Eloise Returns* makes an assertion about Mr. Salomone in the *Eloise* book, not Mr. Salomone the real person.[107] To borrow Searle's model, in which social facts take the form *X* counts as *Y* in *C*,[108] we want to say Salomone is the manager of the Plaza both in the *Eloise* book and in the Plaza Hotel in New York, and that the assertion of *Eloise Returns* was directed to the former context rather

---

[103] *Salomone v Macmillan Publishing Co., Inc.*, 411 N.Y.S. 2d 105 (1978).

[104] Id. at 107.

[105] Id. at 109.

[106] Id. The Court of Appeals later dismissed the complaint on the ground that Salomone could not allege harm to his reputation. *Salomone v Macmillan Publishing Co., Inc.*, 429 N.Y.S. 2d 441 (1980).

[107] Hughes puts essentially the same point, saying the status of facts within fiction can be conceived as the location of the fact: Marge is Homer's wife, but only in the Simpson's show, which is its own place. Hughes, *supra* note 87 at 86.

[108] X is some thing, such as a person, piece of paper, or line on a playing field, Y is an agreement on the status given to X, and C is the context to which that agreement pertains, and in which it is effective.

than the latter. In terms of the defamation tort, assertions in the former context are not 'of and concerning' the 'real' Mr. Salomone.[109]

Finally, the court was wrong because its modesty was counterproductive. Once we recognize that practices and conventions structure the way people interpret expression, a court cannot help but construe them. To demur in such a case is to say that a reasonable reader could have understood the parody as referring to the real world rather than the fictional world of *Eloise*. That is as much a determination as the opposite approach (granting judgment for defendant on 'of and concerning' grounds) would be. The question is the level at which judges intervene, not whether they do so.

This reading of why the *Salomone* court was wrong highlights the importance of conventions and practices in interpreting something as a statement of fact. Elaborating on Peirce in the defamation context, Robert Post points out that the minimum condition for treating a statement as one of fact is a general agreement on standards, procedures, or methods of inquiry about some subject such that a reader would expect reasonable persons engaged in that inquiry to reach the same conclusion. We treat temperature as a statement of fact because of social agreement on tools for measuring temperature; we treat statements characterizing the weather as pleasant as less fact-like (almost certainly as opinion) because there is no such consensus on how to measure 'pleasant'.[110]

This point becomes clearer if we consider the understandings implicit in watching the tapes of Zapruder, Holliday, or Tur. Rather than invoking conventions of fiction to suspend conventions leading us to interpret statements as fact, these films are the product of the camera operators' understanding of what counts as news to a particular audience, and they rely for their force on a variety of assumptions generated by introspection.

Take Holliday. Logically, there is no fact of the matter regarding what counts as 'news' when he looks out from his balcony. But he had the same sense of what counts as extraordinary, and thus worth filming, as you would if you had had his apartment. You know that, in his position, you would have filmed the same thing. Had Holliday watched King being beaten but filmed a bird on a nearby tree, or his neighbor's sprinkler,[111] you would think him weird.[112]

---

[109] The *Salomone* Court's excessive reticence contrasts with the Supreme Court's more assured stance in *Greenbelt Cooperative Publishing Association v Bresler*, 398 U.S. 6 (1970), in which the Court held that no one could construe a story accusing a real estate developer of 'blackmail' in negotiations with city officials as asserting that the developer was guilty of a criminal offense.

[110] Post, *supra* note 102 at 656.

[111] Unless he had some reason to film the sprinkler, as he might if the sprinkler violated water rationing rules and he had a grudge against his neighbor.

[112] For commercial players such as Tur, economics plays a role as well. We know

Socialization influences expression by narrowing the range of expressive acts that can achieve a speaker's (or taper's) intention. That is one of the things Stanley Fish means when he says there is no such thing as 'free' speech,[113] and it is a reason why we must discount somewhat the notion that originality inheres in Tur and Gerrard's choice of what to film.

Such understandings also influence audience perceptions of such films. If Holliday had visited a movie set, filmed a beating staged for a movie, and then posted it on YouTube without disclosing that fact, viewers would feel defrauded.[114] Viewers would feel misled if he photographed a small group of protestors in a way to make them seem large, or photographed a scuffle in a way that suggested a melee. All these misrepresentations can be achieved to a degree by trading on presumptions about spontaneous news filming and on conventions that lead people to extrapolate 'truth' from what they see.

The social influences that create an understanding of what counts as news are weaker than conventions of naming or the experimental method as applied to natural science. For purposes of copyright policy, though, they matter. To take one example, they are not so different from the concept of efficiency, which is relevant to infringement analysis in cases involving software. A finding that efficiency would lead any programmer presented with a particular problem to produce the plaintiff's solution would defeat an infringement claim through application of the merger doctrine.[115] To the extent *Feist* extends the originality requirement to all expression, it is hard to justify a different result for someone like Holliday or Zapruder.

C.

But here we have an apparent quandary. How can expression convey facts – that which *any* person is fated to agree on – while simultaneously conveying the stamp of individuality, or, more modestly, that not trivial spark of creativity, necessary for copyright protection?

---

he is in it for the money, and this knowledge enhances our introspection. If he is in it for the money, we presume the sensational footage is worth more than boring footage. We count on his self-interest to focus the camera on Denny, just as anyone else in his position would do.

[113] Fish, Stanley (1994), *There's No Such Thing As Free Speech, and It's A Good Thing, Too*.

[114] Neil Netanel raises a fascinating and disturbing example of an apparently staged incident. http://balkin.blogspot.com/2008/06/france-2-v-karsenty.html.

[115] *Computer Associates, International, Inc. v Altai, Inc.*, 982 F.2d 693, 708 (2d Cir. 1992) ('filtration' analysis for protectibility of software 'entails examining the structural components at each level of abstraction to determine whether their particular inclusion at that level was "idea" or was dictated by considerations of efficiency, so as to be necessarily incidental to that idea').

One answer is that even with regard to the taping of news events the conventions that lead us to think of an assertion as one of fact can do that job while simultaneously leaving enough room for individual creativity. In some cases that may be true. But in some, I assert, it will not be.

And even in cases where the social forces pushing toward convergence leave some room for individuality – say, with written descriptions rather than recordings – there is something odd about insisting on adornment as the price of protection. When the very concept of a fact is defined by reference to objective conventions and standards it seems strange to demand that authors deviate from those standards, if only by addition, to be free from copiers.[116]

We can escape the oddness by rejecting *Feist*'s erroneous conflation of facts and expressions about them, but even that seems unsatisfying. Granted that the difference between fact and expression often implies some room for variation,[117] but why demand purple prose when simplicity or transparency is best? Why bother with talk of lens selection when a clear picture is all anyone wants, and when we would reach the same result if no such selection had been made?

A couple of practical arguments point in favor of a *Feist*-like requirement, though weakly. An originality requirement might be justified as a rule of evidence. If the agreed standards and methods of inquiry are precise enough, then every author who employs them should be expected to produce substantially similar expression of the facts. Such similarity would say nothing about free-riding, however. A rule encouraging individual variation might help to distinguish copying from independent (though similar) creation, avoiding false findings of infringement.[118]

That argument does not go very far, however. If conventions forcing convergence on some fact were strong enough, it is hard to imagine anyone bringing suit. We do not see news services suing each other over weather forecasts, for example. And it is easy enough to weed out false positives by requiring strong proof of copying where the baseline probability of coincidental

---

116 Cf Judge Leval's comment in *CCC Information Services, Inc. v Maclean Hunter Market Reports, Inc.*, 41 F.3d 61, 66 (2d Cir. 1994), that requiring substantial creativity 'would be counterproductive. The policy embodied into law is to encourage authors to publish innovations for the common good – not to threaten them with loss of their livelihood if their works of authorship are found insufficiently imaginative.' Leval argues that a low degree of creativity is tolerable because protection extends only to original elements, and thus might not be very strong. Id. But since copying is an element in any event, it is not clear, other than as an evidentiary matter, why creativity (rather than simple origination) should be required at all.

117 But see $E=MC^2$.

118 See Lichtman, Douglas, 'Copyright as a rule of evidence', 52 *Duke L.J.* 683 (2003).

similarity is high; the problem is similar to that courts face when two authors each copy a public domain work.

Another justification is that the creativity branch of the originality requirement is trivial. As a practical matter, when we leave the world of parts catalogues, dental procedures, price lists, and similar works – those useful as an input or complement to some endeavor unrelated to expression – and move to the world in which deliberation and debate are the points of expression, the creativity requirement disappears. That is why Zapruder and Holliday have rights.

This justification seems very odd. It holds the rule of *Feist* is justified because, as to 'speech that matters',[119] it is ignored. Nevertheless, I suspect that is what is going on. The legal mind conceives of the Zapruder/Holliday/Tur kind of work as 'news' and thus as core free speech activity. This 'speech' frame entails an unarticulated conclusion that expression within it is copyrightable, and that conclusion entails the findings needed to sustain it.[120] It is bootstrapping.

Why the bootstrapping? Habit, maybe, or possibly an unarticulated error cost analysis leading to a form of risk aversion: It would be worse to deny protection to news coverage that might actually be creative in some abstract sense than to grant protection to Holliday, so courts err on the side of extending protection. That is a plausible, if not provable, account (though its logic is not limited to 'speech'). It does not say, however, what would be bad about denying protection.

Perhaps the bootstrapping reflects normative discomfort with my analysis of the un-creativity of Zapruder, Holliday, and Tur. Perhaps judges have an inkling that, though any socially aware person would do what they did, and thus produce images understood as representing 'facts', there are reasons to deny that there is a single fact of the matter about any news event. Perhaps there is a sense in which we recognize the conventions and practices that lead us to think of things as facts, and the motivations that imply a high degree of uniformity in filming such events (and thus the corresponding absence, for practical purposes, of creativity), do not preclude the value of variation, as is the case with names.

On this view, variation, even if only conceptual, is desirable because all aspects of reality count. Even if we are certain that everyone with Holliday's camera would focus on King and the police beating him, and even if we very much want that to happen, we accept that the (wholly theoretical) idiosyncratic

---

119 *Gertz v Robert Welch, Inc.*, 418 U.S. 323 (1974).

120 In Jane Ginsburg's terms, much newsgathering is expressed in 'low authorship' works, copyright in which 'essentially secures the labor and resources . . . invested in the work'. Ginsburg, *supra* note 19 at 340.

person who films only the several officers standing by adds to our understanding as well. Perhaps the theoretical usefulness of variation creates a background against which it makes sense to treat even the filming of the obvious 'story' as a creative choice. Perhaps courts extend copyright protection reflexively, as an expression of this sense and in recognition that, at least as a conceptual matter, though perhaps not a practical one, the presence of rights implies variation while the absence implies copying, and thus uniformity.

This reaction accords with the conclusion that variation in expression is valuable for fiction and decreases the value of names. It in essence preserves a diversity-enhancing legal framework for such news reports, notwithstanding the strong intuition that there will be no creativity to speak of in many cases. Nevertheless, the variety and creativity in this argument are theoretical, almost ethereal. The manifestations of creativity *Feist* demands do not exist in many news-taping cases, certainly not in the Zapruder of Holliday type of case. My explanation does not justify the state of affairs it tries to explain.

For these reasons, when one looks at the spontaneous news video cases, the claim that creativity is a constitutional mandate seems hollow. What kind of constitutional mandate is it that makes courts announce a doctrine, only to proclaim in the next breath that we should not worry about it too much because in reality it has almost no teeth at all (as all courts do)?[121] And what is the point of pretending to have a requirement that, when push comes to shove, is tolerable only because it is not taken seriously with respect to (what courts seem to think is) the most serious expression? Why do judges and lawyers, as opposed to academics, recoil from the notion of taking *Feist* seriously?

The answer to these questions is that *Feist* rejected the 'sweat of the brow' doctrine in name only. The doctrine lives on the tacit acceptance that spontaneous news reporting is creative, when much of the time that is not true. Courts and lawyers understand that L.A. News and similar firms must cover their costs, even if all they do is point and shoot, so they ignore the supposedly constitutional creativity requirement and extend rights to facilitate pure cost recovery.

That is not to say that one cannot come up with some story about creativity in every case – even Holliday decided when to stop filming, after all. It is instead to say that such stories cannot be taken seriously and in fact are not taken seriously. They are fig leaves for cost recovery.

---

121 Including *Feist*. 499 U.S. at 358.

IV.

That *Feist* did not in fact eliminate pure cost recovery as a basis for claiming rights is a good thing, I think. This Part explains why, and responds to two possible objections.

A.

The price list cases exemplify the main reason copyright should continue to embrace cost recovery, and do so more openly. These are cases in which some person or firm sinks costs into tracking human behavior in certain markets. *CDN, Inc. v Kapes*[122] is the most aggressive of these cases, so it offers a good example of the genre and my claim. CDN published a newsletter for coin dealers. It listed wholesale prices for virtually all collectible coins and was used extensively by dealers. Kapes ran a website that posted retail prices for coins. He generated these by copying CDN's wholesale prices and marking them up according to a formula he devised.

CDN sued Kapes for infringement. Kapes defended by arguing that the CDN's prices were facts and therefore not copyright subject matter. (Only the prices were at issue, not CDN's whole catalogue, which Kapes did not copy.) The district court found that CDN created the prices, so *Feist* did not bar CDN's claim.

The Ninth Circuit agreed.[123] It treated the prices as individual compilations of the data generated by a creative process:

> if CDN did nothing more than discover and report the prices paid by dealers in transactions throughout the country, the prices would not be copyrightable. But it did much more than this. The prices listed are not mere listings of actual prices paid;

---

122 197 F.3d 1256 (9th Cir. 1999).

123 The district court found:

> CDN's process to arrive at wholesale prices begins with examining the major coin publications to find relevant retail price information. CDN then reviews this data to retain only that information it considers to be the most accurate and important. Prices for each grade of coin are determined with attention to whether the coin is graded by a professional service (and which one). CDN also reviews the online networks for the bid and ask prices posted by dealers. It extrapolates from the reported prices to arrive at estimates for prices for unreported coin types and grades. CDN also considers the impact of public auctions and private sales, and analyzes the effect of the economy and foreign policies on the price of coins. As the district court found, CDN does not republish data from another source or apply a set formula or rule to generate prices. The prices CDN creates are compilations of data that represent its best estimate of the value of the coins.

Id. at 1260.

> rather, they are CDN's best estimate of the fair value of that coin . . . What CDN has done is use its own judgment and expertise in arriving at that value for the dealers. This process imbues the prices listed with sufficient creativity and originality to make them copyrightable.[124]

The court's focus on process is correct but its analysis is incomplete. If the notion of a fact is derived from agreement on standards or methods of inquiry that compel a conclusion, then the standards and methods of inquiry are the right place to look for creativity. But the court's language does not explain why these sources implied a range of prices, nor what that range was. If any reasonable person replicating CDN's inquiry would be, in Peirce's words, fated to reach the same price as CDN, then CDN's price expresses a fact even though it is the product of a process.[125]

In *CDN,* as in all price list cases, there is an inverse relation between the creativity (meaning subjectivity) of a process and the usefulness of the prices the process produces. That CDN had a good reputation and its prices were widely used implies that its customers found CDN's prices conformed to actual buying and selling. That in turn implied that its pricing methodology captured the relevant variables well, which suggests that others employing the same methodology to analyzing the same behavior would produce the same price.[126]

The Ninth Circuit's failure to ask whether replication would produce the same result undercut its statement that it was 'wholly irrelevant' to its decision that CDN's process 'takes much time and effort'.[127] *Feist* compelled some such statement, but the gap between the court's reasoning and its result cannot be sufficiently explained without reference to CDN's costs.[128] Dennis Karjala

---

124 Id. at 1261.

125 Dennis Karjala offers a similar process understanding of facts, and suggests that '[i]n principle, there is only one answer for the average value of a particular car' in any of the categories used by the plaintiff in *CCC Information Services, Inc. v Maclean Hunter Market Reports*, 44 F.3d 61 (2d Cir. 1994). Karjala, Dennis S. (2003), 'Distinguishing Patent and Copyright Subject Matter', 35 *Conn. L. Rev.* 439, 479. That may be definitionally true of the word 'average', but the relevant inquiry is into the sociology of knowledge, not the semantic meaning of mathematical terms. It is not necessarily true of all pricing inquiries. Dan Burk gets this point right in his 'Method and Madness in Copyright Law', *supra* note 78 at 593–94, though I see the implications of the point differently than he does.

126 The method might be a proper subject matter for trade secret, but it was not copied so there could be no copyright issue about it.

127 197 F.3d at 1260.

128 I do not read *CDN* as coming close to extending protection to ideas, which worries Professor Hughes. Hughes, *supra* note 87 at 72. When the court said 'CDN does not, nor could it, claim protection for its idea of creating a wholesale price guide,

is right to say the *CDN* Court's references to *Feist* on this topic were 'lip service' and that '*CDN* simply uses anti-misappropriation notions to force the defendant to do its own work in determining the value estimates rather than to protect the creative selection or arrangement of compiled data . . .'[129] Thank goodness.

Kapes and similar cases, such as *CCC Information Services, Inc. v Maclean Hunter Market Reports, Inc.*,[130] trivialize the creativity requirement in essentially the same way that 'speech' cases such as Zapruder and Holliday do.[131] *Kapes* and *CCC* identify a process and, discovering choice points within the process, pronounce that the choices entail creativity. We never know if the choices were creative in any meaningful sense, or ones that were so constrained that any reasonable researcher would have to make them. We have good reason to believe that, if the prices are useful enough to bother copying them, the choices were highly constrained.[132]

---

but it can use the copyright laws to protect its idea of what those prices are', its second reference to ideas was shorthand for expression, in the sense that Part IV of this chapter will receive protection for my ideas about property rules and liability rules.

129 Karjala, *supra* note 125 at 480.

130 44 F.3d 61 (2d Cir. 1994).

131 The directory cases are consistent with this claim, though not uniformly so. Consistent with *Feist*, *BellSouth Advertising & Publishing Corp. v Donnelley Information Publishing, Inc*, 999 F.2d 1436 (11th Cir. 1999) (*en banc*), held a regional business yellow-page directory was not copyrightable. On the other hand, in *Key Publications, Inc. v Chinatown Today Publishing Enterprises,* 945 F.2d 509 (2d Cir. 1991), the court held that a directory of businesses of interest to Chinese Americans was copyrightable, though the defendant's similar work did not infringe. The idea of such a directory would not be protectable, of course, and the court located the necessary originality in the categories into which the author sorted the (factual, and thus not copyrightable) data. The categories no doubt helped users find what they wanted to find, but I suspect the gathering of the data – the sweat that went into the project – generated most of the usefulness of the directory. The same is true of *BUC International, Corp. v International Yacht Counsel, Ltd.*, 489 F.3d 1129 (11th Cir. 1997), in which the court held that a directory of yachts for sale was copyrightable. The court noted that there had been no standard manner of presenting such data prior to the plaintiff's directory, but did not deny the degree of constraint inherent in describing a boat. If buyers tend to care about a few variables – price, size, and so on – then there would be significant limits on variation, which would not, however, imply that there was no need to cover the costs of compiling the data.

132 Unless they are enacted into law, I do not agree with Hughes's conclusion that price lists are social facts in the sense Searle used the term. Hughes, *supra* note 87 at 60. Searle's model requires a token of some sort, the *X* term, that is given a status and function, the *Y* term, in a context C, the status being a product of a sufficient social agreement that X counts as Y in C. CDN and CCC simply publish prices. Absent compulsion, I am free to disregard them in a way I am not free to deny that a $20 bill is money. Nor is pricing naming. For one thing, naming does not require research into behavior in order accurately to reflect it (though research might be done to assess a

For Professor Karjala and most academics this is a problem with *CDN*. I disagree. I think, rather, it is a creative way of getting past the faulty analysis in *Feist*. As between *Feist* and fairness (defined as allowing those who produce useful expression to cover their costs by excluding free riders), the latter is the better choice.[133]

In addition to whatever Lockean impulses are at work in this assessment, and there surely are some, as there are in the cases, I offer two practical arguments. I'll return to news reporting for my examples. The first is that the denial of copyright could result in less widespread dissemination of a work than would be secured by the extension of copyright.[134] The second is that it probably would result in the creation of fewer works.

Suppose *Feist* were taken seriously, and Holliday sought counsel before handing over his tape to a TV station. He would be advised to try to extract the full value of his tape from his first transaction. Once shown, the tape would be copied and Holliday would make no further sales. Such a situation might generate a reasonable fraction of the revenue to be had from copyright.[135] But the result would still probably entail relatively high transaction costs and a relatively lumpy price structure, with high prices for the first transaction and low if any prices thereafter, akin to the pricing structure seen in subscriptions to academic journals.[136]

Alternatively, a Holliday or a Tur could set up a website and charge on a pay-per-view basis. Particularly if one believes that much of the social value of such tapes comes from widespread viewing, that result is hardly a prescription

---

name's market appeal). Names are stipulated. For another, variation in pricing may in some cases be useful; a range may be more helpful than a point estimate if that estimate misleads. Names do not benefit from being cast as a range. (Hughes is right, however, that if prices are legislatively mandated, they become facts to the extent of the mandate.) Because social fact analysis is ultimately empirical analysis, it is possible that people agree to treat price list prices as social facts, and that no bargaining for used cars occurs. I doubt that, however. Price lists may influence bargaining, but that is different from having the status of a $20 bill.

133 My defense of the price list cases is not about prices but recovery of costs needed to produce expression as a primary product. Where expression is a by-product, as it was in *New York Mercantile Exchange, Inc.* v *Intercontinental Exchange, Inc.*, 497 F.3d 109 (2d Cir. 2007), *cert denied* 128 S.Ct. 1669 (2008), the part number cases are the appropriate analogy. The Second Circuit was right about that, though its discussion of authorship, compelled by *Feist*, was necessarily awkward.

134 The always-acute Jessica Litman explains this point quite well. Litman, Jessica (1991–92), 'After *Feist*', 17 *U. Dayton L. Rev.* 607, 611.

135 The first buyer might act as lead negotiator for a syndicate of major outlets, for example. But that involves transaction costs and delays.

136 Liebowitz, Stanley (1985), 'Copying and Indirect Appropriability: Photocopying of Journals', 93 *J. Poli. Econ.* 944.

for enhancing public discourse.[137] (Note that neither problem exists for the part number cases; the need to sell parts efficiently ensures publication in that case.)

Of course, another result might simply be that Zapruder and Holliday get nothing, or next to nothing, from the first buyer, and the public gets the work at essentially zero marginal cost.[138] That would be a happy story so long as the loss of revenue does not imply the loss of future works. For amateurs such as Zapruder and Holliday, it almost certainly would not. They did not sink costs for the particular purpose of producing the expression for which they are known. Copyright seems to give them a windfall that is hard to justify.

Which leads my to my second point. Tur and Gerrard, who make their living from expression they must sink costs to produce, get no windfall. They need protection, *Feist* or not. The difference between them and Holliday is similar to the difference between firms such as CDN and Southco: The former sink costs to produce expression as a product, while the latter produce expression either as a byproduct of some other process, such as making tools, or at least in a sense incidental to cost-recoupment concerns.[139] Without protection, the former would not produce their works, while the latter would.[140]

This point in turn leads to what I see as the most plausible argument for protecting Zapruder and Holliday – that it is imprudent to try to assess the cost recovery needs of every video taper. The argument is plausible – the cost of recording devices and of distribution has fallen to very low levels, implying more recording by more people with more heterogeneous cost structures than we are used to seeing with firms such as L.A. News. I have a lot of sympathy for the view that courts should not tinker with the rights structure as a means of back-door price and cost regulation.

---

137 And, in the real world, it wouldn't work. The site would be hacked, the content copied, and dissemination made.

138 That is in fact what happened with Holliday.

139 The same could be said of the page numbers in which Westlaw unsuccessfully sought copyright protection in *Matthew Bender & Co. v West Publishing Co.*, 158 F.3d 693 (2d Cir. 1998).

140 Justin Hughes captures this point nicely. He argues that '[m]ost human facts are "side effects" of human activity', Hughes, *supra* note 87 at 59. It is a fact that I go to the store, but my going to the store is unrelated to any concern for creating that fact; it is food I want, not rights in what I see on the way or in representations of the trip. Hughes contrasts such byproducts of activity with 'human facts that result from an act that was the *intentional creation of information qua information* through the *intentional creation of expression qua expression*'. Id. His resulting test for protection (described as an elaboration of the merger doctrine) is basically a test extending rights where cost recovery is needed to induce expression and denying rights where it is not needed.

B.

A couple of points are commonly raised against cost recovery. One is that it does not deal easily with all cases, and may produce bad results in some. That is true. It has a hard time with standardized price lists for medical procedures,[141] for example, where the expression is a product of a process intended to produce it, but where it is also a component of a larger bureaucratic process that may be the primary source of cost recovery, such as medicine or dentistry.

Cost recovery also has a hard time with legislative adoption of model codes. The leading case on the subject holds that users may copy the text of a law even if they may not copy the identical text of the model code from which the law itself was copied.[142] That is a defensible but not obvious answer, one that cannot turn on a metaphysical distinction between the same words as code and as model code. The question should boil down to whether the cost of legislation (which might be considerable) should be borne by the public at large or by the equivalent of user fees imposed only on those persons likely to deal with the law.[143] But those cases are simply hard cases under any view; their difficulty for cost recovery makes no particular point against it.

A second, more formal objection is that patent law, not copyright, is the place to look for cost recovery for highly constrained work. Dan Burk endorses this view.[144] He traces it to the delphic *Baker v Selden*,[145] which denied copyright protection to ledger pages needed to practice a system of double-entry accounting.[146] The point gets some modern force from *Bonito Boats v Thunder Craft Boats*,[147] which held a Florida statute forbidding copying of boat hull

---

141 *American Dental Ass'n v Delta Dental Plans Ass'n*, 126 F.3d 977, 979 (7th Cir. 1997) (Easterbrook, J.).

142 *Veeck v S. Bldg. Code Congress Int'l, Inc.*, 293 F.3d 791 (5th Cir. 2002) (*en banc*).

143 My instinct is to distinguish laws that apply to many people and relate to general conduct not just their business from laws that in effect pertain to a small group of people and are in substance inputs to their works. Laws against theft or libel would fall into the first category; building codes (needed and used mostly by contractors) would fall into the second. Recognizing rights in the first type of laws would conflict with strong intuitions about due process, and probably is not necessary to cover the relatively modest cost of general conduct rules. Recognizing rights in the second type of law seems less problematic from a due process perspective and easier to justify on economic grounds.

144 Burk, *supra* note 78, at 607.

145 101 U.S. 99 (1879).

146 For a thorough discussion, see Samuelson, Pamela (2007), 'Why Copyright Law Excludes Systems and Processes from the Scope of its Protection', 85 *Tex. L. Rev.* 1921.

147 489 U.S. 141 (1989).

designs was pre-empted by the Patent Act's policy of allowing free competition in things within patent subject matter but ineligible for patent protection. Justice O'Connor wrote, and described the result as pragmatic, to boot.[148]

Bonito Boats dealt with state law, not federal, but the basic idea that a scope of protection implies a corresponding area of freedom support's Burk's view. He would deny copyright protection to works that can be shown right or wrong relative to the world as it is.[149] In his terms, 'monovalent works' are for patent law, 'multivalent' works are for copyright.[150] Burk rightly identifies the price list cases as cost recovery cases, and asserts '[y]ou cannot use copyright as a general misappropriation statute without doing enormous violence to the structure of the copyright system, and ignoring all of the limiting parameters that the statute lays out'.[151]

'Violence' is hyperbole, and signals the presence of a formal argument rather than a practical one. Formalism may be a pragmatic approach in some cases, but I do not think this is one. Burk identifies no harm the price cases have done, and I do not think there is any. Conventional economic analysis suggests contrary rulings would have put price aggregators at risk, or reduced distribution of prices by forcing them to shift to restricted online access. And many things within copyright's subject matter are useful because they reflect reality, and can sensibly be called right or wrong; maps and charts exemplify the point.[152] Protection of such works is more consistent with copyright's history than is *Feist*.[153] Neither formal nor practical considerations support this argument in this context.

V.

I want to make one brief and final point. The debate over creativity, including the subset of arguments concerning convergence, is distinct from the debate over property rules and liability rules. There is nothing illogical about having a property rule even in a name. We do that to a degree with the right of publicity. We also do it to a degree with expression that is literally unique, such as the Zapruder, Holliday, and Tur tapes.

---

148 Id. at 156.

149 Burk, *supra* note 78, at 608.

150 Id. at 602.

151 Id. at 616.

152 17 U.S.C. §101 (definition of pictorial, graphic, or sculptural works).

153 On which see Ginsburg, *supra* note 19; Brauneis, Robert, 'The debate over copyright in news and its effect on originality doctrine', *supra* Chapter 2.

My convergence analysis suggests that the only case in which a property rule is plainly inferior to a liability rule is a case where it is also inferior to the exclusion of expression from the subject matter of copyright. That is to say, where variation is undesirable, and where the relevant costs are not costs of producing expression, it would be better to have mandatory, court-priced licensing than to have injunctions. But it would be better still not to grant rights in expression at all.

Parts numbers fall into this category but price lists do not. For one thing, not all price lists are the product of forces that can be identified well enough to sustain the expectation of convergence that justifies treating a statement as a fact. For another, prices are the point of price lists, so cost recovery is in play. Operating system software – even Windows – falls into this category as well. It meets neither of my two elements for exclusion: variation over time is desirable (that is innovation), and there are lots of costs of expression to cover.

Widespread adoption of a price or operating system does not change these facts. The fact of a monopoly or near-monopoly position is a different type of fact than the social facts that fit Searle's model of *X* counts as *Y* in *C*. If I feel my coin or car is worth more than some price list specifies, widespread adoption of the prices by insurers or even by the government does not trump my price. Insurers might have to pay at least that amount if the law orders them to,[154] but that command does not make the price *the* price for anyone other than the insurer, and it is not even the price for the insurer absent the additional (and I agree significant) step of proclaiming it so by legislation.

Whether to treat widely adopted expression with a property rule or liability rule depends on whether costs of expression have to be covered, the difficulty of estimating damages, the relationship between pricing and evolution of the standard, if any (a *de facto* standard such as Windows evolves continuously and at great expense), and similar variables. It would be a mistake either to exclude such expression from copyright or assign judges the task of setting its price or determining its configuration. Different works might require different treatment, but the basic principles remain constant. Neither widespread adoption of expression nor convergence sufficient to say expression refers to a social fact implies judicial pricing; either would be relevant to the inquiry.

CONCLUSION

I hope to have shown that the sweat of the brow doctrine lives on and that this is a good thing. It would be better if *Feist* were gutted so the analysis could be

154 See Hughes, *supra* note 87 at 68.

more candid. I also hope I have specified more precisely the relationship between copyright and the usefulness of convergence and variation in expression.

Conventional analysis holds that the proper domain of copyright extends only to (as Dan Burk puts it) 'multivalent' works, meaning works for which variation is affirmatively desirable.[155] I believe that from the practical point of view, variation plays a role, but a negative one. Copyright should not extend to types of works for which variation reduces the usefulness of expression and for which rights are not needed to facilitate cost recovery. Where a high degree of similarity – even uniformity – is expected, copyright should only be extended to cover the costs of expression (though not of unrelated activities). Where variation is desirable, copyright should extend in all cases.

---

155 Burk, *supra* note 78 at 605–06.

PART III

Alternatives to copyright: trade secret, tort, and *sui generis* protection of facts

8. The challenge of protecting trade secret information in a digital world

Elizabeth A. Rowe

I. INTRODUCTION

Trade secret law provides protection for facts, ideas, inventions and information. Part of the appeal of choosing trade secret protection over other kinds of intellectual property protection, is the relative ease with which a business can claim such protection and the broad scope of information that is protectable.[1] A business can, for example, protect trade secrets without complying with a government registration system,[2] and without observing any specified formalities. It is also not difficult to identify which materials might be eligible for trade secret protection. A trade secret can be any information of value used in one's business that has been kept secret and provides an economic advantage over competitors.[3] Thus, the kinds of information that can be protected include everything from customer lists to marketing strategies and chemical formulas.[4] Accordingly, the kind of proprietary information and innovative concepts that tend to fall outside the copyright paradigm are within the ambit of trade secret law.

---

1 See Taylor, Brooks W. (2005), 'You Can't Say That!: Enjoining Publication of Trade Secrets Despite the First Amendment', 9 *Computer L. Rev. & Tech. J.* 393, 394–95 (discussing reasons why corporations rely on trade secret protection).

2 Copyright protection may attach without registration, but registration is necessary before a plaintiff files suit for infringement. Thus, prior to registration, a copyright owner is in a similar situation to the owner of a trade secret who does not know whether the targeted material will indeed be protectable. Registration of a copyright provides a presumption of validity. See *Bibbero Systems, Inc. v Colwell Systems, Inc.*, 893 F.2d 1104, 1106 (9th Cir. 1990).

3 See Unif. Trade Secrets Act § 1 (amended 1985), 14 U.L.A. 538 (2005); Restatement (First) of Torts § 757 cmt. b (1939).

4 See, for example, *PepsiCo v Redmond*, 54 F.3d 1262, 1265–70 (7th Cir. 1995); *ConAgra, Inc. v Tyson Foods, Inc.*, 30 S.W.3d 725, 728–30 (Ark. 2000); *McFarland v Brier*, No. C.A. 96-1007, 1998 WL 269223, at *3 (R.I. Super. Ct. 13 May 1998).

Trade secrets are important to the economy because they protect and encourage innovation.[5] They are important to businesses of all sizes, from the smallest entities to the largest multi-national corporations.[6] Trade secrets encompass approximately 80 per cent of the assets of some companies,[7] and prior to obtaining patent protection, virtually all inventions are covered by trade secret protection.[8] The survival of a company may depend on its ability to protect its trade secrets.

The biggest challenge for trade secret protection is maintaining secrecy. The digital world complicates this problem and indeed vastly increases the likelihood of destroying the trade secret status of misappropriated information. Securing secret information is critical because once a trade secret has been disclosed, even if inadvertently, it ceases to be a trade secret.[9]

There is an inherent tension between the need to keep information secret and modern technological methods that allow the information to be easily accessed, reproduced, and disseminated. This chapter exposes why the lure of greater efficiency that comes from the technological tools in the digital world can expose trade secrets to even greater risks than previously existed.

II. THE DIGITAL WORLD

Computers have become ubiquitous tools in the workplace, with approximately 80 million people using computers at work.[10] Beyond the workplace, computers are also widely used in homes.[11] Computer technology, including

---

5 See *Kewanee Oil Co. v Bicron Corp.*, 416 U.S. 470, 493 (1974); see also Lao, Marina (1999), 'Federalizing Trade Secrets Law in an Information Economy', 59 *Ohio St. L. J.* 1633, 1633–34 (noting that corporations are increasingly relying on trade secret protection).

6 See generally id.; Merges, Robert P., Peter S. Menell, and Mark A. Lemley, (2006), *Intellectual Property in the New Technological Age* 35 (4th edn.) (discussing the importance of trade secrets to small companies).

7 See Hutchins, John P. (2006), 'The Corporation's Valuable Assets: IP Rights Under Sox', in *26th Annual Institute on Computer & Internet Law* 291 (PLI Intellectual Property, Course Handbook Series No. 859).

8 See *Bonito Boats v Thunder Craft Boats*, 489 U.S. 141, 155 (1989).

9 For a general discussion about choosing trade secret protection over patent protection see generally Beckerman-Rodeau, Andrew (2002), 'The Choice Between Patent Protection and Trade Secret Protection: a Legal and Business Decision', 84 *J. Pat.& Trademark Off. Soc'y* 371; Pooley, § 3.01[1] [a].

10 *Computer and Internet Use at Work in 2003*, United States Department of Labor, http://www.bls.gov/news.release/ciuaw.nr0.htm last visited on 21 August 2006.

11 See Park, Daniel W. (2004), 'Trade Secrets, The First Amendment, and Patent Law: A Collision on the Information Superhighway', 10 *Stan. J. L. Bus. & Fin.* 46, 47.

the Internet, has changed the way in which business is done, and in many ways contributes to greater efficiency and productivity.[12] The new technology has also affected how trade secrets are stored, accessed, and disseminated. Ironically, however, because trade secret information is now easier to store, easier to access, and easier to disseminate, it is easier than ever to misappropriate trade secrets. Accordingly, the challenge of protecting trade secret information in today's world is a daunting task.

A. Easier Storage and Accessibility

The very ease with which large amounts of information can now be stored rapidly, transported quickly and later accessed in the original format provides greater incentive and opportunity for it to be removed. For someone intending to steal trade secret information which has been stored electronically there is no need to photocopy hundreds of pages of documents, and load them into boxes or folders to leave the building. It is now a simple matter to either download the information, within seconds, onto a thumb size storage device which fits easily into a pocket, or attach the information to an e-mail sent to an outside account where it can later be easily retrieved. The risk of misappropriation involving new storage devices is already evident in many trade secret misappropriation cases. For example, in one case an employee downloaded the equivalent of 1.5 million pages of his employer's trade secret information by attaching a thumb drive to his desktop computer.[13] In another case, a departing employee transferred, among other things, a sensitive 500-page document to his home computer while working for the plaintiff, but after he had already accepted employment from the plaintiff's principal competitor.[14] He did it by downloading the files from his employer's computer system to a zip drive and then later transferred the information from the zip drive to his home computer.[15]

The use of servers to consolidate, store and publish information can also pose risks to trade secrets. Information which previously might have been locked away and scattered across many offices can now be accessed immediately by

---

12 See generally Matwyshyn, Andrea M. (2004), 'Symposium: Personal Jurisdiction In The Internet Age: Of Nodes And Power Laws: A Network Theory Approach To Internet Jurisdiction Through Data Privacy', 98 *Nw. U. L. Rev.* 493, 499 (discussing trends in the Internet economy).

13 *Anadarko Petroleum Corp. v Davis*, No. H-06-2849, 2006 U.S. Dist. LEXIS 93594, at * 18–19 (S.D. Tex. Dec. 28, 2006).

14 *Diamond Power Int'l, Inc. v Davidson*, 540 F. Supp. 2d 1322, at 1329 (N.D. Ga. 2007).

15 Id. at 1330.

every employee in the organization.[16] This permits employees to download the trade secret information onto personal laptops or miniaturized storage devices.[17]

Finally, laptop computers epitomize information portability. They enable employees to take valuable data to any location. When an employee connects her corporate laptop to wireless networks such as public Wi-Fi connections or 'hot spots', information stored on the laptop is susceptible to hackers.[18] In addition, the theft of a laptop can expose a company's most sensitive information, posing challenges to data security and trade secret protection. The personal data of about 26 million veterans and military troops was recently exposed when a burglar stole a laptop from the home of an employee of the Department of Veterans Affairs.[19] If this kind of theft led to a large scale exposure of trade secrets, it could be devastating to a company, as the trade secret protection in all of the now public data would be lost.

B. Easier Dissemination

Trade secret law only protects secret information.[20] With the click of a mouse or the push of a button e-mail, the Internet, and even cell phones can expose trade secrets to potentially millions of people within seconds. Once the trade secret becomes public, the trade secret owner may not be able to prevent third parties, including competitors, from using it. Worst still, however, the trade secret owner faces the complete loss of trade secret status. Accordingly, these technologies pose grave risks.

---

16 See, for example, *Four Seasons Hotels and Resorts v Consorcio Barr*, 267 F.Supp. 2d 1268, 1283 (S. D. Fl. 2003) ('The Lotus Notes server was connected to all of the servers for all Four Seasons' worldwide to allow e-mail communication. Aside from that, it also provided access to Four Seasons' corporate databases which provided other information.').

17 See, for example, *Liebert Corp. v Mazur*, 357 Ill. App. 3d 265, 267 (Ill. App. Ct., 2005) (an employee downloaded sensitive pricing information from the company server onto his laptop computer).

18 See Paola Singer, 'A Secure Laptop on the Go', *The Wall St. J.*, 13 May 2008, at D1.

19 Yip, Pamela 'Firms Ready to Put Leash on Laptops: Companies Expect Employees to "Guard Them Like a Wallet" to Prevent Theft and Protect Sensitive Data', *The Dallas Morning News*, 16 July 2006, at 1D.

20 See *Ruckelshaus v Monsanto Co.*, 467 U.S. 986, 1002 (1984) ('Information that is public knowledge or that is generally known in an industry cannot be a trade secret'); *Kewanee Oil Co. v Bicron Corp.*, 416 U.S. 470, 475 (1974) ('The subject of a trade secret must be secret, and must not be of public knowledge or of a general knowledge in the trade or business').

1. E-mail

E-mail can accomplish most transfers of files and other data with little effort. Even without sending attachments, confidential information can also be exchanged in the text of the message. Many trade secret cases involve employees transmitting files containing trade secret information through e-mails. In a case prosecuted under the *Economic Espionage Act*,[21] a product development manager gained access to secret product information belonging to a customer of his former employer.[22] When he later accepted new employment from a competitor of that customer, he downloaded the secret information and e-mailed them to his new employer.[23] In another case, an engineer who had knowledge of secret software source codes was terminated from work.[24] In resentment, he sent e-mail messages to several competitors of his former employer, offering the secret software source codes for sale.[25] All messages were sent from an alias e-mail account at a public library so that it would be difficult to uncover the true identity of the sender.[26] To his surprise, the competitor brought those messages to the attention of his former employer.[27] His identity was eventually revealed when the FBI's Computer Hacking and Intellectual Property Squad detected accesses to the alias e-mail account through his home Internet connection.[28]

Trade secret information can also be transmitted by employees from their corporate e-mail account to their private e-mail accounts and then to competitors.[29] In a case that made headlines recently, seven former Citibank employees were accused of e-mailing secret client data from work to their personal e-mail addresses before leaving to join a competitor.[30] As a result of these

---

21 18 U.S.C. 1832 (2006).

22 United States Dep't of Justice, Intellectual Property Cases: Silicon Valley Engineer Indicted for Stealing Trade Secrets and Computer Fraud, http://www.usdoj.gov/criminal/cybercrime/zhangIndict.htm (last visited 4 July 2008).

23 Id.

24 United States Dep't of Justice, Intellectual Property Cases: Former Engineer of White Plains Software Company Receives Two Years in Prison for Theft of Trade Secret, http://www.usdoj.gov/criminal/cybercrime/kissaneSent.htm (last visited July 4, 2008).

25 Id.

26 Id.

27 Id.

28 Id.

29 See, for example, *Posdata Co. v Kim*, No. C-07-02504 RMW, 2007 U.S. Dist. LEXIS 48359, at * 7–8 (N.D. Cal. 27 June 2007).

30 Nur Dianah Suhaimi, 'Stealing Office Data? Computer Forensics Can Track You Down', *The Straits Times* (Singapore), 27 January 2008, *available at* 2008 WLNR 1549360.

bankers' use of Citibank's trade secret information to lure away clients, Citibank is alleged to have lost about $50 million of business.[31]

2. The Internet

Because the value of a trade secret lies in its secrecy, most misappropriators who have acquired another's trade secrets and plan to use them for their own competitive advantage, have no incentive to publicize the secret.[32] Thus, historically, trade secret misappropriation cases do not implicate disclosure of the secret, other than in a very limited fashion, such as to a new employer. The culture of the Internet, however, has led to a higher likelihood that those in possession of other's trade secrets will make them public, rather than continuing to keep them secret for personal gain. The great ease with which virtually anyone can post information on the Internet coupled with its 'disinhibiting effect'[33] and a general decline in employee loyalty in the workplace,[34] have allowed disgruntled employees to achieve the ultimate revenge against their former employers by destroying trade secrets.

When a trade secret is posted on the Internet it will most likely be deemed to have lost its trade secret status.[35] Even when a party posting trade secret information may not have intended to cause harm to the trade secret owner, the nature of the Internet is such that the secret nonetheless could be destroyed.[36]

Unlike other mass media, the Internet has no editors who scrutinize submissions and decide what materials will be published. Any person sitting at a

---

31 Id.

32 See, for example, *DVD Copy Control Ass'n v Bunner*, 10 Cal. Rptr. 3d 185, 195 (Ct. App. 2004) (noting that a defendant in a trade secret case typically 'has as much interest as the plaintiff has in keeping the secret away from good faith competitors and out of the public domain').

33 Lidsky, Lyrissa Barnett and Thomas Cotter (2007), 'Authorship, Audiences, and Anonymous Speech', 82 *Notre Dame L. Rev.* 1537, 1575 (discussing the phenomenon whereby users of the Internet are less inhibited when expressing themselves).

34 See generally Stone, Katherine (2001), 'The New Psychological Contract: Implications of the Changing Workplace for Labor and Employment Law', 48 *UCLA L. Rev.* 519, 540, 542; Aaron, Benjamin and Matthew Finkin (1999), 'The Law of Employee Loyalty in the United States', 20 *Comp. Lab. L. & Pol'y J.* 321, 339.

35 See *Religious Tech. Ctr. v Netcom On-Line Commc'n Servs., Inc.*, No. C-95-20091 RMW, 1997 U.S. Dist. LEXIS 23572, at *40–41 (N.D. Cal. 3 January 1997); *Religious Tech. Ctr. v Lerma*, 908 F. Supp. 1362, 1368 (E.D. Va. 1995); *DVD Copy Control Ass'n v Bunner*, 10 Cal. Rptr. 3d 185, 192–93 (Ct. App. 2004). But see DVD Copy Control Ass'n, 10 Cal. Rptr. 3d at 190 (finding that the mere posting of information on the Internet does not destroy a trade secret).

36 See, for example, *Jerome Stevens Pharms., Inc. v Food & Drug Admin.*, 402 F.3d 1249, 1250, 1254 (D.C. Cir 2005) (reversing district court dismissal, holding that FDA could be liable for misappropriation of trade secrets where it posted plaintiff's trade secrets on its website for five months, and remanding).

computer can post information onto the Internet, resulting in immediate and irreparable harm. 'Once a trade secret is posted on the Internet, it is effectively part of the public domain, impossible to retrieve',[37] and a trade secret owner generally has no satisfactory recourse.[38] In some cases trade secret owners may also have to overcome First Amendment defenses as courts could reason that injunctions to prevent a defendant from publishing trade secrets would be an unconstitutional prior restraint on speech.[39]

III. MANAGING THE RISKS

Effective protection of trade secret information in this digital era requires both legal and technical approaches.[40] The goal is not necessarily perfect security, since employees often must be granted access to the information for optimal functioning of the business' operations. The trade secret owner needs an infrastructure in place to protect its secrets; one that includes specific processes and technological measures. Conducting a risk analysis of potential threats to the company's trade secrets should be comprehensive, paying attention to people, processes, and technology. Reliance on technological measures alone will not be sufficient.

At a minimum, companies should give careful deliberation to policies regarding remote access to company computer networks and systems, telecommuting, e-mail and Internet usage, and access rights to sensitive information.[41] Some companies may even choose to ban camera-phones or other recording devices, where such devices could easily expose certain secrets.[42] Closer regulation and monitoring of lap tops might also be advisable. Boeing

---

[37] *Religious Tech. Ctr. v Lerma*, 908 F. Supp. 1362, 1368 (E.D. Va. 1995).

[38] For a more detailed discussion of the legal significance of the effect of trade secrets appearing on the Internet, see Rowe, Elizabeth A. (2007), 'Saving Trade Secret Disclosures on the Internet through Sequential Preservation', 42 *Wake Forest L. Rev.* 1; Rowe, Elizabeth A. (2007), 'Introducing a Takedown for Trade Secrets on the Internet', 2007 *Wisconsin L. Rev.* 1041.

[39] See, for example, *Ford Motor Co. v Lane*, 67 F. Supp. 2d 745, 750, 753 (E.D. Mich. 1999).

[40] See generally McShane, Antony J. and Sarah E. Smith, 'Implement an Effective Trade Secret Protection Plan – Before It's Too Late', *Intell. Prop. Today*, July 2003, at 16 (outlining strategies for developing a trade secret protection program).

[41] See McShane, Antony J. and Sarah E. Smith, 'Implement an Effective Trade Secret Protection Plan – Before It's Too Late', *Intell. Prop. Today*, July 2003, at 16.

[42] See, for example, Gillmor, Dan 'Picture This, Institutions Are Losing the Ability to Control the Creation and Distribution of Images – and Camera-phones are Just the Beginning', *CIO Insight.com*, 6 April 2006, available at 2006 WLNR 14748715 (discussing Samsung Electronics ban on camera-phones inside its facilities).

Co., for instance, 'requires employees to access most sensitive information through company servers instead of downloading the data to a laptop . . . [and] employees working with payroll data must use a cable lock to physically secure their laptops to a desk at all times . . .'[43] ING America requires the installation of encryption software on all laptops before they can leave the premises.[44] For both of these companies, their policies are in reaction to having suffered recent laptop thefts.[45] Fortunately, no trade secrets were reportedly exposed with those incidents; there are no second chances at protection once the secrets have been exposed.

The potential problems regarding Internet disclosures should be another area of serious concern for trade secret owners. Thus, the goal ought to be keeping their trade secrets from leaking onto the Internet in the first instance. When, however, a trade secret is revealed on the Internet despite the owner's best efforts, any chance of saving the trade secret from destruction lies in the trade secret owner's acting with utmost urgency to prevent further dissemination of the secret. This includes notifying the website operator and the person posting the information (if known) and requesting that the trade secrets be removed.

Absent voluntary compliance, the only currently available judicial instrument to effectuate removal of a trade secret posted on the Internet is in the form of injunctive relief from a court. The speed with which information can be circulated over the Internet, coupled with the time and expense involved in seeking injunctive relief, suggests that a more expedient and efficient mechanism is necessary to fill the gap until a court can intervene.[46] Accordingly, one cannot overstate the importance of being proactive in trying to ensure that trade secrets are secure and that trade secret owners remain vigilant.

IV. CONCLUSION

Trade secret misappropriation is pervasive, and no company is immune. The very technological tools in use today that increase the efficiency with which

---

43 Id.

44 Id.

45 The Boeing thefts, which occurred in November 2005 and April 2006, exposed thousands of current and former employees' social security numbers and addresses. The ING laptop stolen in June 2006 contained retirement plan information on 13,000 employees. Id.

46 For a detailed analysis and discussion of this shortcoming and a proposal for legislative action to create a takedown mechanism for trade secrets, see Rowe, 'Introducing a Takedown', *supra* note 38 at 1046–48.

companies do business create challenges for trade secret protection. They make trade secrets easier to store, easier to access, easier to disseminate, and more portable, thus increasing the risks that trade secrets will be destroyed. According to an FBI report, the mobility of trade secrets makes them 'one of the country's most vulnerable economic assets'.[47]

As this chapter has illustrated, trade secrets that are stored on a computer must be given special protection, and attention must be paid to their accessibility and portability.[48] The precise nature of the security measures required will not only vary from one company to another, but within each company as well. Security measures that may be reasonable at one point in time based on the circumstances may no longer be reasonable when those circumstances change,[49] and risk assessment should be a continuous process. Ultimately, optimal protection of trade secrets will require greater awareness and vigilance by trade secret owners before the misappropriation occurs in order to better anticipate and ultimately stem the inappropriate dissemination or disclosure of the secrets.

---

47 Fed. Bureau of Investigation, Strategic Plan 2004–2009 40 (2004), *available at* http://www.fbi.gov/publications/strategicplan/strategicplanfull.pdf (last visited 1 June 2008).

48 See Lans, Maxine S. 'Can You Keep the Lid on your Trade Secrets?', *Marketing News*, 29 August 1994, at 9 (discussing practical suggestions to protect trade secrets, including computer related trade secrets).

49 See *Picker Int'l Corp. v Imaging Equip. Servs., Inc.*, 931 F. Supp. 18, 23 (D. Mass. 1995).

9. The third party problem: assessing the protection of information through tort law

Sharon K. Sandeen*

INTRODUCTION

A lot of attention has been paid to the question whether intellectual property (patents, copyrights, trademarks, and trade secrets) and other forms of information are property and should be treated as such.[1] To many owners and creators of information, the characterization of information as property provides the moral and legal imperative for its protection.[2] However, property law has its limits.[3] Although characterizing information as property may

* Professor of Law, Hamline University School of Law, St. Paul, Minnesota, U.S.A. © 2008 Sharon K. Sandeen. The author wishes to thank Professor Robert Brauneis of The George Washington University Law School for inviting her to contribute to this book. She is also thankful for the research assistance of Karly Kauf, Rachel Knudson, and Emily Sipiorski. Finally, the author is forever indebted to Beverly Rubens Gordon for first teaching her about torts. Hopefully, she did her masterful instruction justice.

1 See for example, Lemley, Mark A. (2005), 'Property, Intellectual Property, and Free Riding', 83 *Texas L. Rev.* 1031; Mossoff, Adam (2003), 'What is Property? Putting the Pieces Back Together', 45 *Ariz. L. Rev.* 371; Lessig, Lawrence (2002), 'The Architecture of Innovation', 51 *Duke L.J.* 1783; Kieff, F. Scott (2001), 'Property Rights and Property Rules for Commercializing Inventions', 85 *Minn. L. Rev.* 697; Radin, Margaret Jane (1996), 'Property Evolving in Cyberspace', 15 *J.L. & Com.* 509; and Brennan, Timothy J. (1993), 'Copyright, Property, and the Right to Deny', 68 *Chi. Kent L. Rev.* 675.

2 See for example, Lessig, Lawrence (2004), *Free Culture: How Big Media Uses Technology and the Law to Lock Down Culture and Control Creativity*, (The Penguin Press, NY), Chapter 10, p. 117, quoting Jack Valenti ('Creative property owners must be accorded the same rights and protection resident in all other property owners in the nation.') and Herman, Bill D. (2008), 'Breaking and Entering My Own Computer: The Contest of Copyright Metaphors', 13 *Comm. L. & Pol'y* 231, n. 101 and 102 (providing examples of the property metaphor in public policy debates).

3 See Carrier, Michael A. (2004), 'Cabining Intellectual Property through a Property Paradigm', 54 *Duke L.J.* 1.

enable information owners to exact *ex ante* compensation from those who desire easy access to their information, it does not necessarily provide the basis for a viable cause of action against those who come to possess or use such information after its initial authorized distribution.[4] Additionally, a property characterization, alone, does not explain why information owners need more protection for 'their property' than is already provided to them under current law.

This chapter looks beyond the property/not property debate to focus instead on what seems to be at the heart of the information industry's interest in greater protection for information: curing what this author refers to as 'the third party problem'.[5] Currently, information owners can use a combination of legal doctrines – principally copyright, trade secret and contract law – to protect information that they voluntarily choose to share with others.[6] However, for reasons that are explained in Section I of this chapter, none of these bodies of law provide absolute protection, particularly with respect to information that falls into the hands of a third party.[7] To the extent information is protected by copyright, information owners enjoy the greatest level of protection because third parties can be sued for direct infringement or based

---

4 See Haddock, David D. and Fred S. McChesney (1991), 'Do Liability Rules Deter Takings?', in Meiners, Roger E. and Bruce Yandle (eds.) *The Economic Consequences of Liability Rules*, 29 ('Protecting property rights by rules that require *ex ante* compensation is fundamentally different from protecting them by rules that tolerate *ex post* compensation.').

5 See also Reichman, J.H. and Pamela Samuelson (1997), 'Intellectual Property Rights in Data?', 50 *Vand. L. Rev.* 51, 145 (describing their version of the third party problem: 'The common denominator facing [members of the information industry] is that the fruits of their investment usually consist of aggregates of valuable information that are embodied on or near the face of products sold in the open market. Because trade secret law does not normally cover such products, third parties who rapidly duplicate the embodied information they contain deprive innovators of the lead time needed to recoup their investment, without contributing, directly or indirectly, to the overall costs of research and development.').

6 Other theories of legal protection for information include privacy law and various statutory rights (see for example, the Plant Variety Protection Act, Pub. L. No. 91-577, 84 Stat. 1542, codified at 7 U.S.C. § 2321-1611, the Semiconductor Chip Protection Act of 1984, Act of 8 November 1984, Pub. L. 98-620, 98 Stat. 3347, codified at 17 U.S.C. § 901–914, and the Vessel Hull Design Protection Act, Act of 28 October 1998, Pub. L. 105-304, 112 Stat. 2860, sec. 501, codified at 17 U.S.C. §1301–1332. See also Reichman, J.H. (1994), 'Legal Hybrids Between the Patent and Copyright Paradigms', 94 *Colum. L. Rev.* 2432 (1994). Additionally, as noted by Lawrence Lessig, technology, social norms and the operation of markets also plays an important role in protecting information. Lessig, Lawrence (1999), *Code and Other Laws of Cyberspace*, (Basic Books).

7 'Third party' is used herein to mean a person with whom the information owner does not have a direct relationship.

upon principles of vicarious liability, contributory infringement or inducement. Trade secret law provides lesser protection for information that falls into the hands of third parties because a claim of trade secret misappropriation is usually dependent upon the existence of a close relationship between the trade secret owner and the alleged misappropriator. Contract law, while extremely useful in filling gaps in protection that exist under copyright and trade secret law, provides the least possible protection against third parties due to the well-established rule that only parties who are in privity are bound by the obligations of a contract.

The question addressed by this chapter is: Given the incomplete solutions to the third party problem that are provided by copyright, trade secret and contract law, should information owners be given additional means for protecting their information and, if so, how?[8] One possible means of expanding protection for information is to lift some of the limitations that exist on the current scope of copyright, trade secret and contract law. Another approach is to adopt a *sui generis* law to protect some defined sub-set of information. This chapter focuses on a third option: the use and possible expansion of existing tort theories of third party liability.

The chapter begins with an overview of the existing means of protecting information with particular attention to the policy rationales behind the limitations that are placed on such protection. Obviously, any effort to expand the protection that is currently provided for information must consider why it is limited and whether there is a sufficient public policy argument for altering those limits. In Section II, the ways in which the third party problem are addressed under US intellectual property laws, including the Uniform Trade Secret Act (UTSA), are discussed. In Section III, the means by which the information industry might seek to solve the third party problem are summarized.

In Section IV, a variety of tort doctrines that impose third party liability are examined with a focus on the rationales that underlie such doctrines. The chapter concludes in Section V by exploring whether the rationales that underlie existing tort doctrines of third party liability might justify extended forms of protection for information.

As will be seen, the challenge for information owners who want additional solutions to the third party problem is to articulate a sufficient rationale for such protection while respecting the important public policies that underlie the limits that exist on the scope of copyright, trade secret and contract law.

[8] This is not the first article to address the question whether the information industry needs additional means of protecting information. See for example, Reichman, J.H. and P. Samuelson (1997), 'Intellectual Property Rights in Data?', 50 *Vand. L. Rev.* 51 (suggesting unfair competition and liability rule approaches for providing greater protection instead of *sui generis* laws).

Merely labeling information as a form of property does not go far enough. Instead, information owners must be able to identify ancillary benefits to society that make the imposition of liability without fault worthwhile or otherwise explain why the acts of a third party should constitute actionable wrongdoing. Being able to identify the 'independent wrongs' of third parties appears to hold the most promise for increasing protection for information.

I. FRAMING THE PROBLEM: CURRENT LIMITS ON THE SCOPE OF PROTECTION FOR INFORMATION

While there are three principal bodies of law – copyright, trade secret and contract – that provide means of protecting information,[9] for important public policy reasons none of them provide absolute protection. Thus, before considering why greater protection for information may be justified, it is important to understand the reasons for the limitations on protection that exist under current law.

A. Overview of the Scope and Limits of US Copyright Law

Under the 1976 Copyright Act, information owners enjoy automatic federal protection for all original works of authorship once they are fixed in tangible form.[10] However, not all information can qualify as an original work of authorship and, even if it does, not all uses of copyrighted materials are prohibited. Although US copyright law provides protection for a broad range

---

9 Both the term 'information' and the field of 'information law' do not have well accepted meanings within the academy. Some view the field of information law in the sense it is used in this chapter, that is, the study of legal doctrines and theories related to information *per se*. See Nimmer, Raymond T. (1996–2008), *Information Law*, §12 (West) and Lipton, Jacqueline (2003), 'A Framework for Information Law and Policy', 82 *Or. L. Rev.* 695. Others view information law as being 'primarily concerned with the issues arising from the use of information within a specific technological context', such as the written press, television, radio broadcasting, and telecommunications. Larouche, Peirre *On the Future of Information Law as a Specific Field of Law*, Tiles Discussion Paper, DP 2008-020, p. 221 (May 2008), available at http://papers.ssrn.com/sol13/papers.cfm?abstract_id=1140162.

As used herein, 'information' is defined to mean 'knowledge or facts communicated about a particular subject, event, etc.' *Shorter Oxford English Dictionary* (5th edn., 2002). Consistent with the UTSA's definition of a trade secret, 'information' includes 'a formula, pattern, compilation, program, device, method, technique, or process'. Uniform Trade Secrets Act (amended 1985), §1, definition of 'trade secret'.

10 17 U.S.C. § 102(a).

of works,[11] there are several doctrines that limit the scope of such protection.[12] Pursuant to the concept of originality, information owners can only protect information if it contains a modicum of creativity and only to the extent of such creativity.[13] If information owners have merely compiled pre-existing factual information, the compilation is not protected under copyright law.[14] As explained by the Supreme Court in the case of *Harper & Row*: 'Copyright does not prevent subsequent users from copying from a prior author's work those constituent elements that are not original . . . as long as such use does not unfairly appropriate the author's original contributions.'[15]

The definition of copyrightable subject matter set forth in the US Copyright Act limits the scope of protectable information even further. Section 102(b) states that copyright protection does not extend to 'any idea, procedure, process, system, method of operation, concept, principle, or discovery, regardless of the form in which it is described, explained, illustrated, or embodied in such work.'[16] This limitation is designed, in part, to create a line of demarcation between information that can be protected under patent law and information that can be protected under copyright law.[17] It also codifies the idea/expression dichotomy that was recognized in the seminal case of *Baker v Selden.*[18] In that case, the US Supreme Court held that copyright law does not protect an idea, but only a particular expression of the idea.[19] Related to the idea/expression dichotomy is the merger doctrine,

---

[11] See 17 U.S. C. § 102(a) (defining 'works of authorship' to include: (1) literary works; (2) musical works, including any accompanying words; (3) dramatic works, including any accompanying music; (4) pantomimes and choreographic works; (5) pictorial, graphic, and sculptural works; (6) motion pictures and audiovisual works; (7) sound recordings; and (8) architectural works; see also 17 U.S.C. § 101 ('[a] "compilation" is a work formed by the collection and assembling of preexisting materials or of data that are selected, coordinated, or arranged in such a way that the resulting work as a whole constitutes an original work of authorship.').

[12] See generally Litman, Jessica (1997), 'Reforming Information Law in Copyright's Image', 22 *U. of Dayton L. Rev.* 587 (detailing the history and purpose of the limits that are placed on copyright protection).

[13] *Feist Publications, Inc. v Rural Telephone Service Co., Inc.*, 499 U.S. 340, 345–346 (1982).

[14] Id. at 347–349.

[15] *Harper & Row Publishers, Inc. v Nation Enterprises*, 471 U.S. 539, 547–548 (1985) (citation omitted).

[16] 17 U.S.C. § 102(b).

[17] See US Patent and Trademark Office and the US Copyright Office, Patent-Copyright Laws Overlap Study, (May 1991).

[18] 17 U.S.C. § 102(b) and *Baker v Selden*, 101 U.S. 99 (1879).

[19] *Baker v Selden*, 101 U.S. 99, 102.

which precludes copyright protection for those things that can only be expressed in one or a few ways.[20]

Even if information is protected by copyright law, a large number of limiting doctrines are set forth in the Copyright Act which preclude enforcement of copyrights in certain circumstances.[21] As the US Supreme Court observed in the case of *Sony Corp. of America v Universal City Studios, Inc.*, '[copyright] protection has never accorded the copyright owner complete control over possible uses of his work'.[22] For instance, pursuant to the fair use doctrine, copyright owners will be denied relief when a defendant's use of copyrightable material is deemed to be a fair use.[23] Of particular relevance to the third party problem is the first sale doctrine that precludes copyright owners from complaining about the subsequent distribution of their works once they are initially sold or distributed to a second party.[24]

Although the limits that are placed on the scope of copyright law may seem unreasonable to many information owners because they do not go far enough to protect their investments, they reflect an important balance that Congress has struck between the public's interest in encouraging creativity on one hand and the public's need for information and the interests of free competition on the other.[25] As explained by the US Supreme Court in *Feist Publications, Inc. v Rural Telephone Service, Inc.*:

> It may seem unfair that much of the fruit of the compiler's labor may be used by others without compensation. As Justice Brennan has correctly observed, however, this is not 'some unforeseen by product of a statutory scheme.' . . . It is, rather, 'the essence of copyright,' . . . and a constitutional requirement. The primary objective

---

20 See *Morrissey v Proctor & Gamble*, 379 F. 2d 675, 678 (1st Cir. 1967) ('When the uncopyrightable subject matter is very narrow, so that "the topic necessarily requires," . . . if not only one form of expression, at best only a limited number, to permit copyrighting would mean that a party or parties, . . . could exhaust all possibilities of future use of the substance.').

21 See 17 U.S.C. §§ 107–122.

22 464 U.S. 417, 432 (1984).

23 17 U.S.C. § 107.

24 17 U.S.C. § 109(a); see also *Vernor v Autodesk, Inc.*, No. C07-1189RAJ, 2008 WL 2199682 (W.D. Wash., 20 May 2008) (holding that a purported 'license' was actually a sale for the purpose of determining whether the first sale doctrine applied) and Rice, David A. (1990), 'Licensing the Use of Computer Program Copies and the Copyright First Sale Doctrine', 30 *Jurimetrics J.* 157, 172.

25 *Fox Film Corp. v Doyal*, 286 U.S. 123, 127 (1932) ('The limited scope of the copyright holder's statutory monopoly, like the limited duration required by the constitution, reflects a balance of competing claims upon the public interest: creative work is to be encouraged and rewarded, but private motivation must ultimately serve the cause of promoting broad public availability of literature, music, and the other arts.').

> of copyright is not to reward the labor of authors, but '[t]o promote the Progress of Science and useful Arts.' . . .[26]

If a particular body of information does not contribute something 'new' and 'creative' to the arts, then the reward of copyrights is deemed to be too great a price for the public to pay. As importantly, the limits that are placed on the scope of copyright protection are essential to ensuring that the Copyright Act does not violate the First Amendment.[27]

B. Overview of the Scope and Limits of US Trade Secret Law

In the absence of copyright protection (or in addition to weak copyright protection), information owners can attempt to protect their information under trade secret law. However, like copyright law, the scope of trade secret protection is limited for a number of important reasons. Thus, not all information can be protected as a trade secret and, even if protected, the length of such protection is unpredictable and often outside the control of the trade secret owner.

Pursuant to the Uniform Trade Secrets Act (UTSA), which is applicable in most states of the United States, to be protected as a trade secret information must: (1) not be generally known or readily ascertainable (that is, it must be 'relatively secret'); (2) be the subject of efforts that are reasonable under the circumstances to protect its secrecy; and (3) derive independent economic value from the fact that the information is secret.[28] If information has been released to the general public or within a trade, or can be readily gleaned from available sources, it is not a trade secret.[29] Also, even if information was once a trade secret, such protection can be lost through no fault of the information owner. This is because, in contrast to the scope of protection provided under patent law, it is not a violation of trade secret law for a person or company to

---

26 *Feist Publications, Inc. v Rural Telephone Service Co., Inc.*, 499 U.S. 340, 349, internal citation omitted; see also *Harper & Row Publishers, Inc. v Nation Enterprises*, 471 U.S. 539, 589, *Twentieth Century Music Corp. v Aiken*, 422 U.S. 151, 156 (1975) and US Constitution, Article I, § 8, cl. 8.

27 See *Eldred v Ashcroft*, 537 U.S. 186, 190 (2003) (noting that the fair use doctrine is what prevents the Copyright Act from being unconstitutional under the First Amendment); see also, Litman, Jessica (1997), 'Reforming Information Law in Copyright's Image', 22 *U. of Dayton L. Rev.* 587, 601 ('. . . a large part of the reason that there has seemed . . . to be little risk of an important collision between copyright law's exclusive rights and first amendment values is that these limitations have preserved the public's access to the ideas, facts, concepts, systems, processes and methods, which, although embodied in protected works, belong from the moment of their creation to the public domain.').

28 UTSA, §1, definition of 'trade secret'.

29 UTSA, §1, cmt. to section 1.

use or disclose information that they acquired through independent research or reverse engineering.[30] Moreover, when a third party independently develops information and thereafter publicly disseminates it, such dissemination destroys the trade secret status of that information wherever and by whomever it is held.[31] If information that was misappropriated ends up in the hands of a third party and he neither knew or had reason to know that it was misappropriated, the subsequent public dissemination of the information destroys its trade secret status.[32]

While eliminating all or some of the limits that are placed upon state trade secret law might seem like an easy fix to the third party problem, the ability of states to legislate in the area of unfair competition (of which trade secret law is one example) is limited by principles of federal preemption.[33] As the US Supreme Court explained in *Sears, Roebuck & Co v Stiffel Co.*:

> Obviously a State could not, consistently with the Supremacy Clause of the Constitution, extend the life of a patent beyond its expiration date or give a patent on an article which lacked the level of invention required for federal patents. . . Just as a State cannot encroach upon the federal patent laws directly, it cannot, under some other law, such as that forbidding unfair competition, give protection of a kind that clashes with the objectives of the federal patent laws.[34]

Although the Supreme Court in the case of *Kewanee Oil Co. v Bicron Corp.* subsequently held that state trade secret law is not preempted by federal

---

30 UTSA, §1, cmt. to section 1, listing 'proper means' to acquire trade secrets.

31 Milgrim, Roger M. (1996–2008), *Milgrim on Trade Secret*, §1.04, pp. 1-297–298 (M. Bender) ('Although evidence of intensive and extensive efforts to maintain secrets may be probative that information itself is a trade secret, the most elaborate secrecy, however, will not elevate public knowledge to the status of a trade secret.').

32 See *Religious Tech. Ctr. v Netcom On-Line Commc'n Servs., Inc.*, No. C-95-20091 RMW, 1997 U.S. Dist. Lexis 23572, at 30 (N.D. Cal. 3 January 1997) ('posting works to the Internet makes them "generally known"') and *Religious Tech. Ctr. v Lerma*, 908 F. Supp. 1362, 1368 (E.D. Va. 1995). But see Rowe, Elizabeth A. (2007), 'Introducing a Takedown for Trade Secrets on the Internet', *Wis. L. Rev.* 1041 (proposing a means to limit the effects of Internet postings on the trade secret status of information).

33 See Sandeen, Sharon K. (2008), 'Kewanee Revisited: Returning to First Principles of Intellectual Property Law to Determine the Issue of Federal Preemption', 12 *Marq. Intell. Prop. L. Rev.* 299 (detailing the history of federal preemption as applied to state trade secret law and citing *Sears, Roebuck & Co. v Stiffel Co.*, 376 U. S. 225 (1964), *Compco Corp. v Day-Brite Lighting, Inc.*, 376 U.S. 234, 238 (1964), *Lear, Inc. v Adkins*, 395 U.S. 653 (1969), *Goldstein v California*, 412 U.S. 546 (1973), *Kewanee Oil Co. v Bicron Corp.*, 416 U.S. 470 (1974), and *Bonito Boats, Inc. v Thunder Craft Boats, Inc.*, 489 U.S. 141 (1989) as the critical Supreme Court cases on the issue).

34 *Sears, Roebuck & Co. v Stiffel Co.*, 376 U. S. 225, 230–231.

law,[35] it did so based upon a narrow conception of that law.[36] It is for this reason that the UTSA (which was adopted after *Kewanee*) was purposefully designed to be an imperfect alternative to the protection that is accorded under federal patent law.[37] Any effort to expand the scope of trade secret law or to adopt a new state-based tort to provide greater protection for information will undoubtedly be challenged on preemption grounds.

C. Overview of the Scope and Limits of US Contract Law

Pursuant to principles of freedom of contract, two or more parties are generally free to agree among themselves on most subjects.[38] Thus, the owners of information may contract to provide all or some of their information to another under specified conditions.[39] Usually, if the information owner desires to maintain control over the use and dissemination of its information, the contract will include a series of obligations that require the recipient of the information to maintain its confidentiality. For instance, it is standard practice in the software industry to couple the licensing of software with a promise that restricts the use and dissemination of the software.

Like copyright law and trade secret law, contract law does not provide information owners with perfect, gap-free protection. First, there are a number of legal doctrines that make certain contractual arrangements unenforceable.[40]

---

35 *Kewanee Oil Co. v Bicron Corp.*, 416 U.S. 470, 492.

36 Id. at 490 ('Where patent law acts as a barrier, trade secret law functions relatively as a sieve.'); see also Sandeen, 'Kewanee Revisited: Returning to First Principles of Intellectual Property Law to Determine the Issue of Federal Preemption', 12 *Marq. Intell. Prop. L. Rev.* 299, 332–333.

37 Sandeen, Sharon K. (2005), 'A Contract by Any Other Name is Still a Contract: Examining the Effectiveness of Trade Secret Clauses to Protect Databases', 45 *IDEA* 119, 151–152 (detailing the history and purpose of the UTSA).

38 See for example, *Lochner v New York*, 198 U.S. 45 (1905) (while the notion that economic due process can be used as a basis for invalidating state legislative action has long been debunked, the right of parties to contract freely within the confines of valid legislative or regulatory restrictions remains in force). A principal proponent of the use of contract law to strengthen protection for information is Raymond Nimmer who has written extensively on what he has dubbed 'Information Law.' See Nimmer, *Information Law*, § 12.

39 See Van Houweling, Molly Shaffer (2008), 'The New Servitudes', 96 *Geo. L.J.* 885 (giving a careful analysis of the various ways information owners attempt to use contract law to fill gaps in intellectual property protection).

40 Lord, Richard A. *Williston on Contracts*, § 64:1 (explaining the consequences of unenforceable contracts and giving some examples) and Nimmer, *Information Law*, § 12.09–12.13. See also Lemley, Mark A. (1999), 'Beyond Preemption: The Law and Policy of Intellectual Property Licensing', 87 *Cal. L. Rev.* 111, 163–168 (discussing state public policy limits on intellectual property contracts).

Secondly, even if the underlying contract is enforceable as between the parties to the contract, and a breach of contract can be proven, the remedies that are available for the breach are limited and do not ordinarily include injunctive relief.[41] Thirdly, and of particular relevance to the third party problem, contractual obligations are not typically enforced against third parties to the contract.[42] Rather, as is discussed in greater detail *infra*, the principal means of bringing a third party into an action for breach of contract is to allege that the third party committed the tort of intentional interference with contract.[43]

As with the limits that are imposed on copyright and trade secret protection, the limits of contract law are not a set of arbitrary rules that can be altered on a whim. Rather, they reflect important public policy considerations that need to be taken into account before any change in the law is made. For instance, the rules concerning the non-enforceability of certain contracts are typically designed either to protect a party who is deemed to be incapable of freely entering into a contract or to prevent transactions that are deemed to be socially undesirable.[44] The remedies that are available for breach of contract were consciously limited for important economic reasons and in order to differentiate contract and tort wrongs.[45] At its core, the rule of privity is intended to put individuals on clear notice of their extra-legal (that is, private contractual) obligations.[46]

---

41 See generally *Williston on Contracts*, § 64:1 (noting that the primary remedy for breach of contract is an action for damages and that equitable relief is granted in 'rare instances') and Chapter 67, 'Specific Performance and Other Equitable Remedies'.

42 See *Williston on Contracts*, §37:1 ('Under the traditional common-law rule, only parties in privity of contract could be sued on the contract.') and Merges, Robert P. (1997), 'The End of Friction? Property Rights and Contract in the 'Newtonian' World of On-Line Commerce', 12 *Berk. Tech. L. J.* 115, 119 (discussing 'The Problem of Privity'); see also *Bonfils v McDonald*, 84 Colo. 325 (1928), *citing* Black's Law Dictionary, p. 943 ('Privity of contract is that connection or relationship which exists between two or more contracting parties.').

Even though the third party beneficiary doctrine is a well-recognized exception to the requirement of privity, it only applies in very specific fact situations that generally require knowledge of the third party beneficiary and some relationship between the promisee and the alleged third party beneficiary. See *Williston on Contracts*, §37:1. Moreover, it is a doctrine that allows a third party to sue a promisor for breach of contract; it is not a basis for a party to a contract to sue a third party.

43 See Section IV.

44 *Supra* note 40.

45 *Williston on Contracts*, § 64:2 (explaining the limited bases for an award of damages for breach of contract).

46 See Epstein, Richard A. (2005), 'Rebuilding the Citadel', in Madden, M. Stuart (ed.) *Exploring Tort Law*, (Cambridge Univ. Press) Chapter Seven, p. 230 (noting the 'horrific consequences if A could be required to pay money to B and C solely because the latter two have agreed on that outcome.').

II. HOW EXISTING IP LAWS SOLVE THE THIRD PARTY PROBLEM

One of the hallmarks of US federal laws governing intellectual property rights is the way they solve most of the third party problem by imposing liability without requiring proof of intent or knowledge of the existence of the subject IP rights. Rather, by carefully defining the scope of rights that are enjoyed by patent, copyright and trademark holders, the US Congress decided what actions, by any person, would be actionable; in effect, creating *sui generis* strict liability torts.

In the case of copyright law, although a defendant's intent and knowledge of the existence of copyrights can affect the amount of damages that are awarded to a plaintiff,[47] anyone who, without the permission of the copyright owner, reproduces or distributes a copyrighted work or violates any of the other exclusive rights that are listed in section 106 of the Copyright Act is liable for copyright infringement.[48] Thus, if information is protected by copyright law, it does not matter whether there was a direct relationship between the information owner and the party who is accused of infringement. They can be perfect strangers. The obligation to respect the copyrights follows the work of authorship wherever it goes.

Copyright law goes an additional step in trying to solve the third party problem by imposing liability in certain circumstances for what is referred to as 'indirect infringement'.[49] As expressed in the recent US Supreme Court case of *Metro Goldwyn-Mayer Studios, Inc. v Grokster, Ltd.* there are actually three theories of indirect copyright infringement: (1) vicarious liability; (2) contributory infringement; and (3) inducement.[50] Generally, vicarious copyright liability is imposed in a manner that is consistent with the common law principle of *respondeat superior*; that is, it is based upon the existence of a relationship of control between the primary wrongdoer and a third party.[51] Contributory infringement is established when the third party defendant, with the requisite level of knowledge, acts to assist the copyright infringement in some manner, either by contributing to the infringement directly or by provid-

---

[47] 17 U.S.C. § 504(c).

[48] 17 U.S.C. § 501.

[49] See generally Nimmer, Melvin B. and David Nimmer (2008), *Nimmer on Copyright*, §12.04 (Lexis Nexis).

[50] 545 U.S. 913 (2005); see also Alfred Yen (2006), 'Third-Party Copyright Liability After' Grokster, 91 *Minn. L. Rev.* 184.

[51] *Nimmer on Copyright*, § 12.04[A][1]–[2]; see also Yen, 'Third-Party Copyright Liability After Grokster', 91 *Minn. L. Rev.* 184, 200, *citing Shapiro, Bernstein & Co. v H.L. Green Co.*, 316 F. 2d 304, 307 (1963).

ing the means to infringe.[52] As set forth in *Grokster:* 'one who distributes a device with the object of promoting its use to infringe copyright, as shown by clear expression or other affirmative steps taken to foster infringement, is liable for the resulting acts of infringement by third parties'.[53]

Under US patent law, anyone who violates any of the exclusive rights prescribed by the Patent Act is liable for patent infringement without regard to their intent or their lack of actual knowledge of the existence of the patent rights.[54] Also, like copyright law, US patent law attempts to address the third party problem by prohibiting various forms of indirect infringement.[55] Section 271(b) of the US Patent Act states that '[w]hoever actively induces infringement of a patent shall be liable as an infringer'.[56] Section 271(c) describes the circumstances under which a third party can be held liable for patent infringement by offering to sell or selling components of a patented device.[57]

US trademark law provides that anyone can be liable for infringing another's trademark simply by adopting and using in commerce a mark that is likely to be confused with a pre-existing mark.[58] As with copyright and patent law, the defendant in a trademark infringement action need not have actual knowledge of the existence of the pre-existing trademark and need not intend to infringe such trademark. In addition, in order to deal with the situation where someone other than the direct infringer engages in activities that facilitate trademark infringement, US trademark law recognizes two doctrines of indirect infringement: contributory infringement and vicarious infringement.[59]

Liability under the UTSA is based primarily upon the existence of a trade secret and a relationship between the trade secret owner and the defendant.[60]

---

52 *Nimmer on Copyrights*, § 12.04[A][3] and Yen, 'Third-Party Copyright Liability After Grokster', 91 *Minn. L. Rev.* 193–94, *citing Gershwin Publishing Corp. v Columbia Artists Management, Inc.*, 443 F. 2d 1159, 1162 (1971).

53 545 U.S. 913, 936–37.

54 35 U.S.C. § 271(a); see also Chisum, Donald S. (2007), *Chisum on Patents*, § 16.01 (Lexis Nexis), 'Direct Infringement' and § 16.02[2], 'Knowledge and Intent'.

55 See generally *Chisum on Patents*, Chapter 7, 'Contributory Infringement'.

56 35 U.S.C. § 271(b).

57 35 U.S.C. § 271(c).

58 See Horwitz, Ethan and Benjamin Levi (1996), 'Fifty Years of the Lanham Act: A Retrospective of Section 43(A)', 7 *Fordham Intell. Prop. Media & Ent. L. J.* 59, 63 (noting that in adopting the Lanham Act: 'Congress intended to eliminate a showing of willfulness or intent to deceive as a prerequisite for winning a trademark protection action').

59 McCarthy, J. Thomas (1996–2008) *McCarthy on Trademarks and Unfair Competition*, §§ 25:17–25:15 (Thomson Reuters/West).

60 See Sandeen, Sharon K. (2005), 'A Contract By Any Other Name Is Still a Contract: Examining the Effectiveness of Trade Secret Clauses to Protect Databases', 45 *IDEA* 119, 124.

Generally, if a relationship exists between the trade secret owner and the alleged wrongful possessor of information that gives rise to an express or implied duty of confidentiality, it is easier for a trade secret owner to successfully plead and prove a claim for trade secret misappropriation. However, because the risk to trade secrets that is posed by third parties was a primary concern of the drafters of the UTSA, the definition of 'misappropriation' includes two scenarios where the existence of a relationship between the trade secret owner and the defendant is not critical, and consequently, where a claim against a third party may lie.

First, a person or entity may be liable for trade secret misappropriation by virtue of the manner by which they acquire the trade secret information. If they engage in wrongful behavior – such as theft, bribery or electronic espionage – to acquire plaintiff's trade secrets, they can be held liable for trade secret misappropriation regardless of whether they had a direct relationship with the trade secret owner.[61] The applicable duty (not to steal, bribe, etc . . .) is defined by the UTSA and not by the duties that may flow from a close relationship. The second scenario concerns the provisions of the UTSA that impose liability for trade secret misappropriation upon those who 'knew or had reason to know' that their acquisition of trade secrets was derived from or through a person who misappropriated such trade secrets.[62] Under this scenario, the focus is on the third party's knowledge at the time he disclosed or used (or threatened to disclose or use) the trade secrets.

III. POSSIBLE ADDITIONAL SOLUTIONS TO THE THIRD PARTY PROBLEM

As the foregoing summary reveals, there are several ways that third parties can currently be held liable for violating the intellectual property rights of others. What the information industry is concerned about, however, is how to control the downstream use and dissemination of information when: (1) the information is not protected by copyright or trade secret law; (2) there is no binding and enforceable contract between the information owner and the persons who possess and use the information; and (3) the persons who possess and use trade secret information do not know or have reason to know that the information is a misappropriated trade secret.

In order to expand the scope of legal protection for information beyond that which currently exists, the information industry has three options. First, it can

61 UTSA, §1, definition of 'misappropriation'.
62 Id.

advocate for a change in existing law to narrow the current limits that are placed on the scope of existing protection. For instance, with respect to contract law, the information industry might advocate for a change in the privity requirement (for example, advocate for the creation of a third party promisor theory of liability). One problem with this approach is that it is difficult to effectuate change to existing laws of general applicability for the benefit of one industry without also affecting other industries. While one perceived problem might be fixed, a change in the law may have unintended consequences and, in the end, the information industry might not like the change.[63] The push-me/pull-you nature of changes to laws of general applicability is one reason courts and legislators are (or should be) reluctant to alter well-established legal doctrines to address the concerns of one industry. Moreover, as noted above, any effort to revise the limits that are currently placed upon the scope of copyright, trade secret and contract law would create greater conflicts with the public policies that underlie such limits and, in the case of trade secret law, may result in federal preemption (that is, invalidation) of state trade secret law.[64]

A second option is to advocate for the passage of a *sui generis* law that would deal specifically with the third party problem. US law is replete with examples of statutes that are designed to solve industry specific problems. However, it is not easy to draft such laws, particularly when the subject matter of a *sui generis* law would overlap substantially – and arguably be inconsistent with – established legal principles. Of particular concern to many commentators is the fact that the adoption of a *sui generis* law to protect information would undermine the balance between free competition and the creation of incentives for innovation and creativity that existing intellectual property laws seek to achieve.[65] It might also conflict with various provisions of international agreements that limit the scope of protection to be provided to intellectual property rights.[66]

A third option, and the one that is the focus of the remainder of this chapter, is to urge the development of one or more new torts that would impose

---

63 Most information owners are also information users and, thus, at the same time they benefit from existing laws that protect their information, they also benefit from limits that are placed upon such protection when they use the information of others.

64 *Supra* notes 33–37.

65 Reichman and Samuelson, 'Intellectual Property Rights in Data?', 50 *Vand. L. Rev.* 51 (discussing the debates surrounding the E.U. Database Directive and the pros and cons of a *sui generis* approach).

66 See generally Agreement on Trade Related Aspects of Intellectual Property Law Rights, 15 April 1994 [the 'TRIPS Agreement'], Marrakesh Agreement Establishing the World Trade Organization, Annex 1C, Legal Instruments – Results of the Uruguay Round, 33 I.L.M. 1197 (1994).

liability on third party information users in certain circumstances. This could either take the form of a new statutory tort (that is, a *sui generis* tort) or a tort that is developed at common law.[67] In either case, for reasons that are explained in more detail, *infra*, it is imperative for the information industry to be able to articulate a rationale for a new tort that goes beyond the mere assertion of personal property rights. Based upon existing tort theory, and in light of the limits that are placed upon copyright, trade secret and contract law, the information industry must either: (1) articulate a reason for the imposition of strict liability (that is, liability without fault); or (2) identify a set of actions, knowledge and intent by a third party that would justify the imposition of liability based upon fault.

IV. EXISTING TORT THEORIES OF THIRD PARTY LIABILITY

The search for a tort theory to solve the third party problem is complicated by the fact that there are a number of potentially overlapping, three-party scenarios that currently give rise to tort liability. The first scenario – the *indirect victim scenario* – arises where a person or entity breaches a duty that is owed to another and, in the process, causes harm to a third party.[68] This is similar to the third party beneficiary scenario of contract law and, like that scenario, is not directly applicable to the third party problem because it concerns the identity of who can sue, not who can be sued. However, the reasoning of cases that have expanded the scope of potential tort victims to include third parties provide a glimpse into the factual circumstances that may justify a solution to the third party problem.

The second three party scenario – the *comparative (or contributory) negligence scenario* – involves multiple individuals (or entities) who each owed a duty to the plaintiff and who acted negligently (or intentionally) to contribute

---

[67] Pursuant to applicable international agreements, countries arguably have more flexibility to adopt laws to prohibit wrongful acts and unfair competition than they do to adopt more stringent intellectual property rights. See for example, TRIPS Agreement, Article 39(1).

[68] A classic example of this scenario is where a mother suffers emotional distress as a result of witnessing her child being harmed by the negligence of another. See for example, *Dillon v Legg*, 68 Cal. 2d 728 (1968). Similarly, one theory of auditor liability is based upon the indirect victim scenario. In such cases, the direct victim is the auditor's client and the indirect victim is a third-party who relied upon the audit. See for example, *Bily v Arthur Young & Co.*, 3 Cal. 4th 370 (1992) (explaining the rationales behind auditor liability to third parties).

to the plaintiff's harm.[69] While, theoretically, this scenario might apply to the third party problem to the extent third party possessors and users of information owe a duty of care to an information owner, it does not directly apply to the problem because, under current law, the use of unprotected, publicly disseminated information does not create such a duty.[70] Ordinarily, the duty that gives rise to negligence liability arises from the nature of the defendant's activities and the foreseeability that such activities will result in harm to others.[71] Particularly in light of the limits that are placed upon the scope of copyright, trade secret and contract law, it is not foreseeable that the mere use of unprotected information will harm anyone.

In the third scenario – the *strict liability scenario* – two different factual situations are typically presented. In one, the plaintiff is injured with little or no intentional or negligent act on the part of the third party but under circumstances where policy makers (used herein to include both legislators and judges) have decided to provide the plaintiff with a remedy.[72] The second factual situation involves what William Prosser referred to as 'imputed negligence', but which is more often referred to as vicarious liability.[73] This is where a third party is held liable for the negligent or wrongful acts of another due to a relationship that exists between the negligent actor and the third party.[74]

The fourth scenario – the *multiple wrongful acts scenario* – arises when two or more parties engage in wrongs that each cause harm to the plaintiff. As so

---

69 This is often referred to as 'contributory liability' and, together with vicarious liability, is often labeled 'secondary liability'. Generally, tort law addresses this scenario by determining whether to (and if so, how best to) apportion liability among the contributory actors.

70 *Supra* Section I.

71 Prosser, William L. (1971), *Handbook of the Law of Torts* [hereinafter *Prosser on Torts*], § 1, p. 6 (4th edn. West) ('The law of torts . . . is concerned with the allocation of losses arising out of human activities. . . . The common thread woven into all torts is the idea of unreasonable interference with the interests of others.'). See also the famous case of *Palsgraf v Long Island R. Co*., 126 N. E. 99 (NY 1928).

72 Classic examples of this scenario include the liability that is imposed upon the owners of wild animals and upon those who engage in ultra hazardous activities. *Prosser on Torts*, Chapter 13 (noting that the activities that traditionally gave rise to strict liability were unusual or abnormal, that is, unexpected).

73 *Prosser on Torts*, § 69.

74 Perhaps the best known example of this form of strict liability is the doctrine of *respondeat superior* whereby principals are held responsible for the tortious acts of their agents. Restatement (Third) of Agency, § 2.05 (2008); see also Sykes, Alan O. (1988), 'The Boundaries of Vicarious Liability: An Economic Analysis of the Scope of Employment Rules and Related Doctrines', 101 *Harv. L. Rev.* 563. So-called 'enterprise liability' is a form of vicarious liability, but instead of shifting liability from a wrongdoer to another, it imposes liability on the enterprise for the wrongs of a member of the enterprise. *Prosser on Torts*, § 72.

described, this scenario is similar to the comparative negligence scenario, but it is discussed separately because it typically involves intentional acts by the third party defendant. Under this scenario, the plaintiff often has a cause of action against the defendant-second party for primary wrongdoing and a separate cause of action against the defendant-third party for what might be considered secondary wrongdoing. A good example is the tort of intentional interference with contract where the primary wrongdoing is the breach of contract and the secondary wrongdoing is the interference with the contract.[75]

Further complicating the search for a tort theory to solve the third party problem is the fact that policy makers have not always been clear or consistent about the rationales that underlie the creation of third party liability.[76] Generally, there are two extremes in the imposition of third party liability and a number of doctrines that fall between the two extremes. On one extreme is the assignment of 'strict liability' based generally upon the policy maker's decision of who to benefit and who to burden.[77] On the other extreme is the imposition of liability based upon a high degree of moral responsibility (that is, 'fault'); typically, a wrongful act coupled with a specific intent to cause harm.[78] In between these two extremes are justifications for tort liability that either tilt more toward the strict liability or the fault side of the tort liability continuum. There is often an added element related to the relationship that exists between the defendant (second party) and the third party.

Guido Calabresi and Jon Hirschoff identified some of the public policy considerations that might underlie a preference for a strict liability regime over a fault-based regime, labeling them 'distributional considerations':

---

75 See Crapster, Gary C. et al. (2005), 'Interference with Contractual and Economic Relationships', in Solen, David A. et al. (ed.), *Business Torts Litigation*, (ABA) Chapter 2, p. 55.

76 See Fletcher, George S. (1972), 'Fairness and Utility in Tort Theory', 85 *Harv. L. Rev.* 537, 544 (discussing strict liability, he said: 'Yet the law of torts has never recognized a general principle underlying these atomistic pockets of liability.').

77 As William Prosser noted in 1971, 'there is a "strong and growing tendency, where there is blame on neither side, to ask, in view of the exigencies of social justice, who can best bear the loss and hence shift the liability where there has been no fault".' *Prosser on Torts*, § 75. See also Calabresi, Guido and Jon T. Hirschoff (1972), 'Toward a Test for Strict Liability in Torts', 81 *Yale L. J.* 1055, 1077–1080.

78 As noted by William Prosser in his 1941 treatise on the law of torts, '[u]ntil about the close of the nineteenth century, the history of the law of torts was that of a slow and somewhat unsteady progress toward the recognition of "fault" or moral responsibility as the basis of the remedy'. Prosser, William L. (1941), *Handbook of the Law of Torts*, (West) p. 427.

> These preferences may reflect a desire to distribute or fractionalize losses, often called *spreading*. They may reflect a preference for moving toward a given *distribution of wealth*, such as greater wealth equality, better treatment for higher castes, or better treatment for castes which in the past have been poorly treated. They may instead reflect a desire to further what might be viewed as *dynamic efficiency goals* – as might occur by favoring the doers, the entrepreneurs in society. Finally they may reflect society's notion, if it has one or if it has many, of rewarding individuals' merits – of *recognizing their just deserts*.[79]

Similarly, William Prosser listed the considerations underlying theories of imputed negligence as: (1) who can afford the loss; (2) who can insure against the loss; (3) what is fair; and (4) who is privileged by the activity.[80] Others have noted that strict liability is often imposed on third parties due to the nature of the activities in which they are engaged.[81] Because third parties have chosen to engage in certain activities, and presumably profit from them, it is argued that as a matter of fairness they should be liable for any harm that results from those activities.[82]

As a matter of tort theory, it is ordinarily not enough for a person to act badly or even to cause harm to another. Tort liability will be imposed only when policy makers deem the actions or non-actions of a defendant to be 'tortious'.[83] In the absence of a decision to impose strict liability, ordinarily the defendant must owe a duty of care that allows him to reasonably foresee that his actions will cause harm to another. In the case of a negligence cause of action, it is the nature of the defendants' activities that lead courts to recognize a duty of care.[84] In the case of intentional torts, it is the defendant's actions coupled with defendant's knowledge (*scienter*) or intent (*mens rea*) to

---

[79] Calabresi and Hirschoff, 'Toward a Test for Strict Liability in Torts', 81 *Yale L. J.* 1055, 1077–1080, emphasis added.

[80] *Prosser on Torts*, § 73.

[81] Keating, Gregory C. (2001), 'The Theory of Enterprise Liability and Common Law Strict Liability', 54 *Vand. L. Rev.* 1285, 1286 ('Fault liability pins the costs of the nonnegligent accidents that are the long-run price of an activity's presence in the world on the random victims of the activity. Enterprise liability pins those accident costs on the activity – the enterprise – which imposed the nonnegligent risks responsible for the injuries at issues.').

[82] See Englard, Izhak (1993), *The Philosophy of Tort Law*, (Dartmouth Publishing Co.) p. 51 ('The modern basis for the doctrine of vicarious liability is a combination of considerations: a person who employs others to advance his own economic interest should in fairness be placed under a corresponding liability for losses incurred in the course of the enterprise . . .').

[83] See generally Restatement (Second) of the Law of Torts, §6, (ALI 1965), defining 'tortious conduct'.

[84] See generally Restatement (Second) of the Law of Torts, Chapter 12, *Negligence; Palsgraf v Long Island R. Co.*, 162 N.E. 99.

engage in a specific act and/or cause a specific harm that justifies the imposition of tort liability.[85]

Because the ability of a defendant to reasonably foresee injury to a person or entity with whom he or the plaintiff has no direct relationship or contact is limited, courts are generally reluctant to impose negligence liability in such situations (that is, third party victims are limited in their ability to successfully sue negligent actors). Thus, a better means for a third party victim (for example, the information industry in the scenario that is the topic of this chapter) to successfully assert a fault-based theory of liability is to plead and prove the commission of an intentional tort; that is, the information industry should try to articulate an 'independent wrong' that policy makers will be willing to recognize as 'tortious'.

V. THE CASE FOR THIRD PARTY LIABILITY RELATED TO NON-IP INFORMATION

Summarizing the foregoing, the creation of third party tort liability is ordinarily based on one or more of the following considerations:

1. distributional considerations based upon perceived ancillary benefits to society, including economic considerations and judicial efficiency concerns;
2. the risky nature of the third party's activities leading either to a general duty of care or strict liability;
3. the existence of a relationship between the defendant and the third party that enables the third party to control or influence the defendant;
4. a determination of who is in the best position to bear or prevent the loss;
5. a general desire to punish wrongful acts, particularly those that are engaged in with intent to harm; and
6. general considerations of fairness and social justice.

Thus, efforts to establish a new tort to solve the third party problem should focus on these considerations.

Looking first at possible distributional considerations, it may be possible for the information industry to articulate one or more ancillary societal benefits that would be derived from added protection for information. For instance, as some have already suggested, it might be argued that due to the shift from

---

[85] See generally Restatement (Second) of the Law of Torts, Chapter 2, *Intentional Invasions of Interests in Personalty.*

the Industrial Age to the Information Age, greater protection for information is needed to encourage sufficient (or more) investment in the collection and development of information.[86] An obvious problem with this argument is that it runs counter to established copyright policy – particularly the decision of the US Supreme Court that explicitly rejected the 'sweat of the brow' doctrine – and the public's interest in a rich public domain.[87] Moreover, since many of the owners and holders of information are also the users of information, the alleged societal benefits of greater protection for information are arguably illusory.[88] As the software industry has learned from recognition of business methods patents, with greater protection of information often comes more difficult and costly competition.

Based upon the second factor that is listed above, the information industry could attempt to fashion an argument for strict liability based upon the nature of third party activities. As noted above, Congress has already done this with respect to aspects of patent, copyright and trade secret law by specifically identifying acts that will give rise to third party liability even in the absence of knowledge of the underlying intellectual property rights or an intent to harm.[89] But what is it about the activities of third parties – likely to consist of the acquisition, disclosure or use of otherwise unprotected information – that might justify the imposition of strict liability? Can it be argued that third parties are engaging in activities *vis-à-vis* information owners that are akin to ultra hazardous (that is, abnormal, unusual or unexpected) activities?[90] Or, more broadly, is there a particular class of information users that policy makers should burden with strict liability?

As noted above, often the imposition of strict liability is based upon a decision that a third party – or more accurately, the class to which the third party belongs – is in a better position to bear or prevent the loss. Ordinarily, however, the size of the class is relatively small. The third parties who are the focus of the information industry's concern (apparently everyone who uses information without the express permission of the information owner) comprise a very large class of potential third party defendants. That is the point of US information policy; all members of the public should be able to freely use publicly available information unless it is protected by copyright law. Certainly, we do

---

86 See for example, Nimmer, Raymond T. (1996), 'Information Age in Law: New Frontiers in Property and Contract', 68 *JUN N.Y. St. B. J.* 28.

87 *Feist Publications, Inc. v Rural Telephone Service Co., Inc.*, 499 U.S. 340, 353.

88 See also Bitton, Miriam (2006), 'A New Outlook on the Economic Dimension of the Database Protection Debate', 47 *IDEA* 93 (exploring the incentive rationale behind pleas for greater protection for information).

89 *Supra* Section II.

90 *Supra* note 72.

not want to impose strict liability upon such a large class. But is there a smaller class of information users upon which it would be fair to impose strict liability related to their use of otherwise unprotected information?

In the abstract, it might be argued that the makers of information sharing technologies or internet service providers (ISPs) comprise two subsets of information users that may be made subject to strict liability for losses occasioned by the downstream (that is, third party) use of information. In the minds of many information owners, technology manufacturers and ISPs have created the third party problem by enabling the quick and wide-spread dissemination of information. If the efforts to impose general tort liability upon such entities (as opposed to strict liability) are any indication, however, this strategy does hold much promise. Usually, when given the choice between punishing technology manufacturers and ISPs, or providing greater protection for information owners, Congress and the courts have sided with the former.[91] Moreover, imposing strict liability on the manufacturers of technologies that have improved information sharing would be akin to killing the goose that laid the golden egg because those are the very technologies that have enabled the growth of the information industry.

In the absence of a reason to impose the classic form of strict liability, it is theoretically possible for the information industry to argue for the imposition of vicarious liability based upon some relationship that exists between the defendant and the third party. As noted above, however, ordinarily the type of relationship that gives rise to vicarious liability is one of control and supervision.[92] Clearly, information owners can attempt to rely upon existing theories of vicarious liability if, factually, a third party is the employer or principal of the second party.[93] However, the mere transfer of information from a second party to a third party does not create a relationship, let alone one that is marked by elements of control and supervision. There is nothing about the receipt of unprotected information that would put a third party on notice of a duty not to use or disclose that information. In the case of an employee or agency relationship, the third party either knows or can reasonably intuit that the relationship imposes obligations upon him that make the imposition of vicarious liability fair. The same cannot be said about the transfer of information between a second and third party. Without some advance notice of the nature of the information, third parties cannot know what obligations they have with respect to the handling and treatment of otherwise unprotected information.[94]

---

91 See for example, *Sony Corporation of America v Universal Studios, Inc.*, 464 U.S. 417 (1984).

92 *Supra* notes 73–74.

93 Id.

94 Although similar difficulties exist with respect to publicly distributed materi-

The fact that information owners are clearly in the best position to prevent and bear the loss of their information is another factor that tips against the imposition of vicarious liability. As they create and compile information, information owners have the power to control its dissemination. As long as they keep their information to themselves, they do not need any legal remedies unless they are victims of theft, in which case they can rely upon trade secret law and a variety of criminal laws to protect their interests. Once they make the voluntary choice to disseminate their information, and presumably profit thereby, however, it is difficult to see why information owners should not bear the burden of loss that results when their information ends up in the hands of third parties. As between the information owner and the third party, the third party is least able to differentiate between protectable and unprotectable bits of information. Thus, it seems reasonable to require information owners to pre-designate the information to be protected before it is released to the public by either taking care to create an original work of authorship that is protected by copyright law or by only releasing information under circumstances that give rise to a duty of confidentiality under principles of contract of trade secret law.

The fact that the third party problem is most acute when the subject information is not protected by copyright, trade secret or contract law makes it difficult for information owners to argue that third party liability should be based upon fault related to the character of the information. As noted previously, for important public policy reasons, the scope of protection for information is limited and, therefore, it is not wrongful or blameworthy for individuals to read, learn from, use, collect, share, or copy unprotected, publicly available information.[95] However, this does not mean that third parties cannot be held liable for other wrongful or blameworthy conduct; that is, conduct that is disconnected from the character of the information to be protected.[96] Borrowing from the case of *Della Penna v Toyota Motor, U.S.A., Inc.*,[97] it appears that the most promising argument for the information industry is to articulate a wrong that is not dependent on the IP status of the underlying information.

---

als that are protected by copyright, there is a process that a third party can follow to determine the copyright status of a work. The steps are: (1) look for a copyright notice; (2) verify the copyright status of the work; and (3) consider the nature of the work (that is, is it an original work of authorship) and the date of its creation.

95 *Supra* Section I.

96 See for example, *International News Service, Inc. v Associated Press*, 248 U.S. 215 (1918) ('We need spend no time, however, upon the general question of property in news matter at common law, or the application of the copyright act, since it seems to us the case must turn upon the question of unfair competition in business.').

97 *Della Penna v Toyota Motor Sales, U.S.A., Inc.*, 11 Cal. 4th 376, 393 (1995).

Although theories of negligence and strict liability tend to get most of the attention among tort scholars, there is a long history in the United States of the recognition of new intentional torts.[98] As the previous discussion of the tort of intentional interference with contract reveals, the idea that third parties can be liable for independent (albeit potentially interdependent) wrongs is also not new.[99] Thus, although the existence of well-developed doctrines of intellectual property law may make it more difficult to fashion new torts due to issues of federal preemption, the potential for independent wrongdoing that requires a judicially or legislatively created tort remedy remains. Conceptually, the scope of potential wrongdoing goes beyond mere unfair competition,[100] or even so-called economic torts, to include any set of actions that might be classified as an intentional tort.

A review of the elements of a number of intentional third party torts reveals that they have three essential features: (1) some wrongful act by the third party; (2) a degree of knowledge on behalf of the third party; and (3) a *mens rea* requirement that may range from a mere intent to act to a specific intent to harm. For instance, the tort of intentional interference with contract typically requires the third party to have knowledge of the existence of the contract and to act intentionally to disrupt the performance of that contract.[101] The independent wrong that is at the heart of this tort relates to society's interest in the sanctity of contracts.[102] The tort of intentional interference with prospective economic advantage, although similar to the tort of intentional interference with contract, involves an entirely different independent wrong because, by definition, it does not implicate society's interest in the sanctity of contracts.[103] As detailed by the California Supreme Court, a plaintiff who alleges interference with prospective economic advantage 'must plead and prove . . . that the defendant not only *knowingly* interfered with the plaintiff's

---

[98] See Dobbs, Dan B. (2006), 'A Restatement (Third) of Intentional Torts?', 48 *Ariz. L. Rev.* 1061, 1079 ('The simple picture is this. Tort law is divided into three domains: intentional torts, negligence, and strict liability. The most serious level of fault is expressed in the intentional tort domain; a lesser degree of fault in negligence; and no fault at all in strict liability.').

[99] *Supra* note 75.

[100] See Reichman and Samuelson, pp. 139–140 (discussing an unfair competition approach to the information industry's dilemma).

[101] *Supra* note 75.

[102] *Della Penna v Toyota Motor Sales, U.S.A., Inc.*, 11 Cal. 4th 376, 392–393.

[103] Id. at 393 ('Our courts should, in short, firmly distinguish the two kinds of business contexts, bringing a greater solicitude to those relationships that have ripened into agreements, while recognizing that relationships short of that subsist in a zone where the rewards and risks of competition are dominant.').

expectancy, but *engaged in conduct* that was wrongful by some legal measure other than the fact of interference itself'.[104]

The tort now referred to as '*INS* misappropriation' illustrates the general requirements of an intentional tort in the context of the alleged wrongful use of publicly available information. In the case of *International News Service, Inc. v Associated Press*, the plaintiff complained of defendant's alleged wrongful use of news reports that, at that time, were not protected by copyright law.[105] After repeatedly noting the unprotected status of the new reports, the Court explained what the defendant did wrong:

> Stripped of all disguises, the [acts of defendant] amounts to an unauthorized interference with the normal operation of complainant's legitimate business precisely at the point where the profit is to be reaped, in order to divert a material portion of the profit from those who have earned it to those who have not; with special advantage to defendant in the competition because of the fact that it is not burdened with any part of the expense of gathering the news.[106]

As later refined in the case of *National Basketball Association v Motorola, Inc.*, an *INS* claim requires proof that: (1) plaintiff gathers information at a cost; (2) the information is time sensitive; (3) defendant's use of the information constitutes free-riding; (4) defendant is in direct competition with plaintiff; and (5) the ability of others to free-ride on plaintiff's information would reduce plaintiff's incentives to compile the information.[107]

As another example of an information-related independent wrong that is not dependent on the IP status of information, consider the case of identity theft. At its very basic, identity theft is the use of someone else's personally identifiable information without permission.[108] Although some of this information may be private in the sense that it is not generally known or disseminated, much of it may be publicly available. Although publicly available personally identifiable information (such as one's address and phone number) is unlikely to be protected under copyright, trade secret or contract law, there are few people who would consider the use of such information to be proper if it is for the wrongful purpose of assuming someone else's identity. However,

104 Id. at 393, emphasis added.

105 248 U.S. 215 (1918).

106 Id. at 240.

107 105 F. 3d 841 (2nd Cir. 1997); see also Gordon, Wendy J. (1992), 'Asymetric Market Failure and Prisoner's Dilemma in Intellectual Property', 17 *U. Dayton L. Rev.* 853, 863–65 (elaborating on the essential features of the *INS* tort from an economic perspective).

108 See for example, 18 U.S.C. § 1028: see also Jasper, Margaret C. (2006), *Identity Theft and How to Protect Yourself*, 2nd edn., (Oceana Pubs.) Appendix 15 (providing a list of US state laws prohibiting identity theft.).

the fact that the same information can be collected, organized, and sold by multiple database brokers also suggests that there are circumstances where the unauthorized use of personally identifiable information is not troubling enough to require a legal sanction.[109] The reason that remedies are provided in one situation and not in the other is because a wrong can be articulated that is not solely dependent on the nature of the information; rather, the wrong is principally dependent upon the commission of an intentional act that is deemed by policy makers to be tortious or criminal.

Based upon the foregoing, the key to solving the third party problem under existing third party tort theories is for the information industry to identify an intentional act that third parties are engaging in which should be deemed tortious. This, of course, is the appeal of a property characterization; it is easy to label an action as tortious when it involves the unauthorized use of someone else's property. However, in light of the limits that exist on the property aspects of information, the claim of wrongdoing is unsupportable without more. Again, borrowing from the language of *Della Penna*, the third party must have engaged in conduct that was wrongful by some legal measure other than an interference with a property right.[110] Or, in the parlance of US copyright law, the information industry must articulate 'extra elements' that make the actions of the third party different from copyright infringement.[111]

Articulating what the third party users of unprotected, publicly available information have done wrong is a difficult task. Consistent with the nature of tort law, the wrongfulness of a third party's actions will, in the final analysis, depend on what the third party did and why he did it; that is, it will require a very fact-specific inquiry. Before the particular facts of a case reveal themselves, however, it is possible to hypothesize about the types of activities that might give rise to liability.[112]

---

[109] In many cases where identity theft has been deemed a wrong, we have chosen to make the wrong punishable as a crime instead of providing for a civil action. Id.

[110] *Della Penna v Toyota Motor Sales, U.S.A., Inc.*, 11 Cal. 4th 376, 393.

[111] See for example, *Data Gen. Corp. v Grumman Sys. Support Corp.*, 36 F. 3d. 1147, 1164 (1st Cir. 1994); *Dun & Bradstreet Software Servs. v Grace Consulting, Inc.*, 307 F. 3d 197 (3rd 2002); *Trandes Corp. v Guy F. Atkinson Co.*, 996 F. 2d 655, 660 (4th Cir. 1993).

[112] As detailed by Jerome Reichman and Pamela Samuelson, courts might consider a number of 'market-oriented criteria' to determine if a third party's actions are wrongful. These include: (1) the quantum of data appropriated by the third party; (2) the nature of the data appropriated; (3) the purpose for which the third party appropriated the data; (4) the degree of investment initially required to bring that data into being; (5) the degree of dependence or independence of the third party's own development effort and the substantiality of his investment in such efforts; (6) the degree of similarity between the contents of the database and a product developed by the third party; (7) the proximity of the markets in which the database owner and the third party

First, there is the question of how the information was acquired. If a third party comes to possess unprotected information honestly (that is, it was not acquired by bribery, theft, or electronic espionage), then he should not be punished for the mere possession of such information. If the information was acquired improperly, for instance through theft or artifice, then the act of acquisition might be punished in some fashion even if the information is otherwise unprotected by copyright, trade secret or contract law.

Secondly, there is the question of how the third party has used or disseminated the information. For instance, there may be something improper with the way the information is labeled or presented by the third party. If the third party claims to have compiled and verified the information, when in fact it was compiled by another or was not verified, then claims for fraud and misrepresentation might be made. To the extent the information contains the trademarks or other markings of the plaintiff, an argument might also be made that the distribution of the information by the third party resulted in trademark infringement of trade disparagement.[113]

Thirdly, there may be some wrong that arises from the nature of the relationship between the second-party defendant (that is, a rightful recipient of the information) and the third party.[114] For instance, perhaps there is an express or implied duty of confidentiality that the third party owes to the second party that would make it reasonable to impose liability on the third party. This, of course, would be very similar to the action against knowledgeable third party's that is set forth in the UTSA,[115] so the challenge would be to explain what the wrong is when the information is not protected by trade secret law. Perhaps the requisite duty would arise with respect to such information only if the relationship was in the nature of a trust or fiduciary relationship.

Fourthly, although the intellectual property status of the information is irrelevant because this analysis assumes the subject information is not protected by intellectual property law, the nature and character of the information might still be important in determining if the actions of a third party should give rise to a new intentional tort. As noted in *INS*, there is something wrong with direct competitors using time-sensitive information within a short period of time after it is initially released to the public.[116] Perhaps there are

are operating; and (8) how quickly the user was able to come into the market. Reichman and Samuelson, 'Intellectual Property Rights in Data?', 50 *Vand. L. Rev.* 51, 142–143.

113 See for example, *Dastar Crop. v Twentieth Century Fox film Corp.*, 539 U.S. 23 (2003).

114 In this regard, this article assumes that there is no direct relationship between the information owner and the third party.

115 *Supra* note 62 accompanying text.

116 *Supra* note 106.

other sub-classes of information that are deserving of special protection akin to that provided to time sensitive information.

Finally, and perhaps most importantly, the motives of the third party must be considered. Generally, the more egregious the activities of the third party, and the greater the specific intent to cause harm, the more willing policy makers are to recognize new intentional torts.[117] Under principles of unfair competition, however, there is a privilege to compete,[118] so the required motive should be different from a desire to beat a competitor in the marketplace.

CONCLUSION

If an information owner does not have a viable copyright, trade secret or contract claim against a party who is alleged to wrongfully possess or use his information, he must rely upon tort law for a potential solution.[119] By reviewing existing theories of third party liability under tort law, this chapter has demonstrated that, in the absence of a legislative decision to extend greater protection to information, the best option for the information industry is to fashion arguments that focus, not on the character of the information that is sought to be protected, but on the 'independent wrongful acts' of the third party defendant. In light of the limits that are placed upon the scope of intellectual property rights, the classification of information as a form of personal property does not matter; what matters is convincing policy makers that the particular manner in which a third party has acquired, disclosed or used unprotected publicly available information should not be condoned in a civil society.

---

[117] *Prosser on Torts*, §7, p. 30 ('There is a definite tendency to impose greater responsibility upon a defendant whose conduct has been intended to do harm, or is morally wrong. More liberal rules are applied as to the consequences for which he will be held liable . . .').

[118] See generally Restatement (Third) of the Law of Unfair Competition, § 1, *General Principles*, 'The Freedom to Compete'. (ALI 1995).

[119] See Epstein, 'Rebuilding the Citadel', *Exploring Tort Law*, Chapter Seven, pp. 240–242 (discussing the tort/contract divide).

10. The componentization of information

Kristen Osenga*

INTRODUCTION

Information is 'the oxygen of the modern age'.[1] Despite its importance, or perhaps because of it, conventional wisdom has long been of the view that information wants to, or even needs to, be free. This idea has been extended to encompass not just raw data, but also information products such as databases and software. These products – products whose primary value lies in organizing, providing context, and distributing information content – have often been the subject of debate over whether and to what extent these works should be protected. The tension between information being free and information products being protected is particularly acute in our technological society, where computers and the Internet have made the collection, storage,

* Associate Professor, University of Richmond School of Law.

For a full discussion of the ideas presented in this chapter, see 'Information May Want to Be Free, But Information Products Do Not: Protecting and Facilitating Transactions in Information Products', 30 *Cardozo Law Review* 101 (2009).

I would like to specifically thank Justin Hughes, Tom Cotter, Jay Kesan, Jim Gibson, and Corinna Lain for their thoughtful and detailed comments on this chapter. I am also grateful to the participants at the George Washington/Software and Information Industry Association conference '*Feist*, Facts, and Function: IP Protection for Works Beyond Entertainment'; the Intellectual Property Scholars Conference at DePaul University College of Law; the Intellectual Property & Communications Law and Policy Scholars Roundtable at Michigan State University College of Law; the Southeastern Association of Law Schools annual meeting; and Faculty Colloquia at the University of Emory School of Law and the University of Richmond School of Law for their comments at the earlier stages of this manuscript. Finally, I appreciate the excellent research assistance provided by Jennifer Jones. Comments are welcome at kosenga@richmond.edu.

1 See Ronald Reagan, *Guardian* (14 June 1989). In less dramatic fashion, information has also been called 'one of the nation's most critical economic resources'. See *Information Infrastructure Task Force, National Information Infrastructure Agenda for Action* 7 (1993) (quoted in Yu, Peter K. (2008), 'The Political Economy of Data Protection' at 2 (available at http://ssrn.com/abstract=1046781, 83 *Chicago Kent L. Rev.*); Boyle, James (1996), *Shamans, Software, and Spleens: Law and the Construction of the Information Society* 2 (Harvard University Press).

management, delivery, reproduction, and transfer of enormous quantities of data as simple as clicking a mouse button or typing a keystroke.[2] Even print compilations of information can be easily transformed into digital format using today's technology.[3]

Yet while the combination of ever-improving technology and ever-increasing access to and availability of information creates low barriers to entry into the information product market, it also facilitates misappropriation of these works. It is natural for creators of these goods to seek some form of protection to inhibit misappropriation and allow recoupment of investments made in the creation of these information products. For the most part though, traditional intellectual property law has failed to provide this protection. Copyright law specifically prohibits protection of ideas and facts; patent law, while not particularly excluding information products, has been generally, and increasingly, held by the courts to not extend to these works. To fill the void left by intellectual property law, producers of information products have resorted to other legal and non-legal mechanisms to prevent misappropriation of their works. These alternative constraints, however, shift the decisions of access and control to private parties who may not honor the public welfare goals of intellectual property law, such as disclosure and fair use.[4] As a result, instead of information qua information products being free, it is often effectively more propertized than it would have been under a traditional intellectual property scheme.

Although protection for information products was debated long before the products were widely electronic, the issue has taken on renewed importance as these products become increasingly ubiquitous. The primary argument advanced by proponents in this debate is that protection is necessary to provide incentives to a creator to produce the protected work.[5] The exclusive rights provided by most protection schemes afford the creator an artificial lead-time to exploit his creation and potentially recoup costs sunk into developing the product. Proponents argue that information products, maybe more so

---

[2] See Reichman, J.H. and Pamela Samuelson (1997), 'Intellectual Property Rights in Data?', 50 *Vand. L. Rev.* 51, 64–5.

[3] See id. at 67. As true as this statement was in 1997, in the decade that has passed since Reichman and Samuelson published their article, the advances in technology have increased exponentially.

[4] See Burk, Dan L. and Julie E. Cohen (2001), 'Fair Use Infrastructure for Rights Management Systems', 15 *Harv. J. Law & Tech.* 41, 51.

[5] See, for example, Lemley, Mark A. (1997), 'The Economics of Improvement in Intellectual Property Law', 75 *Tex. L. Rev.* 989, 993 ('Intellectual property law is fundamentally about incentives to invent and create. While there are a number of noneconomic theories offered to explain both copyright and patent law, both the United States Constitution and judicial decisions seem to acknowledge the primacy of incentive theory in justifying intellectual property.').

than other works, require some grant of exclusivity to support optimal creation, because the costs of developing an information product are typically front-loaded and the costs of appropriating, duplicating, and transmitting an existent information product are typically low. On the other hand, there are two main arguments advanced by those opposed to protection: first, that information has to be free, and secondly, that even in an environment of uncertain protection, information products are being produced. As to the first, most information is presumptively free for use so long as it is acquired fairly.[6] Information is often considered to be part of the public domain, free for anyone to access and use, and further considered to be 'the building block of knowledge' and 'a cardinal element in securing competition in a free market economy'.[7] As to the second, commentators opposed to protection for information products argue that it is speculative, at best, to presume that creators of these works require such incentive.[8]

Regardless of the merits of the debate, up to now, the decision has been seen as binary – either there should be protection or there should not be. This simplistic view, however, neglects an important facet of reality: the absence of protection does not guarantee that information will be free. In fact, evidence suggests that information products are routinely covered by other, more onerous, protection mechanisms that prohibit uses of information that traditional intellectual property protection would permit.[9] The fact that producers of these works are relying on alternative protection schemes remove much credibility from the second oppositional argument discussed above: the fact that information products may be flourishing in the absence of intellectual property protection is not the same as flourishing in the absence of *any* protection.

The incentive to produce these works is instead found in whatever other protective means the creators can wrangle to obtain at least the perception of exclusivity, but these alternate means lack the oversight and safety valves that can be implemented in an intellectual property scheme.[10] This scheme of

---

6 See Zimmerman, Diane Leenheer (1992), 'Information as Speech, Information as Goods: Some Thoughts on Marketplaces and the Bill of Rights', 35 *Wm. & Mary L. Rev.* 665, 665.

7 See Bitton, Miriam (2006), 'A New Outlook on the Economic Dimension of the Database Protection Debate', 47 *IDEA* 93, 100.

8 See Eisenberg, Rebecca S. (2002), 'Patents on DNA Sequences: Molecules and Information', in N. Elkin-Koren and N.W. Netanel, eds *The Commodification of Information* 417, 430.

9 See, for example, Lipton, Jacqueline (2006), 'Information Property: Rights & Responsibilities', 56 *Fla. L. Rev.* 135, 144; *Bowers v Baystate Techs., Inc.* 320 F.3d 1317 (Fed. Cir. 2003); *ProCD, Inc. v Zeidenberg*, 86 F.3d 1447 (7th Cir. 1996).

10 See generally Lipton, Jacqueline (2003), 'Balancing Private Rights & Public Policies: Reconceptualizing Property in Databases', 18 *Berkeley Tech. L.J.* 773.

incomplete protection under intellectual property laws and potential over-reaching protection under a patchwork quilt of alternate means leads to a system with unclearly defined coverage and rights. In turn, this further hampers the flow of information because the increased protection obtained by the creator comes at the expense of increased transaction costs for disseminating the work[11] and difficulties in negotiating access and use of the information products.[12]

What is needed is a different approach, one that appreciates the value added to raw information when it is included in an information product while preserving, and perhaps enhancing, the free flow of the information itself. This scheme needs to provide a well-defined system of rights in information products to both encourage creation of these works and facilitate transactions related to access and use of the products, and yet be flexible enough to ensure that innovation is not stifled because the necessary information has become propertized. The proposal outlined below considers information products that have both information components that typically remove these works from protection and structural components that add value to the information components by organizing the data, providing context to the data, and facilitating distribution of the data in a useful fashion. The proposed scheme uses these components to clearly define the boundaries of the works and protection, as well as requirements for and appropriate levels of protection for these works.

Section I discusses the current state of protection available for information products under the traditional intellectual property regimes of patent and copyright law. I conclude that neither of these systems sufficiently covers information products; indeed, these laws expressly exclude most of these works from protection. Section II describes alternative protection schemes that have been applied to information products in the absence of intellectual property protection, ranging from non-intellectual-property legal schemes to alternative non-legal mechanisms, as well as a number of legislative and academic proposals directed towards the protection of information products. I critique the inability of these means to provide adequate protection without over-reaching. Section III explains the advantages of providing protection for information products and proposes a *sui generis* protection scheme that addresses the concerns previously discussed while still permitting a creator of information products to reap some benefits for his investment in the work. The resulting scheme avoids over-reaching while still providing the advantages that accrue in protecting information products. Further, by clarifying the boundaries of

---

11 See Siebrasse, Norman (2001), 'A Property Rights Theory of the Limits of Copyright', 51 *Univ. of Toronto L.J.* 1, 10–11.

12 See id. at 56–57.

protection and implementing a liability-type regime, the scheme facilitates transactions in information products and may actually promote the free flow of information.

I. INTELLECTUAL PROPERTY COVERAGE FOR INFORMATION PRODUCTS IS INSUFFICIENT

Although the debate about whether information products should be protected remains, reviewing the current state of protection for these works demonstrates that a new scheme is required. Quite naturally, the first sources to examine for the protection for new, innovative, or creative works are the traditional intellectual property regimes – namely patent law and copyright law. Neither of these regimes, however, provides adequate coverage for information products and, in fact, they actually exclude many of these works from protection in whole or in part.

A. Patent Law

A patent provides an inventor an exclusive right over his invention for a period of 20 years from the filing of an application for patent.[13] For a patent to be granted, the patent application must describe a new, useful, and non-obvious invention in sufficient detail to permit a person of ordinary skill in the art to practice the invention based on that description.[14] Patents are granted on a wide range of inventions, and statutory subject matter for patenting includes processes, machines, manufactures, or compositions of matter.[15] While these categories are generally broad enough to cover nearly every imaginable invention, there are three judicially-created exceptions to works that otherwise fall into these categories.[16] Abstract ideas, laws of nature, and natural phenomena may not be patented.[17]

Although neither the statutory provisions nor the interpreting case law explicitly excludes information,[18] information products have been barred from patent protection based on a number of theories. First, some information products, such as databases, do not fit comfortably within any of the enumerated

---

13 35 U.S.C. § 154(a).

14 The requirements for patentability of an invention are provided by 35 U.S.C. §§ 101, 102, 103, and 112.

15 35 U.S.C. § 101.

16 See, for example, *Diamond v Chakrabarty*, 447 U.S. 303, 309 (1980).

17 See id.

18 See Eisenberg, *supra* note 8, at 419.

statutory categories (process, machine, manufacture, or article of composition). In the same vein, case law has long excepted information products under the 'printed matter doctrine', which presumes that printed articles are excluded from patent eligibility.[19] The printed matter doctrine has been updated for today's technology to prohibit patenting of storage media including information, where the stored information represents the only new or inventive portion.[20] Secondly, even if the information product falls within one of the four statutory categories, it may fall within one of the judicially-created exceptions to patent eligible subject matter – abstract idea, law of nature, and natural phenomena. For example, in early case law, software was denied patent protection because courts considered the invention to be simply an abstract idea.[21] At other times, because the software included an algorithm or equation that described the natural world, the work was held to be unpatentable because it fell within the law of nature exception.[22] In the last few decades, it has been unquestioned that software inventions are eligible for patenting, but recent administrative and legal decisions indicate that the unquestioned patentability of these works may be ending, based in part on a revival of the abstract idea rejection.[23] Thirdly, there is a policy argument against the patenting of information. Patents are granted on the basis of a bargain between the patentee and the public, granting the inventor a limited-time exclusionary right in a tangible application of an invention in exchange for free disclosure of information to the public about the invention.[24] In the case of information products, because the work often does not provide any new disclosure to the public, the patent bargain becomes less attractive to the public.[25] Thus, at best, patent protection for information products is incomplete and uncertain; at worst, patent protection for information products simply does not exist and is considered inappropriate.

B. Copyright Law

Protection under copyright law grants exclusive rights to creators of original expressive works.[26] The rights generally attach when the work is created and

---

19 See, for example, *In re Sterling*, 70 F.2d 910, 912 (CCPA 1934).

20 See, for example, *In re Nuijten*, 2006-1371 (Fed. Cir. 2007) (Linn, J. dissenting) at 15.

21 See, for example, *Gottschalk v Benson*, 409 U.S. 63 (1972).

22 See, for example, *Parker v Flook*, 437 U.S. 584 (1978).

23 I have written elsewhere about the unfortunate revival of abstract idea rejections of software inventions. See Osenga, Kristen 'Ants, Elephant Guns, and Statutory Subject Matter', 39 *Arizona St. L.J.* 1087 (Winter 2007).

24 See Eisenberg, *supra* note 8, at 425.

25 See Eisenberg, *supra* note 8, at 427.

26 17 U.S.C. §§ 102(a), 106.

last for a period of the life of the author plus 70 years.[27] Similar to patent law, however, copyright protection is generally unavailable for information products for many reasons. First, although the list of statutory categories of works for which copyright protection is available is fairly extensive and quite inclusive, bare information has been explicitly excluded from copyright protection under a doctrine known as the idea/expression dichotomy, codified at § 102(b) of the Copyright Act: '[I]n no case does copyright protection for an original work of authorship extend to any idea, procedure, process, system, method of operation, concept, principle or discovery'.[28]

Secondly, both information and information products have failed to qualify for protection under the originality doctrine, which states only original works of authorship are eligible for protection, where originality is demonstrated by a work that is independently created by its author and demonstrates a minimal level of creativity.[29] Although the threshold of originality is quite low, the courts have largely defined the requirement in the negative, describing what will not suffice to obtain protection, with facts uniformly being found deficient.[30]

Thirdly, information products will most often be considered 'compilations'[31] and will likely fail the originality requirement associated with that type of work. Although the compilation may include pre-existing materials or data, the originality requirement is met only when the selection, coordination, or arrangement of the information meets the threshold of originality.[32] Even if a particular information product meets this requirement, the protection is quite weak; for these works, the underlying data 'may be freely copied because copyright protects only the elements that owe their origin to the compiler – the selection, coordination, and arrangement of facts'.[33]

Both the idea/expression dichotomy and the originality requirement (generally and with respect to compilations) serve to facilitate a balance between encouraging creativity on one hand and permitting access to information and

---

[27] 17 U.S.C. § 302(a).

[28] 17 U.S.C. § 102(b).

[29] See *Feist Publications, Inc. v Rural Telephone Serv. Co.*, 499 U.S. 340, 358 (1991) (noting that 'facts are never original').

[30] Shipley, David E. (2007), 'Thin But Not Anorexic: Copyright Protection for Compilations and Other Fact Works', 15 *J. Intell. Prop. L.* 91, 93. At least one commentator has argued that not all facts are created equal and that 'created facts' may be sufficiently original to satisfy the originality requirement. See Hughes, Justin (2007), 'Created Facts and the Flawed Ontology of Copyright Law', 83 *Notre Dame L. Rev.* 43, 59.

[31] 17 U.S.C. § 101.

[32] See id.

[33] See *Feist*, 499 U.S. at 359.

ideas on the other.[34] To reach this sense of balance, copyright law even grants partial property rights, extending protection to the 'form in which the author has chosen to cast her thoughts or concepts and not to the thoughts or concepts themselves',[35] thereby leaving the information free from protection. Finally, the idea/expression dichotomy ensures that copyright, generally, is completely consistent with the First Amendment's requirement that information be generally free.[36]

A primary difficulty in applying the doctrines of idea/expression and originality, however, comes in determining how to categorize information: Which portion of a work is unprotectable idea and which portion is protectable expression? What portion of a compilation represents originality of selection, coordination, or arrangement?[37] For works other than information products, the line between idea and expression is often easy to draw – either the expression is the whole creation, as in the case of a fiction novel, or the expression can be distinguished clearly from the idea, as in the case of a household ornament.[38] Information products, however, typically reside at some point at or near the division between idea and expression, or may even encompass both in a non-severable fashion.[39]

While copyright law may have initially, albeit superficially, seemed hospitable to protecting information products, the courts have squarely addressed both the idea/expression dichotomy and the originality requirement for the two primary types of information products – databases and software – and have concluded that any protection under copyright is quite limited. The originality requirement as applied to compilations, such as databases, is set forth in the Supreme Court's *Feist Publications v Rural Telephone Service Co.*[40] opinion; the dividing line between idea and expression in software works is explored by the Second Circuit in *Computer Associates International v Altai, Inc.*[41]

From the *Feist* case, which involved telephone white pages, the Supreme Court provided the following analysis with respect to copyright protection for databases: (1) facts are not independently eligible for copyright; (2) that facts are compiled by industrious collection or sweat of the brow does not alter the

---

34 See Boyle, *supra* note 1, at 56–57.
35 See Zimmerman, *supra* note 6, at 666.
36 See id. at 669.
37 See id. at 668–69.
38 See Dreyfuss, Rochelle Cooper (1988), 'Information Products: A Challenge to Intellectual Property Theory', 20 *N.Y.U. J. Int'l L. & Pol.* 897, 903.
39 See id. at 904.
40 499 U.S. 340 (1991).
41 982 F.2d 693 (2d Cir. 1992).

non-copyrightable nature of the facts; and (3) collections of facts (and databases generally) become eligible for copyright protection only through a showing of creativity in the unique or original selection, coordination, or arrangement of the facts.[42] Court opinions subsequent to *Feist* demonstrate that this burden of originality often keeps factual compilations from copyright protection.[43] Various, seemingly useful, databases, such as specialized yellow pages, catalog numbers for parts, data about collectibles or car values, and classifications and taxonomies, have all been denied protection.[44] To avoid falling outside the scope of copyright protection, database owners have sought to qualify for copyright protection by injecting arbitrary creativity into the selection and arrangement of facts in their databases.[45] Unfortunately, in doing so, the database creator is often decreasing the product's utility, which derives value from having a comprehensive (albeit obvious) selection of facts provided in an easy to use (but unoriginal) arrangement.[46] Thus, for many databases, an important category of information products, copyright protection is simply not available.

The scope of protection for computer programs has similarly provided courts with the opportunity to clarify the application of the idea/expression dichotomy. Much software appears to encompass expressive features (for example, in the visual portions or graphical user interfaces) as well as idea or functional features (for example, the working algorithms that drive the program's behavior). Underlying both of these outwardly visible features is the code itself, the computer language that instantiates both the expressive and functional aspects that are apparent to a user of the program. Computer code itself has been found to include both idea and expression components as well.[47] Thus, the answer to the question of whether software is a copyrightable expression or a non-copyrightable (and potentially patentable) functional idea is both.[48] It is determining the placement of this line between functional ideas and creative expression that creates difficulty in obtaining copyright protection for software.

In the *Altai* case, the Second Circuit attempted to solve this difficulty and determine what portion of software is covered by copyright protection; the

---

42 See *Feist*, 499 U.S. at 358.

43 See Shipley, *supra* note 30, at 99.

44 See id.

45 See Gibson, James (2004), 'Re-Reifying Data', 80 *Notre Dame L. Rev* 163, 181 (2004).

46 See Shipley, *supra* note 30, at 130.

47 See Samuelson, Pamela et al., (1994), 'A Manifesto Concerning the Legal Protection of Computer Programs', 94 *Colum. L. Rev.* 2308, 2310.

48 See Madison, Michael J. (2005), 'Law as Design: Objects, Concepts, and Digital Things', 56 *Case W. Res. L. Rev.* 381, 414.

result of this attempt is the widely adopted, yet difficult to apply 'abstraction-filtration-comparison' test.[49] Both the district court and the Second Circuit struggled to apply traditional copyright law to computer programs. The district court recognized computer software has two aspects – a static structure, which is the text of the code and the arrangement of the instructions, and a dynamic structure, which is the way the program runs and reacts to user inputs.[50] Because the court determined that the dynamic component is simply a process or idea and thus can not protected by copyright law, the court analyzed only the static, source code, portion of the software at issue, and found no infringement.[51]

On appeal, the Second Circuit did not limit its review to only the static portion of the software, but held instead that some non-literal structures of computer programs may be protected by copyright to prevent the clever infringer from merely rewriting the code to avoid liability;[52] the difficulty is in deciding which elements are eligible, leading the court to develop the abstraction-filtration-comparison test. In applying the test, a court is to first 'dissect the allegedly copied program's structure and isolate each level of abstraction contained within it'.[53] Next, the court determines whether the inclusion of each level of abstraction 'was idea or dictated by considerations of efficiency, so as to be necessarily incidental to that idea; required by factors external to the program itself; or taken from the public domain'.[54] The components required by idea or efficiency are not eligible for copyright protection; the remaining, expressive portions are protectable and, as the last step of the *Altai* test, are compared with the corresponding portion of the allegedly infringing product to determine infringement.[55]

The first step, isolating levels of abstraction, represented an important acknowledgement that software exists on many levels and that the idea/expression dichotomy may be relevant at each of these levels.[56] However, the second step of filtering out idea and expression at each level is much more

---

49 See, for example, Mtima, Lateef (2007), 'So Dark the CON(TU) of Man: The Quest for Software Derivative Work right in Section 117', 69 *U. Pitt. L. Rev.* 23, 95 n. 226.

50 See *Computer Assocs. Int'l v Altai, Inc.*, 775 F.Supp. 544, 560 (E.D.N.Y. 1991) ('*Altai I*').

51 See *Altai I*, 775 F.Supp. at 560.

52 See *Altai*, 982 F.2d at 706.

53 See id. at 707.

54 See id.

55 See id. at 710.

56 See, for example, Isztwan, Andrew G. (1993), 'Computer Associates International v Altai, Inc.: Protecting the Structure of Computer Software in the Second Circuit', 59 *Brooklyn L. Rev.* 423, 448–9.

difficult to apply and has been quite controversial.[57] In any case, it is clear that copyright protection does not extend to many of the more important, functional aspects of computer programs. Thus, as with databases, the more useful portions or embodiments of software lie beyond the protection of copyright law.

Even if an information product, such as a database or software program, was found to meet both the requirements of originality and expressiveness discussed above, there is a third doctrine in copyright law – fair use – that could easily decimate any protection obtained. Fair use is a defense to copyright infringement that essentially allows, in certain circumstances, unauthorized use by someone other than the copyright owner.[58] Although it began as a judicially created doctrine, fair use has been codified and applies to all copyrighted works.[59] It has particular applicability to databases and software and likely eviscerates any protection that may otherwise be available.

II. WHY ALTERNATIVE LEGAL AND NON-LEGAL MECHANISMS DO NOT WORK

In the absence of traditional intellectual property protection under either patent law or copyright law, creators of information products have sought various alternative legal and non-legal mechanisms to provide some manner of exclusivity in which to reap a benefit from their development investments. Legal theories advanced include quasi-intellectual property doctrines, such as liability under trade secret and misappropriation, as well as non-intellectual property

---

57 See, for example, Chon, Margaret (1993), 'Post Modern "Progress": Reconsidering the Copyright and Patent Power', 43 *DePaul L. Rev.* 97, 112; Perdue, Mark D. and Robert A. Felsman (1996), 'Recent Developments in Copyright Law', 4 *Tex. Intell. Prop. L.J.* 459, 469.

58 See Denicola, Robert C. (1981), 'Copyright in Collections of Facts: A Theory for the Protection of Nonfiction Literary Works', 81 *Colum. L. Rev.* 516, 524 (defining fair use as a 'privilege in others than the owner of a copyright to use the copyrighted material in a reasonable manner without his consent, notwithstanding the monopoly granted to the owner by the copyright.').

59 See 17 U.S.C. § 107. The fair use analysis is based on four non-determinative factors: (1) the purpose and character of the use, including whether such use is of a commercial nature or is for nonprofit educational purposes; (2) the nature of the copyrighted work; (3) the amount and substantiality of the portion used in relation to the copyrighted work as a whole; and (4) the effect of the use upon the potential market for or value of the copyrighted work. The second factor, the nature of the work, nearly always weighs against the creators of databases and computer programs because these works already reside at the margin of copyright coverage due to their information content.

claims in contract and trespass, among others. Non-legal options have included using technological or operational mechanisms that provide some measure of exclusivity, or at least some sort of artificial lead-time, to the creator of the information product. As appealing as these options may seem, they each have one or more significant flaws – most yield incomplete coverage, some are unlikely to withstand judicial scrutiny, some are difficult to apply on a large scale, and all fail to provide the oversight and safety valves that are essential in traditional intellectual property regimes. As a result, resort to these mechanisms leads to both overprotection and under-protection of information products.

A. Trade Secret Protection

Trade secret protection is often considered an auxiliary to the traditional intellectual property regimes and so would seem to be a natural next choice for an information product's creator seeking to protect his investment. Trade secret protection, a state law mechanism, generally covers valuable or commercial information to the extent that information is kept secret.[60] However, many information products derive some or all of their value from the fact that the information can be used publicly, and thus these works are not eligible for trade secret protection. Also, because trade secret protection arises from state law, there may be variations from state to state that make enforcement more costly or difficult.[61] Finally, as a matter of policy, trade secret law is typically disfavored because it actually inhibits, rather than promotes, the flow of information via the disclosure or dissemination encouraged by the traditional intellectual property regimes.[62] As such, even if trade secret coverage is available

---

60 See, for example, *Ruckelshaus v Monsanto Co.*, 467 U.S. 986, 1001–02 (1984) (defining a trade secret as 'information which is used in one's business, and which gives him an opportunity to obtain an advantage over competitors who do not know or use it . . . the extent of the property right therein is defined by the extent to which the owner of the secret protects his interest from disclosure to others'); Bagley, Constance E. and Gavin Clarkson (2003), 'Adverse Possession for Intellectual Property: Adapting an Ancient Concept to Resolve Conflicts between Antitrust and Intellectual Property Laws in the Information Age', 16 *Harv. J. L. & Tech.* 327, 332. Know-how protection, a contractual agreement to share information, is similar in that it too relies on the secrecy value of the information and is governed by state law. See, for example, Reichman, J.H. (1994), 'Legal Hybrids Between the Patent and Copyright Paradigms', 94 *Colum. L. Rev.* 2432, 2454.

61 Many states (specifically 42 states and the District of Columbia by 1999) however, have based their trade secret laws around the Uniform Trade Secrets Act so the variations may be insignificant. See Bagley and Clarkson, *supra* note 60, at 332.

62 See, for example, Katopis, Chris J. (1997), 'Patients v Patents?: Policy Implications of Recent Patent Legislation', 71 *St. John's L. Rev.* 329, 378.

for information products and the differences in the laws across the various states are insignificant, trade secret protection is inappropriate because it lacks the safety valve of disclosure.

B. Misappropriation

The misappropriation doctrine, which prohibits the unauthorized taking of another's works, has also been used as a mechanism for protecting products where other intellectual property regimes do not seem to apply,[63] as is the case with many information products. It was in precisely this circumstance that the Supreme Court gave life to the doctrine in *International News Service v The Associated Press* case.[64] International News Service (INS) obtained over wire service many news stories that had been gathered and prepared by the Associated Press (AP) and published the stories before AP could.[65] The news stories prepared by AP were not eligible for intellectual property protection because the works failed to meet the originality and expression requirements.[66] Further, the news stories were not subject to trade secret protection because the stories had not been kept secret.[67] Yet, the Court upheld an injunction against INS, prohibiting it from using AP's news bulletins in this way, basing the liability of INS on the notion of misappropriation.[68] This expanded liability for misappropriation, however, was limited to 'hot news' and may have signaled discomfort with the result.[69] More recent cases applying the misappropriation doctrine have reinforced and heightened the 'hot news' limitation.[70] Although the 'hot news' requirement serves as a safety valve to limit the scope of misappropriation coverage, it also limits the ability of the doctrine to provide adequate protection for the majority of information products, which often include information beyond merely 'hot news'.

---

63 See Brill, Charles (1998), 'Legal Protection of Collections of Facts', *Comp. L. Rev. & Tech. J.* 1, 20.

64 284 U.S. 215 (1918).

65 See id.

66 In particular, the Court would not credit AP with ownership of the news simply because AP happened to report it, nor could AP claim copyright because INS was not simply taking AP's expression, but rather using the unprotectable facts. See id. at 234–37.

67 See id.

68 See id.

69 See Zimmerman, *supra* note 6, at 721.

70 See, for example, *Nat'l Basketball Assoc. v Motorola Inc.*, 105 F.3d 841 (1997) (applying an *INS v AP* analysis and requiring a quite narrow 'hot news' component to avoid preemption by copyright laws).

C. Contract

Because traditional intellectual property regimes, as well as the schemes like trade secrets and misappropriation that have developed at the margins of intellectual property, fail to provide sufficient protection for information products, creators of these works often turn to other legal means, like contract, to limit the use (or misuse) of the products. Databases and software in particular have often found protection via contract and have been subject to both negotiated and shrink-wrap licenses.[71] Where a negotiated contract involves the usual agreement between the two participating parties, shrinkwrap licenses typically go into force when the customer opens the packaging that encloses the product, even though the customer may not actually get to review the terms of the license until after it has already been entered and the customer certainly did not take part in negotiating the terms.[72] Although the validity of shrinkwrap licenses has been questioned, they have uniformly been found valid and enforceable.[73]

Contract law certainly provides an appealing alternative to traditional intellectual property protection. Like intellectual property regimes, contracts carry the force of law. Businesses are comfortable and familiar with contracts, probably even more so than intellectual property. Further, contracts can be written to restrict virtually any legal behavior. And above all, shrinkwrap licenses, as are common in the information product industry, permit a one-sided determination by the creator of what types of access and use are permissible.

Despite this allure, however, there are disadvantages to using contract law to protect information products. The first disadvantage is that effective use of contract law may be difficult in practice for a number of reasons. While contractual protection may be useful for information products used by a small number of consumers, it may become unwieldy to actually police and enforce as the number of users grows.[74] Also, because of the easily transferable nature of information products, the enforceability of the contractual provisions may be compromised because contract terms can only be enforced against parties in privity; once the information product is released to a non-associated third party, there is no recourse against that third party who was not privy to the

---

71 See Brill, *supra* note 63, at 24.

72 See generally, Lemley, Mark A. (1995), 'Intellectual Property and Shrinkwrap Licenses', 68 *S. Cal. L. Rev.* 1239; Lipton, Jacqueline D. (2006), 'IP's Problem Child: Shifting the Paradigms for Software Protection', 58 *Hastings L.J.* 205, 221 n. 96 (2006).

73 See id. See also *ProCD Inc. v Zeidenberg*, 86 F.3d 1447 (7th Cir. 1996).

74 See Brill, *supra* note 63, at 25.

contract.[75] Further, because contract law is a state law creation, it is not uniform domestically and contracts are difficult, if not impossible, to enforce globally.[76] The second disadvantage is that contract law provides little or no oversight or safety valves and thus allows protection of information beyond the scope that may be deemed acceptable by the public. Because of the importance of freely flowing information, a protection scheme such as contract that permits the creator great latitude in keeping information from being used is not an acceptable protection scheme.

D. Trespass to Chattels

Although trade secret, misappropriation, and contract law have been the primary non-intellectual property legal sources used to protect information products, some courts have taken far more creative approaches to craft what they consider fair resolution in cases of misappropriation of information products. One such approach is trespass to chattels.[77] Generally speaking, this tort involves the unauthorized interference with or use of another's personal property that results in damage.[78] One court stretched this doctrine to apply to a situation where a 'web crawler' program was systematically obtaining auction information from websites.[79] Although the unauthorized interference or use was clear, the requisite damage was not; rather the court based its reasoning on the potential damage that would (or could) result after the computer system crashed under the aggregate effects of many of these web crawler programs.[80] Despite the novelty and creativity of the application of this doctrine, there are significant limitations to its widespread use, such as being limited to works residing on servers and applying only to activity that can cause server or network damage.[81] Finally, even though the trespass to chattels claim is unlikely to create a viable level of protection for most information products, it

---

75 See Sandeen, Sharon (2005), 'A Contract by Any Other Name is Still a Contract: Examining the Effectiveness of Trade Secret Clauses to Protect Databases', 45 *IDEA* 119, 147; Brill, *supra* note 63, at 25; ProCD, 86 F.3d at 1454 ('Contracts . . . generally affect only their parties.').

76 See Bitton, *supra* note 7, at 160.

77 See, for example, *eBay v Bidder's Edge*, 100 F.Supp.2d 1058 (N.D. Calif. 2000).

78 See *Thrifty-Tel, Inc. v Bezenek*, 54 Cal. Rptr. 2d 468, 473 (Cal. App.. 1996); Bitton, *supra* note 7, at 166.

79 See *eBay*, 100 F.Supp.2d at 1069–70.

80 See id. at 1069–72.

81 See *Intel Corp. v Hamidi*, 71 P.3d 296, 306–7 (Cal. 2003) (finding no trespass to chattels where there was no physical harm to the computer system); see also Bitton, *supra* note 7, at 167.

is disfavored because it too lacks any sort of oversight or safety valves: essentially, if there is damage to the creator based on access to the information product, liability may be found, but there is no effort to protect and facilitate the use of information generally.

E. Other Legal Protection

In certain limited circumstances, other legal theories may provide potential protection for information products. For example, criminal law may be used to protect many features of electronic databases and software, based on computer crime and anti-hacking statutes.[82] Privacy and confidentiality laws may provide a level of protection for databases that contain certain types of personal data.[83] However, these theories are available only in specialized circumstances and do not provide broad or certain coverage. Further, none of these theories have the built in safety valves or oversight necessary for appropriate coverage of information products.

F. Non-legal Mechanisms

Despite the wide variety of legal means that have been applied to protect information products, the extent of coverage available for these works and the ease of obtaining that coverage remains quite uncertain, both for practical and doctrinal reasons. Thus, creators of information products have also explored non-legal mechanisms, such as technological measures and creative business plans, to obtain the artificial lead-time or measure of exclusivity required to protect some of their investment in the creation of these works.

1. Technological mechanisms

The most common non-legal mechanism for protecting information products is the use of technological safeguards to prevent against unauthorized access, uses and appropriation of these products.[84] Digital rights management (DRM) tools may be used, for example, to limit who may access the work, the duration for which access is allowed, and the ability to reproduce or retransmit the

---

[82] See Ginsburg, Jane C. (2007), 'A Marriage of Convenience? A Comment on the Protection of Databases', 82 *Chicago-Kent L. Rev.* 1171, 1172 (noting that the Computer Fraud and Abuse Act, 18 U.S.C. § 1030(a), which prohibits unauthorized, damaging access to computers for the purpose of obtaining information, may be useful against competitors who 'copy frequently updated information from a "dynamic" database'); Bitton, *supra* note 7, at 148.

[83] See Bitton, *supra* note 7, at 149.

[84] See Yu, Peter K. (2006), 'Anticircumvention and Anti-anticircumvention', 84 *Denv. U. L. Rev.* 13, 14.

work.[85] Anti-circumvention laws, which then prohibit the disabling or hacking of DRM tools, provide a layer of legal protection on top of the technological layer.[86] For example, the Digital Millenium Copyright Act (DMCA) makes illegal the circumvention of DRM tools that control access to a work if done with the intent to violate any rights under copyright law.[87] Beyond DRM technology, the way some information products are naturally configured provides additional options for technological safeguards. For example, many database management systems are set up so that the access of the entirety (or even a substantial portion) of the contained database is difficult, if not impossible.[88]

While not perfect, DRM technology and limited access rights have been used with some success to protect investments in information products. The most significant disadvantage with DRM technology (and taking advantage of the natural configurations of these products) is that it can be, and often is, used to limit access to information content that should not be so limited and thus inhibit information flow.[89] The creator can use these means to include and obtain protection over more content than he might be able to get under a legal scheme. For example, the creator might use DRM to prohibit any copying of a computer disk containing an information product, even though a purchaser of a computer disk is typically permitted to make a back up copy for personal use. While this may encourage the creators of these works by providing enhanced protection, this method is not favorable because the over-inclusion of content being protected will likely inhibit, not facilitate, information flow, especially in the absence of associated oversight and safety valves.

2. Business schemes

One of the main justifications for providing a protection scheme for information products is to give the creator of the work an artificial lead-time to receive some level of compensation for his efforts. As discussed above, this is particularly critical for information products, as the cost of development is front-end loaded and the end-product is easily duplicable and transferable. While legal schemes and technological measures provide an artificial lead-time in order for the creator to recoup his investment, business schemes have been used to give the creator a different sort of advantage over his competitors and a means

---

85 See Burk, Dan L. (2004), 'DNA Rules: Legal and Conceptual Implications of Biological "Lock-Out" Systems', 92 *Calif. L. Rev.* 1553, 1563.

86 See Yu, *supra* note 84, at 14.

87 See 17 U.S.C. § 1201.

88 See Bitton, *supra* note 7, at 142.

89 See Burk, Dan L. and Tarleton Gillespie (2006), 'Autonomy and Morality in DRM and AntiCircumvention', 4 *Triple C* 239, 244, *available at* http://triplec.uti.at/files/tripleC4(2)/Burk-Gillespie.pdf.

to obtain compensation for the development costs associated with the information product. Although it is often necessary to use one of these other means in conjunction with the business scheme, the below described options may decrease the amount of artificial lead-time or exclusivity that a creator needs to reap the desired reward. One exemplary business scheme is the providing of added value to the information product in the form of additional services or products.

The provision of auxiliary services or bundling of related products is particularly useful in the information products industry. There are a number of successful examples of this business model, particularly in the open source software industry.[90] One such company is Red Hat, which has been built around the model of providing services to accompany Linux, an open source software product that specifically cannot be protected by typical protection schemes.[91] In the absence of being able to protect the software product, Red Hat has developed value and a consumer following for its particular accompanying services, which gives them an advantage over other companies that can also distribute Linux products. Database providers may provide similar valuable services such as possession of the infrastructure for service, ongoing enhancement, and maintenance.[92] Database providers may also bundle the actual database with powerful proprietary search engines or management systems.[93]

III. INTERNATIONAL AND PROPOSED SCHEMES

The lack of protection for information products is not new, nor is it unique to the United States. In the international arena, improved protection systems for information products have been implemented, although it is unclear whether the schemes are successful. In this country, legislators and academic commentators have offered numerous proposals over the years aimed at providing improved protection for information products in this country, but none have

---

90 In the open source software industry, participants specifically eschew intellectual property protection for their products. Instead, the open source movement is based on a protocol of openness and sharing. Yet, even with their works being unprotected, some companies have created businesses around these products. See Raymond, Eric S. (2001), *The Cathedral and the Bazaar*. Although open source creators opt for a lack of protection, the business models that have been used in this industry are applicable to the information product arena as well.

91 See id.; Red Hat, http://www.redhat.com; Linux Online, http://www.linux.org.

92 See Bitton, *supra* note 7, at 127.

93 See Greenbaum, Dov S. (2003), 'Commentary: The Database Debate: In Support of an Inequitable Solution', 13 *Alb. L.J. Sci. & Tech.* 431, 483–84.

been implemented. In any case, both the international schemes and the proposed systems are fairly similar to the legal and alternative means described above, and thus suffer from the same shortcomings.

A. International Protection

The most visible international protection for any form of information product is found in the European Union (EU) Directive on the protection of databases (Database Directive).[94] The Database Directive was developed in 'response to perceived needs to harmonize protection within the EU and to provide greater protection for the investment in the creation and maintenance of databases.'[95] The Database Directive sought to achieve this greater protection in two ways: harmonizing the standard for granting copyright protection in databases and implementing a *sui generis* protection scheme for databases that failed to qualify for copyright protection.

First, the Database Directive harmonizes copyright protection for databases in member countries, basing protection on the original selection or arrangement of the data.[96] This provision, requiring members to grant copyright protection in databases that 'by reason of their selection or arrangement of their contents constitute the author's own intellectual creation',[97] is not unlike the *Feist* standard in the United States. As discussed above with respect to protection for information products under copyright law, this provision of the Directive fails to adequately protect most useful databases.[98]

Secondly, the Database Directive creates a *sui generis* right for the protection of databases that do not qualify under the originality requirement for copyright protection, so long as a substantial investment, either qualitative or quantitative, has been made in obtaining, verifying, or presenting the contents

---

[94] Directive 96/9/EC of the European Parliament and of the Council of 11 March 1996 on the legal protection of databases, OJ 1996 L 077/20 (Directive).

Other countries have examined protection for databases as well; these analyses often turn on a review of 'originality,' like the *Feist* decision in the United States, and so will not be independently reviewed in this chapter. For a detailed treatment of protection available for databases in countries such as Australia, Canada, China, and Russia, see Gervais, Daniel J. (2007), 'The Protection of Databases', 82 *Chicago-Kent L.Rev.* 1109, 1148–1157.

[95] See Davison, Mark (2006), 'Database Protection: The Commodification of Information', in Guibault, L. and P.B. Hugenholz (eds) *The Future of the Public Domain*, 167, 168.

[96] See Article 3(1) of the Directive.

[97] See id.

[98] See notes 45–46, *supra*, and accompanying text.

of a database.[99] The *sui generis* right lasts for 15 years, but can be extended (theoretically, into perpetuity) if the database is updated and maintained. This right is infringed where a qualitatively or quantitatively substantial portion of the database is taken, either via extraction or reutilization, without authorization.[100] Although the *sui generis* right facially appears to grant sufficient, but not overreaching, rights to creators of information products, the European Court of Justice (ECJ) has substantially limited the right in practice.[101]

Finally, the impact of the Database Directive on the information product industry and the future of the Database Directive are unclear. In December 2005, a working paper evaluating the Database Directive was released, concluding that '[t]he economic impact of the "sui generis" right on database protection is unproven. Introduced to stimulate the production of databases in Europe, the new instrument has had no proven impact on the production of database.'[102] However, the database industries were also surveyed for the report; these business concerns indicated their belief that the *sui generis* protection was critical for their continued success.[103] Although the effect, if any, is unclear and there are critics calling for repeal or at least change to the *sui generis* protection scheme, the EU has not yet changed course and, given the perception of the database industry, may not.

---

99 See Article 7(1) of the Directive.

100 Extraction refers to the transfer of the contents of a database to another medium by any means. See Article 7(2)(a) of the Directive. Reutilization refers to making available to the public the contents of a database, either by distribution, renting, or putting on-line. See Article 7(2)(b) of the Directive.

The *sui generis* right also includes a fair use exception, permitting member states to allow an exception from infringement by unauthorized taking of portions of the database in three circumstances: (1) where the reproduction of a non-electronic database is for private purposes; (2) where the sole purpose is illustration for teaching and scientific research, as long as the source is indicated and only to the extent justified; and (3) where the use is for purposes of public security or for administrative or judicial procedures. See Article 9 of the Directive; Lipton, *supra* note 9, at 154–56. Although the fair use exception in the United States weighs heavily against creators of information products, the fair use exception provided by the Directive is more fairly applicable and does not eviscerate the protection granted as extensively as the fair use provision in the United States.

101 C-203/02 *The British Horseracing Board Ltd and Others v William Hill Organisation Ltd.*, *available at* http://europa.eu.int/comm/internal_market/copyright/prot-databases/jurisprudence_en.htm.

102 See Commission of the European Communities, DG Internal Market and Services Working Paper, First Evaluation of Directive 96/9/EC on the legal protection of databases at 5 (Brussels, 12 December 2005) (Working Paper); see also Davison, *supra* note 95, at 188, citing Working Paper at 1.4. Davison also offers reports on litigation stemming from the Directive. See id.

103 See Working Paper, *supra*; Bitton, *supra* note 7, at 113.

B. Proposed Legislation

In this country, lawmakers have debated some form of protection for databases for at least the last decade.[104] Beginning in the mid-1990s, the United States submitted a database protection treaty proposal to the World Intellectual Property Organization (WIPO) that was similar in scope to the European Union Database Directive.[105] In fact, the proposed treaty arguably provided stronger protection to database compilers, with a renewable term of 25 years and a DRM provision that prohibited circumvention of technology limiting access.[106] A parallel bill was simultaneously introduced in Congress, but was widely opposed and failed to move out of the Judiciary Committee.[107] Two years later, database protection was once again introduced in Congress; while the initiative passed the floor of the House twice, once on its own[108] and once as part of the Digital Millennium Copyright Act,[109] it never made it to the Senate Floor. The drama played out in the same way the very next year.[110] Each of these bills was influenced by property rules and called for the creation of a *sui generis* right, again similar to that provided by the Database Directive in Europe. However, the failure to enact these proposed bills seem to have less to do with the substantive merits of the rights provisions and more to do with politics: each of these proposals was met with significant and 'well-orchestrated' opposition by key United States' companies, such as AOL and AT&T, and academics.[111]

Taking a different tactic and with the aim of appeasing the domestic business concerns, the 108th Congress next took up the issue by proposing liability-type

---

104 See Davison, *supra* note 95, at 174.

105 See Committee of Experts on a Possible Protocol to the Berne Convention, *Proposal of the United States of America on Sui Generis Protection of Databases*, 6th Sess., Geneva, WIPO Doc. BCP/CE/VII/2-INR/CE/VI/2 (May 1996); WIPO had also proposed an independent database treaty. See Brill, *supra* note 63, at 35.

106 See Brill, *supra* note 63, at 35.

107 See id. at 41; Database Investment and Intellectual Property Act of 1996, H.R. 3531, 104th Congress, 1996.

108 See Collections of Information Antipiracy Act, H.R. 2652, 105th Congress, 1998; 144 Cong. Rec. 9,681 (1998).

109 See 144 Cong. Rec. 18,783 (1998).

110 Collections of Information Antipiracy Act, H.R. 354 (1999). This bill reached the floor of the full House, but went no further.

111 See Hughes, Justin (2003), 'Of World Music and Sovereign States, Professors and the Formation of Legal Norms', 35 *Loy. U. Chi. L.J.* 155, 186–87; see also, Yu, *supra* note 1 at pp. 4–5 (noting that the proposals failed because the biggest database producers at the time were not American corporations and that the domestic companies were most concerned about their ability to use others' databases if the legislation had passed).

protection for databases, hoping to garner more enthusiastic support.[112] Unfortunately, these proposals fared much the same as the property-type bills that preceded them and never even reached the full House. Very little action has been seen in this area since 2004 and there has been no indication that protection for information products will be taken up by Congress in the near future.

C. Commentator Proposals

Given the disadvantages and failures of existing and proposed legal mechanisms to cover information products, it is not surprising that commentators have embraced the task of either proposing new solutions or, if not providing a solution, at least discussing the factors of a successful proposal.[113] Unfortunately, most of the academic proposals approach the problem of protection for information products by only addressing one type of work, such as only software or only databases. Further, even in their limited scope, the proposals still embody many of the disadvantages noted above for the existing schemes, and thus none represent a favorable solution for protecting information products.

Some commentators propose implementing protection through modifications to existing intellectual property regimes or utilization of alternate areas of current law. For example, Michael Steven Green argues that by re-examining how we think about copyright, and particularly the originality

---

112 The 108th Congress actually proposed two bills: the Database and Collections of Information Misappropriation Act, 108 H.R. 3261, and the Consumer Access to Information Act of 2004 (108 H.R. 3872). The key feature of HR 3261 was its basis in misappropriation law. Infringement would have consisted of making available, in commerce, a quantitatively substantial portion of the information contained in a database, if '1) the database was generated, gathered, or maintained through a substantial expenditure of resources or time, 2) the unauthorized making available in commerce occurred in a time sensitive manner and inflicts injury on the database or [related products or services],' and 3) the ability to free ride would lessen the incentive to create the database initially. These elements are not unlike the elements created in the *INS v AP* case described above – again with the focus on the time-sensitive nature of the included data. The bill also included significant exceptions, similar to fair use. HR 3872 was also based on misappropriation and followed a 'hot news' type model.

113 This list is merely exemplary; there are far too many articles on this topic, with new pieces being added frequently, to list them all here. See, for example, Gibson, *supra*; Greenbaum, *supra*; Reichman and Samuelson, *supra*; Gervais, *supra*; Ginsburg, Jane C. (1997), 'Copyright, Common Law, and Sui Generis Protection of Databases in the United States and Abroad', 66 *U. Cin. L. Rev.* 151; Pachnanda, Amol (2003), Comment, 'Scientific Databases Should Be Protected Under a Sui Generis Regime', 51 *Buffalo L. Rev.* 219 (2003).

requirement and the idea/expression dichotomy, there is room to cover 'collective facts' or compiled data.[114] Stacey Dogan and Joseph Liu argue that courts can apply, and indeed have been applying, copyright law in a manner that allows protection of software information products.[115] Dov Greenbaum suggests an alternate structure to aid in protecting databases – the databank.[116] A databank would be a simple depository of information to be used for scientific research and ineligible for protection; a database, by comparison, is a highly organized data structure that provides tools for analyzing the data and should be eligible for protection under a modified copyright protection scheme.[117] Daryl Lim suggests that antitrust law can be used to limit access to and use of databases without altering the current intellectual property regimes.[118]

Many influential commentators have proposed *sui generis* protection schemes for different sorts of information products. Jane Ginsburg, Pamela Samuelson, and Jerome Reichman have all proposed a new right of protection for database-type information products.[119] Pamela Samuelson and Peter Menell have proposed *sui generis* protection for software-type information products.[120] Other commentators, such as Dan Burk and Charles McManis, have argued for *sui generis* protection for alternative information products like genetic sequences and traditional knowledge.[121]

---

114 See Green, Michael Steven (2003), 'Copyrighting Facts', 78 *Ind. L. J.* 919, 957–63.

115 See Dogan, Stacey L. and Joseph Liu (2005), 'Copyright Law & Subject Matter Specificity: The Case of Computer Software', 61 *N.Y.U. Ann. Surv. Am. L.* 203, 206 ('Courts have, on the whole, successfully adapted copyright doctrines in a way that respects the underlying copyright policies, as applied to the unique aspects of computer software.').

116 See Greenbaum, *supra* note 93, at 500.

117 See id.

118 See Lim, Daryl (2006), 'Regulating Access to Databases Through Antitrust Law: A Missing Perspective in the Database Debate', 2006 *Stanford Tech. L. Rev.* 7, pp 8, 30 *et seq.*

119 See Ginsburg, Jane C. (1997), 'Copyright, Common Law, and Sui Generis Protection of Databases in the United States and Abroad', 66 *U. Cincinnati L. Rev.* 151, 171–76 (proposing *sui generis* protection for databases); Reichman, J.H. and Pamela Samuelson (1997), 'Intellectual Property Rights in Data?', 50 *Vanderbilt L. Rev.* 51, 64–109 (same).

120 See Menell, Peter S. (1987), 'Tailoring Legal Protection for Computer Software', 39 *Stanford L. Rev.* 1329 (proposing *sui generis* protection for software); Samuelson, Pamela et al. (1994), 'A Manifesto Concerning the Legal Protection of Computer Programs', 94 *Columbia L.Rev.* 2308, 2332–2432 (same).

121 See Burk, Dan L. (1989), 'Copyrightability of Recombinant DNA Sequences', 29 *Jurimetrics J.* 469 (proposing a copyright-like protection scheme for biotechnology inventions); McManis, Charles R. (2003), 'Thinking Globally, Acting

Still other commentators, although avoiding proposing a solution to the problem of protection for information products, have provided suggestions for shaping a new regime or altering an existing regime to cover these works. For example, Jim Gibson argues that any workable solution should exploit the technological architecture surrounding databases, regulating the extent to which developers can impose architectural restraints that limit access, which can further be buttressed by 'technolegical' measures.[122] Jacqueline Lipton proposes reconceptualizing the protection of information products as a system of property rights and responsibilities.[123] Her system envisions balancing the competing interests of information products creators and the public through the imposition of significant legal duties on information property rights holders, including obligations such as facilitating scientific, technical, or educational use of the information; ensuring the accuracy and accessibility of personal information; and protecting cultural rights.[124]

As discussed above, current means available for protecting information products either result in under-protection, depriving the creator of the work the opportunity to recoup the resources invested in the development of the product, or over-protection, keeping information that would otherwise be available to the public from being accessed or used. In the very worst cases, both under-protection and over-protection may occur. For example, in the case of a database consisting mostly of facts that the creator has attempted to cover by contract law, his level of protection may be insufficient if a third-party obtains a copy of the database because of privity issues in contract. Yet, through the use of this very same contract, the creator may limit access to and use of mere facts that would otherwise be unprotectable. While the numerous articles and proposals for new or improved protection for information products clearly demonstrates the need, none address the dual concern of providing adequate protection while maintaining a free flow of information.

IV. PROTECTING AND FACILITATING TRANSACTIONS IN INFORMATION PRODUCTS

Despite the best intentions to keep information 'free' by denying protection under traditional intellectual property regimes, the reality is that an improved

---

Locally', 11 *Cardozo J. Int'l & Comp. L.* 547, 563 (discussing *sui generis* protection for traditional knowledge). See also Pleune, S. Benjamin (2001), 'Trouble with the Guidelines: On Urging the PTO to Properly Evolve with Novel Technologies', *J. Tech. L. & Pol'y* 365 (proposing DNA-specific *sui generis* legislation).

122 See Gibson, *supra* note 45, at 189–190.

123 See Lipton, *supra* note 9, at 165.

124 See id. at 172–3.

protection scheme is necessary to truly facilitate information flow. I propose a *sui generis* protection scheme for information products that defines clear rights and boundaries, aimed at clarifying the rights of the creator of the work while also facilitating transactions in the information, both with an eye towards encouraging the free flow of information. My proposal focuses on the overall work (both the information and structural components) and, unlike many academic and legislative proposals, is applicable to multiple types of information products.

Many of the objections to the protection of information are based on the idea that we do not want 'information' itself to be protected; that is, we are against the protection of the information as the 'thing'. This is the essence of propertization or commodification of information. My proposal instead seeks to provide the protection necessary to encourage the development of information products while being conscious of the concerns that are raised when information is propertized. The main tenet of my proposal is that information should be protected not as the 'thing', but rather as a component of the 'thing'. Thus, the 'thing' being protected is the information product as a whole, which consists of both a structural component and an information component. In doing so, I aim to provide a better definition of precisely when information qua information products will be protected. I also center this proposal largely on a liability-type regime, which along with the clarified boundaries of protection, should encourage transactions in information and information products and, at bottom, the flow of information.

In order to provide improved protection for information products while still facilitating the free flow of information, I propose a system that better defines the scope of coverage for a wide range of information products and incorporates liability-type rules; these two improvements – clarifying the boundaries of protection and altering the remedies available – should, when taken together, ease the concerns about enclosure and even facilitate the flow of information. The coverage is tailored to protect not simply data, which offends the notion that information should be free; rather the system covers only data that has enhanced value based on the added structural component.

A. Components

The information products contemplated to be covered by this proposal are those that include both an information component and a structural component. A component is commonly defined as 'a constituent part'.[125] In the technical

125 See *Microsoft Corp. v AT&T Corp.*, 127 S.Ct. 1746, 1755 n 11 (2007) (citing *Webster's Third New International Dictionary of the English Language* 466 (1981)).

arts, such as software, componentization is defined as breaking a system into interchangeable parts, each of which encapsulate a portion of functionality.[126] Applying this idea of componentization to information products, consider a work where the information component can be interchanged and where the structural component organizes the information component, gives the information component context and meaning, and facilitates distribution of the information component. A simple example of this idea is a database of telephone listings. The same structural component still provides the context, but the information component that provides the real functional data is interchangeable. However, it is possible too to conceive of a different structural component, perhaps with fields for only last names and phone numbers, in which the same information components may be used. The components of the information component are interchangeable in this respect as well. This notion of components and interchangeability can be extrapolated to cover every type of information product for which this system may be used.

Although the composition of information components may vary across the spectrum of information products, there is some information that would not fit within this scheme. Simple information about a tangible (or even intangible) item or information resulting from a process would be unlikely to fall into the category of information product to be protected under this scheme. However, information that would not, by itself, constitute an information component can, in relation to other pieces of information and within a viable structural component, become an information component.[127] This introduces the further notion that the information component as combinable – that is, the information should be able to be combined with other information or components.[128] Even information that is quite detailed can fall outside the notion of an information component. For example, instructions for building a device would not likely be an information component, because even though detailed, it could not be combined with other components nor could it be interchangeable.[129]

Many types of information products may include both an information component and a structural component and thus will be eligible for coverage under the proposed scheme. Two information products for which the system

---

[126] See, for example, Define meaning of componentization, *available at* http://looselycoupled.com/glossary/componentization (last visited 10 March 2008).

[127] This idea is not dissimilar from Michael Steven Green's idea of protection for 'collective facts'. See Green, *supra* note 114. However, I do not believe, as Green does, that copyright law is the best avenue for covering collective facts and thus propose a *sui generis* system.

[128] See *Microsoft Corp.*, 127 S.Ct. at 1748 (discussing the difference between simple information, such as a blueprint, and information which can be combined with other components, such as software).

[129] See id.

has immediately recognizable applicability are databases and software; however, the system has potential application for protecting other existing information products.

1. Databases

Databases are the most natural type of information products to envision in the proposed protection scheme. In modern times, the term generally refers to any compilation of data that is typically organized and utilized via a database management system, providing a bridge between the data and the end user.[130] The information component of the database, literally the data, is organized by the structural component, the fields of the database, that also give context and meaning to the information component. The structural component further facilitates distribution of the data, or information component, in a useful fashion.

2. Software

Software is slightly more difficult to envision as an information product, in part because software is difficult to define or classify.[131] One definition of software is 'a set of instructions, not mere knowledge, but a certain arrangement of matter that makes a computer perform.'[132] Working from this definition, the information component of software is the set of instructions. The structural component is then the particular arrangement of those instructions that organizes the instructions, provides context and meaning to the instructions as the organization or arrangement is the basis for the instructions to cause the computer to behave in a certain fashion,[133] and facilitates the distribution of the instructions or information component.

3. Additional information products

While databases and software provide the simplest examples of information products that would be eligible for protection under this proposal, there are

---

130 See id. Although most databases today are electronic, printed databases could also be covered by this proposal. '[A] database is [simply] an organized and indexed collection of information that allows users to access and organize heterogeneous data in an efficient fashion.' See id.

131 One of the difficulties in classifying software as an information product may be that, unlike databases, software can be and has been viewed in multiple ways. *Microsoft Corp.*, 127 S.Ct. at 1754 (quoting *Fantasy Sports Properties, Inc. v Sportsline.com, Inc.*, 287 F.3d 1108, 1118 (Fed. Cir. 2002)).

132 See Radin, Margaret Jane 'Incomplete Commodification in a Computerized World', in Elkin-Koren, N. and N.W. Netanel, (eds) *The Commodification of Information* 403.

133 See Samuelson, Pamela et al. (1994), 'A Manifesto Concerning the Legal Protection of Computer Programs', 94 *Colum. L. Rev.* 2308, 2316.

other works that both have an information component and a structural component. Some examples include genetic sequence inventions, geo-spatial data, real estate appraisal systems, and certain types of indigenous knowledge. Many of these works have been likened to specialized forms of databases, where the information component is given value by virtue of the organization provided by the structural component.[134] Because these products can be characterized in this manner, they too would fall within the proposed scheme.

B. How Does the Proposed Scheme Work?

The two most important aspects of the proposed scheme are that a creator's rights in the information product are clearly defined and that the system is based largely on liability, rather than property type rules.[135] First, clearly defined rights are important to encourage creators of information products to make the necessary investment in developing their product, but also to facilitate transactions in information and information products. As economists note, the purpose of a property regime is to 'ensure that resources are allocated to their highest valued use' in order to increase monetary reward and, to achieve this goal, the system must clearly define property rights.[136] The clearly defined rights then facilitate for private bargaining,[137] permitting parties to

---

[134] See, for example, Reichman and Samuelson, *supra* note 2, at 135 ('Conceivably, . . . genetically engineered life forms could also fall within the broad definition of database in that they are "assemblies . . . of . . . materials arranged in a methodical or systematic way".'); Eisenberg, Rebecca S. (2002), 'Patents on DNA Sequences: Molecules and Information', in Elkin-Koren, N. and N.W. Netanel (eds) *The Commodification of Information* 417 (likening genetic sequence inventions to scientific information, rather than chemical entities); Janssen, Katleen and Jos Dumortier (2006), 'The Protection of Maps and Spatial Databases in Europe and the United States by Copyright and the Sui Generis Right', 24 *J. Marshall J. Computer & Info L.* 195; Simon, Bradford S. (2005), 'Intellectual Property and Traditional Knowledge: A Psychological Approach to Conflicting Claims of Creativity in International Law', 20 *Berkeley Tech. L.J.* 1613; Goldman, Eric 'Real Estate Appraisals and Copyrighting Facts', posted on Concurring Opinions blog 1/28/2007 (available at http://www.concurringopinions.com/archives/2007/01/real_estate_app.html).

[135] The difference between 'property rules' and 'liability rules' was elucidated by Guido Calabresi and A. Douglas Melamed in their seminal work on this topic, 'Property Rules, Liability Rules, and Inalienability: One View of the Cathedral', 85 *Harv. L. Rev.* 1089 (1972). Under a property rule, the owner has the right to exclude others; under a liability rule, the owner has no right to exclude but can demand compensation or damages. See id. at 1105–06.

[136] See, for example, Galbraith, Christine D. (2007), 'A Panoptic Approach to Information Policy: Utilizing a More Balanced Theory of Property in Order to Ensure the Existence of a Prodigious Public Domain', 15 *J. Intell. Prop. L.* 1, 33.

[137] See id; Siebrasse, *supra* note 11, at 56–57.

effectively negotiate for use of and access to the information product on the basis of perceived value. As the law currently stands, it is unclear what rights, if any, a creator has in any given information product, which makes bargaining impossible and thereby inhibits transactions in information products and the underlying information.

Secondly, a key feature of the proposed system is that much infringing behavior is viewed from a liability-type perspective. It may seem counter-intuitive, after advocating above for clearly defined property rights, to propose that a system that relies, at least in part, on liability rules. However, that rights are available for information products has been clarified by this system. Also, there are regularly substitutions of fuzzy, ambiguous rules for clear entitlements, even in property-type systems.[138] In fact, at least one commentator has argued that 'muddy rules' will encourage bargaining where transaction costs are high, for example on the Internet.[139] The proposed system defines the outer extents of protection available, but leaves the details to a 'muddy', liability-type analysis in order to facilitate transactions and allow for the flexibility required to avoid concerns about propertizing information.[140]

One way to view the liability-type regime is to consider that potentially infringing behavior resides on a spectrum. In property law, the inquiry is typically binary: Is there trespass or not?[141] Instead, for the protection of

---

138 See, for example, Rose, Carol M. 'Crystals and Mud in Property Law', 40 *Stanford L. Rev.* 577, 578.

139 See Burk, Dan L. (1999), 'Muddy Rules for Cyberspace', 21 *Cardozo L. Rev.* 121, 138. Other commentators have also noted that property rules may be more efficient where borders are fuzzy. See Epstein, Richard 'Transaction Costs and Property Rights: Or, Do Good Fences Make Good Neighbors?', at 6–7 (Chicago Working Papers in Law & Economics, 2d Series) (March 1996) (*cited in* Burk, *supra* at n 29).

140 See Calabresi and Melamed, *supra* note 135 (suggesting that liability rules may be preferable where transaction costs are high, such that a party who places high value on the work can simply take it and compensate the owner for the loss); Burk, 'Muddy Rules', *supra* note 139, at 140 ('More often, the uncertainty created by the muddy standard tends to channel buyers and sellers into less costly informal structures.'). This idea is controversial and has won both supporters and detractors. Compare Ayres, Ian and Eric Talley (1995), 'Solomnic Bargaining: Dividing a Legal Entitlement to Facilitate Coasean Trade', 104 *Yale L.J.* 1027 with Kaplow, Louis and Steven Shavell (1995), 'Do Liability Rules Facilitate Bargaining? A Reply to Ayres and Talley', 105 *Yale L.J.* 221; Kaplow, Louis and Steven Shavell (1996), 'Property Rules versus Liability Rules: An Economic Analysis', 109 *Harv. L. Rev.* 713.

141 To be sure, there is some 'muddiness' even in this simple inquiry. Dan Burk explains this using the common idea of tying a boat up to a dock. Normally, permission from the dock owner is required and the dock owner is free to exclude others from tying up their boats. However, in the case of a deadly storm or other exigent circumstances, a sailor may tie up to a dock without permission and will simply be liable for any damages incurred, thus turning the simple question of trespass into a liability inquiry. See Burk, 'Muddy Rules', *supra* note 139, at 127–28.

information products, the real analysis should question how bad the offending behavior was. At one end of the spectrum, there is no protection for the information component separate from the structural component. This means that there is no liability for simply possessing the information. There is also no liability where the information component has been reverse engineered or independently created. At the other end of the spectrum, there is full coverage for infringement via unauthorized access or appropriation of the entire information product, consisting of both the information component and the structural component. Because the information product as a whole has been taken, this is better treated under a property-type regime and the system contemplates injunction as a potential remedy for this.

The more difficult inquiry occurs when something less than the whole is taken, and this is where the liability-type rules will be used. For a concrete example, consider a database that includes the names of all of the law professors that teach at law schools in the United States, their contact information, and their areas of teaching and research.[142] This database would most likely fail to be protected under copyright law, because its selection of data is not unique (all law professors are included) and because its arrangement is obvious (for example, by law school or by subject matter taught). Under the proposed protection scheme, however, this database would fare better. Because the information component is not independently protectable and reverse-engineering is permitted, I can – should I wish – go to every law school's website and gather up this information on my own, without incurring any liability for possessing or using the information thereafter. On the flipside, I can not copy wholesale the database (either in print or electronic form), as this would be taking the whole information product, both the information component and the structural component. In that case, I would be subject to traditional property remedies, including an injunction if appropriate.

What is the result, however, if I merely take a portion of the database – if I copy only the information component related to intellectual property professors in the structural framework? Or if I only take a portion of the structural framework, such as only some of the fields, and all of the information contained therein – for example, if I take only the names and e-mail addresses of all of the professors in the database? What if I am merely using the database to verify a single fact?[143] These situations are where a liability-type

142 Such a database is maintained by the American Association of Law Schools (AALS) and is generally protected via contract law. See http://www.aals.org/services_directory.php.

143 See National Research Council Committee for a Study on Promoting Access to Scientific and Technical Data for the Public Interest (1999), *A Question of Balance: Private Rights and the Public Interest in Scientific and Technical Databases* 34 (distin-

regime provides the appropriate response. Where portions of the information component and framework have been taken, the remedy will not be an injunction but rather a system of damages to compensate the creator of the information product. As with many liability regimes, the amount of damages will be determined by looking at a number of factors, such as how much of the information product was taken, the reason the information product was taken, the relationship between the creator of the information product and the party who took the information without consent, and the effect of the taking on the market for the original information product.[144] The effect of this inquiry will be to permit free or cheap access to portions of an information component within one of these works subject to the value the information has to the user, permit access to the information components in cases of good reason (such as educational investigation or research), and permit the creation of new inventions (both traditional and information products) so long as the effect is not to take away from the market for the original information product.

The benefits of this scheme are clear. The creator of the information product benefits from an artificial lead-time in which to try to recover his development investment, but others can effectively make a decision about what and whether it is worth for them to use the information. Thus, if the information is necessary for innovation in another field, it will be available for some cost; if the information product is simply being taken to compete with the original information product, it will be unavailable or available at an inflated cost. Because of the factors that are considered in determining the cost for the transactions (liability damages), there is an element of fair use that protects innocent and de minimis users, as well as educational and research users. The scheme is dynamic, not tied to any one information product, not tied to any particular technology, and most importantly, encourages bargaining outside of the legal system. The owner of the information product has the incentive to bargain, because only in the face of complete, wholesale infringement is there going to be injunctive relief – there is no benefit to acting as a hold-out. Further, the user wishing to access and use the information product has an incentive to bargain, because the boundaries of the protection covering the information product are going to be more clearly defined than exist today.

---

guishing using a database as an end user – to verify a fact or perform a personal task – versus using a database for a derivative use – which 'builds on a preexisting database and includes at least one, and frequently more, extractions from one or more databases to create a new database').

144 In these instances, where portions of an information product are taken, it is important to remember that the value of information is not simply related to the quantity of information taken, but the value in being able to obtain the necessary information quickly, without having to do the searching and gathering. See Gervais, *supra* note 94, at 1159–60.

Most uses of the information component and information product are going to result simply in monetary remedies and thus a priori negotiations are in all parties' best interests.

One criticism raised with respect to this proposal is that all information is currently available for a cost and that it is unlikely that this proposal will result in increased bargaining or negotiation between the information product creator and the user desiring access. However, at least anecdotally, there is evidence that information product creators do not always behave in a rational manner and readily deny access to information, even when a reasonable price has been offered.[145] This proposal addresses this problem by prohibiting the creator of information products to hold-out against an offer; if the creator chooses to deny access, a party wanting to use the information product can always simply misappropriate the product and pay damages later.

CONCLUSION

While legislators and commentators debate whether information products should be protected, creators of these works are seeking self-help coverage for the information products under a panoply of alternative legal and non-legal mechanisms. This results in the simultaneous under-protection of information products, to the detriment of the creator, and over-protection of these products, which inhibits information flow. Yet preserving the free flow of information is precisely why intellectual property protection has traditionally not been offered for these works.

This chapter proposes a *sui generis* protection scheme that seeks to address these issues of under-protection and over-protection. The proposed system clarifies that rights are available in information products, which should both provide incentives for increased creation of these works and should facilitate transactions in these works (and the underlying information). The system, however, is also flexible, relying on liability-type remedies for most types of infringement to keep information freely flowing. This too should encourage negotiations and transactions for these products because injunctive relief will rarely be available. Denying protection for information products does not ensure that information is free, in fact, the opposite seems to be true; information may want to be free, but information products do not.

---

145 See, for example, Burk, 'Muddy Rules', *supra* note 139, at 158 ('One might expect serious "holdout" problems to arise in [the informational goods] environment, as every copyright holder attempts to capture the full value of every use of his works.').

Index